Heresies of Catholicism…
The Apostate Church

Heresies of Catholicism...
The Apostate Church

John Schroeder

iUniverse, Inc.
New York Lincoln Shanghai

Heresies of Catholicism...The Apostate Church

All Rights Reserved © 2003 by John Schroeder

No part of this book may be reproduced or transmitted in any form or by any means, graphic, electronic, or mechanical, including photocopying, recording, taping, or by any information storage retrieval system, without the written permission of the publisher.

iUniverse, Inc.

For information address:
iUniverse, Inc.
2021 Pine Lake Road, Suite 100
Lincoln, NE 68512
www.iuniverse.com

ISBN: 0-595-27499-4 (pbk)
ISBN: 0-595-65682-X (cloth)

Printed in the United States of America

To: Jesus who saved me;

And to Claudia, the precious
Christian lady who gave me
my most prized possession—
my King James Bible;
and just two months later, gave
herself to me in holy wedlock.

Contents

Preface ix
Foreword. xi

CHAPTER 1   From Patchwork Gospel To Tradition's Trap 1
    The twin heresies that paved Rome's road to apostasy.

CHAPTER 2   The Goddess Man Has Made 33
    Re-invented: worship of another "Queen of Heaven."

CHAPTER 3   The Great Imposters 69
    Of fraud, forgery, and papal "piracy."

CHAPTER 4   The Money Machinery 100
    Wealth-makers: temporal punishment, Purgatory, indulgences.

CHAPTER 5   The Seven Dwarf Syndrome 130
    Salvation by works doesn't work.

CHAPTER 6   The Aposta-Seeds 170
    Satan the sower; Rome the reaper.

CHAPTER 7   The Sacrifice That Isn't 188
    "It is finished" means it is finished.

CHAPTER 8   The Apparition Addiction 202
    Marian visions: Don't look. Listen.

CHAPTER 9   The Catechism Cataclysm 244
    Exposed: Rome's contradiction affliction.

CHAPTER 10   The Sword and the Lamp 269
    Equipment for life everlasting.

Preface

If you are a Roman Catholic, you may have received this book as a gift, clearly an indication that someone loves you very much and is concerned for the eternal destiny of your soul.

When I was a Catholic, had someone given me a book like this, my first inclination would have been to round-file it in the nearest waste basket. But so convinced was I that Catholicism was the one true religion established by Jesus on the Apostle Peter, that I would have read it just to prove the author wrong and the Catholic Church right.

And when I received—as a gift—my first Bible, that's exactly what I did, measured the Bible's teachings against Catholic doctrines to prove the rightness of my religion.

But that approach created so much confusion I was forced to reverse the process, thereafter measuring the Catholic teachings against biblical doctrines. The better part of twenty years has been spent doing just that, and this book is the result.

Within these pages, what Rome teaches is measured against the divine Word of God. If you proceed beyond this point, that is the one fact I pray you will keep in mind as you read—it is the divine Word of God Himself against which Catholic doctrine is being measured.

May God bless you.

Foreword

Dear Reader:

When I met the author 20 years ago he was attending the Catholic Mass seven days a week. Though sincere in his spiritual desires, he was sincerely wrong in his spiritual pursuit. Nine months earlier the Lord had delivered him from a destructive addiction to alcohol. One of the actions required by his recovery program was to depend entirely upon God for deliverance. In order to do that, he believed he would have to return to the Catholic religion from which he had been many years "fallen away." His daily attendance at Mass was the product of that belief.

During our very first meeting, he confessed to me that he felt at a standstill spiritually and didn't know why. As a former Catholic myself I **knew** why! And three days later I presented him with a Bible; not the Catholic bible he requested, but a King James study Bible that, to this day, remains his Bible of choice. He consumed the Word of God like a starving man. In less than two weeks he had read the New Testament from Matthew through Revelation. But because the Bible lacks most of the teachings he had learned growing up in the Catholic Church, he ended up both puzzled and confused.

Thereafter, much energy was expended correcting his perspective from subjective—that is, comparing Scripture to Catholic doctrine—to objective, comparing Catholic doctrine to the Word of God. He fought hard to retain his faith in Catholicism, nearly exhausting my capacity to repeat over and over again, *"John, you don't compare the Bible to Catholic doctrine, you compare Catholic doctrine to the Bible whose Author is the Holy Spirit."* As the precious Word of God brought truth to his soul, he eventually realized how he had been deceived all his life, and how impossible it is to "work" one's way to heaven.

When that realization took hold, he experienced the joy and relief that only the new birth in Christ can produce. It was then, I believe, that this book was born in his mind. Born as a means of reaching other deceived souls—not directly necessarily—but by informing born again Christians of Catholicism's numerous heresies and what Catholics believe, thereby equipping them to become more effective witnesses for Jesus.

During the past 20 years, he has diligently read and studied the precious Word of God, his heart ever burdened by the Lord to bring truth to Catholics.

This book is the product of his obedience to God. It is our prayer—his and mine for we are now one flesh—that the Lord bless the distribution of this work with the salvation of many Catholics.

In His service, Claudia Schroeder

1

From Patchwork Gospel To Tradition's Trap

"My covenant will I not break, nor alter the thing that is gone out of my lips."

Psalm 89:34

To professing Catholics of the 21st century, the Roman Catholic Church is the oldest—and in fact is the only—church founded by our lord Jesus Christ. The church's teaching ministry has been eminently successful in establishing and maintaining this belief as if it were an established fact of history. Utilizing what is termed "apostolic succession," Rome has convinced the faithful that their religion of today, in its leadership, its doctrines, and its liturgy, is virtually unchanged from what the Apostles left with their immediate successors. In Chapter 2 of the 1994 Catholic Catechism, Article 2 entitled "The Transmission of Divine Revelation," fosters the notion that Christ left His Gospel and the dissemination of it exclusively in the hands of the Catholic Church. The Apostles "own position of teaching authority" is alleged to have been passed on directly to those first bishops of the "Catholic" Church, and from them to all succeeding popes and bishops down through the annals of time.

In Part 2 of the '94 Catechism, Article 3, entitled "The Sacrament of The Eucharist," contains several entries conveying the impression that the Catholic Mass and the doctrine of bread and wine becoming Christ's literal flesh and blood had their origin in the apostolic church. The office of the popes is alleged to have originated with Peter, and by association, this teaching imputes great antiquity to the 19th century doctrine of papal infallibility. Christ is supposed to have instituted all seven of the Catholic sacraments before His ascension, and infant baptism supposedly was practiced right from the church's inception. Mary's Immaculate Conception, her sinless life, her cradle-to-the-grave virginity, all recent doctrinal additions, are taught as if they had been articles of faith preached by the Apostles. This deliberate "aging" of doctrines reflects the tireless efforts of Rome's apologists to create for Catholicism a reputation of great antiquity, stability, and holiness combined with absolute, God-given authority. Proof that these efforts have yielded the desired results is found in the fact that Catholicism as it presently exists is thought by a vast majority of the faithful to be the exact same faith instituted by Jesus and passed on by His Apostles.

Of course, if Catholicism really **IS** the one and only Church founded by Jesus, its organization, its doctrines, and its liturgies should dovetail with what is known about the apostolic Church. But, when we consult the written records—those found in the Bible, the history books, and the writings of early Church saints—we are hard pressed to find how today's Roman Catholic Church is even remotely related to the Church instituted by Christ and propagated by His disciples. What we **do** find is a religion, not of grace, but of works, governed not by independent bishops, but by a self-styled monarch, and *"teaching for doctrines the commandments of men."* (Mat 15:9) Hence, all of Rome's propaganda notwithstanding, Catholicism's antiquity is self-assumed, and has no relationship whatever to the truth. All the claims of longevity are just that, and only that—claims unsubstantiated by history, the Holy Scriptures, or the writings of early church saints. Rome is undaunted in the face of reality and truth, however, adamantly insisting that Catholicism is the one and only true church founded by Christ. Therefore, of Catholicism's numerous heresies, this must be considered the first, for it is the one from which all the others derive their existence. Moreover, it is a chief cause of Rome's well-documented antipathy to the Scriptures, a matter given extensive coverage later in this chapter.

What our Lord left on earth was left not just to 12 Apostles, but to 120 disciples who were in the same upper room together on the first Pentecost. These all were indwelt by and filled with the Holy Spirit who empowered them to carry the salvation message throughout the world. Not one of those 120 disciples was a Catholic. Nor were Peter, James, John, Thomas, or any of the other Apostles Catholics. Their immediate successors—Clement, Ignatius, Polycarp, Linus, Cletus, etc.—were **Christians**, not Catholics. When, in the middle of the 2nd century, Polycarp, bishop of Smyrna, was martyred, the crowd of onlookers called him the "father of **Christians**." Referring to himself, Polycarp declared, "I am a **Christian**!" In the Bible we read, *"And the disciples were called Christians first in Antioch."* (Act 11:26)

The Council of Nicaea, AD 325-225 years removed from the apostolic church—was a synod of **Christian,** not Catholic, bishops. It was convened and supervised by the emperor, Constantine, an alleged convert to **Christianity**, not Catholicism. At the time, there were at least 1800 known **Christian**, not Catholic, churches, each one independent of the others, each led by its own bishop. The Council was attended by 318 of those bishops, but Sylvester, the sitting bishop of Rome, (who is listed by the Vatican as a Catholic pope,) was not among them. Historically, the designation "Catholic" is not found in common usage until the fifth century. Church historian, Eusebius, writing in the 4th century, recorded events of Christendom's early years without once mentioning a Catholic Church. Near the start of the 5th century, Augustine, bishop of Hippo in Africa, was called by his mother a "Catholic Christian."

Possessed of these **facts**, we conclude that what was passed on by Christ's disciples to their successors was not a religious denomination—Catholicism—but the simple grace-based **Christian** faith instituted by our Lord. History, the Bible, the writings of the early church saints, these offer no support whatever for Rome's claims that Catholicism was the one and only true church founded by Jesus; nor that Christ ordained Peter as bishop of Rome and the first pope. The so-called "holy sacrifice of the Mass," was unknown in the apostolic church; the Lord's Supper was a memorial, not a reenactment, of Calvary, and there were no priests allegedly endowed with the power to take the place of Jesus here on earth. Baptism was not mandatory for salvation or receipt of the Holy Spirit. No works were required of the individual who wished to be saved, only faith in Christ Jesus. ***"And they said, Believe on the Lord Jesus Christ, and thou shalt be saved, and thy house."*** (Acts 16:31) ***"And Crispus, the chief ruler of the synagogue, believed on the Lord with all his house; and many of the Corinthians hearing believed and were baptized."*** (Acts 18:8)

No one, this writer included, disputes the fact that the Roman Catholic Church emerged from apostolic Christianity. So did the eastern branch of Christendom, known today as the Orthodox Church. So did the Anabaptists, the Arians, The Docetists, the Marcions, the Ebionites, the Gnostics, etc. All emerged from the same Christian roots and are eloquent proof that common beginnings do not guarantee truth will be the end result.

The Gospel Christ entrusted to His followers has never been added to, taken from, or altered in any way. It and it alone is the benchmark against which the one and only true church is measured and identified. What God's Word said in the first century is what God's Word says today: ***"By grace are you saved through faith, and that not of yourselves; it is the gift of God, not of works lest anyone should boast."*** (Eph. 2:8, 9) Salvation faith is a free gift from God. It can't be bought with all the good works or penances in the world. ***"Except a man*** *be born again, he cannot see the Kingdom of God."* (John 3:3) A new spiritual birth is necessary, and occurs when the Holy Spirit indwells the believer. *"For God so loved the world, that He gave His only begotten Son, that whosoever believeth in Him should not perish, but have everlasting life."* (John 3:16) The new birth results from belief in all that Christ is, all that He said, and all that He did. It has never been limited to persons of any one particular denomination, but to *"whosoever believeth."*

This basically is the Gospel left to us by Christ, the one His disciples preached and recorded. Like Jesus, it is the *"same yesterday, today and forever."* (Heb 13:8) That verse should apply as well to Catholicism if it is the one true church founded by Christ. But it does not apply because of Rome's own self-generated problem—its **"Patchwork Gospel"**—which completely obviates that unsubstantiated claim. History is a hard task master, and it shows that from the time it assumed an identity of its own, becoming the Catholic, rather than the Christian church, Catholicism has been "patching" the immutable Gospel of Christ with one doctrine after another, none of which is supported in the Scriptures, nor was orally transmitted by Christ's Apostles. By inference, this makes the God of Scripture appear to be both inept and unjust. Inept, because His original Gospel allegedly was incomplete, insufficient, and had to be "patched" numerous times over many centuries. Unjust because the original converts were denied privileges and benefits enjoyed by later converts to the "complete Gospel" whose latest "patch" was added in 1965.

This "Patchwork Gospel" that Rome created, and now is forced to live with, actually is the strongest rebuttal to any and all claims that the Roman Catholic Church is the one and only Church instituted by Christ. It is painful to admit that in 52 years as a Catholic I never once realized that the God of Catholicism needed hundreds and hundred of years, and numerous "patches" to the original, to get His Gospel "right" in my generation. Neither did I realize that the Jesus of Catholicism is a wholly different Jesus than the Savior known and preached by His Apostles. In retrospect, I accepted all of the church's doctrines as having been a part of the religion since the time of Christ. I did not know, for example, that the critically important doctrine of transubstantiation—the assertion that ordinary bread and wine becomes the physical body and blood of Jesus—has been an article of faith only since the 13th century. Through the parochial school training I received, I fully believed the following, which is from a book entitled, *"The Faith of Millions—The Credentials of the Catholic Church."*

> "When the priest announces the tremendous words of consecration, he reaches up into the heavens, brings Christ down from His throne, and places Him upon our altar to be offered up again as the victim for the sins of man. It is a power greater than that of the saints and angels, greater than that of the Seraphim and Cherubim. The priest brings Christ down from heaven, and renders Him present on our altar as the eternal victim for the sins of man—not once but a thousand times! The priest speaks and lo! Christ, the eternal and omnipotent God, bows His head in humble obedience to the priest's command."

Aside from the fact that the above is unscriptural, blasphemous, and utter nonsense, it points up the problem Rome has created for itself by periodically "patching" strange new doctrines into God's original and only Gospel, the one Gospel that identifies the Church He left on earth. Since transubstantiation was not declared an article of faith until 1215 AD, Catholic liturgy did not "bring Christ down from heaven" prior to that date. How, then, could this doctrine be a product of "apostolic succession" when, 1) there were no priests in the apostolic Church, and, 2) when a gap of more than 1200 years separates it from the Apostles? And, would God feed His flock mere bread and wine prior to AD 1215; then begin feeding them His actual body and blood after that date? Hardly.

Catholics, (me, too, when I was one) accept without question that the Apostle Peter was a Catholic and the first pope. They believe that Jesus ordained him with the words from Matthew 16:18, ***"Thou art Peter, and upon this rock I will build my church."*** But the Bible itself, history, and the writings of the early church saints show this belief to be seriously in error. In fact, if it were not for some forged documents appearing in the third century, documents that even Rome admits are blatant frauds, there is little likelihood Peter ever would have been touted as a bishop of Rome and the first pope. The Apostle Paul was a far better candidate because of his lengthy, biblically recorded, stay in Rome, plus his own claim to having the oversight of all the churches. (2 Cor 11:28) All evidence considered, the papacy has not existed from the time of Christ. It was permanently "patched-in" many hundreds of years later when a second set of forged documents gained acceptance for a time as genuine and trustworthy.

In regard to the critical matter of church leadership, a monarchy headed by one individual called the pope was not what Christ bequeathed to His Apostles. In the book of Acts, in nine Pauline epistles and the First Epistle of Peter, it is evident that there were many churches, each independent of the others, all comprising the one Church whose unifying element was common faith in Jesus, His atoning sacrifice, and His bodily resurrection. That the existence of numerous independent churches met with Christ's approval is supported by our Lord's letters to seven of them in the book of Revelation. He did not address one letter to one church ruled by one bishop occupying a position of supremacy over all the churches. He addressed seven letters to seven "Messengers" who were the leaders of seven separate independent churches; and He revealed His very presence among them. *"These things saith he that holdeth the seven stars in his right hand, who walketh in the midst of the seven golden candlesticks,"* (Rev 2:1) In his Galatians epistle, Paul acknowledges a multiplicity of churches in that area alone by addressing his letter "unto the **churches** of Galatia." (Gal 1:2)

Further evidence that the apostolic church was made up of many individual, independent, churches, is found in letters generated by Clement and Ignatius, two renowned first-century saints. Especially in letters of Ignatius, it is apparent the independent churches were headed by bishops, presbyters and deacons. Polycarp, bishop of the Smyrna church, awaiting arrest and martyrdom, prayed for the safety of the churches, not the Church singular. Regarding the installation of new bishops, Ignatius in his letter to the Philadelphia church, constrained the **church members to *elect* a new bishop.** In so doing he contradicts Rome's "apostolic succession" claim in which the faithful are led to believe bishops appointed by the Apostles appointed bishops to succeed themselves, who appointed bishops to succeed themselves, who then appointed bishops to succeed themselves, etc., all the way down to the present time. Likewise, in Clement's letter to the church at Corinth, he related how the Apostles wanted bishops they had appointed replaced, as death removed them. They were to be replaced by

> "...other approved men...with the *consent* of the whole church."

Clement, a bishop of Rome, (AD 92-101) never claimed that he was a supreme bishop with authority over all other bishops. And, the cited quote from his letter to the Corinthian church shows to be in error the Catholic belief that new bishops could only receive their appointment from existing bishops, or a "pope." The churches obviously enjoyed the right to approve individuals who aspired to leadership positions, another serious blow to Rome's "apostolic succession" crutch. If, however, one measure of the true church founded by Jesus is, in fact, "apostolic succession," Rome is in really deep trouble because of the eastern branch of Christendom, existing today as the Orthodox Church.

Since the days of the Apostles, eastern churches have maintained absolute independence from Rome, and do not embrace Catholicism's "Patchwork Gospel." Ignatius, bishop of Antioch, and Polycarp, bishop of Smyrna, were two of many eastern bishops, first-century successors to the Apostles. Both men were protégés of John the Evangelist. Through them and others, apostolic organization and authority would have passed to all succeeding Eastern Church bishops right down to the present time, thereby, obviating Rome's claim of exclusivity through "apostolic succession." For the record, today's Orthodox Church is comprised of independent fellowships each with its own governing bishop, an exact extension of apostolic church organization.

It was the 6th century—500 years after the Apostles—before the doctrine of purgatory began to attract attention as a possible future doctrinal "patch." It was not made an article of faith until AD 1274 by the Second Council of Lyons. It was reconfirmed by the Council of Trent in the 16th century because of attacks on it by the Reformers. Indulgences, temporal punishment, mortal and venial sin—doctrines symbiotically related to purgatory—also were unknown to the apostolic church and were "patched-in" many hundreds of years later. Is it unfair to question where in eternity all the souls went who died before purgatory and its related doctrines were "patched-in?"

Unreported to Catholics is the fact that the apostolic church had no priests. Their Old Testament function—offering the sacrifices—was eliminated forever by Calvary. And early efforts aimed at re-establishing a Levitical-type priesthood were condemned by Jesus, Himself, in the Book of Revelation. (Rev 2:6, 15) The Roman Catholic priesthood, then is a much later development, another example of Rome's "patchworking." Likewise, confession of sins to another human being was unheard of in the days of the early church. The Bible says we are to confess sin directly to God. That was apostolic church practice according to the episode in Acts where Peter rebuked Simon for trying to buy power to confer the Holy Spirit. Peter said, *"Repent therefore of this thy wickedness, and pray God, if perhaps the thought of thine heart may be forgiven thee."* (Act 8:22) If Peter was bishop of Rome and the first pope, and if Catholic Confession was a doctrine known to the Apostles, why didn't Peter "hear" Simon's confession, give him absolution, and send him on his way a forgiven sinner? Or, why did Clement's 1st century letter to the Corinthian church include the following observation?

> "The Lord, brethren, stands in need of nothing: and he desires nothing of anyone, except that confession be made to him. For, says the elect David, *'I will confess unto the Lord…'*"

As doctrinal "patches" go, the one that mandated confession of sins to a priest was another late comer. First declared a doctrine in the 12th century, it was formalized as an article of faith 100 years later—in AD 1216—during the Second Lateran Council, the same **western-church synod** that decreed the doctrine of transubstantiation. In my years as a Catholic I was uninformed and, therefore, unaware that—like the ones I have cited—doctrines I believed were instituted by Jesus, were, in reality, very late additions to the religion, and were simply "the commandments of men."

When Jesus bowed His sacred head on Calvary's cross, and in agony whispered, *"It is finished,"* (John 19:30) the Gospel of salvation was complete. Animal sacrifice was ended; the Levitical priesthood was eliminated; the Temple was done away with. All replaced by simple faith in our Lord's sinless deity, His once-for-all-sacrifice, and His glorious resurrection from the grave. Through this simple faith came forgiveness of sins, reconciliation with God, and adoption into His household for all eternity. Before the foundation of the world, before there was an Adam, an Eve, or an original sin, that plan of redemption for fallen mankind was in place. (1 Pet 1:20) Jesus, through His sinless life, sacrificial death and grave-conquering resurrection, executed and completed that plan. There was nothing partial about it. Nothing was left undone because God is a God of completeness. He did not create a partial universe, a partial world, or—as the evolutionists claim—partial people. Neither did Jesus leave behind a partial Gospel. Nothing, absolutely nothing, was left out of the Gospel entrusted to His Apostles and disciples. The New Testament, compiled and ratified long before there was a Catholic Church, contains every doctrine received, preached, and recorded by them; every doctrine a lost soul needs for deliverance from sin and admission into heaven's eternal bliss.

Catholics who firmly believe that their religion is the one and only founded by Christ are sorely mistaken and deliberately misled. The numerous doctrinal "patches" applied to Catholicism down through the ages are mute, unimpeachable testimony to the contrary. The sacraments, (works necessary for salvation), are "patches" added hundreds of years after the passing of the Apostles and their successors. Likewise, the priesthood, the papacy, Purgatory, mortal and venial sin, temporal punishment, indulgences, verbal confession, the Mass liturgy, transubstantiation. Canonization of "saints," the Marian doctrines, and "Tradition" as a doctrinal source equal to God's divine Word, also are late additions to a Gospel made whole, entire and eternal by those sacred words, *"It is finished."* Sadly, not even one of the aforementioned doctrines is supported by Scripture, nor by oral transmissions of traditions observed and practiced by the Apostles or the apostolic church. Catholicism's motto—**semper eadem,** (ever the same)—should be changed to **nunquam eadem,** never the same.

The fallacy of Rome's claim to be the one true church is clearly exposed by its own history of adding strange new doctrines from time to time. For Catholics, it means they've never had one complete set of truths, one, single, immutable pathway to salvation. What applies today may be altered, added to, or eliminated tomorrow. In fact, Rome has today's Catholics doing a lot more to be "saved" than Catholics living before most "patches" became articles of faith. For example, weekly Mass attendance was not mandatory until the 12th century. Holy Communion was not necessary for salvation before that, and neither was confession of sins to a priest. From all the evidence, only one conclusion is possible—Catholicism really isn't the one true church at all. Rather, it's a denomination whose roots can be traced to early Christianity, but whose "Patchwork Gospel" betrays it as a purveyor of heresy, an apostate church.

In subsequent chapters, Rome's most flagrant anti-Scriptural "patches" will be reviewed, starting in chapter two with the numerous Marian heresies. Chapter three will be devoted to the fraud-based papal office, and other chapters will critique Purgatory, temporal punishment, indulgences, mortal and venial sin, transubstantiation, Confession, the Mass, apparitions, etc. For the remainder of this chapter, however, a "patch" Rome calls "Tradition" will be the object of study, because the fallout from it produced the second of Catholicism's many heresies, and a fitting twin for the one just dealt with. Obviously meant to solve problems, "Tradition" has served only to emphasize the apostate condition into which Catholicism had lapsed by the 16th century when Martin Luther's Bible reading produced the launching pad for a Reformation that had been in the making for over 300 years. How "Tradition" came to be an article of faith, what effect it has had on the Roman Catholic view of Scriptures, the inescapable trap that has resulted, these comprise a fascinating but tragic story, one that began in AD 1546 in Trent, Italy.

By the 16th century, Catholicism had added so many doctrinal "patches" the Council of Trent, (AD 1545-63) had to take drastic action to justify their establishment as articles of faith. One of its most critical tasks was to protect and preserve at any cost the illusion that Catholicism is the true and only church founded by Christ, empowered by Him to "create" doctrines not found in Scripture. Reformers were challenging every "patched" doctrine. Justification and indulgences, which brought the opening sally, were only the tip of the iceberg. Purgatory, temporal punishment, sacraments, the priesthood, the papacy, the Mass, transubstantiation, and more, all came under fire from the Reformers. Their watchwords were four in number: **sola Scriptura, sola gratia, sola fide, sola Christus.** Only Scripture, only Grace, only Faith, and only Christ.

For Rome, the stakes were enormous. To admit *sola Scriptura* would have been an unmitigated disaster. Doctrines not found in the divine Word—all the ones that had been "patched-in" over a period of ten centuries—would have been exposed as man-inspired, and simply could not have been defended. Equally repugnant to the Vatican was the Reformers' insistence that justification is exclusively by the grace of God, whose free gift of faith in Christ's sacrifice produces forgiveness of sin and assures eternal life in heaven. Admitting to that would have wiped out the sacraments and all other works that had been "patched-in" as necessary for salvation. But the most perplexing problem of all for the assembled prelates, may well have been what to do about its own Office of the Inquisition, which office, for over 300 years, had been executing those very advocates of the four "only's" that the Council was convened to deal with.

One could have predicted that Rome would not capitulate without a fight, for the nearly absolute power Catholicism had wielded over western churches since the 9th century is not something willingly relinquished. But it is doubtful that anyone—even the most avid Reformer—had the slightest inkling that Trent's prelates would do the unthinkable. Compelled to deal with a challenge that had rapidly gotten out of control, deal with it they did. On the 8th of April, AD 1546, the Council issued a decree that met the *sola Scriptura* issue head-on, and, as far as Rome is concerned, disposed of it for all time. That wordy decree included the following excerpt:

> **(The Synod) "following the example of the orthodox Fathers, receives and venerates with an *equal affection* of piety and reverence, all the books of both the Old and of the New Testament...*as also* the said *Traditions* as well those (traditions) appertaining to faith as to morals, as having been dictated either by Christ's own word of mouth or by the Holy Ghost, and preserved in the Catholic church by a *continuous succession.* Let all, therefore, understand, in what order, and in what manner, the said Synod, after having laid the foundation of the Confession of Faith, will proceed, and what testimonies and authorities (Praesidiis) it will mainly use in confirming dogmas, and in restoring morals in the Church."**
> (Emphasis mine.)

With this astonishing "declaration of independence," Rome notified the Reformers, and all posterity, that Catholicism was free from reliance on divine Scripture alone, (***sola Scriptura***) for its doctrine, was not in the least encumbered or bound by it, and was, in fact, at liberty to use other "testimonies and authorities"...(read that, Tradition)..."in confirming dogmas." Thus was severed for all time whatever was left of Catholicism's relationship to the church instituted by Christ. The Word of God that Rome hadn't paid much attention to for ten centuries anyway, was formally evicted from its rightful position of exclusivity and preeminence, its value as the source of doctrine virtually eliminated. The numerous "patches" added to the Gospel from the 6th century on were—in retrospect—attributable to that which was venerated "with an equal affection of piety and reverence,"—(the said **Traditions**)—which allegedly had been "preserved in the Catholic church by a continuous succession."

Nor was that infamous Council content to stop at giving itself the authority to deviate from God's divine Word in matters of faith, doctrine, organization, etc. It must also appoint itself the sole custodian and interpreter of the very Scriptures it held in such low esteem. To wit:

> **"Furthermore, in order to restrain petulant spirits, it (Trent) decrees, that *no one*, relying on his own skill, shall—in matters of faith, and of morals pertaining to the edification of Christian doctrine—wresting the sacred Scripture to his own senses, *presume to interpret* the said sacred Scripture contrary to that sense which holy mother Church—whose it is to judge of the true sense and interpretation of the holy Scriptures—hath held and doth hold; or even *contrary to* the unanimous consent of *the Fathers*; even though such interpretations were never (intended) to be at any time published. Contraveners shall be made known by their Ordinaries, and be punished with the penalties by law established."** (Emphasis mine.)

From these Council of Trent decrees it is clear that the second of Catholicism's many heresies is Rome's teaching that it alone has been entrusted with God's revelation of Himself to mankind—both the divine Scriptures and Catholicism's alleged Traditions—and the very interpretation of it to boot. Since escaping from the Roman Catholic Church I never cease to be amazed at these kinds of claims. During my years as a Catholic I was not aware of them. I would be surprised if one out of a thousand of the faithful today are aware of them, either. For example, to justify this second great heresy, Rome claims that the Catholic Church actually pre-dates the New Testament, and is responsible for the assembly and ratification of its canon. But historical fact gives the lie to such preposterous claims.

The renowned church historian, Eusebius, AD 260-339, writing early in the fourth century records the following in Book 1, Chapter 4:4:

> "....but although it is clear that we are new and that this new name of *Christians* has really but recently been known among all nations, nevertheless our life and our conduct, with our doctrines of religion, have not been lately invented by us, but from the first creation of man, so to speak, have been established by the natural understanding of divinely favored men of old."

Had the Roman Catholic Church existed at the time it is certain Eusebius would have so noted the fact. He didn't. In AD 397, (still nearly 200 years before Catholicism) the Council of Carthage was convened, and Rome maintains that this convocation determined the New Testament canon. Not so says history. The representatives to that council merely confirmed the 27 New Testament books that were listed by Athanasius, Bishop of Alexandria, (an Eastern Church) 30 years before, and had been confirmed in AD 393 at the Synod of Hippo. But even before that, in the very beginning of the second century, Polycarp, Clement, Justin Martyr and, a bit later, Irenaeus, Bishop of Lyons, were quoting in their writings from most of our New Testament books. F. F. Bruce relates that the writings of Irenaeus alone in about AD 180, showed canonical acceptance of the four Gospels, the Acts, Romans, I and II Corinthians, Galatians, Ephesians, Philippians, Colossians, I and II Thessalonians, I and II Timothy, Titus, I Peter, I John and the Revelation. In other words, at least 21 of our 27 New Testament books were considered Holy Scripture more than 400 years before the Roman Catholic Church became an identifiable entity. Catholicism did not pre-date the New Testament; did not spearhead verification of its canon; is not its exclusive custodian, nor its God-appointed interpreter.

It will come as no surprise that the Council of Trent declarations cited earlier remain in effect to this day. They have never been modified; never been abrogated. In fact the Second Vatican Council, (1963-65) enthusiastically embraced them along with the rest of Trent's myriad decrees and condemnations. Today, the church's official position is unchanged and is boldly reiterated on pages 26 and 27 of the 1994 Catechism.

> "....the (Catholic) Church, to whom the transmission and interpretation of Revelation is entrusted, does not derive her certainty about all revealed truths from the holy Scriptures alone. Both Scripture and Tradition must be accepted and honored with equal sentiments of devotion and reverence."

The baseless, unsupported claims and autocratic proclamations emanating from Rome are nothing but brazen falsehoods, ugly heresies that foster the one-true-church illusion held so resolutely by the laity. These far-fetched claims are accepted by Catholic faithful as justification for Rome's various, unscriptural mandates—in this case, that "Tradition" is to be given honor and reverence equivalent to the very Word of God. Not only are their claims lacking the support of history, the Bible, and saints of the apostolic church, they contradict the very Scriptures Rome claims authority over.

Our Lord told the religious Jews that, *"the Scriptures cannot be broken."* (John 10:35) By this He clearly indicated that His Word is not to be demeaned, avoided, ignored, changed, or added to. In Psalm 89:34, quoted on the first page of this chapter, He declared that He would not break His covenant—in the New Testament, His promise of salvation by grace and faith alone—nor would He change (or allow to be changed) a single one of His Words. In the Galatians letter of Paul, those who preach a gospel different from the one he preached—his came directly from the lips of Jesus—are cursed, not once, but twice. (Gal 1:8, 9) Additional warnings against tampering with Scripture are found in Deuteronomy, Proverbs, and Revelation, and will be seen later on.

By exalting "Tradition" Rome has trapped the faithful in a belief system centered on "the commandments of men," not on the Gospel of the Savior who died for their sins. Since the word tradition is suggestive of long established customs and practices it is fair to insist that the many doctrines Rome has "patched-in" over a period of fifteen-hundred years be traceable to the early church, orally transmitted by the Apostles and their immediate successors. From all available records, however, such is not the case by any stretch of the imagination. And when the 1994 Catechism is consulted for Rome's definition of "Tradition," we see at once why none of the added doctrines is traceable to the Christian Church of the first four hundred years

> (Tradition is) **"…distinct from Sacred Scripture, though closely connected to it. Through tradition…the church, in her doctrine, life and worship perpetuates and transmits to every generation all that she herself IS, all that she BELIEVES.** (Emphasis mine.)

"Tradition" as Rome sees it, is not a compendium of early church customs and practices at all. It's simply **"all that she herself is,"** and **"all she believes,"** masquerading as apostolic hand-me-downs. To rationalize fifteen centuries of error; to justify her heretical view that not all truths **revealed by God** are to be found in His Scriptures, Rome resorts to "Tradition" that really isn't traditional at all. The whole thing is suggestive of an incomplete Bible, a partial Gospel, a capricious deity who improvises as He goes along. In the Scriptures, however, tradition does not inspire what Rome describes as "sentiments of devotion and reverence." Quite the opposite. Eleven out of thirteen times the word appears in the New Testament, it refers to that which is displeasing to God. Cf. Mat 15:3,6; Mar 7:8, 13; Col 2:8; I Pet 1:18. Only twice is it used in a favorable sense. (2 Th 2:15, 3:6) But, in neither instance can it be construed as justification for "patching-in" doctrines never known to, nor verbally passed on by, the original 120 disciples and their successors.

It was mentioned previously that the Trent declarations of 500 years ago have never been abrogated, nor so much as modified in the slightest degree. On the contrary, they have been enthusiastically ratified and even reinforced with the passing of time. For instance, today's Catholics, besides being denied the liberty to interpret Scriptures for themselves, also are denied the freedom to interpret "Tradition," whatever that may be at any given time. The 1994 Catechism puts it this way:

> "The task of giving an authentic INTERPRETATION of the Word of God, whether in written form or in the form of Tradition, has been ENTRUSTED to the living, teaching office of the CHURCH ALONE." (Emphasis mine.)

Way back in the dark ages, the Roman church began to recognize the danger to itself of exposing the laity to the Word of God. Experience showed that problems resulted when individuals got their hands on Scriptures produced in their own language. At first, this was successfully countermanded by making Latin the only approved language for Scripture, liturgical rites, prayer, communication, etc. This effectively kept God's Word out of the hands of the common people who were Latin illiterate. But later on, as the Scriptures began to appear in more and more native languages—Anglo-Saxon, Gothic, Germanic, Slavic, Coptic, Armenian, etc.—more stringent controls became necessary. Only Latin Vulgate Bibles were approved. Those published in other languages were condemned and ownership of them prohibited. Any native-language Bibles found were summarily confiscated and destroyed. Among those suffering that fate were the Gothic Bibles of the Ostrogoth, Theodoric, the Lollard Bibles of Wycliffe, and the Old English texts that became popular in England as far back as the 10th Century.

Rome's obsession to control both the message of Scripture and the interpretation of it has never been more evident than in its treatment of Godly dissenters such as Wycliffe, Tyndale, Savonarola, Huss, the Cathari, the Waldenses, etc. Wycliffe was excommunicated for translating the Bible into English in 1382. After death, his bones were exhumed, burned and tossed in the river. Tyndale, for his English translation of the Bible, Savonarola and Huss, for preaching *sola scriptura* and *sola gratia*, all were burned alive. The Cathari, also called the Albigenses, and the Waldenses, for their insistence on justification by faith, were exterminated as heretics.

The 16th century Council of Trent forbade publication of the Scripture except by those to whom Rome had issued a proper license. By the 19th century, no fewer than six different popes ruled against all efforts aimed at making the Scriptures available to the general public. Pius VII said that the indiscriminate distribution of Bibles in native languages **"…produced more harm than benefits… was eminently dangerous to souls."** Gregory XVI was vehemently opposed to making the Scriptures freely available to all people. Leo XIII in 1897 forbade the publication or reading of Scriptures in native languages.

There is an obvious antipathy to God's Word in the Vatican, expressions of which sometimes are nothing short of incredible. Ignatius Loyola who founded the Jesuit order, in his "*Rules For Thinking With The Church*," expressed his disdain for Scripture in Rule #13 which states:

> **"I will believe that the white that I see is black if the hierarchical Church so defines it."**

One of Loyola's fellow Jesuits had this to say about God's Word:

> **Without the authority of the Church, I would believe St. Matthew no more than Titus Livius."**

To Polish Cardinal Stanislaus Hosius, who presided over the Council of Trent, is credited the following statement about the value of God's Word:

> **"Except for the authority of the Holy Mother Church, the Scriptures would have no more weight than the fables of Aesop."**

In a recent general letter to Roman Catholic bishops from current pope, John Paul II, the church "party-line" regarding ***sola scriptura*** is rigidly adhered to.

Addressing a "resurgence of fideism" (faith alone) that has been observed, he writes as follows:

> "One currently widespread symptom of this fideistic tendency is a 'biblicism' which tends to make the reading and exegesis of Sacred Scripture the sole criterion of truth. In consequence, the Word of God is identified with Sacred Scripture alone, thus eliminating the *doctrine of the Church* which the Second Vatican Council stressed quite specifically. Having recalled that the word of God is present in both Scripture and Tradition, the Constitution Dei Verbum continues emphatically: 'Sacred Tradition and Sacred Scripture comprise a single deposit of the word of God entrusted to the Church…' Scripture, therefore, is not the Church's sole point of reference. The 'supreme rule of her faith' derives from the unity which the Spirit has created between Sacred Tradition, Sacred Scripture, and the Magisterium of the Church in a reciprocity which means that *none* of the three *can survive without the others.* (Emphasis mine.)

Imagine standing before the Judgment Seat of Christ and telling our blessed Savior that His divine Word—Sacred Scripture—was no more valuable than Aesop's Fables; that it could not have survived apart from Catholicism's "Sacred Tradition" and its Magisterium. *"Heaven and earth shall pass away, but my words shall not pass away."* (Matt 24:35) May God be merciful to such proud but horribly deluded men, and to all who are taken in by them. In that same letter to the bishops, John Paul II included the following admonition:

> "Moreover, one should not underestimate the danger inherent in seeking to derive the truth of Sacred Scripture from the use of one method alone, ignoring the need for a more comprehensive exegesis which enables the exegete, together with the whole Church, to arrive at the full sense of the texts."

Evangelicals who have tried witnessing to Catholics without an understanding of the Catholic mentality, express dismay that unregenerate sinners can be so biblically illiterate and so arrogant at the same time. Often in the most contemptuous manner, Catholics will let it be known that their interest is not in what the Bible says, but in what the Catholic Church teaches. That is what I have come to call the **"Tradition Trap."** It has been created by Rome's numerous statements and mandates devaluing Scripture, while at the same time demanding "equal" honor and reverence for "Sacred Tradition." It holds Catholics tenaciously in the grip of what Rome says without regard, interest, or fear for what God's Word says. What Rome says and what the Bible says, however, are as far apart as Rome is from the true "eternal city"—Jerusalem.

Rome says it alone has been entrusted with Sacred Scripture. God's Word says: *"**All scripture is given by inspiration of God, and is profitable for doctrine, for reproof, for correction, for instruction in righteousness:**"* (I Tim 3:16) No indication therein that Rome or anyone else is appointed exclusive custodian of Scripture. And, no indication in the following that it has been given exclusive interpretive authority, either. *"**…the anointing which ye have received of him** (the Holy Spirit) **abideth in you, and ye need not that any man teach you: but as the same anointing teacheth you all things, and is truth, and is no lie, and even as it hath taught you, ye shall abide in him.**"* (I John 2:27) It is the indwelling Holy Spirit that interprets and teaches, not the Roman church.

Taken as a whole, the Council of Trent decrees and the 1994 Catechism references previously cited, comprise a perfect blueprint for the establishment of a **religious cult.** Rome **endows itself** with absolute authority over what is taught, what is to be believed, how Scriptures are to be interpreted. New doctrines and teachings, products of "Tradition," can be introduced at any time. Yet none of this can be attributed or traced to the Church instituted by Christ. All of it is simply the Montanist heresy of the 2nd century reprised. Its founder, Montanus, was a mystic who experienced trances in which he allegedly received new revelations directly from the Holy Spirit. This implied what Rome's "patchworking" also implies—that Christ's Gospel was incomplete, that the Holy Spirit was adding to it via special revelations given only to Montanus and his followers. The early Church wisely declared Montanism a heresy. It still is. Christ's Gospel required no new revelations then or since then. Holy Spirit revelation ended with the Book of Revelation.

Some time ago, my wife and I had a conversation with a practicing Roman Catholic couple who knew that I was raised in a Catholic home. The subjects covered were of a doctrinal nature touching on numerous areas where Catholic teachings conflict with God's Word. Our friends continually referred to what they had learned from their Catholic education while my wife and I adhered strictly to Biblical truth. At one point the dear lady fairly shouted at me, "John, you were **raised** a Catholic! "You **know** better!" By this I was supposed to understand that all Catholic teaching is correct—the truth—and any conflicting beliefs have to be in error. When my wife suggested that a lack of Bible knowledge was seriously affecting their beliefs, the angry lady's husband exclaimed: "Ah, the Bible is just a bunch of words on paper!" I, for one, have nothing but fear for the pitiful soul who—at the seat of Judgment—tells our Lord His Bible was "just a bunch of words on paper."

While on the one hand Rome admits that the Bible is the inspired **Word of God,** and even suggests that Catholics read it, little real enthusiasm for Scripture has been generated, and control of the message received is never relinquished. Catholics, under pain of sin, abide at all times by Rome's interpretations. In this way, Rome solidifies its position of absolute authority over the faithful, discourages in-depth Bible study, and prevents a mass exodus of its members into evangelical, Bible-directed Christianity.

In our day the Roman Catholic Church has further diminished the credibility of the Bible in Catholic circles by accepting as fact the Darwinian theory of evolution, and sanctioning the evil campaign of the infamous Jesus Seminar. By embracing the theory that all organisms—man included—are evolved from "primeval slime," the church capitulates to the forces of evil who promote the belief that the first eleven chapters of Genesis are nothing more than myth. So insensitive is Rome to Biblical truth that they fail to see—or choose to ignore—that every Christian doctrine has its foundation in the first eleven chapters of Genesis. Destroy belief in the historicity of Genesis and you destroy the very foundations of Christianity! *"If the foundations be destroyed, what can the righteous do?"* (Psa 11:3) The last time Rome dabbled in a scientific matter, Galileo was censured for agreeing with Copernicus that the earth revolves around the sun and not vice-versa. This time Rome has not only picked the wrong "horse" again, but by so doing has stepped all over the divinely revealed Word of God. (Cf. I Tim 3:16.) Following is a news item that must have had the atheists, agnostics and humanists jumping for joy. Words of John Paul II are in bold type.

> NEWSBRIEF: Chicago Tribune, Friday 10/25/96.
> POPE BOLSTERS CHURCH SUPPORT FOR EVOLUTION
> By Stevenson Swanson, Tribune staff writer. Dateline: New York.
> "In a major statement of the Roman Catholic Church's position on the theory of evolution, Pope John Paul II has proclaimed that the theory is *'more than just a hypothesis'* and that **evolution is *'compatible with Christian faith.'***
> In a written message to the Pontifical Academy of Sciences, the pope said the theory of evolution has been buttressed by scientific studies and discoveries since Charles Darwin. '**…it is indeed remarkable that this theory has progressively taken root in the minds of researchers following a series of discoveries made in different spheres of knowledge,**' the pope said in his message Wednesday. '**The convergence, neither sought nor provoked, of results of studies undertaken independently from each other constitutes, in itself, a significant argument in favor of this theory…**'*If taken literally,*

the Biblical view of the beginning of life and Darwin's scientific view would seem irreconcilable. In Genesis, the creation of the world, and Adam, the first human, took six days. Evolution's process of genetic mutation and natural selection—the survival and proliferation of the fittest new species—has taken billions of years, *according to scientists…*'
The Pope's message went much further in accepting the theory of evolution as a valid explanation of the development of life on Earth, with one major exception: the human soul. '*If the human body* **has its origin in living material which pre-exists it the spiritual soul is immediately created by God,**' the Pope said." (Emphases mine.)

In the foregoing, we see one of the self-appointed "guardians" of the Holy Scriptures, one of the self-styled "infallible" popes, denying the truth of God's revealed Word as recorded in the book of Genesis. He who claims for Rome, and for Rome alone, the right to interpret God's Word, publicly endorses the Devil's evolution lie with statements that refute the veracity of the divine Scriptures. This thinly veiled attack on the Bible concludes with doubt being cast upon the origin of the human body that God says in Genesis was formed on the sixth day of creation out of the dust of the earth—not over eons of time by way of ever advancing speciation.

Of all the ironies associated with the Vatican's claims (A) to be the one true church, and (B) to be the sole custodian and interpreter of the Scriptures, this one—the endorsement of Darwinian evolution—most visibly and successfully shatters the laity's trust in the Bible. Darwin's theory of evolution, which everywhere is taught as fact, is a blatant repudiation of God's Word, and in no sense or way is it "compatible with Christian faith." The "baggage" that accompanies it for the unsuspecting Catholic includes elimination of the six days of creation, replacement of them with a naturally occurring universe in existence for billions of years following an imagined "Big Bang" or a collapsed ultra-dense cloud. It presumes the existence of pain, suffering and death before Adam's original sin, thereby contradicting God, whose Word says death came as a result of Adam's sin. **"Wherefore, as by one man sin entered into the world, and death by sin; and so death passed upon all men, for that all have sinned:"** (Rom 5:12)

This endorsement of Darwinian evolution by the leader of nearly a billion souls amounts to a subtle declaration that God has deceived us; has led us to believe that the first eleven chapters of Genesis contain an historical account of ex nihilo creation, man's fall into sin, God's judgment via Noah's flood, the confusion of languages, and the migration of nations. Catholics who subscribe to their pope's doubts about the veracity of the Scriptures should ask themselves some hard questions. To wit:

Did our Lord purpose to deceive us when He referred to Genesis as historical? *"But from the beginning of the creation God made them male and female.*" (Mar 10:6) *"For in the days that were before the flood they were eating and drinking, marrying and giving in marriage, until the day that Noe entered into the ark."* (Mat 24:38) Our Savior was not deceiving us.

The writer of Hebrews referred to the sacrifices of Cain and Abel recorded in Genesis 4. *"By faith Abel offered a more excellent sacrifice than Cain, by which he obtained witness that he was righteous."* (Heb 11:4) Was this an attempt to deceive us? Peter spoke of God's judgment on Sodom and Gomorrha. *"And turning the cities of Sodom and Gomorrha into ashes condemned them with an overthrow, making them an ensample unto those that after should live ungodly."* (2 Pet 2:6) Was Peter somehow misinformed? Not likely.

By accepting Darwinian evolution as fact, (with the stipulation that at some point in time God breathed a soul into some form of animal life that then became a man) the Roman Catholic church has committed doctrinal suicide. Without the initial chapters of Genesis as historical fact, there is no foundation for ex nihilo creation, (2 Pet 3:4, 5) original sin, judgment, suffering and death, blood atonement, clothing, marriage, the promised Savior, on and on.

Moreover, Darwinian evolution is bad science; it is, in fact, no science at all. True science is based on observation, testability, replication, and affirmation or falsification, none of which are applicable with respect to the origin of all things for the simple reason that there were no eye witnesses except God Himself. Former evolution supporters, though still unwilling to believe in ex nihilo creation, have been jumping Darwin's sinking ship by the dozens for several years now. Gould, Hoyle, Behe, big important figures in the scientific community, have, along with numerous others, abandoned entirely Darwin's gradualization ideas. And, unbeknownst to Rome, or deliberately overlooked by it, there is not a scientist living on this earth who can produce one unimpeachable **proof** that molecule-to-man evolution ever happened. Three immutable natural laws stand as insurmountable barriers against it, and, though John Paul II appears not to know it, **all**—not some—**all genetic mutations are harmful!** Most actually are fatal, thus eliminating entirely the possibility that genetic mutations result in the formation of new, advanced species. In truth, all real scientific evidence points to "intelligent design"—creation by a sovereign, omnipotent deity.

For the Catholic Church to so diminish the integrity, yea the very truth, of God's divinely revealed Scriptures is to spawn doubts that Rome has any respect at all for our Lord's Words. *"…had ye believed Moses, ye would have believed me; for he wrote of me. But if ye believed not his writings, how shall ye believe my words?"* (John 5:46, 47) A critical question for the Vatican, especially when at the same time it is sanctioning the egregious work of the infamous Jesus Seminar. For those unfamiliar with this evil group, let me explain.

Some years ago, a collection of self-styled Bible scholars got together for the express purpose of determining which of the words attributed to Jesus in the Bible were, in fact, spoken by Him. The group is made up of individuals representing many denominations including Roman Catholics. Their efforst have been directed at analyses of the four Gospels with an eye to determining which of the words in red letters were actually spoken by our Lord during His earthly ministry. This, mind you, 2000 years after the fact! Meetings have been held every so often for several years, at least one of them at Catholic Notre Dame University in South Bend, Indiana.

Reports coming out of these sessions indicate they don't put much confidence in the Holy Spirit's ability to inspire and direct the composition and compilation of God's divine Word. In 2 Peter 1:20, 21, credit for the Scriptures is given to the Holy Spirit, not to mortal men. ***"For the prophecy came not at any time by the will of man, but holy men of God spake as they were moved by the Holy Ghost."*** In Paul's second letter to Timothy he instructs that young Christian as follows: ***"All Scripture is given by inspiration of God."*** (2 Tim 3:16)

It's clear that the Jesus Seminar participants do not subscribe to those Biblical assurances, for published progress reports indicate they have already determined very few of the words red-lettered in our Bibles were actually spoken by our Lord. This conclusion has been arrived at by majority vote. Certain passages containing the words of Jesus were reviewed by the group during each of the meetings, at the end of which, voting was done to establish whether or not the reviewed words came from the lips of the Lord. A participant casting his vote via a black ball was expressing his conviction that Jesus never said the critiqued words. A gray ball cast was notification a slim possibility existed that Christ said such words, while the casting of a red ball indicated agreement that Jesus really spoke the words in question. At last report, these people were in the process of producing their own version of the four Gospels. When it's published, our Lord may become known to its readers as the "silent Jesus."

These actions on the part of the Roman Catholic Church—giving credence to the bankrupt Darwinian evolution theory, and sanctioning the ill-conceived Jesus Seminar by participating in its evil enterprise—are merely modern examples of the Vatican's antipathy to Scripture. Such publicized endorsements effectively undermine the laity's confidence in the Bible, and are a clear indication why so few Catholics read it; why others say, "Ah, the Bible is just a bunch of words on paper!"

When Satan set out to destroy the man and woman God had created perfect in every way, his avenue of attack centered on the Word of God. **"Yea, hath God said, 'Ye shall not eat of every tree of the garden?'"** This, or course, is an intentional misquotation of Genesis 2:17 in which God made only one tree off limits. **"Ye shall not surely die."** A deliberate contradiction of God's admonition that eating fruit of the forbidden tree would result in certain death. Finally, **"For God doth know that…ye shall be as gods, knowing good and evil."** (Gen 3:5) Here Satan infers God has a hidden motive not favorable to His creatures, and known only to Satan himself. This strategy—assaulting God's Word—successful there in the Garden of Eden, has remained Satan's most effective weapon for the corruption of souls through all the succeeding ages. In the Roman Catholic religion—in its practice of "patching" the Lord's Gospel while continually devaluing His divine Word—Satan has found a most useful ally.

> **"Yea hath God not said His Gospel is incomplete? Hath He not said it lacketh many truths? Hath He not periodically revealed new truths from TRADITION to the great high priest who sitteth in the Vatican?"**

Three times—twice in the Old Testament, once in the New—mankind is forbidden to add to or to take from the Word of God. Yet this is exactly what the Vatican has done by: 1) **adding dogmas** not found in Scripture; 2) by **adding books** to the Bible that both the Jews and early Christians rejected as uninspired; and 3) by **publishing Catechisms** that have replaced the Bible as Catholicism's number-one teaching tool. These all are in violation of God's divine Word. *"You shall not add unto the word which I command you neither shall you diminish aught from it, that you may keep the commandments of the Lord your God which I command you."* (Deut 4:2) Clearly, mankind is prohibited from tampering with Scripture as given by the Holy Spirit.

In the book of Proverbs we find this admonition: *"Every word of God is pure: He is a shield unto them that put their trust in Him. Add thou not unto His words, lest He reprove thee, and thou be found a liar."* (Pro 30:5,6) Because God's Word is true and everlasting, this Scripture bluntly decrees **the Catholic Church is a liar!**

Once again—in the very last book of the Bible, and in its very last chapter—God's warning is repeated, and its gravity emphasized by the addition of anathemas not previously stated. The divine Word of God—not the finite word of Rome—reads as follows: ***"For I testify unto every man that hears the words of the prophecy* (message)** *of this book if any man shall add unto these things, God shall add unto him the plagues that are written in this book: and if any man shall take away from the words of this book, God shall take away his part out of the book of life, and out of the holy city, and from the things which are written in this book."* (Rev 22:18, 19)

Unfortunately, for devout Catholics who are entrusting their souls to their religion instead of to their Savior, the Vatican "marches to the beat of a different drummer." Besides inventing so-called "Tradition" as justification for the numerous "patches" it has imposed upon God's Gospel, **the Council of Trent added to the Bible itself** by including books the Jews and the apostolic church had summarily rejected. These books known as the Apocrypha were excluded by the Jews from the Old Testament Scriptures for three reasons: 1) historical inaccuracies; 2) blatant heresy; and 3) absence of Holy Spirit inspiration. Ditto the early Church Christians who unanimously approved the long accepted Old Testament while settling on the canon of the New Testament. For fifteen centuries Christianity had a 39-book Old Testament and a 27-book New Testament. After Trent, the Catholic Church had a new expanded Bible that could no longer be called the Word of God. And to make sure this arrogant insult to a Holy God would be accepted by the faithful as "sacred and canonical," one of Trent's 125 curses was pronounced upon any who would dissent from the Council's action.

> "…**But if any one receive not, as** *sacred and canonical,* **the said** (Apocrypha) **books entire with all their parts, as they have been used to be read in the Catholic church, and as they are contained in the old Latin Vulgate edition; and knowingly and deliberately contemn the traditions aforesaid, let him be anathema** (cursed). Note: Jerome's Latin Vulgate, a 5th century product, did include the Apocryphal books, but **not** as sacred Scripture.

Imagine for a moment doing something the Word of God expressly forbids, and then pronouncing a curse upon all those who disagree. Amazing. Catholicism, the self-appointed custodian and sole interpreter of God's Word, applies "patch" after unsupported "patch" to God's immutable Gospel for ten centuries, invents a thing called "Tradition" to justify their forbidden actions, tops these off with the addition of spurious books to their Bible, and then declares "cursed" all those who spurn such absolute folly. Thanks be to God for comforting Scriptures like this one: ***"Who is he that condemneth? It is Christ that died, yea rather, that is risen again, who is even at the right hand of God, who also maketh intercession for us."*** (Rom 8:34)

The Council of Trent was the ultimate disaster for the Catholic Church. Not even one of the doctrinal "patches" attacked by the Reformers as unsupported in Scripture was repudiated by the assembled prelates. Luther's contention, based solidly on the Word of God, that justification is by faith alone, and not by works, not only was rejected by the Council, but also was condemned. Luther was excommunicated, and all were cursed who hold to his belief that, ***"The just shall live by faith."*** (Hab 2:4; Rom 1:17)

> "If anyone shall say that justifying faith is nothing else than confidence in the divine mercy pardoning sins for Christ's sake, or that it is that confidence alone by which we are justified, let him be accursed."

Not just anyone, but the very Holy Spirit of God said long ago, ***"For by grace are ye saved through faith; and that not of yourselves; it is the gift of God, not of works, lest any man should boast."*** (Eph 2:8, 9) Does the Trent curse apply to the One who gave us that sweet promise? And this one: ***"Not by works of righteousness which we have done, but according to His mercy He saved us by the washing of regeneration, and renewing of the Holy Ghost."*** (Tit 3:5) And this one: ***"Verily, verily, I say unto you, he that believeth on me hath everlasting life."*** (John 6:47) Unlike Roman Catholic officials who are held captive in their own "Tradition Trap," the early Christian leaders clung tenaciously to the Scriptures. In his Book 4, Chapter 28:8, church historian, Eusebius, expresses the 4th century Christian view of contemporaries who were deserting and twisting the Word of God.

> "…They have treated the Divine Scriptures recklessly and without fear. They have set aside the rule of ancient faith; and Christ they have not known. They do not endeavor to learn what the Divine Scriptures declare, but strive laboriously after any form of syllogism which may be devised to sustain their impiety."

Had the Roman Catholic religion existed in the 4th century when Eusebius wrote his history of the young Christian Church, the above-cited quotation may well have been aimed straight at the Vatican. There in the Lateran's hallowed halls, the Scriptures have been treated with reckless abandon, downgraded to mere equality with the words of sinful men, twisted, added to, ignored, and all without fear of the mighty, eternal, King of Kings from whom those Scriptures emanated. Not only has Catholicism failed to observe what God's Word declares, it has tried every way to keep the trusting laity from obedience to that Word as well. Faced with ever increasing availability of printed Bibles in more and more native languages, the Council of Trent chalked up one more mark against itself and Catholicism by authorizing a Jesuit, Robert Bellarmine, to produce an extra-biblical publication which became known shortly thereafter as the Trent Catechism. In it were found no contradictions to Rome's numerous heresies. None of the Reformers' Scriptural doctrines were found there, either.

Many Catholic Catechisms have been published since that first one in the 16th century. All have been, and continue to be, tightly controlled purveyors of the Vatican-approved Catholic "party line." They are extra-biblical, meaning they are not authorized—in fact, are condemned—by the Word of God. They offer, nonetheless, a fascinating study in how nimbly Rome skips through momentous doctrinal upheavals and changes, and how subtly they discourage the study of divine Scripture. My personal favorite has to do with papal infallibility which has been a declared article of faith only since the year AD 1870. In that 19th century, and prior to the First Vatican Council out of which came the infallibility declaration, a popular Catechism was one published in Scotland by Stephen Keenan, a Catholic priest. When first it appeared in 1851, it featured the following question and answer regarding papal infallibility;

Q. Must not Catholics believe the pope in himself to be infallible?
A. This is a Protestant invention; it is *no article of Catholic faith*.

In 1851, it seems, papal infallibility was nothing more than a Protestant "invention." Catholics were not bound under pain of sin to believe it. It was not a doctrine; not an article of faith. The pope was as prone to err in that era as any other mortal soul. But when the Keenan Catechism was reprinted just 20 years later—one year after Pius IX "patched" papal infallibility into the Catholic Church repertoire of added doctrines not supported by Scripture—its treatment of the same subject had undergone a major face-lift.

Q. Is the pope infallible?
A. Yes, the pope is infallible.
Q. But some Catholics, before the Vatican Council, denied the infallibility of the pope, which was impugned by this very Catechism.
A. Yes, they did so under the usual reservation, insofar as they then could grasp the mind of the church, and subject to her (the church's) future definitions, thus implicitly accepting the dogma.

A most amazing organism is the Roman Catholic Church. One day a doctrine is not a doctrine. The next day it becomes a doctrine. All who denied it yesterday must believe it today, because their denial yesterday was with the reservation that Rome might change its mind today. Such unmitigated insolence on the part of those who claim custodial authority over God's divine Word. Who dares trust his or her immortal soul to a church whose "mind" can be changed any time expediency dictates? How can one ever be certain that today's already heretical doctrine of Mary as co-mediatrix with Christ, will not tomorrow become the doctrine of Mary co-redeemer, co-savior with our Lord, of all who "believe on her name?" How long before today's "infallible" pope declares himself not just "vicar of Christ" but Christ Himself? These are very real possibilities, not in the least far-fetched. For a church that is not restricted in its beliefs and declarations by the Word of God, is a church unpredictable; a church unreliable; an apostate church, no less deadly than the "Mystery Babylon" of Revelation.

Another Catechism—the "Full Catechism of The Catholic Religion"—presents an excellent study in the art of discouraging Bible reading. Authored by Joseph Deharbe, and re-published in 1979, the hardbound version sells in Catholic book stores for 17.95. In it, the Catholic Church is projected as the lone *"pillar and ground of truth,"* (Cf. 1 Tim 3:15) For this reason, the church allegedly cannot erroneously interpret the Word of God. Therefore, the individual Catholic is forbidden to interpret Scriptures, for two given reasons. First, no individual can understand the Scriptures like the Holy Spirit who gives the Vatican their true meanings. Second, **"The Holy Scripture is a Divine and mysterious book,"** containing certain things not easily understood. (Cf. 1 Pet 3:16) Only those possessing the **"learning and piety"** necessary should read the Bible, and then only approved translations with annotations endorsed by Rome.

R.A. Torrey, the great 19th century evangelist, commenting on the concept that the Bible is a difficult book and hard to be understood, expressed his belief like this:

> **"I am always suspicious of profound explanations of Scripture, explanations that require a scholar or philosopher to understand them. The Bible is a plain man's book.** (Cf. Mat 11:25) **In at least ninety-nine cases in a hundred the meaning of Scripture lies on the surface—the meaning that any simple-minded man, woman or child who really wants to know and obey the truth would see in it."**

When Vatican VIPS say in effect, "We only are the ones who compiled, preserved, and disseminated the Holy Scriptures, (none of which is true,) therefore we have the exclusive right to their interpretation," they can be compared to the telegraph operator who, upon starting his shift, finds a message for a group of people already typed out and packaged for delivery. As he delivers it, he declares, "I'm the only one who can tell you folks what this message means." In the case of God's divine Word, every born again believer is indwelt by the Holy Spirit—the very author of the Scriptures—and by Him is empowered to interpret them quite correctly. (Cf. 1 John 2:27.)

It is apparent that Jesus did not consider His Word to be "mysterious" or difficult to understand, for he urged the unbelieving religious Jews to, **"Search the Scriptures; for…they are they which testify of me."** (John 5:39) Why would our Lord urge people—especially unbelievers—to search into what He knew they would be unable to comprehend? Such would only engender confusion, and the Bible tells us God is not the author of confusion. (Cf. 1 Cor 14:33) In a similar vein, Luke expressed admiration for the Bereans to whom Paul and Silas preached the Gospel. Of them he said, **"These were more noble than those in Thessalonica, in that they received the Word with all readiness of mind, and searched the Scriptures daily, whether those things were so."** (Act 17:11) Does Rome think its laity is of lesser intelligence than the common folk of Berea in Paul's lifetime?

This second great heresy of Catholicism—that Rome is the sole custodian and interpreter of God's Word—is, as has already been noted, propagated very effectively through Catechisms and the teachings they contain. Add to this the personal influence of the clergy, the trust placed in the priest by his parishioners, the Rome-fostered illusion that only in the pastor resides the "oracles" of God, and what you end up with is a brainwashed flock, unable and unwilling to contest even the most outlandish claims and dogmas—the Marian heresies, for example. On page 27 of the 1994 Catechism, even the manner in which the laity is to accept Rome's teachings is dictated.

> **"Mindful of Christ's words to His apostles: 'He who hears you hears me,' the faithful receive with docility the teachings and directives that their pastors give them in different forms."**

How clever of the Vatican to suggest in the above that "hearing" the teachings and directives of their pastors is equivalent to hearing the very words of our Lord. For this reason, of course, the laity is instructed to accept whatever they are taught submissively and without doubting, questioning, or disputation of any kind. Unfortunately, this is exactly how the Vatican's teachings are received by multi-millions of the Catholic faithful, (me, too, when I was one). It accounts for the stonewalling experienced by evangelical Christians who try to witness to these sadly misled folks. A Catechism statement—"...**the Church...does not derive her certainty about all revealed truths from the Holy Scriptures alone,**" should have Catholics jumping out of their seats shouting, **"Why not!? Why would God leave important truths out of His Bible!?"** But, instead of demanding answers to that and numerous similar questions, Catholics (me, too, when I was one) find it easier to "receive with docility" only what Rome chooses to feed them. What Rome chooses **not** to feed them, though, is critical to the eternal destination of their souls.

In the epistle of Paul to the Galatians, God's Word reveals two vitally important facts that are hidden from the Catholic faithful. *"But I certify you, brethren, that the gospel which was preached of (by) me is not after man. For I neither received it of man, neither was I taught it, but by the revelation of Jesus Christ."* (Gal 1:11, 12) Fact the first: what Paul preached he received directly from the lips of our Lord, and there is not the slightest suggestion it was anything less than a complete Gospel. *"But though we, or an angel from heaven, preach any other gospel unto you than that which we have preached unto you, let him be accursed. As we said before, so say I now again, if any man preach any other gospel unto you than that ye have received, let him be accursed."* (Gal 1:8, 9) Fact the second: to preach anything other than what Paul preached is twice cursed in God's Word. The oft "patched" gospel of Catholicism is not even close to the complete Gospel Paul and the other Apostles preached. Those who preach and teach it do so at their own peril.

In His wonderful "Olivet Discourse" our blessed Savior said, *"And THIS Gospel of the kingdom shall be preached in all the world for a witness to all nations; and then shall the end come."* (Mat 24:14) Christ said, *"THIS"* Gospel, not an incomplete Gospel needing "patches" to perfect it. Later, toward the end of that famous sermon, Jesus said. *"Heaven and earth shall pass away, but my words shall not pass away."* (Mat 24:35) "Sacred Tradition," so-called by the Council of Trent bunch, has been granted equal status with the Word of God by the Vatican VIPS; but it was not so honored by our Lord. He said it was His Words that would not pass away; not His Words **and** the "Sacred Tradition" unveiled at Trent, Italy in the 16th century.

When a religion departs even partially from the written *Logos*—the *Word* as it is preserved in our Bibles—there is only one way it can go—astray. In each of the heresies discussed in this and following chapters, the Catholic church either has added to God's Word, twisted God's Word, taken away from it, or ignored it entirely, always to the detriment of its trusting members. Justification by faith alone in Christ's atoning sacrifice—the very foundation of the Gospel given to

Paul directly by Jesus—has been replaced in Catholicism by a works-based, Tradition-driven theology not found anywhere in divine Scripture.

The Bible contains many warnings about false teachers and teachings, some of which have been referred to already. The one that follows seems especially apropos. *"Now the SPIRIT speaketh expressly that in the latter times some shall depart from the faith, giving heed to seducing spirits and doctrines of devils; speaking lies in hypocrisy: having their consciences seared with a hot iron; forbidding to marry and commanding to abstain from meats."* (1 Tim 4:1-3) In AD 1079, the Catholic Church forbade priests to marry; commanded them to remain celibate throughout their lives. That order has never been rescinded; continues in force to this day, and has resulted in the kind of shocking immorality previously associated only with pagan religions of bygone days and the cults of this generation. Catholicism completed fulfillment of the prophecy in First Timothy—about the same time as the celibacy decree—when Rome commanded the faithful, under penalty of serious sin, to abstain from meat on all Fridays and certain "fast" days throughout the year.

According to Eusebius, historian of the early Christian church, certain of the Apostles were married, among them both Peter and Philip. The latter had four daughters *"which did prophesy."* (Act 21:9) Obviously there was no such thing as celibacy in the early church. Nor were the early Christians bound to observe certain days of the week or abstain from certain foods. Says Eusebius in his Book 1, Chapter 4, the patriarchs, Abraham, Isaac and Jacob:

> **"…did not care about observing Sabbaths, nor do we. They did not avoid certain kinds of food, neither did they regard the other distinctions which Moses first delivered to their posterity to be observed as symbols; nor do Christians of the present day do such things."**

The early Christian church, predecessor to the Roman Catholic Church, was not under bondage to commandments not found in the Word of God. No one was placed under penalty of sin for missing a Lord's Day gathering. Bishops, deacons, elders, presbyters, could be married or not married as they themselves were led. No foods were forbidden them. No works were prescribed as necessary for salvation. "Sacred Tradition" was unheard of. The Scriptures alone contained their articles of faith, their doctrine. As a former Catholic who had no knowledge of the Word of God other than what Rome fed me, it now seems so appropriate to me that the longest chapter in the Bible is Psalm 119 which has 176 verses. Appropriate, because the entire psalm is focused on the wonder, the beauty, the comfort, the truth, the guidance, and the protection to be found in God's precious Word. *"Thy word have I hid in mine heart, that I might not sin against thee."* (Psa 119:11) *"This is my comfort in my affliction: for thy word hath quickened me."* (Psa 119:50) *"For ever, O LORD, thy word is settled in heaven."* (Psa 119:89) *"Thy word is a lamp unto my feet, and a light unto my path."* (Psa 119:105 *"Thou art my hiding place and my shield: I hope in thy word."* (Psa 119:114)

The Apostle, Peter, declared a bishop of Rome and the first pope by the Catholic church, believed what the Vatican seems not to believe. When a saddened Jesus asked the twelve, *"Will you also go away?"* it was Peter who expressed the group's sentiments. *"Then Simon Peter answered him, Lord, to whom shall we go? Thou hast the words of eternal life."* (John 6:67, 68) They are found in every Bible, those wonderful words of eternal life. They are not found in so-called "Sacred Tradition," Catechisms, papal "bulls" and encyclicals, pastoral observations or "Patchwork" doctrines. Because they are God's Word, they are found only in God's Word.

In these pages we have seen overwhelming evidence that Rome lies when it claims to be the original, the true, and the only church founded by Christ Jesus. Its "Patchwork gospel" is a very visible contradiction to that claim, for it is **not** the Gospel given us by Jesus. It is **not** the Gospel preached by Paul, Peter, Philip, John, all the other Apostles, as well, and the early **Christian Church**. The Vatican's gospel is **not** the Gospel Jesus referred to in Matthew 24 as "**THIS Gospel**." Furthermore, in its organization, its doctrines, its liturgies, and its extensive statuary, the Roman Catholic Church is radically different from the church left on earth by Christ. Is it descended from apostolic Christianity? Of course, just as numerous other sects, faiths and denominations are rooted in the early church. But is it the one and only true church? Not according to history and the Word of God. That's simply one of Rome's many lies. Another is Rome's claim to have been appointed sole custodian and interpreter of the divine Scriptures. This is Catholicism's second great heresy and is as unsubstantiated as the first, 1) by God's Word, 2) by history, and, 3) by the early church saints. Hundreds of years before there was a Catholic church, the Old and New Testaments were compiled and ratified. Rome had nothing to do with their compilation or approval, and any authority Rome claims with respect to the Bible is self-assumed and has not come from Jesus.

In all truth, the Vatican's well-documented antipathy to the Bible, reflected in its record of banning, and/or discouraging the study of it, more than disqualifies Rome from any kind of say-so with respect to the divine Scriptures. Its expedient manufacture of an umbrella called "Sacred Tradition," under which doctrines not found in the Bible can be introduced and justified, is just further proof of Rome's very active disdain for the Word of God, and its unswerving opposition to the Bible as the one and only rule of faith.

Would our Lord have entrusted His divine Word and its interpretation to a Vatican crowd that denies the historicity of Genesis by endorsing microbe-to-man evolution? Would He entrust His most precious Word to a Vatican crowd whose leaders say it's downright dangerous to seek for truth in the Word of God...who say the Bible is **"...eminently dangerous to souls?"** Rome's audacity impugns the intelligence of a holy God, Creator of all things, for it implies the kind of stupidity that entrusts the wolf with the protection of the sheep. *"...I am not ashamed of the gospel of Christ: for it is the power of God unto salvation to every one that believeth; to the Jew first, and also to the Greek. For therein is the righteousness of God revealed from faith to faith: as it is written, The just shall live by faith."* (Rom 1:16, 17) The Apostle, Paul, was not ashamed of the Gospel Christ bequeathed to His followers, the complete Gospel clearly set forth in the Bible. Why should popes be so afraid of it if their motives are pure?

The twin heresies looked at in this chapter are deeply implanted in the minds of most Roman Catholics, even those not-so-devout souls for whom a forty-minute Mass on Saturday night or Sunday morning is a sufficient amount of spirituality for the week. And so long as they accept Rome's false claims of exclusivity, antiquity, and absolute God-given authority, it's nearly impossible to help them achieve a saving relationship with the Lord Jesus Christ. They literally are caught in Catholicism's **"Tradition Trap,"** and only an open-minded comparison of what they've been taught with what the Bible says can free them from it.

That in itself—gaining the Catholic's respect for God's Word—can prove difficult in the extreme and engender much disappointment. One missionary to a "Catholic Country" told me of instances where Catholics to whom he had given a King James Bible tore out a page right in front of him, rolled their tobacco in it, and smoked the resulting "cigarette," smiling smugly at him the whole time. Fortunately, most evangelical Christians attempting to witness to a Catholic will not be subjected to a similar experience. But they are likely to get a lot of, "Ah, the Bible is just a bunch of words on paper!" and/or, "I don't care what the Bible says, that's not what the Catholic Church teaches."

Catholics firmly believe that their church is the one and only true church founded by Jesus, but even if this were true, the Catholicism of today has very little in common with the Christian Church our Lord left to the Apostles. Today's Catholic Church is like the company that got started producing fine bread, but after a short time switched over to baking rum cakes. Likewise, the product Rome is marketing in this generation is a far cry from what early Christendom brought to the table. Some of the ingredients are the same, but the end product has an entirely different flavor. And, what bread-maker, converted to the production of rum cakes, would have the audacity to forbid others to produce fine bread? Rome is expert at claiming, forbidding, and condemning, but, as if ignoring an unsavory fact will make it go away, the Vatican maintains an uncharacteristic silence about the period of 800 plus years when pope after pope curtailed or banned entirely the reading of the Bible by the Catholic faithful. Nothing is said in Catholic educational institutions or the local parish church about the persecution—rather, the execution—of holy men of God who brought or sought to bring the Word of God to the general populace. Moreover, the rank immorality of popes, (those guardians of the Sacred Scriptures) that extended from the ninth to at least the 17th century is never mentioned in polite Catholic conversation.

In succeeding chapters, Catholic doctrines—all "patches" to God's Gospel—will be measured against Bible teachings, same as in this chapter. It's the way I was liberated from Rome's "Tradition Trap," the way former priests and nuns also have come to a knowledge of the truth. I pray it will be useful to evangelical Christians in helping Catholic relatives, friends, co-workers, etc., come to a realization that it doesn't take a cardinal with a red hat, or a pope with a staff and crown to grasp the salvation message found in the Word of a loving and merciful God.

2

The Goddess Man Has Made

> *Fear ye not, neither be afraid: have not I told thee from that time, and have declared it? Ye are even my witnesses. Is there a God beside me? Yea, there is no God; I know not any.* (Isa 44:8)

Of all the beautiful, soul-stirring ceremonies that have become a part of the Roman Catholic religion, perhaps the most beautiful and soul-stirring are those associated with the worship of Mary, the mother of Jesus. For example, besides the two holy days of obligation honoring her (August 15, Assumption, and December 8, Immaculate Conception) the entire month of May has been designated as Mary's month, a month whose culmination features processions, lovely hymns, and the crowning of Mary's statue with a headpiece of fresh flowers interwoven with gold ribbon and lace.

As the congregation sings "*Tis The Month Of Our Mother,*" and "*Bring Flowers Of The Fairest,*" little girls in crisp white dresses scatter rose petals in the main aisle ahead of a young lady who carries on a satin pillow the crown she has been chosen to place upon the head of the great Queen's statue. In the sanctuary, boys in white cassocks and pink surpluses swing censors filled with sweet smelling incense in the direction of Mary's statue. The procession winds solemnly to the altar rail and the young lady with the crown respectfully advances to the side altar—Mary's altar—where a ladder awaits. Slowly, with great reverence and devotion, she mounts the ladder, then lovingly, carefully, glowing all the while, she places the crown upon the statue's head. It is all so beautiful; so uplifting!

Unfortunately, it's heresy. More than heresy, it's blasphemy! It's man at his most arrogant, making a goddess out of a created being. This in defiance of the true, the one and only God, the very Creator of all things, the One who said: **"Thus saith the LORD the King of Israel, and his redeemer the LORD of hosts; I am the first, and I am the last; and beside me there is no God."** (Isa 44:6) The entire "Cult of Mary" as it is called in the 1994 edition of the Catholic Catechism, is a satanic diversion taking glory from the One who died that we might have eternal life. Mariology is absolutely without any foundation in God's Holy Word. It is based entirely on fables, fantasy, spurious documents and "Traditions" that have been built on them. This humble maiden chosen by God to bring her own Savior into the world has been elevated by Rome to the status of **Theotikos** (mother of God) and **Regina Caeli** (queen of heaven). This, without Scriptural support of any kind. Yet the Catholic faithful are commanded under the penalty of grievous sin to accept as divine truth all of the following about Mary the mother of Jesus:

1. She was conceived immaculate, without a sin nature, in her mother's womb.
2. She is the Mother of God by virtue of being the one who gave birth to Jesus.
3. She lived a completely sinless life, the result of her Immaculate Conception.
4. She remained a virgin throughout her life; even after Jesus was born.
5. At the time of her death, her body was "assumed" into heaven and did not decay.
6. She is, with Christ, the co-mediatrix between God and man.
7. She now reigns as "Queen of Heaven."

In the 1994 Catholic Catechism thousands of words are devoted to doctrines about Mary. Many Scriptural references are given, but not a single one offers unqualified support for belief in any of the dogmas enumerated above. All rationale that directly supports Rome's teachings about Mary are based on the inductive reasoning of error-prone human minds, people who simply came to believe things about Mary that, over many centuries, were assimilated into Rome's "Tradition Trap." Some of these teachings were originated by spurious documents dating from the 4th and 5th centuries, hundreds of years after the deaths of the Apostles and their immediate successors. Others are, quite obviously, the result of men's fertile imaginations. All are—I repeat—completely unsubstantiated or supported by even one Scripture from the Word of God. And, as we compare each of the Marian doctrines to what is written in the Bible, it will become crystal clear that the Roman Catholic church beliefs about Mary, the mother of Jesus, are heretical beyond a shadow of a doubt. They are, in fact, a prime example of extra-biblical "revealed truths" (Cf. chapter 1) Rome attributes to "Tradition" and the private revelation of the Holy Spirit.

IMMACULATE CONCEPTION: SINLESS LIFE.

Certainly two of the most fallacious teachings about Mary are her imagined Immaculate Conception, and her alleged freedom from sin throughout her life. According to these doctrines, Mary, whose father was a mortal and a sinner like all of us, was conceived in her mother's womb free from the sin nature (called "original sin") inherited by all descendents of Adam, and remained sinless throughout her life. Such teachings are found nowhere in either the Old or the New Testament, and are at once in conflict with the written Word of God. For the Bible tells us only the man Christ Jesus—whose father was God the Holy Spirit—was born and endured without sin. *"For he hath made him to be sin for us, who knew no sin; that we might be made the righteousness of God in him."* (2 Cor 5:21) Scripture also tells us that every individual except our Lord is guilty of sin. *"As it is written, There is none righteous, no, not one."* (Rom 3:10) and: *"For all have sinned and come short of the glory of God."* (Rom 3:23)

A thorough study of both Testaments reveals a total absence of information about Mary's birth, her parents, her childhood, anything. The Apostles of Jesus and the early church saints knew nothing of Mary's origins, either, for there are no such references in any of their writings. As a matter of historical fact, the very first known appearance of this idea is traced to the 4th century when Augustine was bishop of Hippo. A sect known as Pelagians, whose chief spokesman was Julian of Eclanum, believed that Mary the mother of Jesus had been born without sin and was, therefore, free from the power of the "demons." In defending the clearly stated Biblical doctrine that all mankind inherits a sin nature from the original sin of Adam, Augustine pointed out to the heretic Julian of Eclanum that if Mary the mother of Jesus had been freed from the power of the demons, it was not the result of her natural birth, but the result of her being **born again** by the grace of God, as described in the third chapter of John's Gospel. That should have put to rest for all time any suggestions that Mary's conception was in some way special or different. But in the 13th century, about 800 years after Augustine, the Immaculate Conception matter enjoyed a renewal of support. Not, however from Thomas Aquinas, the famous doctor of the Roman Catholic Church. Aquinas declared quite emphatically that Mary the mother of Jesus was conceived with the stain of original sin—an inherited predisposition to sin—as are all descendents of Adam and Eve. In his ***Brevis Summa de Fide***, Aquinas addressed the matter this way:

> **"Certainly Mary was conceived with original sin, as is natural. If she would not have been born with original sin, she would not have needed to be redeemed by Christ, and, this being so, Christ would not be the universal Redeemer of men, which would abolish the dignity of Christ."**

It is interesting to note in the Catholic Catechism that not a single early Church father is cited as a reference for the Immaculate Conception doctrine. Nor, in fact, are there any Scriptures invoked to support it. Oh, there are included some quotes by early Church patriarchs, but none have to do with Mary's supposed Immaculate Conception. By their inclusion, however, the apathetic faithful and less than astute student can be led to believe that this is a doctrine of great antiquity, one that has come down through the ages as an accepted "Tradition," one that can be traced back to apostolic times. But if it is, in fact a church "Tradition," founded on the doctrines held by the early Church, all evidence for this is conspicuous by its absence from the 1994 Catechism. What is found there are the conclusions of pope's and councils, all of them far removed from the Christian Church founded by Jesus. How then, with no record of support for it in Scripture or among the early Church fathers, with emphatic opposition to it on the part of Augustine of Hippo and Thomas Aquinas, how could the doctrine of the Immaculate Conception ever have been declared an article of faith of the Roman Catholic Church?

John Duns Scotus was his name and the Immaculate Conception doctrine can be attributed almost exclusively to his efforts. His life spanned the years AD 1266-1308, the latter part of which he spent as a Franciscan monk and self-styled Catholic theologian. As a teacher in Paris in 1306 Duns Scotus gave new life to the Immaculate Conception doctrine that Augustine and Aquinas had emphatically opposed. His espousal of it marked the turning point for a belief that, if not completely moribund at the time, was at least in a deep coma. His own order adamantly opposed his position. Pope Sixtus IV, himself a Franciscan, distanced himself from the **cause celebre** that resulted. Duns Scotus was threatened with trial by Philip the Fair's ongoing heresy inquisition, and either fled or was transferred to Cologne, the place of his death. End of story? Not by a long shot.

The popularity of Duns Scotus saw great growth in the century following his death, and by the 16th century, this obscure Franciscan monk had become the darling of Catholic theologians, his adherents first rivaling and then surpassing those of Aquinas. And with his popularity grew the popularity of the Immaculate Conception doctrine. Several popes supported it. The councils of Basel (AD 1439) and Trent (AD 1546) endorsed it. It even prospered, may have greatly benefited, from the chaos of the Protestant Reformation and the Catholic Counter-Reformation.

It was not until December 8, 1854, however, that Pius IX, declared the Immaculate Conception to be a dogma of the Roman Catholic Church. In a document entitled **Ineffabilis Deus,** he said the doctrine had been revealed by God, (Cf. Chapter 1, Montanism) and must be accepted and believed by all the faithful under penalty of sin. The Word of God, the Apostles, early Christian Church fathers, and both Augustine and Aquinas were overruled! The heretic Julian of Eclanum and his sect, the Pelagians, with a major assist from John Duns Scotus, had somehow convinced "god" to make this doctrine known to Pius IX. From page 124 of the 1994 Catechism we have the **word of Pius IX** that Mary was conceived free of sin.

> **"The most Blessed Virgin Mary was, from the first moment of her conception, by a singular grace and privilege of Almighty God and by virtue of the merits of Jesus Christ, Savior of the human race, preserved immune from all stain of original sin."**

History indicates that Pius IX made this declaration on his own and without the benefit of a church council. It was a grave contradiction of the Holy Scriptures that insist only one person—Christ Jesus our Lord—was born without the Adamic nature that leads inevitably to sin. *"For we have not an high priest which cannot be touched with the feeling of our infirmities; but was in all points tempted like as we are, yet without sin."* (Heb 4:15) Which raises the question: what "god" revealed this to Pius IX?

In the 20th century, Pius XII defended the Immaculate Conception dogma, citing as its Scriptural support God's words to the serpent after Adam sinned. *"And I will put enmity between thee and the woman, and between thy seed and her seed; it shall bruise thy head, and thou shalt bruise his heel."* (Gen 3:15) From this first Messianic prophecy, Rome has somehow been able to determine that Mary was conceived without a sin nature and sinless for life. This same Scripture has been cited by the Vatican VIPS as justification for Mary's elevation by the Catholic Church to her status as "Queen of Heaven." Amazing? Incredible? Astounding? Yes, yes, yes. Factual? Not even close!

Genesis 3:15 has nothing to do with Mary, the mother of Jesus, other than to prophecy that our Lord would be conceived in the womb of a virgin by the power of the Holy Ghost. The woman referred to is the nation of Israel out of whose ranks the Redeemer was to come. The word "enmity" is the key to understanding the prophecy. When God said there would be enmity between Satan and the woman, He was foretelling the war that Satan would wage against God's chosen people—the children of Israel—throughout history, and even to this present time. Nowhere in the Bible are we informed of any attempt by Satan to destroy Mary. But we have ample proof of his efforts to corrupt and crush the nation of Israel, thereby frustrating God's plan and promise that the Savior would be born a Jew.

The Bible tells us, moreover, that the prophesied enmity between Satan and Israel will even carry over into the very last times. The same "woman" of Genesis 3:15 is seen again in Chapter 12 of Revelation. *"And there appeared a great wonder in heaven; a woman clothed with the sun, and the moon under her feet, and upon her head a crown of twelve stars. And she being with child cried, travailing in birth, and pained to be delivered".* (Rev 12:1, 2) *"...and the dragon (Satan) stood before the woman which was ready to be delivered, for to devour her child as soon as it was born. And she brought forth a man child, who was to rule all nations with a rod of iron: and her child was caught up unto God, and to his throne. And the woman fled into the wilderness, where she hath a place prepared of God, that they should feed her there a thousand two hundred and threescore days."* (Rev 12:5, 6) *"And the dragon was wroth with the woman, and went to make war with the remnant of her seed, which keep the commandments of God, and have the testimony of Jesus Christ."* (Rev 12:17) In these verses, certain phrases leave no doubt that the woman described is the nation of Israel, not Mary, the mother of Jesus. The crown of twelve stars worn by the woman unquestionably marks her as a figure of the twelve tribes of Israel. The woman's flight into the wilderness is prophetic of God's plan to prevent total annihilation of Israel during the "time of Jacob's trouble." (Jer 30:7) And the phrase, "the remnant of her seed," can only refer to Jewish converts to Christianity during the great Tribulation.

That Catholic theology insists the woman in Genesis 3 and Revelation 12 is Mary, the mother of Jesus, is proof positive that Rome's agenda—in this case the Immaculate Conception doctrine—takes precedence over the Word of God, and actually contradicts sound exegesis. No wonder Rome doesn't want Catholics interpreting the Bible on their own! The earthly mother of the man Christ Jesus died and was buried two millennia ago. It is the nation of Israel—referred to as "the woman" both in Genesis and Revelation—who will flee into the wilderness for God's protection during the coming tribulation. But Catholics are not permitted to believe that. They must believe Pius XII's lie that the woman is Mary, our Lord's mother.

Another justification for the Immaculate Conception doctrine, according to Catholic theologians, is found in a familiar passage of Scripture recorded in the Book of Luke. It is the passage that relates the angel Gabriel's appearance to Mary announcing the news of her selection as the vessel through which Israel's promised Messiah will be brought into the world. Catholic teaching contends that the angel's words to Mary were, *"Hail, FULL of grace."* Since only a sinless soul could be addressed in that manner, Rome cites this Scripture as proof of Mary's Immaculate Conception and sinless life. Numerous other Scriptures—some previously quoted—quite explicitly rule out Mary's alleged freedom from sin, so something must be wrong with Rome's translation of God's Word. Sure enough, when the Greek text is consulted, it's obvious that Gabriel has been misquoted by the Vatican.

In the Gospel of John, our Lord is described by the evangelist as *"FULL of grace and truth."* (John 1:14) In the Greek, the phrase translated, "full of grace," is *pleres charitos*. In the entire New Testament, this is the **only use of that phrase**, and it pertains to the **One**—the only **One**—who truly was without sin. The Greek phrase the angel used to address Mary is *chaire kecharitomene*. A literal translation of that phrase is, "one who is receiving unmerited favor." Thus, the KJV correctly translates John 1:14 as: *"Hail, thou that art highly favoured, the Lord is with thee: blessed art thou among women."* There simply is no **honest** way you can get "full of grace" out of the Greek phrase *chaire kecharitomene*. J.M. Carda, a Roman Catholic priest and author, offered this commentary on the subject doctrine: **"The Holy Scriptures do not mention the historical origin of Mary, nor do they expressly allude to any privilege in her conception."** The word *pleres* in the Greek means "filled up to the maximum" or, "completely full." It has no other meaning. It is used once in Scripture in reference to Jesus. It is **not** used in reference to Mary. Conclusions. She was **not** full of grace at conception. She was **not** conceived free of the Adamic nature. She is **not** the Immaculate Conception. She did **not** live a sinless life, only Jesus did.

Just what are the implications of a Mary conceived without a sin nature—without the stain of original sin? Of a Mary who was thus empowered to live a life absent of any sin whatever? Well, first of all, it obviates the need for Jesus to have a divine rather than a human father. If Mary had a human father, and she must have for the Bible does not tell us otherwise; and if she was born free of the

Adamic sin nature, then Jesus, too, could have had a human father and still been sinless. Point number two; if Mary was born free from the inclination to sin and therefore lived a sinless life, then our Lord was not alone the perfect unblemished sacrifice God required for atonement of the world's sins. Mary could have gone to the cross and thereby redeemed mankind. There would have been no reason for God to allow His beloved, only begotten son to suffer the excruciating agonies He went through. Implication the third; a Mary conceived sinless and sin-free for life would not have needed redemption, nor would she have been subject to pain and death. However, she herself acknowledged her need for redemption when she prayed, *"My soul doth magnify the Lord, And my spirit hath rejoiced in God my Saviour."* (Luke 1:46, 47) The fact that Mary suffered death—as do all sinners—is acknowledged in the Vatican by its Assumption doctrine covered later in this chapter.

The implications just cited of a sinless Mary certainly are sufficient to cast the most serious doubts upon the Catholic Immaculate Conception doctrine and her alleged lifelong sinlessness. But it is in God's divine Word that doubts are fully confirmed and this invention of Rome is revealed to be a "doctrine of devils," (1 Tim 4:1) and a "damnable heresy." (2 Pet 2:1) *"...we have before proved both Jews and Gentiles, that they are all under sin; As it is written, There is none righteous, no, not one:"* (Rom 3:9,10) *"there is none that doeth good, no, not one."* (Rom 3:12) *"For all have sinned, and come short of the glory of God;"* (Rom 3:23)

Unless the Roman Catholic theologians have successfully changed its meaning, the little word "all" still encompasses everyone sired by a human father, while excluding none. The Bible is absolutely clear in its teaching that Jesus was perfect and sinless, without spot or blemish, and the only acceptable sacrifice for the sins of the world. On Mary's alleged perfection the Bible's silence is deafening. From the lips of Jesus Himself we have this assurance: *"Verily I say unto you, among them that are born of women there hath not risen a greater than John the Baptist:"* (Mat 11:11) If Mary, the mother of Jesus, was "born of woman"—and she was—then, by the witness of her own Son, she was not greater than John the Baptist. And if the Bible does not teach that John the Baptist was conceived without sin and was sinless throughout his life—and it most definitely doesn't—then Mary was neither, either, amen!

If even further proof of the fallacious nature of the Immaculate Conception doctrine is needed, it can be found in the writings attributed to the early Church saints. Not one of them relates that the mother of Jesus was born without a sin nature. Not one of them expresses admiration for her because of her totally sinless life. Were there any truth in these peculiarly Catholic beliefs, it is certain that at least some of the apostolic church saints would have commented on such a noteworthy and singular blessing. As a former Catholic with dear relations still bound by Rome's "damnable heresies," I am saddened by their trust in what Rome disseminates rather than what is written for all people in the divine Word of God. Jesus, not Mary, is the Star of the story. He is the hero deserving all and getting all of the glory. Mary, the Apostles, John the Baptist, are merely the supporting cast, all in need of forgiveness and redemption by the Leading Man of all time, the Lord Jesus. To Him and to Him alone we are to give glory, honor and praise.

MOTHER OF GOD.

The second Marian heresy, that she is the "mother of God," actually is the oldest, its seeds having been planted in the 5th century. In our day, Catholic theologians have concluded from two passages in the Gospel of Luke that Mary's designation as God's mother is Scriptural. However, any rational human being must reject the contention that a created being—Mary—could be maternal to an eternal, uncaused, uncreated being—God. Certainly she was the mother of the physical child Jesus placed in her womb by the power of the Holy Spirit. She was the mother of His human body and His human nature. His divine nature is from everlasting and had no beginning; is no one's offspring *"Before the mountains were brought forth, or ever thou hadst formed the earth and the world, even from everlasting to everlasting, thou art God."* (Psa 90:2) and in another of the Psalms we are told *"Thy throne is established of old: thou art from everlasting."* (Psa 93:2) There certainly can be no question about the eternal nature of Him who in the Old Testament was called variously **The Lord of Hosts, the Angel of the Lord, Messiah, Emanuel, Prince of Peace, The Mighty God.** How then can Rome conclude that Mary is the Mother of God when she was a mere mortal, a creation of the eternal Word? Rome's explanation, which has a very persuasive ring to it, appears on page 125 of the 1994 Catholic Catechism.

> **Called in the Gospels "the mother of Jesus," Mary is acclaimed by Elizabeth, at the prompting of the Spirit and even before the birth of her son, as "the mother of my Lord." In fact, the One whom she conceived as man by the Holy Sprit, who truly became her Son according to the flesh, was none other than the Father's eternal Son, the second person of the Holy Trinity. Hence the Church confesses that Mary is truly "Mother of God". (Theotokos)**

That has such a logical ring to it one cannot be faulted for accepting it as factual, and concluding that Mary really is the Mother of God. This, of course, is the wisdom of man, not the inspired Word of God, so it is at once suspect and for good reason. Two Bible references are cited in the Catechism apologetic above. The first is an admission that the Gospels always refer to Mary as the "mother of Jesus," never as the mother of God. This is true and moot. It is the second Scriptural citation about Elisabeth's statement to which our attention is directed. For background, Mary has been told by the angel that her cousin Elisabeth also is with child and Mary goes to visit her. Upon hearing Mary's greeting the babe leaps in Elisabeth's womb and she makes the following statements to Mary: *"And whence is this to me that the mother of my Lord should come to me? For, lo, as soon as the voice of thy salutation sounded in mine ears, the babe leaped in my womb for joy. And blessed is she that believed: for there shall be a performance of those things which were told her from the lord."* (Luke 1:43-45)

Before drawing the same conclusion from these statements of Elisabeth as is drawn by Rome, a good question to ask is: who was Elisabeth referring to as her Lord? Was she referring to God or not? There are two Greek words she could have used. The first is **kurios,** which is used 748 times in the New Testament and is translated **master, lord, owner,** but **never God.** The other Greek word she could have used is **Theos** (God)," which is used 1343 times in the New Testament, and **always means God, Deity**. Elisabeth used the first word—**kurios.** She did not refer to Mary as "...the mother of my **Theos** (God)," but rather as "...the mother of my kurios (Lord)." Scripture makes a clear distinction between Lord and God, as can be seen in Mary's response to her cousin. She said, *"My soul doth magnify the Lord (kurios) and my spirit doth rejoice in God (Theos) my (Soter) Saviour."* Another excellent example is found in the Gospel of John, Chapter 20.

"But Thomas, one of the twelve, called Didymus, was not with them when Jesus came. The other disciples therefore said unto him, 'We have seen the LORD.' But he said unto them, 'Except I shall see in his hands the print of the nails, and put my finger into the print of the nails, and thrust my hand into his side, I will not believe.' And after eight days again his disciples were within, and Thomas with them: then came Jesus, the doors being shut, and stood in the midst, and said, 'Peace be unto you.' Then saith he to Thomas, 'Reach hither thy finger, and behold my hands; and reach hither thy hand, and thrust it into my side; and be not faithless, but believing.' And Thomas

answered and said unto him, 'My LORD (kurios) and my GOD.'" (Theos) (John 20:24-28)

There are literally scores of Scriptures from which we conclude that the Jews were not expecting their Messiah to have both a human and a divine nature. They were expecting a man—a man of great power—who would free them from Rome's domination and restore the Davidic Kingdom. This simply cannot be doubted, for even after our Lord had died and risen again, the Apostles were still preoccupied with their Messianic expectation. ***"When they therefore were come together, they asked of him, saying, 'Lord (Kurios) wilt thou at this time restore again the kingdom to Israel?'"*** (Acts 1:6)

When Elisabeth acknowledged Mary as the mother of her "Lord" she was referring to the Messiah whom she expected to be a man. In her mind Mary was to be the mother of the Messiah—Jesus—not the mother of God. It is a certainty that the Messiah would warrant the title of Lord. These Scriptures in Luke are the only ones in the entire New Testament that even faintly suggest that Mary was the mother of God; and when the Jews' Messianic expectations are understood, they offer no real support for such an exegesis. This is especially obvious in the fact that throughout the Gospels Mary is referred to always as the mother of Jesus, but never as ***Theotokos,*** which is the Greek word for "God-bearer."

At the 5th century Council of Ephesus, the title that applied to Mary from apostolic times—***Christotokos,*** that is, "Christ-bearer"—was rejected. The Eastern Church insisted on calling her ***Theotokos,*** and the emerging Catholic Church acceded after some rigorous debate. But this was a council decision at once in conflict with the Scriptures, and a significant departure from sound reasoning as well. In Luke 1:35, the angel told Mary that the child she would bear would be called the Son of **GOD**. He did not tell her she would become the **mother** of God. There **is** a difference. In numerous New Testament Scriptures, Jesus is referred to as, "the only **begotten** Son of God." Now we know that the Second Person of the blessed Trinity is an eternal being, not begotten, but co-equal and co-existent with the Father and the Holy Ghost. Thus, biblical references to Jesus as the "only begotten Son" identify the Christ, the Messiah, not the eternal Second Person of the Trinity. Jesus often used the term, "son of man" in reference to Himself. However he was nearly stoned by the religious Jews when He acknowledged that He was the Son of God. ***"Say ye of him, whom the Father hath sanctified, and sent into the world, Thou blasphemest; because I said, I am the Son of (Theos) God?"*** (John 10:36)

It was not the Second Person of the Trinity that died on Calvary's cross, for God cannot die. It was the man Christ Jesus whose precious, sinless blood was shed there to reconcile mankind to God. And it is the man Christ Jesus who now—in heaven—is the lone mediator between God and His creatures. ***"For there is one God, and one mediator between God and men, the man Christ Jesus;"*** (1 Tim 2:5) It is notable that our Lord never called Mary His mother. In John 2:4 and 19:26 He called her "woman." It's as if He wanted posterity to have a proper view of Himself as the perfect man, the last Adam, and Mary as a vessel chosen for the achievement of God's purposes but nothing more. A fitting wrap-up to this rebuttal of the Catholic heresy that Mary is the mother of God may be seen in the Gospel of Matthew. In an exchange with the oh-so spiritual Pharisees, who, by biblical accounts were as adept as the Vatican at teaching for doctrines the commandments of men, our Lord challenged them to answer a question that exactly equates to the one with which we are here dealing.

"While the Pharisees were gathered together, Jesus asked them, Saying, 'What think ye of Christ? whose son is he?' They say unto him, 'The son of David'. He saith unto them, 'How then doth David in spirit call him Lord, saying, The LORD said unto my Lord, Sit thou on my right hand, till I make thine enemies thy footstool? If David then call him Lord, how is he his son?' And no man was able to answer him a word, neither durst any man from that day forth ask him any more questions." Mat 22:41-46.)

The MAN Christ Jesus is, in fact, a "son of David." The Second Person of the blessed Trinity, is, in fact David's GOD. Likewise, the MAN Christ Jesus is Mary's firstborn son. The DIVINE Second Person of the Trinity is Mary's GOD. Mary, the mother of Jesus, yes. Mary, the mother of God, never.

MARY EVER VIRGIN.

Of all the heresies concerning Mary which are taught to, and believed by, the practicing Roman Catholic, the one considered most ridiculous by born again Christians, is the representation of Mary as "ever-virgin" from the cradle to the grave, even after giving birth to the Lord Jesus. Of this strange doctrine the Bible is so contradictory, and in its own teaching so crystal clear, one is compelled to question the sanity of the minds that conceived it and believed it.

Historically, Christians into the 5th Century believed what the Scriptures clearly assert, that Mary had four sons in addition to Jesus, and at least two daughters. The idea of Mary "ever-virgin" came about as the result of a spurious document entitled the Prot Evangelium of James, also called, The First Gospel of James. Though it had been circulated for some time in the Eastern branch of Christendom, it was rejected as Scripture and disqualified for inclusion in the Bible. It purported to be written by one James the Lesser, and was ostensibly a narrative of Mary's life, Christ's birth, the slaughter of the infants by Herod, and the story of Zachariah, Elisabeth's spouse. Among the unsavory episodes appearing in the manuscript, is a story about Mary and Joseph undergoing the immorality water test described in the Old Testament. (Cf. Num 5:12-31) When an accusation of adultery was lodged against a married woman, the water test was administered to ascertain her guilt or innocence. Though Mary was only betrothed to Joseph at the time of the angel's visit, Jewish law considered her a married woman. In the manuscript, Mary passes the water test and is thereafter the subject of an even more unsavory episode.

Chapters 19 and 20 of the subject work carry a disgusting account that is at the very least highly insulting to this dear, sweet soul who became the mother of our Lord. Supposedly, a midwife who was present at the birth of Jesus, (information not found in God's Word) tells one Salome who also was there, that Mary, a virgin, has borne a child and yet remains a virgin. Salome doubts this and is unconvinced of its truth until she has discovered it for herself, the description of which is disgusting.

This admittedly false document, one of several that figure prominently in Roman Catholic theology, is thought to have originated with a sect known as the Ebionites. These were Jews who believed that Jesus was their Messiah but not a member of the Godhead. In their day, the unconverted Jews tried to counter the rapidly spreading Christian movement by calling Jesus a bastard, and Mary, his mother, an unwed woman of easy virtue. It is believed by historians that the Prot Evangelium of James was an Ebionite attempt to defend against that unholy charge. Be that as it may, there is not one hint in Scripture, nor is there any factual historical support for the belief that Mary retained her virginity from birth to death. And in spite of the subject manuscript, the "ever-virgin" heresy attracted very few adherents until the middle ages when it began to enjoy wider appeal among those who would have a queen in heaven as well as a King of Kings.

For Catholics to believe in the perpetual virginity of Mary, they must first believe that she and Joseph had a marriage in name only, a lifetime platonic relationship. This is a radical contradiction of Rome's own teaching about marriage and its alleged chief purpose—procreation. Even more serious is the conflict set up between this doctrine and God's Scriptural instructions to married couples. ***"The wife hath not power of her own body, but the husband: and likewise also the husband hath not power of his own body, but the wife. Defraud ye not one the other, except it be with consent for a time, that ye may give yourselves to fasting and prayer; and come together again, that Satan tempt you not for your incontinency."*** (1Cor 7:4, 5)

Married couples are here instructed in the very Word of God, to engage in normal conjugal relations. They may for a time—by mutual consent—abstain, but they are commanded to come together again to avoid the temptations arising from overlong abstinence. Neither the husband nor the wife has the right to unilaterally decide on abstention. So, a "sinless" Mary denying Joseph the privileges of the marriage bed would have been committing sin by doing so. For both of them to permanently abstain would have been doubly sinful according to Scripture. Bluntly stated, Mary could not have been **both sinless and ever-virgin** at the same time, as the Vatican instructs the faithful to believe.

The ever-virgin doctrine also requires Catholics to accept Rome's explanation that the half-brothers of Jesus—James, Joses, Simon, and Jude—specifically named in three of the Gospels, were really not Christ's brothers at all, but merely close relations. The following is from page 126 of the 1994 Catechism.

> **Against this doctrine (Mary ever virgin) the objection is sometimes raised that the Bible mentions brothers and sisters of Jesus. The** *Church has* **always** *understood these passages* **as not referring to other children of the Virgin Mary. In fact, James and Joseph, 'brothers of Jesus' are the sons of another Mary, a disciple of Christ, whom St Matthew significantly calls 'the other Mary.' They are close relations of Jesus, according to an Old Testament expression."**

In chapter one it was pointed out that the Vatican has given itself absolute authority over the Scriptures and their interpretation. It also was pointed out that when Catholicism's doctrinal "patches" conflict with the Word of God, Rome invokes its self-assumed right of interpretation. The laity then is bound under penalty of sin to believe what Rome says the Scriptures mean. The foregoing is a premier example of this self-assumed authority in action, and an excellent indication of why Rome has never really encouraged the faithful to read and study the Bible.

In this and numerous other instances, what the Vatican says the **church has always understood** and what the Scriptures really say, are as far apart as New York is from Los Angeles. That there was another Mary who had sons named James and Joses (Mat 27:56) in no way changes or negates Scriptures that specifically name Christ's half brothers, and call them **His brothers**, not kinfolk or relations. In Christ's day, as in our day, certain names were very popular. This is obvious when one begins to count how many Marys how many Simons, how many James, Johns, Josephs, Judes, etc., are named in the Bible. It's very clever of the Catholic apologists to suggest that two of Christ's specifically named half-brothers are the sons of another Mary. But what about the other two half-brothers? Whose sons were they? What was their mother's name? And whose sisters were they whom Scripture calls Christ's sisters?

In the Greek, one of the most precise languages the world has ever known, the word for brother is ***adelphos***; for sister it is ***adelphee.*** And even a very shallow investigation of the way these words are used in the Bible leads to an unshakeable conviction that Mary, the mother of Jesus her firstborn, had four other sons and at least two daughters. In the 4th chapter of Matthew's Gospel we are told that ***"Jesus…saw two brothers, Simon called Peter, and Andrew his brother."*** (Mat 4:18) The Greek word used for "brother" both times is ***adelphos***. Throughout the New Testament we are told that Simon, called Peter, and Andrew were, in fact, blood brothers. Certainly the Catholic apologists would not suggest that these men were merely "close relations" according to an "Old Testament expression."

Again, in the same chapter, Jesus saw ***"other two brothers—James*** (another James), ***the son of Zebedee, and John his brother."*** (Mat 4:21) Once again the Greek word ***adelphos*** is used to establish the blood-brother relationship of James and John. Would the Vatican deny this? Are these men merely close relations in the eyes of the Catholic Church? John the Baptist, (another John) got in trouble for denouncing the marriage of Herod to Herodias who was the wife of Herod's ***adelphos***, Philip. This episode is recorded in Matthew 14. It is an historical fact that Herod and Philip were blood brothers, not just close relations. Rome has never been known to say these men were only cousins.

In the parable of the Prodigal Son recorded in the Book of Luke, Jesus uses the Greek word ***adelphos*** to identify the father's two sons as blood brothers. And the Father, speaking to his eldest son in Luke 15:27, says, ***"Thy adelphos*** (brother) ***is come…"*** In verse 32, same chapter, the father says, ***"…thy adelphos*** (brother) ***was dead…"*** Had the men in the parable been merely close relations and not blood brothers, the parable would have made no sense at all.

One of the most thrilling miracles performed by our Lord was the raising of His friend, Lazarus, from the dead four days after his interment. This astounding act is related in the 11th chapter of the Gospel of John. Five times the Greek word ***adelphos*** is used to describe the relationship of Lazarus as **blood brother** to Mary (another Mary) and Martha. Moreover, the Greek word ***adelphee*** is used the same amount of times to describe the **blood sister** relationship of Mary and Martha to each other and to Lazarus, their ***adelphos***. To my knowledge, the Catholic Church has never denied the blood brother/sister relationship of Mary, Martha and Lazarus. Catholic theologians have never suggested that they were merely close relations.

As one reads and studies the Word of God, it becomes crystal clear that in every single instance where the Greek words ***adelphos*** and ***adelphee*** are used in association with a **specific name or names**, the relationship described is blood brother or sister. **There are no exceptions**, period! Hence, when we read in the Gospel of Matthew, that Jesus had four specifically named half-brothers and at least two sisters, it is impossible to conclude that they were merely close relatives. ***"Is not this the carpenter's son? Is not his mother called Mary? And his brethren, James, and Joses, and Simon, and Judas? And his sisters, are they not all with us? Whence then hath this man all these things?*** (Mat 13:55, 56) As expected, the Greek word used to describe the relationship of James, Joses, Simon, and Judas to Jesus is ***adelphos***. And the Greek word used to describe the relationship to Jesus of His sisters is ***adelphee***.

"Is not this the carpenter, the son of Mary, the brother of James, and Joses, and of Juda, and Simon? And are not his sisters here with us? And they were offended at him." (Mar 6:3) Here again, the words ***adelphos*** and ***adelphee*** are employed to ascertain the relationship to Jesus of the named brothers and unnamed sisters.

In Matthew again, on an occasion when our Lord's family attempted to interrupt Him while He was teaching a crowd, the Bible tells us; ***"Then one said unto him, Behold, thy mother and thy (adelphos) brethren stand without, desiring to speak with thee."*** (Mat 12:47) Based on Roman Catholic theology, the brothers referred to in the passage cited were merely close relatives. But there is neither biblical evidence nor references in the writings of the apostolic church saints to confirm this belief. And, why would someone say our Lord's mother and brothers were outside if he was only guessing at their identities? Wouldn't he have said what you or I would have said? "Sir, some people outside wish to speak with you."

The Word of God mentions only two relatives of Mary—an unnamed sister, (***adelphee***, Mat 19:25) and Elisabeth, her **cousin**, who, in her "old age," gave birth to John the Baptist. This reference of Elisabeth's relationship to Mary appears in the very first chapter of Luke's Gospel. The angel Gabriel, as he nears completion of his mission to inform Mary of her selection as the Messiah's mother, says: ***"And, behold, thy cousin Elisabeth, she hath also conceived a son in her old age: and this is the sixth month with her, who was called barren."*** (Luke 1:36) In this passage, the Greek word translated **cousin** is ***suggenes***. Appearing 12 times in the New Testament, this Greek word—***suggenes***—is always translated **cousin** or **kinfolk.** It is worthy of note that just as Elisabeth is the only cousin of Mary mentioned in Scripture, John the Baptist is the only relative of our Lord that is mentioned other than His immediate family and his unnamed aunt. So, in order to cling to the "ever-virgin" doctrine, one must conclude that the brothers of Jesus referred to in Matthew 12: 46, 47, in Mark 3:31, 32, in Luke 8:20, 21, and John 2:12, really were the brothers of John the Baptist, and therefore only "close relations" of Jesus according to an "Old Testament expression." Once that conclusion is drawn, though, Elisabeth's "Old-age" pregnancy wasn't such a big deal after all because she would have had four more sons and at least two daughters following the birth of John. The only other possibility is that the four boys were the named sons of Mary's unnamed sister; Mary's nephews, Christ's first cousins. But the Bible says they were our Lord's (***adelphos***) brothers, not his (***suggenes***) cousins.

The more the doctrinal disaster of Mary's alleged perpetual virginity is studied, the more contradictory evidence from Scripture and other sources keeps turning up. Quoting from Paul's epistle to the Galations: ***"But other of the apostles saw I none, save James the Lord's brother."*** (Gal 1:19) This is strong internal evidence that the Apostle, Paul, knew James was a blood brother of our Lord. The other James, one of Zebedee's sons, had already been slain by Herod (Cf. Acts 12:2) so the James Paul refers to must be the one who presided at the first church council in Jerusalem, a description of which is recorded in Acts 15. As in other verses cited, the Greek word ***adelphos*** is the one used for **brother** in Galatians 1:19.

The great Jewish historian, Josephus, understood that Jesus was not Mary's only child. In his *ANTIQUITIES XX, 200*, he reports that **"James, the brother of Jesus called the Christ,"** had been put to death. To apostolic church saints—Ignatius, Justin Martyr, Clement, John Chrysostom, Clement, and others—it was a matter of fact that Mary had other children after the birth of Jesus. **"James the Lord's brother"** is referred to by early church historian, Eusebius in his Book 2, Chapter 1:3. And in his Book 3, Chapter 20:1 he refers to **"Jude…the Lord's brother according to the flesh."** Even Jerome, later in the 4th century, knew that our Lord had several half-brothers. But the Catholic popes, the men who supposedly are infallible when it comes to faith and morals and interpretation of God's Word, began as early as the 6th century to promote the perpetual virginity of Mary.

Undoubtedly influenced by the spurious Prot Evangelium of James from the previous century, Gregory I, in the middle of the 6th century, led the "ever-virgin" movement. Hermisdas picked up on Gregory's effort, and then Martin I, at the Synod of Rome, AD 649, issued the following opinion: **"Mary gave birth incorruptibly, keeping her virginity intact even after giving birth."** He condemned those who were not of like mind, but, of course offered no Scriptural support for his position. In the last years of the 7th century, the Council of Toledo issued this unsubstantiated claim: **"Mary conceived as a virgin, gave birth as a virgin, and after childbirth, conserved without losing the modesty of her integrity."** It is the great paradox of Catholicism that popes who claim infallibility and the exclusive ownership and interpretation of Scriptures, line up one after another in opposition to those very Scriptures that reveal Mary had other children after the birth of Jesus. And to make matters worse, they command the laity to believe what they say, thus denying the truth of what God says.

But God's Word says what it means and means what it says. God is not in the deception business, that's Satan's specialty. Nor, as has been previously pointed out, did He give us a partial Gospel requiring periodic doctrinal "patches" to complete it. Had God wanted us to believe in the perpetual virginity of His earthly mother, His Word would have stated clearly that James, Joses, Simon, Jude, and the unnamed sisters were merely *suggenes*—kinfolk—and not *adelphos* and *adelphee*—brothers and sisters. His Word did not so state.

An incident involving the Lord's brothers related in John's Gospel is not there by accident. It emphasizes the near universal rejection of Christ's message by revealing the unbelief that existed in His own immediate family. *"His (adelphos) brethren therefore said unto him, Depart hence, and go into Judaea, that thy disciples also may see the works that thou doest. For there is no man that doeth any thing in secret, and he himself seeketh to be known openly. If thou do these things, shew thyself to the world. For neither did his (adelphos) brethren believe in him.* (John 7:3-5) Citing the unbelief of mere close relations rather than blood brothers could never have as effectively shown the extent of resistance to Christ's ministry that existed among the Jews. Remember, our Lord's family was Jewish. However, the most important reason for inclusion of this incident in God's Word was to reveal the fulfillment of another Messianic prophecy. *"I am become a stranger unto my BRETHREN and an alien unto my mother's CHILDREN"* (Psa 69:8) From prophecy it is obvious the Messiah was not to be an only child. His mother was to have other children in addition to Himself, children who would treat Him as an imposter and would become estranged from Him.

In the Catechism entry cited earlier, Rome states that Christ's named brothers are only **"close relations of Jesus according to an Old Testament expression."** The O.T. expression, however, is not identified and is really of no importance to this issue. What **is** important is to pay close attention to how the Word of God describes the birth of our Lord in Matthew's Gospel. ***"Then Joseph being raised from sleep did as the angel of the Lord had bidden him, and took unto him his wife: And knew her not till she had brought forth her firstborn son: and he called his name JESUS."*** (Mat 1:24, 25) There are two phrases critical to the "ever virgin" issue in those Scriptures.

In any language, the word "until" denotes, and precedes, a future change in current status. With the phrase, ***"knew her not till,"*** God informs us that Joseph's initial celibate condition preceded a change in that condition that took place after our Lord's birth. In other words, Joseph and Mary refrained from normal marital relations during her pregnancy but not afterwards. That other births would result—namely four more males and at least two females—is certainly a very strong possibility.

The second phrase, ***"brought forth her firstborn son,"*** appears only twice in the entire Bible, once in Matthew 1:25, and again in Luke 2:7. In both cases, of course, it is in reference to the birth of our Lord. The word "firstborn" is found 90 times in the Old Testament and 7 more times in the New Testament, but never in conjunction with the action of birthing a child. Put another way, no woman in either Testament, other than Mary, is described as bringing forth a firstborn son or daughter or child. In all cases in the Bible where the word "firstborn" is used it indicates that other births followed. God, speaking at our Lord's baptism called Jesus His **"ONLY begotten Son**." Why, in Matthew 1:25 and Luke 2:7, does God not tell us Mary brought forth her **ONLY** son?

From the many Scriptures reviewed here, from the lack of evidence in the writings of the patristic saints, from the dearth of factual historical evidence, one can only conclude that—contrary to published Catholic doctrine—Mary, the mother of Jesus, had a normal marriage that produced four sons besides our Lord, (half-brothers of Jesus) and at least two daughters, (half-sisters of the Lord). That these things are true is not in the least demeaning to Mary or Jesus. On the contrary, they show Mary to be a loving and beloved wife and mother, virtuous and yet human in every way, the ideal example for every young Christian girl who is drawn to the vocation of wife and mother. They show Jesus, the Second Person of the trinity, to be a compassionate and considerate God who would not deny Mary the joys of a normal marriage, or the rewards of a large family just because she was the vessel chosen to give human life to the Messiah.

Upon entering life as one of His own creations, our Lord removed the veil of His mother's virginity, so that she thereafter might enjoy fully the privileges and pleasures of a made-in-heaven marriage. Upon departing this life as the spotless, unblemished, once-for-all sin sacrifice, He rent the veil of the temple so that we who believe according to His Word might have forgiveness of our sins and access to the very throne-room of heaven. Mary's Vatican-invented cradle-to-the-grave virginity can be dismissed as one more heresy of the apostate church.

MARY'S BODILY ASSUMPTION.

It was on November 1, 1950, that Pope Pius XII added one more heresy to the already crowded Roman Catholic list of man-made, doctrinal "patches." In a document with the impressive Latin title of **Minificentissimus Deus**, he declared that the body of Mary, the mother of Jesus, was not subject to corruption after her death. Instead, said he, by a singular act of God, her body had been "assumed" into heaven, there to be reunited with her soul and spirit. Thus was confirmed into doctrine an unscriptural belief that originated in forged documents traceable to the 5th century.

I was twenty and a Roman Catholic when the Assumption doctrine was formalized by papal decree, and my typically Catholic reaction was, "If the pope says so, it has to be true." But thirty-two years later, after my first reading of the entire New Testament had been completed, my reaction was markedly different. "Where," I wondered aloud, "Is the Assumption of Mary? How did I miss it?" The patient lady who had given me my first ever Bible, and was later to become my wife, had this response: "You didn't miss it. It's not there." And so, like the Immaculate Conception, the Mother of God and the Ever-Virgin doctrines, Mary's Assumption was just one more invention of sinful, mortal men.

It seems eminently fair at this juncture to raise another question, one that Roman Catholics themselves would be well advised to ask. The question is this. If God is the Author of all the Marian doctrines that have been "patched" into Catholicism from time to time over a period of 1500 years, why didn't He reveal them all at once to His Apostles and their immediate successors and have done with it? For at least the first 500 years of Christendom, before emergence of the Catholic church, Christians were denied the "opportunity" to worship Mary as the immaculately conceived, sinless, ever-virgin, mother of God, Queen of Heaven, and co-mediatrix with Christ. Why would **God, who is all just**, have denied the early Christians the "opportunity" to believe in these key doctrines and petition Mary for their various needs as Catholics do today? And, what about the many other doctrines Rome has "patched" in at various times? Why the delay? What possible purpose was served by dragging out over hundreds and hundreds of years their elevation to doctrine status? For example, have popes only become infallible since the year 1870 when Pius IX said they are? And why would

God who is described in His Word as immutable, change from "It is finished" at Calvary, to "Standby for Further Developments" starting at Rome, but not until the 6th century? Unthinkable! When the temple veil was ripped from top to bottom, the Old Testament was ended. The New Testament Gospel of salvation by grace through faith in Christ's work was complete, fellowship with God fully restored. The doctrine of Mary's bodily Assumption into heaven adds absolutely nothing to the good news that Jesus became sin for us in order to give us His righteousness. It and the other Marian doctrines serve only as a distraction from our Lord's sacrifice and triumphant victory over death through His bodily resurrection.

If these doctrines, the Assumption included, could be found in the Scriptures, it would be one thing. Then Catholics would have solid backing for believing Mary was given special privileges from conception to the grave. But the way God's Word reads, there really is no Scriptural support for any of the Marian doctrines. *"...there is no respect of persons with God."* (Rom 2:11) And*..."...your Master also is in heaven; neither is there respect of persons with him.* (Eph 6:9) And... *"But if ye have respect to persons, ye commit sin, and are convinced of the law as transgressors."* (Jas 2:9) And finally... *"And if ye call on the Father, who without respect of persons judgeth according to every man's work."* (1 Pet 1:17) Thus, any special honors heaped upon Mary would conflict with the clearly stated truth that God is not a respecter of persons.

It was earlier noted that Mary—based on the statements of Jesus Himself—was no greater than John the Baptist, and certainly no more than equal in the eyes of Christ with *"whosoever shall do the will of my Father which is in heaven."* (Mat 12:50) Rome rationalizes these many signal honors it has heaped upon the earthly mother of Jesus with the excuse that they really honor our Lord by showing the extent of His love and respect for her. But God's own Word says He will not give His glory to another: *"I am the LORD: that is my name: and my glory will I not give to another, neither my praise to graven images."* (Isa 42:8) From that Scripture alone, investing Mary with special honors and titles, petitioning her as though she were an omniscient goddess, and venerating statues of her, are actions expressly condemned in the divine Word of God. In truth, Mary was created to give glory to God, not to be glorified by God. *"...bring my sons from far, and my daughters from the ends of the earth; Even every one that is called by my name: for I have created him* (her, too) *for MY glory, I have formed him; yea, I have made him.* Isa 43:6, 7) The Vatican promotes the idea that it was a great honor for Jesus to have Mary as His earthly mother; that He was so indebted to her for bearing Him that He instructs the Vatican every now and then to add some new honor, some new glory to her memory. This is utter nonsense. Mary is the one who was honored above all other women in all history when God chose her to bring His only begotten Son into this sinful world. To hold any other view is to contradict God's immutable Word.

As one of the proofs for the validity of the Assumption doctrine, Catholic apologists point to the lack of relics identified as having come from Mary the mother of Jesus. This is supposed to prove that her body was removed to heaven before anyone could "raid" her remains and acquire such "mementos" of her. However, history is not favorable to this postulation. It was not until the persecutions began that the relics of martyred saints became a popular pursuit of those who admired their bravery, and falsely believed that possession of such relics imparted some special spiritual powers. There is no record anywhere to foster a belief that Mary was martyred, and therefore the object of that kind of admiration. As a matter of fact, her death is not reported at all in the Scriptures or the writings of the patristic church saints. Clearly, if Mary's death and alleged bodily Assumption into heaven were events God wanted us to believe He would have caused them to be included in His inspired Word. Remember He did not leave us a partial Bible or a partial Gospel.

Scripture reports that two men—Enoch and Elijah—escaped death by being taken alive to heaven. *"And Enoch walked with God: and he was not; for God took him."* (Gen 5:24) *"…and Elijah went up by a whirlwind into heaven."* (2 Ki 2:11) These incidents, say the Catholic apologists, are evidence that Mary's Assumption would not have been without precedent. And, because of a Scripture in the Book of Jude, they feel that the body of Moses was assumed into heaven much as Mary's supposedly was. *"Yet Michael the archangel, when contending with the devil he disputed about the body of Moses, durst not bring against him a railing accusation, but said, The Lord rebuke thee."* (Jude 1:9) What the dispute over the body of Moses was all about is not explained in Scripture, but the Word of God quite clearly states the fact that Moses was buried. *"So Moses the servant of the LORD died there in the land of Moab, according to the word of the LORD. And he (God) buried him in a valley in the land of Moab, over against Bethpeor: but no man knoweth of his sepulchre unto this day."* (Deu 34:5, 6) As further evidence that Mary's alleged Assumption—that is, her restoration to life through the reunification of her body, soul and spirit—was quite feasible, Rome points to the bodily resurrection of deceased saints after our Lord's Resurrection. *"And the graves were opened; and many bodies of the saints which slept arose, and came out of the graves after his resurrection, and went into the holy city, and appeared unto many."* (Mat 27:52, 53) Rome concludes that these saints did not die again but were assumed alive into heaven, a foreshadowing of what Mary later experienced. One faction within Catholicism believes that Mary never really died, but only slept—this known as her dormition—and while asleep was taken by angels to heaven.

But none of the above proves that Mary's body was assumed into heaven. What is in question is not the **feasibility** of such an occurrence. What is in question is **did it really happen**, and if it did, why did God not see fit to so inform us? He wanted us to know about Enoch, about Elijah, and about the saints restored to life at Christ's Resurrection. Why then is God completely silent about the alleged Assumption of Mary, and, in fact, all of the Marian doctrines? It seems that if Jesus so loved Mary and wanted her invested with such great honors, the first action He would have taken was to have them—not just included—but highly featured in His divine Scriptures. After the first chapter of the Book of Acts, however, there is not one mention of Mary in the 22 additional books of the New Testament, two of which were compiled by men identified as her sons, the half-brothers of our Lord.

Prior to making his declaration, Pius XII, called "Hitler's Pope," by some, reportedly asked all the Catholic bishops throughout the world their opinion of the Assumption doctrine. Their nearly unanimous endorsement of it is cited by Catholic apologists as another proof of its validity. Said Pius XII, himself: **"…the universal teaching of the authorities of the Church by itself gives us a proof."** It is worthy of note, however, that at one time the "authorities of the Church" were nearly unanimous in their belief that Earth, not the Sun, is the center of our galaxy. They were dead wrong. And, if the "authorities of the Church," of our day are in agreement with John Paul II that Darwinian Evolution is an established fact, they are dead wrong again. Point? In the absence of proof from God's Word, the fact that all "the authorities of the Church," approved of the Assumption doctrine is no proof at all.

Catholics as a body are so gullible. They accept without a whimper of disapproval, the proposition that popes need not disclose where in their "Tradition Bank" an extra-biblical doctrine was found. But Pius XII, in formalizing the Assumption dogma, went to great lengths attempting to make it believable. He said Mary was always sharing the lot of Jesus, so she was not required like the rest of us to wait until the end for the resurrection of her body. And, because of her alleged Immaculate Conception her body was not liable to the corruption of the grave anyhow. He also said he found the dogma mentioned in some old time liturgical books, adding that after the apostolic church age, the Assumption doctrine was a subject of study by scholastic theologians. At least one of them, a 15th century theologian, believed it fitting that not only the soul and body of a man—Jesus—should already have attained heavenly glory, but also the soul and body of a woman—namely, Mary. More opinion; still no proof. Continuing with his rationalization of the doctrine, Pius XII cited an early belief that cast Mary as the "new Eve," sinless and holy, a fitting queen of heaven ruling jointly with the King of Kings, Christ Jesus our Lord. The "new Eve" was alleged to have been closely allied with the "new Adam"—Jesus—in the battle to defeat sin and death. Therefore, Pius reasoned, the common cause should produce a common effect, a glorification of Mary paralleling the glorification of Christ. Finally, as our Lord perfectly fulfilled the commandments, He would have perfectly honored His earthly mother, and one of the ways He could have chosen to do this was to assume her lifeless body into heaven.

But there is not a shred of evidence in Scripture to support any of this. As a matter of fact, Mary was not always sharing our Lord's work; she was not allied with Him in the battle to defeat sin and death; and she already was honored above all the other women who ever lived by being chosen to give birth to God's only begotten Son. As for the "new Eve" thing, it is dangerously close to the Babylon Mystery Religion that had a goddess queen intimately involved with her own son and ruling jointly with him. Certainly, Jesus was the "last Adam," but a "new Eve" is nowhere to be found in Scripture.

"Wherefore, as by one man sin entered into the world, and death by sin; and so death passed upon all men, for that all have sinned:" (Rom 5:12) ***"Nevertheless death reigned from Adam to Moses, even over them that had not sinned after the similitude of Adam's transgression, who is the figure of him that was to come."*** (Rom 5:14) ***"For if by one man's offense death reigned by one; much more they which receive abundance of grace and of the gift of righteousness shall reign in life by one, Jesus Christ."*** (Rom 5:17)

In these Scriptures it is obvious that it was not the sin of Eve that brought death into the world, but the sin of Adam who was the "head" of Eve. It is also clear that there was to be a second "Adam," but **not** a second Eve. Lastly, Jesus had no one allied with Him or sharing His lot in the redemption. He did it all by Himself with no help from Mary. Only His blood was shed. Only He deserves the glory that He has justly received from born again Christians, but not from Rome.

In his efforts to justify the Assumption doctrine, Pius XII tried his best to give it an aura of antiquity in keeping with Rome's standard practice. But history is not at all cooperative in the matter. There simply is no evidence that the early church espoused such a doctrine or had even heard of it. But right around AD

300 a manuscript attributed to the Ebionite sect began to circulate. In it was the first suggestion that Mary's body had not decayed but been taken by angels to heaven. Then, early in the 5th century there followed a book variously entitled "Holiest Mother of God Rests," and "The Passing of Mary." Soon after, the same material turned up in a volume entitled, "Dormitio Mariae," compiled by the Ebionite heretic, Leucius. It purported to contain the account of Mary's bodily Assumption into heaven. Like the numerous other spurious documents that figure in the theology of Catholicism, "Dormitio Mariae" was merely a religious fairy tale. It contained serious historical and doctrinal flaws that eliminate any doubt about its authenticity.

To begin with, the account has Jesus demoted to the status of an angel, rather than the Second Person of the triune Godhead, a sure mark of the Ebionite influence. Secondly, salvation is not a free gift of God, but is achieved by various works instead of by faith alone in Christ's Calvary sacrifice. That bit of heresy was later adopted by Catholicism and continues as church doctrine to this day. Thirdly, Paul is not granted equal status with the other Apostles as he is in the Scriptures, another belief linking the whole myth to the Ebionites. Nor is it historically dependable, for it has all the Apostles from all over the known world assembled in Jerusalem, something for which there is no record whatever anywhere.

Briefly, this is the myth—the "Dormitio Mariae." Jesus, as an angel and not the Son of God, tells Mary of her impending death. Mary goes home and gets ready to die by going through a series of rituals to ward off demons. The Apostles come from all over the known world to be there in Jerusalem for Mary's demise. As she sleeps away (dormition) into eternity, her soul is protected by Jesus and Michael the archangel, while her body is buried in a brand new grave located in the biblically famous Kidron Valley. The Apostles remain in Jerusalem for three more days, at which time Paul appears on the scene wanting to know what great mysteries have been revealed to them. Peter, however, opposes giving Paul any information at all. Thereafter, the Apostles leave Jerusalem, returning to their previous places of ministry. End of story? Not quite. Three full days having now elapsed, Jesus and Michael, this time assisted by Gabriel, return with a celestial chariot; they disinter Mary's body, place it in the chariot, and, all together, ascend into heaven.

Such fantasy found but few "takers" in the early centuries of Christianity, and even after the emergence of Catholicism, it was only sparsely subscribed to before the middle ages. Its general acceptance among Catholics had to wait until the 13th century when a forged document falsely attributed to Augustine of Hippo made its appearance. Even then, and until November of 1950, the Assumption doctrine was a "believe it or not matter," no sin attached if an individual chose to reject it.

All in all, there is no legitimate foundation underpinning the Assumption doctrine. There is no biblical support for it, no record of its existence among the patristic saints, no endorsement of it in the annals of church history. Like the other Marian doctrines it's a maverick unsupported and unpredicted in God's Word. Our Lord's Resurrection was clearly foretold in the Book of Psalms: *"For thou wilt not leave my soul in hell; neither wilt thou suffer thine Holy One to see corruption."* (Psa 16:10) Accounts of this prophecy's fulfillment are found in all four Gospels and throughout the remaining 23 books of the New Testament. There are sixty-six books total in the entire Bible. Not one of them contains a prophecy about Mary's body being assumed into heaven, and, of course, where there is no prophecy there is no fulfillment.

Scripture is crystal clear about Enoch being caught up to heaven. *"And Enoch walked with God: and he was not; for God took him."* (Gen 5:24) It is equally clear in the matter of Elijah's departure. *"And it came to pass, as they still went on, and talked, that, behold, there appeared a chariot of fire, and horses of fire, and parted them both asunder; and Elijah went up by a whirlwind into heaven."* (2 Ki 2:11) On such a critical matter as Mary's alleged Assumption the holy Bible is eloquently silent. Why don't Catholics wonder "**WHY?**"

In chapter 8 it will be seen that just four years after Pius IX declared the doctrine of the Immaculate Conception in 1850, a young girl saw visions of a beautiful "lady" who eventually identified "herself" as the "Immaculate Conception." Thus, heaven itself seemed to lend its endorsement to Pius IX's declaration. Not surprisingly, a similar occurrence followed by less than three months Pius XII's declaration of Mary's Assumption.

One Maria Valtorta, (AD 1897-1961) of Viareggio, Italy, had a vision on December 8, 1951, (the feast of the Immaculate Conception) in which she saw the Apostle John witnessing the Assumption of Mary's body into heaven. Valtorta is touted as one of the 18 greatest mystics of all time by at least one highly placed Catholic official, but her vision bears little in common with the "Dormitio Mariae" of the 5th century. Jesus, Michael, and Gabriel are replaced in her vision by a band of angels complete with wings, who carry Mary's body off to heaven. Once again, it appeared heaven had given its approval to a highly controversial doctrine. Valtorta's vision certainly was good news to Pius XII. It is reported that when he read her "The Poem of The Man-God," in which the Assumption vision is related, he ordered, **"Publish this work as it is…Whoever reads it will understand."**

Summing up this entire Assumption matter, the evidence from early church Christians and subsequent archeological finds indicate that Mary had a normal, quite unremarkable death. Her grave was reported to be in the Kidron Valley. Some accounts even pinpointed the grave's location. Churches have been built atop a couple of the locations thought to have contained Mary's remains, and until 1950, the Roman Catholic Church maintained a site known as Mary's Tomb for the edification of pilgrims visiting Jerusalem. It is more than rumor that when the Assumption doctrine was declared, Rome sold the "Tomb of Mary" to the Armenian church. Conclusion? The Assumption is one more heresy declared an article of faith by an imposter whom we know as the Roman Catholic pope. (Cf. chapter 3) And we must ask what "god" revealed to him this biblically unsupported belief. It certainly was not the holy God of Scripture, for He has clearly stated that His glory will not be given or shared with another.

MARY CO-MEDIATRIX.

In Roman Catholic theology Mary has been elevated to a position of co-mediatrix (with Jesus) and supposedly is thereby empowered to act as an advocate for us with our heavenly Father. It is this doctrine that encourages the Catholic faithful to direct their prayers and petitions to Mary instead of directly to the Father in the name of Jesus. Not only is this another flagrant breach of Scripture, it also has given rise to some of the most heart-wrenching practices on the part of both the Catholic laity and clergy. As people look to Mary rather than to our Lord Jesus Christ for intercession with the Father, they perform rites and rituals akin to those of the religious Jews of Jerusalem who caused Christ to weep at their folly. Many clergy and laity alike wear certain medals that are guaranteed—supposedly by Mary—to secure one's eventual acceptance into heaven. Others—making reparation to Mary's "immaculate heart" for the insults of men—attend Mass and receive communion on five consecutive first Saturdays, expecting as a result, Mary's intercession at the hour of death. Frequent recitation of the rosary, a string of beads used for counting fifty prayers to Mary, supposedly imparts special graces and benefits in the quest for salvation.

Of course, endowing Christ's earthly mother with the role of co-intercessor is a blasphemous affront to the blessed Lord Jesus. He earned His place as our only advocate with the Father by His bloody sacrifice on Calvary. He alone is our advocate with the Father. (1 John 2:1) He alone is our high priest, able to intercede for us. (Heb 3:1) He alone has been touched with our infirmities, tempted as we have been tempted but without sin, (Heb 4:15) and burdened by burdens far greater than ours. He is the One to Whom and through Whom we are to direct our prayers. (John 15:16) He is the one alone to Whom and through Whom we are to offer our praise and thanksgiving, our worship. (John 4:24) It is in His sweet name and His alone that we can barge boldly into the very throne room of heaven. (Heb 4:16) In time of abundance and in time of want, it is in and through the name of Jesus, and only Jesus, that we can obtain fulfillment of our petitions.

Although the Catholic hierarchy will deny again and again that Mary is worshiped, she is, in fact, an object of worship for Roman Catholics. Following is a quote taken directly from the 1994 Catholic Catechism, page 253:

"The Church's devotion to the Blessed Virgin is INTRINSIC to Christian WORSHIP."

It cannot be denied that prayer is a very specific form of worship. By encouraging Catholics to pray to Mary, by fostering numerous devotions to her and veneration of her statues, the church is undeniably promoting worship of her who Scripture says should not be worshiped. The most precious Word of God expressly condemns worship offered to anyone or anything other than God Himself. The children of Israel's worship of strange idols and false gods is what brought the judgment of the true God—Jehovah—upon their apostate nation.

Try as they might to assign a co-mediatrix role to Mary, the Vatican crew cannot alter the divine Scriptures. Mary is not, cannot be, a co-mediatrix. She is an abundantly blessed believer who did God's will to the best of her ability. Lacking Scriptural and historical information to the contrary, Mary's body is asleep in Christ Jesus awaiting the time of His return, when both the living and the dead in Christ shall be caught up to heaven, there to remain for all eternity. (1 Thes 4:17) Her soul and spirit certainly are with the Lord, and it is a foregone conclusion that, as the mother of God's only begotten Son, she enjoys a high place in her Father's "house." (Cf. John 14:2) But she is not there as a co-mediatrix to be prayed to and worshiped, else God's Word is lying. *"For there is one God, and ONE MEDIATOR between God and men, the man Christ Jesus."* (1 Tim 2:5) *"But now hath he obtained a more excellent ministry, by how much also he is the mediator of a better covenant, which was established upon better promises."* (Heb 8:6) *"And for this cause he is the mediator of the new testament...."* (Heb 9:15) *"Who is he that condemneth? It is Christ that died, yea rather, that is risen again, who is even at the right hand of God, who also maketh intercession for us."* (Rom 8:34) *"...And to Jesus, the mediator of the new covenant..."* (Heb 12:24)

It could not be made clearer in God's Word that the lone mediator between us and our heavenly Father is the man Christ Jesus. One of the most cherished chapters in the entire Bible is the 14th chapter of John's Gospel. In verse 13, our Lord says to His Apostles: *"whatsoever ye shall ask in my name, that will I do, that the Father may be glorified in the Son."* Verse 15: *"If ye shall ask anything in my name, I will do it."* Earlier in that same great chapter, Jesus told Thomas: *"I am the way, the truth and the life; no man cometh unto the Father but by me."* (John 14:6) It is sheer folly for Roman Catholics to pray to Mary, or, for that matter, to other dead people classified as "saints" by Rome. Mary is not omnipresent to hear the prayers of millions of believers lifting their voices at the same time on every continent of the earth. Nor is she omniscient, knowing the hearts and minds and the very thoughts of earthbound mortals. Only the omnipotent triune God possesses those attributes; only God whose vastness is far beyond our most extensive imaginings. Only God who is so unlimited in his power and intelligence that He could create out of nothing (ex nihilo) us and the universe in which we live.

Our Lord is the "Door"—the only Door—to the "sheepfold" of heaven. (John 10:7) To seek admittance thereto, either in prayer or through faith in something or someone else, classifies the individual who does so as follows: *"**Verily, verily, I say unto you, He that entereth not by the door into the sheepfold, but climbeth up some other way, the same is a thief and a robber.**"* (John 10:1) Roman Catholics are **taught** to be "thieves" and "robbers."

> **"Taken up to heaven she (Mary) did not lay aside this saving office but by her manifold intercession continues to bring us the gifts of eternal salvation. Therefore the Blessed Virgin is invoked in the Church under the titles of Advocate, Helper, Benefactress, and Mediatrix."** (Page 252 '94 Catechism.)

Conceding to Mary a "saving office" and an advocacy position equal to that of the Lord Jesus is an insult to a holy God who was "pleased" to "bruise" His only begotten Son—His Beloved—so that His demand for justice might be satisfied, and unworthy mankind restored to Adamic fellowship with Him. (Cf. Isa 53:10, 11) It is an insult to the man Christ Jesus who willingly underwent the excruciating physical, mental and emotional pain of Calvary to buy our pardon. And it is an insult to the mother of Jesus, blessed by God above all other women, but never by Him elevated to worship-worthy deity. The Vatican's rationale for declaring Mary to be man's "Advocate, Helper, Benefactress, and Mediatrix" is stated as follows on page 252 of the 1994 Catechism:

> "In a wholly singular way she (Mary) cooperated by her obedience, faith, hope and burning charity in the Savior's work of restoring supernatural life to souls."

Those words are a lavish compliment to Mary, but they and the conclusion drawn from them are in conflict with the divine Scriptures. *"But this man, after he had offered one sacrifice for sins for ever, sat down on the right hand of God; From henceforth expecting till his enemies be made his footstool. For by one offering hath perfected for ever them that are sanctified."* (Heb 10:12-14) It was our Lord alone who performed the work of redemption. Only His precious blood was shed. Only He was the *"Lamb of God that taketh away the sin of the world."* (John 1:29) Jesus had no one—needed no one—to assist, cooperate, or contribute in any way toward the payment of man's sin debt. Had the cooperation of others been necessary, there were many of His followers whose **"obedience, faith, hope and burning charity,"** would have qualified them for such a role. But only Christ's blood was precious. Only Christ's blood was shed. And the Word of God tells us that without the shedding of blood there is no remission of sins. (Cf. Heb 9:22) Mary shed no blood; couldn't have as a creature born of Adam's seed and therefore in need herself of a Savior. She was not, is not, and never will or can be co-mediatrix with Jesus no matter how many declarations are forthcoming from the Vatican under the guise of "Sacred Tradition."

I am asked about the great volume of answered prayers attributed to petitions directed to the mother of Jesus, and about the multitude of apparitions claiming to be Mary. Aren't answered prayers and these many apparitions proof of Mary's awesome power and position as co-mediatrix with our Lord? No, these simply are further proof that the divine Word of God never contradicts itself, and is to be trusted in all things. In chapter 8 of this book the subject of Marian apparitions and prayers allegedly answered by her are covered in some depth, and will confirm the truth of the statement just made.

MARY QUEEN OF HEAVEN.

As has been the case with each of the other Marian heresies we have looked at in this chapter, when we turn to the Scriptures, we find no record whatsoever of Mary being crowned Queen of Heaven. Moreover, there is no historical evidence of any kind indicating the early church fathers, the apostolic successors, subscribed to such a belief. What we do find in Scripture—in the Book of Jeremiah—is a negative reference to a queen of heaven worshiped by the children of Israel. A major part of Jeremiah, chapter 44, deals with the vows, incense burnings, cake and drink offerings, etc., that constituted Israel's defiant worship of a so-called queen of heaven, thus angering Jehovah and inviting His divine judgment upon their flagrant idolatry. In Jeremiah 7:18, there appears the first reference to this imagined queen of heaven: *"The children gather wood, and the fathers kindle the fire, and the women knead their dough, to make cakes to the QUEEN OF HEAVEN, and to pour out drink offerings unto other gods, that they may provoke me to anger."*

Later on, in chapter 44, we are privy to the defiance of the children of Israel, paralleled in our day by the Vatican's insistence that Mary, the mother of Jesus, is the Queen of Heaven. To Jeremiah's admonitions, the children of Israel responded as follows: *"Then all the men which knew that their wives had burned incense unto other gods, and all the women that stood by, a great multitude, even all the people that dwelt in the land of Egypt, in Pathros, answered Jeremiah, saying, 'As for the word that thou hast spoken unto us in the name of the LORD, we will not hearken unto thee. But we will certainly do whatsoever thing goeth forth out of our own mouth, to burn incense unto the queen of heaven, and to pour out drink offerings unto her, as we have done, we, and our fathers, our kings, and our princes, in the cities of Judah, and in the streets of Jerusalem: for then had we plenty of victuals, and were well, and saw no evil. But since we left off to burn incense to the queen of heaven, and to pour out drink offerings unto her, we have wanted all things, and have been consumed by the sword and by the famine. And when we burned incense to the queen of heaven, and poured out drink offerings unto her, did we make her cakes to worship her, and pour out drink offerings unto her, without our men?'"* (Jer 44:15-19)

Rome, the self-appointed keeper and interpreter of the Scriptures, ignores God's expressed anger at Israel's worship of an invented queen of heaven, invents one of its own and crowns her the new Queen of Heaven.

> **"Finally the Immaculate Virgin, preserved free from all stain of original sin, when the course of her earthly life was finished, was taken up body and soul into heavenly glory, and exalted by the Lord as Queen over all things, so that she might be the more fully conformed to her Son, the Lord of Lords and conqueror of sin and death."** (Page 252 '94 Catechism.)

Is not the Roman Catholic church as defiant as were the children of Israel in insisting that Mary, a mere creature, is queen of heaven and therefore worthy to be worshiped? What justification is there for the Vatican making such a declaration and commanding the faithful to believe it under the pain of sin? For the answers to these questions, the reader is invited to turn back the clock with me to the 18th century. There, history tells us, was a certain monk named Alfonse Liguori (AD 1696-1787), who began applying the title Queen of Heaven to Mary, the mother of Jesus. It is a distinct possibility that he appropriated this appellation from the writings of a mystic—Maria de Agreda (AD 1602-1665)—who penned a monumental work entitled **"The Mystical City of God,"** a pseudonym for Christ's mother Mary.

Although in Liguori's day, "The Mystical City of God" was a work banned by the Catholic Church, it was not unavailable. And because so much of what Liguori espoused appears in the visionary work of Maria de Agreda, it's almost impossible to believe he was not greatly influenced by her. This will be very apparent when the "Mystical City" manuscript is studied in chapter 8. However, whether Liguori was or wasn't so influenced, it is he who popularized the Mary Queen of Heaven idea, as well as the belief that it was easier to obtain favors from her than from Jesus. This latter belief Liguori based on a silly legend embraced by the monks of his order.

In the legend, there are two ladders, each reaching from earth to heaven. At the top of one ladder—a red one—stands the Lord Jesus. At the top of the second ladder—a white one—stands Mary, our Lord's mother. According to the legend, monks who tried climbing the red ladder to Jesus were unsuccessful. But when they switched their efforts to the white ladder leading up to Mary they made it to heaven quite easily. Thus, via Liguori, was born the belief that is rampant today among the Roman Catholic faithful, that getting to heaven is easier going through Mary than through *"the way, the truth and the life,"* Christ Jesus the Lord. That is blasphemy! There is no other name for it but blasphemy, for it promotes the belief that there are two salvation roads, a very hard one through Jesus and another very easy one through Mary. That, of course, is the "ANOTHER GOSPEL" twice condemned by the Word of God as recorded in Paul's letter to the Galatian churches—Galations 1:8, 9. "Aw, c'mon, Alfonse Liguori is a canonized saint of the Catholic Church; he didn't really **believe** that did he?"

So convinced was Liguori of the dual paths to salvation that he wrote, **"If my redeemer should reject me, I will throw myself at Mary's feet."** But according to God's divine Word no born again believer need ever fear rejection from the One who loved us so much that He left the glory of heaven, and, as a man, shed

His precious blood on the cruel cross of Calvary to expiate the dreadful sins of all mankind. Nevertheless, once Liguori had convinced himself of Mary's redemptive powers, it was an easy step to visualize her as the crowned and reigning Queen of Heaven. It was Liguori's contention—almost certainly gleaned from Maria de Agreda's work—that Mary received her queen's crown from the Blessed Trinity, the Father giving her His power, Jesus giving her His wisdom, and the Holy Ghost giving her His love. Incredible! Astounding! For what Liguori promulgated was God literally breaching His own Word—endowing Mary, a creature, with His own divine attributes, in effect establishing a goddess beside Himself.

One would think that such fantasies would have been met with accusations of heresy and threats of excommunication because of the way God punished the nation of Israel for its idolatry of the same genre. But, no, the allegedly infallible Leo XIII (AD 1878-1903) led the way to acceptance of this Liguori silliness, saying: **"...just as no one can draw close to the Father except through the Son, no one can draw near to Christ except through His mother."** This from an individual Rome says has sovereign authority over God's Word, and is infallible when proclaiming matters having to do with faith (as above) and morals. Can't draw near to Jesus except through Mary? Did he—Leo—never read, ***"Behold, I stand at the door, and knock: if any man hear my voice, and open the door, I will come in to him, and will sup with him, and he with me."*** (Rev 3:20) Jesus craves acceptance by every soul. Can't draw near to Him except through Mary?

Imagine saying that of the Holy One who was thronged by crowds wherever he went when He walked the earth. Imagine saying that of the One who rebuked His Apostles when they tried to keep the little children away from Him. Imagine saying that of the One who ate with Publicans and sinners. Imagine saying that of the One who—against all Jewish custom—deliberately traveled to Galilee through Samaria so he could save a poor lost Samaritan adulteress; the One who called a Publican out of a tree so He could save him; the One who gave Blind Bartimaeus sight when His Apostles rebuked the man for calling to Jesus. How Rome demeans our blessed Lord by inferring that He is stern and unapproachable. In truth, Jesus is the approachable One; the anxious listener to every prayer and supplication of poor needy sinners. He is the almighty King of Kings and Lord of Lords who invites every soul to receive Him by faith, and then come boldly in His name into the throne room of heaven to be heard and comforted.

Following Leo XIII's endorsement of Liguori's hallucination in which Mary is crowned Queen of Heaven, other "infallible" popes began, one after another, to express their approval and support of the myth, and even to add to it. Pius X (AD

1903-14), for example opined that Mary as queen **was *not just a participant with God in passing out graces*, but that she was, in fact, the principal party in that Godly function.** In other words, God who is the source of all grace, turned over the distribution of those graces to a created being. Benedict XV agreed. He said Mary **"...is the mediator with God of all graces."** Pius XII in a radio message to Fatima on May 13, 1946, said, **"...Mary is queen by grace, by divine relationship, by right of conquest,** (whatever that means), **and by singular choice of the Father."**

And where is the Scriptural foundation for all of this? Rome's apologists point without the least bit of embarrassment to Genesis 3:15 and Revelation 12:1, two Scriptures that clearly identify the nation of Israel, not Mary, as the subject woman. Pius XII, by some highly creative inductive reasoning expressed in *Fulgens Corona,* September 8, 1953, was able from Genesis 3:15 alone to arrive at both the Immaculate Conception and Queendom doctrines. He it was who stated that **Mary shared in redeeming us.** LG Paragraph 56 of Vatican Council II adds to Pius XII's statement. **"...by being obedient, she (Mary) became a cause of salvation for herself and for the whole human race."** Mary a *cause* of salvation? What heresy! What blasphemy! Bluntly put, Catholicism teaches that **Mary literally participated in her own redemption, and is one of two causes that brought about the redemption of mankind.**

"Neither is there salvation in any other (name): for there is none other name (but Jesus) under heaven given among men, whereby we must be saved." (Acts 4:12) Mary's alleged Immaculate Conception, lifetime virginity, bodily Assumption and crowning as Queen of Heaven are illicit doctrines that purloin the glory that is due Christ Jesus alone. This stolen glory is then given to Mary, a mere—though highly blessed—creation of Him who has been victimized by the theft. But God is not mocked. Nor will He share His glory with anyone, Mary included. We have his immutable Word on that. *"...before me there was no God formed; neither shall there be after me."* (Isa 43:10)

No matter how many ways the Roman Catholic Church finds to deify Mary, she will not be deified. She will always be Mary, the mother of the man Jesus, wife of Joseph, mother of Christ's half brothers and sisters, cousin of Elisabeth, sinner saved exclusively by the Grace of her Creator, God. No twisting of the Scriptures, no amount of inductive reasoning, no amount of confusing, obfuscating, apologetics will change the truth found in God's divine Word. In Isaiah 44:6 we read: *"I am the first, and I am the last; and beside me there is no God."* And no goddess, either. Mary is a created being. She is neither queen nor mediatrix. According to Jesus, she was not even "good." In the Gospels of Matthew,

Mark and Luke, Christ informed a young ruler that, *"...there is none good but God."* (Mat 19:17; Mark 10:18; Luke 18:19) From the context, our Lord's meaning is clear: only God is perfect, and no created beings—His mother Mary included—can make that claim, or have it made about them.

Like all of us, Mary was a servant assigned a specific task that she carried out admirably. Of such faithful servants, Christ had this to say: *So likewise ye, when ye shall have done all those things which are commanded you, say, We are unprofitable servants: we have done that which was our duty to do."* (Luke 17:10) In doing her duty, Mary did not qualify for deification. When she visited her pregnant cousin Elisabeth, she first acknowledged her need of a Savior, *"...my spirit hath rejoiced in God my Saviour."* (Luke 1:47) Secondly she acknowledged her imperfection when she said, *"For he hath regarded the low estate of his handmaiden:"* (Luke 1:48) The Greek word for the phrase low estate is **tapeinosis,** which conveys one's regret of his or her own moral turpitude and **guilt**.

"...there is no God else beside me; a just God and a Saviour; there is none beside me. Look unto me, and be ye saved, all the ends of the earth: for I am God, and there is none else." (Isa 45:21, 22) In closing this chapter on the heretical Marian doctrines of Catholicism it bears repeating that God alone is our Savior through Christ Jesus our Lord. From other Scriptures quoted we can be sure that only Jesus was born sinless and remained sinless from the cradle to Calvary's cross. He and He alone is our propitiation for sin, and He alone is our advocate with the Father. We can be sure God had no mother, and there is no queen reigning in heaven. Our Lord had no co-savior, no co-mediartix, no "new Eve." Mary was conceived with the same sin nature that all descendents of Adam inherit. She needed salvation just like John the Baptist, Peter, Paul and every believer since. Hers was a normal highly blessed marriage that produced four named sons and at least two unnamed daughters in addition to her firstborn, Jesus. History places her grave with her in it in the Kidron Valley outside of Jerusalem. That said, for our salvation, we need only look to Him—Jesus—not to Him and her.

In the final analysis, the Marian doctrines simply have to be satanically inspired, for they more than any other Catholic teachings, demean the Lord Jesus, disparage His sacrifice, and rob Him of the glory that is His alone. They assign to Mary, His earthly mother, attributes only God Himself possesses. They elevate her to a position to which no created being may aspire or attain. As a result, Mary has become—in the apostate Catholic religion—**THE GODDESS**

MAN HAS MADE. May God have mercy on all who are deceived into worshiping her.

3

The Great Imposters

"For other foundation can no man lay than that is layed, which is Jesus Christ." (1 Co 3:11)

It is a key characteristic of religious cults to have one all-powerful individual as their leader who claims to have a special and exclusive anointing from the deity. In this individual resides, as it were, the very oracles of God, and the declarations made by him or her become commandments to which the cult members must adhere. Invariably, this individual inspires in the cult members an unshakeable faith and trust that enables the leader to exercise total mind control over them, thereby directing both their thoughts and actions. Few would have the temerity to call the Roman Catholic Church a cult, but when its leader—the pope—is measured against the foregoing definition, what other conclusion can be drawn? When he speaks **ex cathedra**—literally, "from his chair"—he is said to be infallible, not subject to error. Therefore, all followers must subordinate themselves to his **ex cathedra** proclamations whether they agree with them or not. Rome says this authority accrues to the successor of the Apostle Peter on whom our Lord allegedly founded His church. Does history, the early church writings and God's Word support what Rome says, or not? This chapter will provide the answers.

Rome's claim—dealt with in chapter 1—that the Catholic Church is the one and only true Church founded by our Lord, rests largely on the assertion that Jesus ordained the Apostle Peter to be the first pope, and on him the church was founded. In the hodgepodge that is Catholic apologetics, Holy Scripture is cited when it can be interpreted to support doctrine and ignored or manipulated when it cannot. In justifying the existence of the papacy, for example, Rome cites Scriptures from all four of the Gospels. But at the same time, it ignores completely our Lord's words to two of the seven Asian churches in the Book of Revelation, words that condemn the very priesthood out of which the papacy evolved.

In His letter to the messenger or bishop of the Ephesian church, Jesus has these words of praise: *"But this thou hast, that thou hatest the deeds of the Nicolaitanes which I also hate."* (Rev 2:6) But in the letter to the messenger of the church at Pergamos, He has this rebuke: *"So hast thou also them that hold the doctrine of the Nicolaitanes, which thing I hate."* (Rev 2:15)

A singularly undesirable trait man has inherited with the Adamic nature is the drive to be a god who makes his own rules, and exercises power over others. This drive is what motivated Satan to challenge God. It was part of the temptation he presented to Adam and Eve. It is the conscious or unconscious motive behind every man's climb to the top of politics, business, academia, etc. That said, let's look again at the *"Nicolaitanes"* whose deeds and doctrine were literally hated by Jesus. It is a composite of two Greek words for sure, possibly three. They are **nikao,** and **laos,** and very possibly a contraction of **thanatos.** The first, **nikao**, means **"power,"** the kind that has been seized or usurped as opposed to power that has been granted or freely received. The second Greek word, **laos,** means the **"common folks,"** in a religious sense, the **laity**. Together, **nikao** and **laos** describe usurped **"power over the laity."** The suffix, **tanes,** may very well be a contraction of **thanatos,** which means **"destructive,"** or **"undesirable."**

If that is the case, and the three Greek words are put together, then the word our Lord employed—*Nicolaitanes*—in the context in which it is twice used, means either, **"destructive power over the laity,"** or **"power over the laity that is undesirable."** The *Nicolaitanes,* then, were a group—perhaps of Jewish converts—who pressed for reestablishment of a priestly order that was forever eliminated by Christ's death on Calvary. Their aim of forming a new clergy exercising ecclesiastical authority over converts to Christianity obviously was displeasing to Jesus. In His Revelation letter to their "messenger"—their "bishop"—our Lord commended the Ephesian church for **"hating"** what the *Nicolaitanes* were trying to do, the very thing that He, too, hated. But the Pergamos church He rebuked because the Nicolaitanes had been admitted to fellowship, and were in the process of achieving—perhaps already had achieved—their objective.

From our vantage point 2000 years after the fact, Christ's letters to the Asian churches, beyond their applicability to conditions extant at that time, were prophetic of seven identifiable periods the Church would pass through during this, the dispensation of Grace. The first period, the apostolic period, lasted only until the persecutions began, and is represented by the Ephesian church. This church resisted the *Nicolaitanes'* efforts, even **"hating"** what they were trying to do. Smyrna represented the church of the persecution period that ended early in the 4th century, about 200 years before Roman Catholicism fully accomplished a successful takeover of western Christendom. The third church period or age began later in the 4th century when Christianity was installed as the official state religion of the Roman Empire. This period is represented by the church at Pergamos. Our Lord's rebukes to this church identify it as a compromising church. And soon after Christianity's installation as the state-sponsored religion, it began embracing the theology and traditions brought in by unregenerate Jews and the diverse pagan worshipers of false gods.

By His Calvary sacrifice, our Lord did away with the Levitical priesthood of Judaism, setting up in its place a "priesthood of believers." His Word tells us, *" Ye also, as lively stones, are built up a spiritual house, an HOLY PRIEST-HOOD, to offer up spiritual sacrifices, acceptable to God by Jesus Christ."* (1 Pet 2:5) And again: *"But ye are a chosen generation, a ROYAL PRIEST-HOOD, an holy nation, a peculiar people; that ye should shew forth the praises of him who hath called you out of darkness into his marvellous light."* (1 Pet 2:9) Christ's once-for-all and once-for-all-time sacrifice obviated further need for animal sacrifices, doing away with those—the Levitical priests—who were responsible to perform them. That's why Jesus "hated" the efforts being made even before the end of the 1st century to reestablish a hierarchy that again would separate between man and God. With the 4th century advent of a compromising Church, the **Nicolaitanes'** objective was well on its way to fruition; was fully achieved by the start of the 6th century when priests began to dress differently from the common people. A priesthood unwanted by our Lord was endorsed and fostered by the emerging Roman Catholic Church as a means of consolidating its authority over the more than 350 independent Christian fellowships in existence in western Christendom by AD 500.

It should come as no surprise to regular readers of the holy Bible that Jesus never intended to have a clergy lording it over the saints who had placed their faith for salvation in His finished work. For, while on earth, He once called His followers together to explain His organizational plan for the Church He would soon establish. *"Ye know that the princes of the gentiles exercise dominion over them and they that are great exercise authority upon them. But it shall not be so among you but whosoever will be great among you, let him be your minister; And whosoever will be chief among you, let him be your servant:"* (Mat 20:25-27) Obviously, then, our Lord was clearly opposed to any group (Are you listening, Rome?) claiming ecclesiastical authority or a higher level of spirituality over His blood-bought saints. There would be preachers and teachers, witnesses and workers, bishops and presbyters, but all equal in the sight of God, all employing the gifts bestowed on them by the Holy Spirit for the edification and advancement of the Body of Christ. He who wished to be chief was to subordinate his selfish aim in servitude to all. No individual or group was to lord it over the flock, a theocracy governed by our Lord from heaven itself.

The very man Rome claims was ordained as Catholicism's first pope, confirmed the policy laid out by Jesus, instructing those who would come after as follows: *"Feed the flock of God which is among you, taking the oversight thereof, not by constraint, but willingly; not for filthy lucre, but of a ready mind; Neither as being lords over God's heritage, but being ensamples to the flock."* (1 Pet 5:2, 3) Peter's use of plurals—i.e. "lords" and "examples"—is a clear signal that there were to be multiple overseers, not one supreme monarch or centralized government. But power and control of the lives of others is a mighty motivator. As early as the start of the 4th century, presbyters in some of the large urban fellowships were being called "priests," and some of the bishops heading up independent fellowships had extended their control to other newer fellowships. Some of the bishops of the Roman fellowship started claiming authority over all other bishops and fellowships. Our Lord's references to the **Nicolaitanes** in the Book of Revelation simply cannot be misconstrued. He was opposed to reestablishment of a clergy, a hierarchy, to say nothing of an outright, all-powerful monarchy occupied by an individual given the title "pope." Nevertheless, the radical changes brought about by Christianity's installation as the state religion, nurtured the spread of the "new priesthood," and emboldened ambitious bishops of Rome to intensify their quest for absolute control over all of Christendom. The fact that the city of Rome had been the seat of the Empire for so long aided their cause, and, for the first time, Scriptures from Matthew's Gospel were cited as proof that Jesus had ordained Peter to be the head of His Church.

It is in the 16th chapter of that Gospel we are informed of an episode that took place in Caesarea Philippi. Our Lord asks His Apostles, *"Whom do men say that I the Son of Man am?"* (Mat 16:13) He is told that the Jewish citizenry believes Him to be John the Baptist, Isaiah, Jeremiah, etc. This prompts our Lord's next question, *"But whom do ye say that I am?"* (Mat 16:15) It is Peter who responds as follows: *"Thou art the Christ, the Son of the living God."* (Mat 16:16) The Greek word that's equivalent to Messiah in Hebrew is "Christ." Therefore, Peter, a Jew, by his confession tells our Lord that the Apostles know Him to be the promised Messiah long awaited by the children of Israel. It is our Lord's response to Peter's confession that the Catholic Church has seized upon as proof for the establishment of the papal office.

In Matthew 16:17 and 18, Jesus said, *"Blessed art thou, Simon Barjona: for flesh and blood hath not revealed it unto thee, but my Father which is in heaven. And I say also unto thee, that thou art Peter, and upon this rock I will build my church; and the gates of hell shall not prevail against it."*

From this translation of the original Greek one might well agree with Rome that our Lord intended Peter to be the foundation on which the Christian Church would be built. It certainly can be interpreted that way in our language. But Greek is a far more precise language than ours. It is, in fact, one of the world's most precise languages in which, for example, the slightest variation in a word ending completely changes the word's meaning. And, when we look at what Jesus said with two key words written in the Greek, an entirely different interpretation of His statement is demanded.

Our Lord said: *"And I say also unto thee, that thou are petros, and upon this petra, I will build my Church,"* etc. In the Greek—and Rome knows this—the words *petros* and *petra* are as far apart in meaning as are **"pebble"** and **"rock"** in English. *Petra* is a feminine gender root word. It means **"huge foundation rock."** *Petros*, on the other hand, is a masculine gender derivative of the root word *petra.* It simply means **"small stone,"** one that can be picked up and skipped across a pond. So what is the true interpretation of Christ's statement to Peter? To what or to whom does the word *petra* refer?

When the entire context of Matthew 16:16 through 18 is reviewed, the true meaning actually is quite obvious; certainly not open to Rome's interpretation at all. In verse 16 Peter makes a factual statement—Jesus is the Jew's promised Messiah, the long awaited Emanuel. In verse 17, our Lord declares that Peter's knowledge of His identity has been divinely revealed from heaven. Then, in verse 18, paraphrased, Jesus says, **"You are *petros* (a small stone) and upon this *petra* (the foundational rock of truth that Jesus is the Christ, the Son of the living God) I will build my Church."**

If Jesus had used *petros* both for Peter's name and for the foundation of His Church, Rome wins. Jesus is in violation of His own organizational plan, and the office of the pope with Peter as its first occupant is forever established. But, because He used *petros* and *petra,* Rome loses, for there is no honest way to harmonize the meanings of these two distinctly different words. Hence, the foundation upon which Christianity is built—and will Rome deny it?—is the truth that Jesus Christ was and is the Jewish Messiah, the Son of the living God, the Savior come down from heaven to reconcile sinful man to holy God.

Another episode quite pertinent to this matter, but ignored by the Vatican, is found in the first chapter of John's Gospel. This incident has Andrew taking Simon, his brother, to meet our Lord who greets him with these words: ***Thou art Simon the son of Jona: thou shalt be called Cephas**, which is by interpreta-*

tion, A stone." (John 1:42) Long before the Caesarea Philippi episode, our Lord had changed Simon's name to a "stone." That John chose to use the Aramaic word **cephas** for stone instead of the Greek word **petros**, in no way changes the facts. John, who was a very close friend and associate of Peter, knew very well that his friend was no foundation rock.

But if these few verses of Scripture were the only ones having to do with the foundation of Christendom, there could remain in the minds of some a conviction that Peter was, in fact, ordained by Jesus to be its first leader, its first "pope." The biblical evidence, however, is overwhelming in its declaration that Jesus, the promised Messiah, is the one, the only, the true foundation upon which the Christian Church is built. Both symbolically, and by direct reference, Jesus is revealed again and again as the foundation "rock," in both the Old and New Testaments.

In the Books of Exodus (17:6) and Numbers (20:11) with the children of Israel traversing the wilderness, our Lord is symbolized in the **rocks** that Moses struck to bring forth water. In the Song of Moses recorded in Deuteronomy 32:1-4, Moses says in verse 4, *"He (the Lord) is the Rock."* Verse 15 tells us that Jeshurun (symbolic name for Israel) *"…lightly esteemed the rock of his salvation."* In verse 18, *"Of the rock that begat thee thou art unmindful, and hast forgotten the God that formed thee."* Lastly, in verse 31, Moses says, *"For their (the enemy's) rock is not as our rock."* Jesus, the instrument of creation and salvation, is beyond question the **Rock** thus referred to in Deuteronomy, chapter 32.

Scripture tells us that our *"God is a consuming fire."* (Deut 4:24) In the Book of Judges, chapter 6, fire comes from a rock, consuming an offering set out by Gideon. Hannah, thanking God for His gift of a man child, prays in First Samuel, chapter 2, *"…neither is there any rock like our God."* (1 Sam 2:2) Chapter 22 in Second Samuel finds David—freshly escaped from King Saul—praying as follows: *"The LORD is my rock, and my fortress, and my deliverer."* (2 Sam 22:2) Later in the same chapter, David poses these questions: *"For who is God, save the LORD? and who is a rock save our God?"* (2 Sam 22:32)

That the Second Person of the blessed Trinity, Jesus, is the **Rock** always referred to in the cited Scriptures cannot be doubted when David's words of Second Samuel 22:47 are carefully studied. From the Books of the Law compiled by Moses, devout Hebrews understood that the Godhead was made up of more than one person. The Hebrew word for God found in Genesis is **Elohim**. It is a remarkable word that is plural in form but is singular in meaning. You would read it "Gods" but with the understanding that it refers to a single deity. Thus, there is one God who is really Gods. Certainly David understood this, for in the cited Scripture he says: *"The LORD liveth; and blessed be my rock; and exalted be the God of the rock of my salvation."* What David said can be paraphrased like this: **"...the Lord (Jesus) is my Rock. Blessed be my Rock (Jesus); and praised be the Father of (Jesus) my Rock who also is my Savior."**

Numerous other Old Testament Scriptures also refer to Jesus as the Rock. He is thusly identified in Psalms 18, 28, 31, 40, 42, 61, 62, 71, 78, 89, 92, 94, and 95. More such references are found in Isaiah as well. Specifically in 8:14, 17:10 and 51:1 there are direct references to Jesus as the rock, and in several other chapters symbolic references are found. Nowhere in the Old Testament is there any indication that someone other than the Lord Jesus is, or will be, the rock upon which humanity may stand redeemed. Great personalities such as Moses, Abraham, Samuel, David, Elijah, Elisha, Jeremiah, Ezekiel, and on and on, none of them ever has been referred to as a rock on which to base our faith. Surely Peter was a great Apostle. But a rock on which Christ chose to build His church Peter was not. And the New Testament is not lacking in evidence to support that statement.

In the Gospels of both Matthew (chapter 7) and Luke (chapter 6) our Lord's parable of the wise and unwise builders is related. The first builder, remember, built his house on a foundation of solid rock. (***Petra*** is the word used for "rock.") When the storm came, his house was unharmed. But the second builder's foundation was nothing but sand, and when the storm came the house fell and was utterly ruined. The parable is so obviously symbolic of Christ as the foundation of our faith that it needs no explanation or analysis.

Turning to Matthew, chapter 27, and Mark, chapter 15, we find the Greek word **petra** is used to describe the kind of material out of which Christ's tomb had been cut. In both accounts of our Lord's burial we are told that His tomb had been hewn out of **(petra)** rock, not **(petros)** rock. Surely a tomb such as the one described could only have been cut out of solid foundation type rock, **(petra),** not the kind of rock or stone that can be picked up and thrown, **(petros).** Is it not also of interest that the ***Rock of Ages*** was entombed for three days in ***solid aged rock***?

The Apostle, Paul, writing in the Book of Romans, Chapter 9, left no doubt in anyone's mind as regards the identity of the rock on whom Christianity is founded. In Romans 9:33, he quotes a familiar Scripture from Isaiah 28:16. Says he, ***"As it is written, Behold, I lay in Sion a stumblingstone and rock (petra) of offence: and whosoever believeth on him shall not be ashamed."*** Because the

Jews rejected Jesus, their *petra,* their promised Messiah, God concluded them in unbelief until such time as the dispensation of the gentiles is ended. Doubtless Jesus was the Rock God laid in Zion; Peter was a sturdy chunk off that rock God used to "throw" the Gospel to the Jews in Jerusalem and the diaspora areas of Pontus, Galatia, Cappadocia, Asia, and Bithynia. (Cf. 1 Pet 1:1)

Chapter 10 in the Book of First Corinthians contains an admonition to Christians to avoid the sinful behavior practiced by the children of Israel. Here, again, we find reference to Jesus, not Peter, as the Church's foundation Rock. Paul relates that the children of Israel, *"...did all drink the same spiritual drink: for they drank of that spiritual Rock that followed them: and that Rock was Christ."* (1 Cor 10:4) Speaking specifically of the foundation upon which the Christian (not the Catholic) Church was to be built, Paul says earlier in First Corinthians, *"For other foundation can no man lay than that is laid, which is Jesus Christ."* (1 Cor 3:11)

From all of this we conclude that when Jesus said *"...upon this rock I will build my church,"* the pronoun "this" did not refer to Peter **(petros)** but rather to the statement made by Peter, *"Thou art the Christ, the Son of the living God."* This must be the case since Peter himself referred to Jesus as the Church's foundation rock in 2:8 of his First Epistle.

In a speech by Catholic bishop Joseph Georg Strossmeyer to the prelates assembled for the AD 1869-70 Vatican Council I, it was revealed that the most renowned Church fathers were of the opinion that the rock **(petra)** referred to by Jesus in Matthew 16:18 was not the Apostle, Peter, but rather the **truth** he had stated, that Christ is the Messiah, the Son of the living God, the Savior of the world. Among the supporters of this interpretation were Cyril, Hilary, Jerome, (of Vulgate fame) Basil, Ambrose, Augustine, Leo the Great, Gregory of Nyssa, and perhaps the most important of all, Chrysostom who, when it came to understanding the precise nuances of the Greek language, was without a peer.

If, in fact, our Lord intended to found His Church upon the "petros" (small stone) of Peter, we should be able to find in the Scriptures that the other Apostles deferred to him as their leader. When the Gospels are consulted, though, we get a strong signal that Christ's Apostles were totally unaware of any preeminence given by the Lord to Peter. In Matthew 20—four chapters **after** the Caesarea Philippi incident—there is an account of Zebedee's sons seeking a commitment from Jesus to sit, one on His right hand, the other on His left hand, in the kingdom of Heaven. This same incident is related in Mark 10:37. In both accounts, the other 10 Apostles, Peter included, were exceedingly displeased with John and James for seeking such exalted positions above their fellows. It is highly unlikely that these "Sons of Thunder" as the Lord called them, would have aspired to such lofty positions if Christ already had appointed Peter to be their leader.

Elsewhere in the Scriptures, the Apostle Paul—not Peter—is God's choice to receive the Christian doctrine directly from the risen, ascended, Lord Jesus. ***"But I certify you, brethren, that the gospel which was preached of me is not after man. For I neither received it of man, neither was I taught it, but by the revelation of Jesus Christ."*** (Gal 1:11, 12) One is left to ponder the question, if Peter was appointed by Jesus to be the supreme leader of His Church, if Peter was the very foundation on which He planned to build it, why was Paul the only one to enjoy that special privilege? In 2 Peter 3:16, we receive the impression that Peter himself was not privy to at least some of what Paul had been given directly from Jesus. In speaking of Paul's letters as Scripture, Peter says they contain certain things that are ***"hard to be understood."*** Had Peter been ordained head of the Church, wouldn't our Lord have made certain that he received the same revelations as were given to Paul?

Equally damaging to Rome's claim that Peter—as bishop of Rome—was the first in an unbroken chain of popes is the total lack of biblical or historical evidence to support this assertion. The final chapter of Paul's letter to the Roman church contains greetings to 27 different individuals, not one of which is Peter. Had he been **the** bishop of Rome, **a** bishop of Rome, or if he even was **just there**, it's hard to believe that Paul wouldn't have greeted him as well. Peter himself, at the end of his First Epistle, salutes the saints on behalf of the ***"church that is at Babylon,"*** (1 Pet 5:13) indicating a later presence in Rome, but only as an "elder" (1 Pet 5:1) and not as bishop of the church. In that same letter, Peter exhorts other "elders" not to act as "Lords over God's heritage," (1 Pet 5:3) but to be examples to the flock.

The great early Church historian—Eusebius—writing in the first quarter of the 4th century, provides us with the only evidence we have of Peter's presence in Rome, and his status while there. In *Eusebius Church History,* Book 2, Chapter 25:1, we read:

> **"…and that they both (Paul and Peter) suffered martyrdom at the same time is stated by Dionysius, bishop of Corinth, in his epistle to the Romans."**

Then Eusebius quotes Dionysius as having said,

> "You have thus by such an admonition bound together the planting of Peter and of Paul at *Rome* and *Corinth*. For both of them planted and likewise taught us in our *Corinth*. And they taught together in like manner in *Italy*, and suffered martyrdom at the same time."

History places Dionysius as bishop of Corinth after the end of the 1st century, so his word most certainly could be trusted that Peter was, in fact, in Rome and was there martyred. In the very first chapter of Eusebius' Book 2, the following is recorded.

> "But Clement in the sixth book of his Hypotyposes writes thus: 'Peter and James and John after the ascension of our Saviour, as is also preferred by our Lord, strove not after honor, but chose James the Just (brother of Jesus) bishop of Jerusalem.'"

Clement lived in the 1st century and was a contemporary of the Apostles. His assertion that Peter, together with the "Sons of Thunder"—James and John—chose Christ's brother to oversee the Jerusalem church, conveys a couple of interesting points. First, Peter was not seeking any preeminence for himself, preferring to do what Jesus directed him to do, namely, *"Feed my lambs; feed my sheep."* (John 21:15, 16) Number two, Peter was not making unilateral decisions like a person having absolute authority.

In his Church History, Book 3, Eusebius has two more entries about Peter that are pertinent to this present study. In chapter 1, he writes:

> "Peter appears to have preached in Pontus, Galatia, Bithynia, Cappadocia, and Asia to the Jews of the dispersion. (Cf. 1 Pet 1:1) **And, having come to Rome, he was crucified head-downwards; for he had requested that he might suffer in this way.**"

No mention here that Peter was in Rome for any great length of time or that he held office as the bishop of Rome. In another entry, Eusebius says Linus was Peter's successor in the episcopate of Rome, but then in chapter 2 of Book 3, he provides this information:

> "After the martyrdom of Paul and Peter, Linus was the first to obtain the episcopate of the church at Rome. Paul mentions him when writing to Timothy from Rome, in the salutation at the end of the epistle."

And, following this contradictory entry that cites Linus as the **FIRST bishop of Rome**, Eusebius creates a very serious problem for the Roman Catholic apologists with the following blockbuster:

> "And at the same time Papias, bishop of the parish of Hierapolis, became well known, as did also *Ignatius, who was chosen bishop of Antioch, SECOND IN SUCCESSION TO PETER,* and whose fame is still celebrated by a great many."

In spite of this entry, it is not likely that Peter was a bishop of Antioch any more than a bishop of Rome, for the Apostles and disciples ***modus operandi*** was to **preach** and **plant** churches, not stick around afterwards to run them. This is borne out by the following Eusebius record:

> "Then starting out upon long journeys they (the Apostles and disciples) performed the office of *evangelists*, being filled with the desire to preach Christ to those who had not yet heard the word of faith, and to deliver to them the divine Gospels. And when they had only laid the foundations of the faith in foreign places, they appointed others as pastors, and entrusted them with the nurture of those that had recently been brought in, while they themselves went on again to other countries and nations, with the grace and the co-operation of God."

This is readily seen from the Scriptures to be a true description of how the Apostles and disciples carried out our Lord's "Great Commission" in the 1st century. Acts includes accounts of three missionary journeys undertaken by Paul, and the First Epistle of Peter, in its salutation, lists some of the places Peter is said to have preached and planted churches. There is one deliberate connection of Peter to the office of bishop of Rome. It is found in a discredited document—a forgery—that received widespread circulation in the 3rd century, and was used by advocates of a monarchial church government to support their cause. The document in question is known as the pseudo-Clementine Letters and Homilies. There is no longer any doubt, however, about its authenticity. It is a deliberate forgery, falsely claiming Clemens Romanus as its author.

Allegedly written to James, the brother of Jesus, after the death of Peter, its claim is that Jesus made Peter the head of His Church, and Peter—before he died—appointed Clement to be his successor. This spurious document has been identified as the only piece of evidence in all of history that deliberately associates Peter with the title bishop of Rome. The document has been termed a "fiction" by scholars, but one that was treated as authentic in the 3rd and 4th centuries. It was in the 4th century that bishops of Rome began their quest for supremacy over all of Christendom. But by its own list of successors to Peter, the Catholic Church acknowledges the pseudo-Clementine Letters and Homilies to be a forgery. After listing Peter as the first pope, the Vatican lists Linus, then Cletus, and then, long after Peter's demise, comes Clement. As for Rome's list of popes, one can never count on tomorrow's list containing the same names seen on it today, for it is an ever changing list with new names added or old names deleted as the case may be. The so-called unbroken chain of popes stretching back to Peter is, in truth, merely another fiction, and does not exist in reality. That subject is dealt with in depth in chapter 9.

On rare occasions there have been voices of reason raised within Catholicism, vainly striving to liberate the church from the grip of heresy. One such voice was that of bishop Strossmeyer who opposed both the office of the papacy and the doctrine of infallibility. In his historic speech at Vatican Council I he spoke as follows:

> **"I conclude victoriously, with history, with reason, with logic, with good sense, and with a Christian conscience, that Jesus Christ *did not confer* any *supremacy on St Peter* and that the bishops of Rome did not become sovereigns of the church, but only by confiscating one by one all the rights of the episcopate."**

In other words, establishment of the papacy was an act of "piracy." To no one's surprise, elements within the Roman church now deny that the good bishop made his volatile speech. When all else fails, rewrite history.

Besides claiming Peter as the rock upon which our Lord built Christianity, Rome also has declared that he was given a) exclusive possession of the "keys to the kingdom of heaven," and b) the authority to make and unmake rules and doctrines here on earth. (Cf. Mat 16:19) In the Scripture verse cited by the Vatican to support these claims, our Lord did not say, "Here are the keys," while handing Peter a set of keys nicely arranged on a holy keychain. What Jesus said was, ***"...and I will give unto thee the keys of***—not to—***the kingdom of heaven.***" Obviously, then, the keys were not to be physical since heaven is not a physical place. They were to be spiritual keys. Also, the keys were to be forthcoming at a future unspecified date. Peter did not have them when our Lord finished speaking. And they were keys **OF** (or about) the kingdom, not keys to OPEN the kingdom, for it was Christ's Calvary sacrifice that enabled the Old Testament saints who had been waiting in Sheol to ascend with Jesus to a newly opened heaven. So what were these keys; when were they received; how were they used, and was Peter the lone recipient?

Answering the last question first, events subsequent to the Caesarea Philippi incident will show clearly Peter was not the lone recipient of the keys. For now, remember that Peter was not alone with Jesus at Caesarea Philippi. When he responded *"Thou art the Christ...."* he was speaking for the group to which Christ had addressed the initial question, *"Who do men say that I the Son of man am?"* In ending the episode our Lord admonished **all** the disciples to keep secret His identity. It is logical, therefore, to conclude he also was speaking to **all** when he promised the keys and dispensed binding and loosing authority.

For the answers to the other questions we must go back through the halls of history to a time 2000 years ago, before we had both the Old and New Testaments—the complete and finished Word of God. Note, first of all, that the Jews of Peter's day still were looking for their promised Messiah—in Greek, the Christ. Their prophets foretold His coming. In Daniel the actual time of His coming was accurately predicted. But the Jews were looking for an earthly king who would restore the Davidic throne to its former power and glory. In spite of Isaiah 53 and other prophecies, the idea of a suffering Messiah who would atone with His blood for the sins of the whole world was as foreign to their thinking as China is to America. They were predisposed to believe that Messiah would lead a successful revolution against the ruling regime and thereby re-establish the autonomy of Israel and the throne of David.

Thus, the real purpose of the Messiah was completely hidden from the Jews of that era. It was first referred to as a "mystery" by our Lord Himself, in Mark 4:11, when He told His Apostles, *"Unto you it is given to know the mystery of the kingdom of God: but unto them that are without,"* (the religious Jews) *"all these things are done in parables."* In the Book of Romans, Paul speaks of the "mystery" in 11:25 and 16:25. In First Corinthians 2:7 it's revealed that the "mystery" was God-planned even before the world was created; and had the forces of evil understood it, they would not have crucified the Savior. Writing in Ephesians 3:3, Paul says Jesus Himself disclosed to him the "mystery" that had been hidden in past ages from the "sons of men" but is now known to Christ's Apostles and prophets. Same chapter, verse 9, Paul says he's been commissioned to *"make all men see..."* the *"mystery, which from the beginning of the world hath been hid in God..."* More references to this "mystery" will be found in Eph 6:19, Col

1:26, 27, 1 Tim 3:9, 16, and in Rev 10:7. Peter, too, in his First Epistle, refers—not by name, but surely by context—to this great "mystery" which even the prophets and God's angels did not understand. (1 Pet 1:12)

The divine purpose of the Messiah, then, to the Jews and the rest of mankind, was shrouded in mystery 2000 years ago. It was still shrouded in mystery to Christ's Apostles and followers even after He had suffered and died on Calvary and had risen from the dead. For we are told in Acts, ***"When they therefore were come together, they asked of him, saying, Lord, wilt thou at this time restore again the kingdom to Israel?"*** (Acts 1:6)

Crucial to the solution of any mystery is possession of the "keys" that can open it to one's understanding. With respect to the kingdom of God, the keys that would unlock its mystery had been hidden since the fall of Adam. These were the very keys that our Lord promised to give Peter, and the first Pentecost is when His promise was fulfilled. Peter—but not only Peter—received the keys that day when the sound of a rushing mighty wind was heard in the upper room where the 120 had assembled, and all were indwelt and filled with Christ's Holy Spirit. This cannot be doubted. Prior to Christ's ascension, Peter and the others did not understand the "mystery" at all. But on the day of Pentecost and the days that followed, Peter and the others clearly grasped its full meaning, clearly understood the "keys" of the kingdom of heaven, and used them to bring at least 8000 souls into a saving relationship with God. These are the "keys" so long hidden, but now known and at the disposal of every born again Christian:

> Jesus is the promised Messiah, the Son of God, the Redeemer.
> By His shed blood is forgiveness of sins, life everlasting.
> Salvation is free to all who believe; all who call on His name.
> God raised Him from the dead to affirm these promises.
> Repent, believe, be indwelt by the Spirit, be baptized.

These spiritual keys are the ones used by Peter and the other Apostles and disciples to unlock the mystery of the kingdom of heaven for 3000 souls on Pentecost Sunday and another 5000 a few days later. These are the keys to the mystery of redemption that had been hidden even from the prophets and God's angels since the time of Adam's fall. They are the only keys to the born again nature that must be experienced for the forgiveness of sins and assurance of eternal life. They reveal the "simplicity" in Christ Jesus spoken of by Paul in his second letter to the Corinthian church. (Cf. 2 Cor 11:3) They are clearly presented to us in God's divine Word, and are available for use by all who name the name of Jesus as their

Savior. Rome's claims to exclusive ownership of them are exposed as mere boast and bluster by the pronoun, **"WHOSOEVER,"** found in John 3:16, John 11:26, Acts 2:21, Acts 10:43, Romans 9:33, Romans 10:13, 1 John 4:15, 1 John 5:1, Revelation 22:17. The keys of the kingdom of heaven are not hanging on a solid gold chain suspended above the pope's opulent throne in the Vatican. They are in the hearts of all believers who have a burden for saving lost souls.

The next claim made by Rome has to do with the binding and loosing authority granted by Jesus during the same Caesarea Philippi episode. *"…whatsoever thou shalt bind on earth shall be bound in heaven: and whatsoever thou shalt loose on earth shall be loosed in heaven."* (Mat 16:19) Wasn't this a clear mandate to Peter to make and unmake rules, regulations, doctrines, etc.? Wasn't it a divine guarantee to Peter of infallibility? On both counts, no. As mentioned above, Peter was not the only Apostle with Jesus on that occasion. Logically the binding/loosing authority was granted to all who were there. And this is confirmed two chapters later.

The setting of Matthew chapter 18 is Capernaum in Galilee. Beginning in verse 15, our Lord instructs His disciples how to deal with a brother who has committed a trespass against another. Our Lord counsels the offended party to pursue redress of the grievance through several specific steps, the last of which—if redress of the grievance still is wonting—is to place the matter before the whole fellowship, the whole church. If this last step also fails, Jesus said, *"…if he neglect to hear the church, let him be unto thee as an heathen man and a publican."* Then, to all His disciples, Jesus said: *"Verily I say unto you, Whatsoever ye shall bind on earth shall be bound in heaven: and whatsoever ye shall loose on earth shall be loosed in heaven."* (Mat 18:17, 18)

But our Lord was not yet finished with His lesson. The next two verses following Matthew 18:18 read like this: *"Again I say unto you, that if two of you shall agree on earth as touching any thing that they shall ask, it shall be done for them of my Father which is in heaven. For where two or three are gathered together in my name, there am I in the midst of them."* (Mat 18:19, 20)

Clearly, Peter was not the only one given the binding/loosing authority, and neither was it limited to our Lord's immediate disciples. Verse 20 extends the authority to any two or three individuals who assemble in Christ's name and in His spiritual presence. These Scriptures deal a fatal blow to Rome's claim that binding/loosing authority was granted exclusively to Peter, and through him, to the imposter popes of Catholicism. Rather, each Christian fellowship enjoys the right to bind and loose in accordance with sound biblical doctrine and practices.

As a Catholic parochial school student many years ago, I was taught that the binding/loosing authority was granted to Peter, and passed on to all Catholic popes. It was what empowered them to make binding faith and morals declarations such as papal infallibility, the Marian doctrines, indulgences, Purgatory, temporal punishment, etc. We accepted this without question, and felt sorry for the non-Catholics who didn't have a pope to lead them. Had we studied the Bible, however, instead of Catholic Doctrine, we would have known that the binding/loosing authority has absolutely nothing to do with making or altering doctrine; that it was given corporately to Christianity, not to Peter alone; and that its divine purpose is threefold. First, it is to protect Christians and Christian churches from evil forces. Second, it is to foster peace and tranquility between believers and within fellowships. Third, it is to facilitate achievement of God's "Great Commission."

The Greek words translated "bind" and "loose" are ***deo*** and ***luo*** respectively. Both are root words; the first means to tie, to bind, literally to fasten in or with chains. The second means to loose and set free what was tied up or chained. Simple enough, but how on earth do they apply to Christianity? Good question, but first let's see how they **don't apply**.

When Jesus commissioned His disciples to carry the Gospel to all nations, He made it clear that the Gospel they would be preaching was **complete**; nothing was missing, and nothing else was needed. He told them they would be, *"Teaching them* (converts) *to observe all things whatsoever I have commanded you."* (Mat 28:20) Earlier, before His death and Resurrection, He had given them a preview of the end times in the famous Olivet Discourse. During that teaching, He told them, *"…THIS gospel of the kingdom shall be preached in all the world for a witness unto all nations; and then shall the end come."* (Mat 24:14)

Our Lord commissioned His followers to teach only what **He** had taught them, and He referred to His teachings as *"**THIS gospel**."* On Calvary's cross, as He bowed His sacred head for the last time, He uttered these words of triumph: *"It is finished."* At that historic moment the work He came to accomplish was completed, as was the Gospel (the good news) that would make what He did known and believed throughout the entire world. Then to spearhead the Gospel's spread among the gentiles, He called Saul of Tarsus and gave him the Gospel from His own divine lips. *"But I certify you, brethren, that the gospel which was preached of me is not after man. For I neither received it of man, neither was I taught it, but by the revelation of Jesus Christ."* (Gal 1:11, 12) He then inspired Paul to write: *"But though we, or an angel from heaven, preach any* *other gospel unto you than that which we have preached unto you, let him be accursed. As we said before, so say I now again, if any man preach any other gospel unto you than that ye have received, let him be accursed."* (Gal 1:8, 9) Twice in the Old Testament, once again in the New, God admonished mankind to keep hands off His inspired Word. It is not to be added to, altered, or taken from. Together, all of this bespeaks a complete Gospel, and obviates use of the binding/loosing authority for adding doctrines to it, or taking doctrines from it. How, then, **does** this God-given authority actually apply in Christianity? Several ways.

In the Book of Acts we find a number of examples of the binding/loosing authority in action in the fledgling Church. In Acts 1:15-26, Matthias, in a binding action by the assembled believers, is chosen to fill the "episcopate" vacated by the suicide of Judas Iscariot. Acts 4:32 through 4:37 relates how the believers bound themselves to community ownership, as opposed to private ownership, of lands and property. *"neither said any of them that ought of the things which he possessed was his own; but they had all things common."* (Act 4:32)

A pressing need that faced the rapidly expanding Jerusalem church was solved by a binding action recorded in Acts 6:1 through 6:6. Gentile widows were being neglected in the daily distribution of food and supplies. This resulted in friction and dissatisfaction that could have produced a serious rift in the Church's unity of purpose. The problem was identified and quickly solved with the creation of a special group of seven who were "bound" to minister equally to all in need. In the reign of Claudias Caesar there came a great dearth in the Holy Land, which, when the saints of the Asian church at Antioch learned of it, they bound upon themselves the burden of providing sustenance to their Judaean brethren. Everyone contributed according to his ability, and the necessities were conveyed to those in need by Barnabas and Saul. (Cf. Acts 11:28-30)

It is reported in Acts 13:8-11 how, on the Isle of Paphos, a sorcerer named Elymas clashed with Paul and Barnabas until Paul bound blindness upon him and he had to be led about. When Jews in Antioch, jealous of the way Paul and Barnabas were making converts, began contradicting them and blaspheming God, Paul and Barnabas left them bound in their unbelief and directed their ministry exclusively to the gentiles. (Cf. Acts 13:46) When their adversaries forced them out of the city, Paul and Barnabas *"shook off the dust of their feet against them, and came unto Iconium."* (Acts 13:51)

The most famous example of the binding/loosing authority is found in Acts chapter 15, beginning in verse 6. A serious disagreement had arisen, caused by Jewish believers who were insisting on a) circumcision for all males among the gentile converts, and b) strict adherence of all gentiles to the Mosaic Law. After much open discussion and input from Peter, Paul, Barnabas, and James, the brother of Jesus, it was decided to **loose** the gentile converts from the rite of circumcision and from keeping the Mosaic Law. Instead, the council **bound** them to *"abstain from pollutions of idols, and from fornication, and from things strangled, and from blood."* (Acts 15:20)

In these examples we see the binding/loosing authority being employed to fill a personnel need, to settle disputes within church fellowships, to assist a fellowship in dire straits, to counteract an attack on a Christian ministry, to dispense with confirmed unbelievers whose aim is to hinder God's work. The binding/loosing authority granted by Jesus to His disciples, and to the Church that grew from their witness, applies also to matters of discipline within the Body of Christ.

In Matthew 18:15-20, our Lord dictates the proper method of dealing with misbehaving believers. After several preliminary steps or warnings, the miscreant who refuses to amend his/her ways, or make required restitution, is to be brought before the assembled church and openly charged. If "guilty" is the assembly's verdict, it has the authority from Christ to **bind** the offender under whatever conditions must be met for continued participation in the fellowship. Where those conditions are complied with, the church has the authority to **loose** the brother from further restrictions. Where they are not complied with the church has the authority to revoke the offender's membership in the fellowship. The effectiveness of this kind of disciplinary action is clearly shown in Paul's letters to the Corinthian church.

The entire fifth chapter of 1st Corinthians is devoted to the importance of a church body dealing with immorality within its membership. Specifically, Paul admonishes the Corinthian believers to deal with one individual who was in an openly sinful relationship with his own father's wife. Paul's instruction to the church—related in 5:13—is to *"...put away from among yourselves that wicked person."* In short, the Corinthian believers were to issue a **binding** order expelling the man from their midst. When the church carried out Paul's instructions, the man repented, but was not restored to his former place of membership in the assembly. This was conveyed to Paul, who then included some additional instructions in 2nd Corinthians 2:5-9.

"But if any have caused grief, he hath not grieved me, but in part: that I may not overcharge you all. Sufficient to such a man is this punishment, which was inflicted of many. So that contrariwise ye ought rather to forgive him, and comfort him, lest perhaps such a one should be swallowed up with overmuch sorrow." No question that the man had repented of his immoral activ-

ity and was overcome with remorse, for Paul continues, *"Wherefore I beseech you that ye would confirm your love toward him. For to this end also did I write, that I might know the proof of you, whether ye be obedient in all things."* In other words, the man was to be **loosed** from the penalty warranted by his former behavior and restored to full fellowship in the congregation of believers.

Binding/loosing authority has nothing to do with adding doctrines to an already complete Gospel. That Catholicism has misrepresented its purposes, in order to justify actions expressly prohibited by the Word of God, is eloquent proof of the extent to which Rome will go in its campaign to underpin the papacy with a semblance of credibility. But the more evidence we examine, the less we see Peter picked to be the rock upon which our Lord would build His Church. Scripture makes it patently clear that Peter received no unique powers or authorities not entrusted to all of our Lord's disciples. Moreover, all the empowerments Christ left with His disciples have been passed on—not to some illicit hierarchy Jesus Himself opposed—but to all born again Christians and the Bible-directed assemblies to which they belong—the Body of Christ. That this is true cannot be doubted, for, as previously noted, *"ye are a chosen generation, a royal priesthood, an holy nation, a peculiar people; that ye should shew forth the praises of him who hath called you out of darkness into his marvellous light."* (1 Pet 2:9)

All believers in the Body of Christ are **priests.** When two or more band together into church units meeting in the spiritual presence of Christ Himself, (Mat 18:20), they are empowered to employ the "Keys **of** the Kingdom of Heaven" to bring lost souls into a saving relationship with the Creator, and declare to them that their sins are forgiven. They also are entitled to use the binding/loosing authority to protect themselves from evil forces and to facilitate achievement of their assigned mission. If they choose to bind themselves to the support of a missionary effort in Uganda, their action will already have been approved in heaven. If they bind themselves to a bus ministry, a home for unwed mothers, a Christian radio outreach, a tract ministry, an association with other Bible-directed assemblies, etc., all already will have been "bound in heaven." When our Lord said, *"Whatsoever ye shall bind on earth shall be bound in heaven: and whatsoever ye shall loose on earth shall be loosed in heaven,"* the tense of the Greek verbs ***dedemena*** (bound) and ***lelumena*** (loosed) gives the following literal translation: ***dedemena***—"shall have been bound," and ***lelumena***—"shall have been loosed." Nothing the churches do is a surprise to our

Father in heaven. If it is in accordance with the Word of God it has already been pre-approved and settled there before the earthly action is carried out.

Rome would have us believe that the Lord reserved these church functions exclusively for the Vatican crowd when there was no such thing as a Vatican crowd in His divine plan. Peter was a "lively stone" like all born again believers, not a foundation rock endowed with infallibility. He sinned, erred, made mistakes as do all who are born with the Adamic nature. His two wonderful epistles show him to be quite satisfied with the Gospel left by our Savior. Nothing in them suggests that he believed the Gospel to be incomplete and in need of "patching." Thus, papal infallibility is—quite honestly—one more Catholic myth based on misrepresentation of the binding/loosing authority. As indicated by the Keenan Catechism entries quoted in Chapter 1, Rome adamantly denied that popes are infallible prior to Pius IX's 1870 declaration. The shocking about face of that declaration—from absolutely not infallible to unquestionably infallible—should have had Catholics stampeding to the exits. But it caused scarcely a ripple. And the Keenan Catechism handling of it is one of the all-time classic examples of Vatican "doublespeak." For purposes of further comment it is reproduced here.

> **Q. Is the pope infallible?**
> **A. Yes, the pope is infallible.**
> **Q. But some Catholics, before the Vatican Council, denied the infallibility of the pope, which was impugned by this very Catechism.**
> **A. Yes, they did so under the usual reservation, insofar as they then could grasp the mind of the church, and subject to her (the church's) future definitions, thus implicitly accepting the dogma.**

If awards were given for "doublespeak," that explanation would win the grand prize hands down. Note the beginning of the lie in the second question. It was not "some" Catholics prior to 1870 that denied papal infallibility; it was THE CATHOLIC CHURCH that denied it and called it a protestant invention! In my 52 years as a Catholic I was never made aware that it is necessary to have **"usual reservations"** about the various doctrines in anticipation that the **"mind of the church"** might change, causing **"future definitions"** of those doctrines to be diametrically opposite of what Rome had taught me to believe as the truth. I should have had a clue, though, when the Friday meat fast was eliminated, the Communion fast was done away with, the Mass in Latin was changed to English, and lay people could do what previously only clergy could do.

At Vatican Council I, out of which came Pius IX's infallibility doctrine, bishop Strossmeyer, a German prelate, tried vainly to convince the assembled delegates to flatly reject the proposed new doctrine. He and Johann J.I. Von Dollinger, were joined by the French delegation in seeking its rejection. Though their efforts were met with defeat, what Strossmeyer feared and foresaw has been a bone in the throat of the Vatican ever since. He predicted that Catholicism's critics would focus their attacks on the infallibility issue against which the church would have no defense. From his impassioned speech, the following:

> "If you decree the dogma of papal infallibility, the Protestants, our adversaries, will mount in the breach, the more bold that they have history on their side, while we have only our own denial against them. What can we say to them when they show up all the bishops of Rome from the days of Luke to his holiness Pius IX?"

In the crass arrogance for which Rome is famous, papal infallibility was declared a must-believe doctrine of the church in spite of the dissenters' objections, and the prediction of repercussions by Strossmeyer. In Cincinnati, Ohio, my hometown, the repercussions were particularly severe because of a debate that had been held there in 1837. Bishop John Purcell, representing the Roman Catholic Church, was challenged by his opponent, Alexander Campbell, a Christian, on—among other things—the matter of papal infallibility. Bishop Purcell said:

> "**Appeals were lodged before the bishop of Rome, though he was not believed to be infallible. Neither is he now. No enlightened Catholic holds the Pope's infallibility to be an article of faith. I do not; and none of my brethren that I know of do**" (Campbell-Purcell Debate p. 26-27.)

"Infallible" popes themselves denied the infallibility of popes. These included Vigilinus, Innocent III, Clement IV, Gregory XI, Adrian VI, and Paul IV. All of this notwithstanding, Pius IX went ahead with his declaration of papal infallibility, and it was a fitting sequel to the equally heretical Immaculate Conception doctrine that preceded it in 1854. What Strossmeyer feared and foresaw—that Protestants would jump on the infallibility thing with a vengeance—came to pass in a hurry. The high jinx of numerous popes—some of which are reported in chapter nine—came under immediate attack, and continues to command the attention of Vatican apologists to this day. The Catholic faithful who have accepted as their lot **"the mind of the Church,"** (Cf. Keenan entry above) would assure their place in heavenly bliss by dumping it, and replacing it with what all born again Christians are promised. To wit: *"...we have the mind of Christ."* (1 Cor 2:16)

In its never-ending quest to convince of Peter's ordination as Catholicism's first pope, Rome is fond of saying the first Church council, the Jerusalem assembly reported in Acts 15, is proof that Peter already was the accepted leader of the Church. Their apologists point out that after Peter spoke, *"then all the multitude kept silence."* (Acts 15:12) The inference, of course, is that what Peter said was decisive. And the faithful, who accept without question anything having the Vatican stamp on it, are convinced Peter's leadership was thus proved, that whatever he said was decisive, final. This, of course, is a deliberate deception of people who are discouraged from reading the Bible.

In the referenced episode, Peter is the first to speak, not the last. Secondly, the multitude kept silent, alright, but to hear Paul and Barnabas relate their experiences among the gentiles. Finally, speaking last, James, the brother of Jesus, presents his judgment of what should be done, and it is his judgment that is ratified and implemented by the whole council. Thus, the gentile converts were "loosed" from any requirement to be circumcised and, at the same time "bound" to refrain from the sins of the pagan idolaters. Peter, a self-professed "elder" was merely a part of the whole Jerusalem church's binding and loosing exercise. At one point, the Jerusalem church sent Peter and John to Samaria to proclaim the Gospel. Not an action one would expect if Peter was thought to be the supreme head of things.

In his letter to the Galatians Paul at one point calls Peter by his Aramaic name—Cephas (stone)—and, well, let's read the verse: ***"And when James, Cephas, and John, who seemed to be pillars, perceived the grace that was given unto me, they gave to me and Barnabas the right hands of fellowship; that we should go unto the heathen, and they unto the circumcision."*** (Gal 2:9) To Paul, Peter was merely one of several who "appeared" to be "pillars;" definitely not a supreme leader. On another occasion, Peter was publicly rebuked by Paul for duplicity in his behavior among the Jews on the one hand and the gentiles on the other. This is hardly what you would expect to happen if Paul were privy to Peter's appointment by Christ as the supreme head of His Church. We know that Paul was respectful of those in authority by his response in Acts 23 when informed that he had used an epithet in referring to the Jewish High Priest. ***"Then said Paul, I wist not, brethren, that he was the high priest: for it is written, Thou shalt not speak evil of the ruler of thy people.*** (Acts 23:5) It is certain that had Paul known Peter was Christ's choice to be the foundation rock of His Church, and the first supreme leader of it, he never would have openly rebuked him, then published the fact in a letter. In fact, had the Catholic Church chosen to designate Paul as the first supreme head of Christianity instead of Peter, they could have made a really good case that would have been extremely difficult to refute. For three reasons. First, it was Paul, not Peter, who received his doctrine directly from the Lord Jesus. *"For I neither received it of man, neither was I taught it, but by the revelation of Jesus Christ."* (Gal 1:12) And in his first letter to the Corinthian Church, *"For I have received of the Lord that which also I delivered unto you."* (1 Cor 11:23) Second, Paul, himself, seemed to have greater authority than others by his own admission. *"Beside those things that are without, that which cometh upon me daily, the care of all the churches."* (2Cor 11:28) In addition to all of the trials and responsibilities he had enumerated in preceding verses, here Paul indicates that the care or oversight of all the Churches fell upon his shoulders as well. Third, there is no question whatever about Paul's Roman residency. The Bible tells us he most certainly was there. But Rome has never claimed that Paul was a pope, even though internal Biblical evidence would have more readily supported that claim.

Peter was chosen instead, certainly because of the misinterpretation of Scripture that occurred long ago. And, though Paul indicated in the Scripture cited above that he had responsibility for the Churches, Peter never made such a claim that we know of. *"The elders which are among you I exhort, who am also an elder and a witness of the sufferings of Christ, and also a partaker of the glory that shall be revealed."* (1 Pet 5:1) Here, Peter simply classifies himself as one among many Elders, and not the first bishop of Rome or supreme head of Christianity. To have been a bishop of Rome would have required Peter to establish residence there, and to be the leader of one of the churches meeting there. But there is no evidence anywhere in the New Testament that he did this. Nor is there reliable historical evidence for his having lived in Rome and been one of its bishops.

He was a Galilean fisherman; his wife was there; he may have had a son named Marcus. His wife accompanied him in his travels. These are the Biblical bits of information we have about Peter, certainly not enough on which to base a key doctrine. As has been pointed out previously, at the end of Paul's letter to the Romans, he addresses greetings and accolades to thirty people, twenty-seven of them by name. Peter is not one of the twenty-seven. Since the three unnamed are women, we can conclude Peter was not yet in Rome when Paul wrote that letter. Why, if he was chosen head of Christ's church and the first bishop of Rome, does Paul not acknowledge him in the last chapter of Romans? He, Peter, should have been there governing the Roman church and Paul should have known it. Only the spurious forgery previously mentioned—the pseudo Clementine Letters and Homilies—specifically declare Peter was a bishop of Rome. Strangely, although the Clementine Homilies long ago were admitted by Rome to be spurious forgeries, they are still being quoted by Catholic sources in conjunction with Rome's doctrines of papal sovereignty and "binding/loosing" authority. An internet page named the ETW—Eternal Word Television, Global CATHOLIC Network—on the date of February 4, 2002, published the following which is quoted verbatim with the alleged words of Peter in italics.

> **"In the same sense the second epistle of Clement to James II (Homilies, Introduction [221]), Peter is represented as having appointed Clement as his successor, saying:** *'I communicate to him the power of binding and loosing so that, with respect to everything which he shall ordain in the earth, it shall be decreed in the heavens; for he shall bind what ought to be bound and loose what ought to be loosed as knowing the rule of the Church.'* **(3:215). Thus Jesus invested the leaders of this church with the....etc."**

Is it not shameful that a document known to be a forgery and a falsehood is still being quoted (by those who know it to be a forgery and a falsehood) to prove that certain of their man-made doctrines are true and were originated by our Lord Jesus? Who can believe anything at all that such a shameless church says must be believed? On the one hand they say bishop Strossmeyer's speech at the 1869-70 Vatican I never happened, while at the same time quoting from a proven, admitted forged document to justify the office of the papacy. Who can trust anything that has Rome's stamp on it?

If all the facts that we have cited to show that Peter was 1) not the Rock on which the Church was to be built, 2) not endowed with authority to make or alter doctrine, 3) not appointed the first bishop of Rome...if all these facts are true...and they are...where on earth did all this stuff about bishops of Rome and Popes and infallibility come from? The forged pseudo-Clementine Letters and Homilies of the third century certainly originated the idea of a monarchial church ruler, and even though **Augustine** (AD 354-430) taught that the **"Rock"** in Matthew 16:18 **was Jesus,** not Peter, his monumental work—*"The City of God"*—helped the movement along.

History shows that the first bishop of Rome to base a claim for preeminence on Matthew 16:18 was Calixtus I in the 3rd century. And it is instantly obvious that his misinterpretation of that Scripture set the tone for the papacy program from then on. Had he been accomplished in the Greek language, and known the

Pauline Scriptures cited above, he could have claimed descent from Paul as supreme overseer of the Church, and who could have said "nay"? But the famous Tertullian, bishop of Carthage at the time, referred to Calixtus I as a "usurper" for speaking of himself as "bishop of bishops." Then, midway through the same century, Stephen I, bishop of Rome from AD 253-257, admonished the North African church about its baptismal practices. Cyprian, bishop of Carthage, refused to yield to Stephen I. He said each bishop had the preeminence in his own jurisdiction. Even when Constantine, early in the 4th century, issued his edict of toleration and convoked the Council of Nicaea in A.D. 325, headship of the Church was not centralized in the bishop of Rome.

By the end of the 4th century there were five bishoprics each operating independently from the others, and headquartered in Jerusalem, Antioch, Alexandria, Constantinople, and Rome. The bishops were called Patriarchs or "Papa" which translated into English is "pope." They enjoyed equal status one with another. Each had complete control in his own jurisdiction. In AD 385, Siricius became bishop of Rome and shortly thereafter claimed absolute authority over all of Christendom. His claim went unheeded and ten years later the Roman Empire split into two separate divisions—east and west. This resulted in a gradual centralization of authority over the eastern churches in the bishopric of Constantinople, and henceforth Rome's struggle for total control of Christendom found an implacable enemy in Constantinople and the Eastern Churches.

Innocent I was bishop of Rome early in the 5th century. (402-417) He referred to himself as "Ruler of the Church of God." He sought to become the arbiter of all major disputes within all of Christendom but was unsuccessful. An Eastern Church council (whose secretary was Augustine) decreed that anyone appealing to Rome for a decision of any kind was to be excommunicated from the African church.

Midway through the 5th century, the Huns, the Visigoths and the Vandals were cutting the once-invincible Roman Empire to pieces. It was the perfect time for a strong man to arrive on the scene and that man turned out to be Leo I, bishop of Rome from AD 440-461. There still was no "papacy" at the time, but Leo took unto himself the title of "Primate of all Bishops." To get this claim validated he appealed to a secular source, Valentinian III, ruler of the Western Roman Empire. Imagine, the self-styled Vicar of Christ having to receive from a secular source approval to be the Vicar of Christ. The lust for power makes for strange bedfellows.

It was Leo I who persuaded both Attila the Hun and, a few years later, the Vandal Geneseric, to spare the city of Rome from destruction. Apparently emboldened by these successes, Leo proclaimed himself the "Lord of the whole Church." He declared that to resist his authority would result in condemnation to hell. (Cf. Rom 8:34) He promoted the death penalty as punishment for heresy, directly contradicting Christ's instructions to His church: ***"But I say unto you, Love your enemies, bless them that curse you, do good to them that hate you, and pray for them which despitefully use you, and persecute you."*** (Mat 5:44) It was Leo I who first introduced the idea of an exclusive universal papacy, but the assemblage of bishops from all over the world who came to the Council of Chalcedon (AD 451) denied Leo's claim. Thus, contrary to all of Rome's claims that the papacy has been in existence since Peter, there still was no pope at the end of the 5th century. In fact, to find the first bishop of Rome who established absolute unopposed control over the western churches, it is necessary to jump ahead 100 years to the very end of the 6th century.

Gregory I, bishop of Rome from AD 590-604 has been called by historians the first pope even though he refused to so identify himself. With absolute control established over all of the Western churches—Italy, Spain, Gaul, and the newly converted England, Gregory I functioned as, and exercised the powers of, what shortly thereafter would become known as the papacy. In spite of this, he adamantly refused to be called "Universal Bishop," and when the bishop of Constantinople applied this title to himself an irritated Gregory said it was haughty and vicious to do so. Because of his attitude toward the pretensions that seem always to accompany the assumption of great power, Gregory must be judged as one who stepped forward to fulfill the needs of the time in which he lived, without any intention of establishing a precedent that would affect all future generations.

His were turbulent times; actually the beginning of the dark ages. Rome had fallen in AD 476 to the Goths. Anarchy was the rule. The Lombards were pillaging and plundering out of control. It was Gregory I who was able to exercise a positive influence over the various warring factions and bring a semblance of order out of the chaos that marked those dark days. Yet he never claimed to be the Vicar of Christ, the supreme authority of the Church, or gifted with infallibility. In a letter to the emperor, Maurice, Gregory wrote:

> **"I confidently affirm that who so calls himself, or desires to be called Universal Priest, (Pontifex Maximus), in his pride goes before antiChrist......St. Peter is not called Universal Apostle....Far from CHRISTIAN (not Catholic) hearts be that blasphemous name."**

In another of his letters, this one to the bishop of Antioch, Gregory wrote that the title Universal Bishop was, **"Profane, superstitious, haughty, and invented by the first apostate."** I think it can be safely said that Gregory I would have been opposed to establishment of the office of the papacy as it evolved over the years after his death.

To give an entire history of the development of the Roman Catholic papacy after the reign of Gregory I, how it became a powerful temporal kingdom that lasted for 1100 years, would fill several books. It has been our purpose here simply to show that Rome's insistence that the office of the papacy has always existed and been a known entity since the days of Peter is utter nonsense without any foundation in Biblical or historical fact. The only evidence that supports Rome's claim—documents known as a) the pseudo Clementine Letters and Homilies from the 3rd century, and b) the Pseudo-Isidorian Decretals dated AD 857—have been proven to be deliberate forgeries produced to convey the belief that the papacy existed right from the beginning of Christianity. Thus the only evidence to support such a claim—because of their proven corrupt nature—is no evidence at all.

Peter was not the first Pope. Historically and biblically, he was not even the first bishop, or a bishop of Rome. Christ did not establish the office of the papacy, nor appoint one to be the supreme leader of His Church. There are a number of church offices mentioned in the New Testament, none of which would apply to a supreme leader. People identified by title include Apostles, disciples, evangelists, and prophets (preachers), pastors, and teachers; (Eph. 4:11) offices listed are bishops, deacons, and elders. (I Tim. 3 and 5) The title pope is from the Latin "papa" which means father, and the only time it receives the specific attention of our Lord further diminishes Rome's claim to the office of the papacy.

Matthew Chapter 23 contains a strong message from our Lord about who should and who should not be called "father" in a spiritual sense. The chapter records an episode in which Jesus is speaking to both His disciples and the "multitudes." Beginning in Verse 8, Jesus says: *"But be not ye called Rabbi: for one is your Master, even Christ; and all ye are brethren. And call no man your father upon the earth for One is your Father, which is in heaven. Neither be ye called masters: for One is your Master, even Christ. But he that is greatest among you shall be your servant. and whosoever shall exalt himself shall be abased; and he that shall humble himself shall be exalted."* (Mat 23:8-12)

On several occasions, one of them briefly mentioned earlier, our Lord had great opportunities to confirm the fact that He had selected Peter to be the first supreme leader of His church, the "Rock" upon which it would be built. In Mark 9:33-37, in Mark 10:37-44, in Luke 9:46-48, in Luke 22:24-30 and in Matthew 20:21-27, accounts are given of the Apostles disputing among themselves who was to be "greatest" (read that, "leader") among them. Our Lord never said, "Look, gentlemen, I have already appointed Peter at Caesarea Philippi to be your supreme leader." In Luke 20, he said there would be not one throne for Peter, but 12 thrones,—one for each Apostle—on which they would sit to judge the tribes of Israel. Repeating what was pointed out earlier, our Lord clearly stated His wishes regarding organization of His church as follows: **"But Jesus called them to him, and saith unto them, Ye know that they which are accounted to rule over the Gentiles exercise lordship over them; and their great ones exercise authority upon them. But so shall it not be among you but whosoever will be great among you, shall be your minister: And whosoever of you will be the chiefest, shall be servant of all"** (Mar 10:42-44)

Jesus could not have made it any clearer that His Church was not to concentrate power in a central source. He Himself was to be with the Church always until the end of the age. His Holy Spirit indwelling believers was to be the power that would keep His church free from the influx of heresy. His hatred of the Nicolaitanes, expressed in two of His Revelation letters to the Asian churches, reveals his profound opposition to a priesthood of any kind, much less a ruling monarch called "papa"—father.

Following our Lord's ascension into heaven, the Apostle John was given the final cap to the New Testament—The Revelation of Jesus Christ. By His letters to the messengers (bishops) of seven Asian Churches, (Rev Chapters 2, 3), our Lord strongly endorses their independence from each other. Each of the letters concludes with the following admonition: **"He that hath an ear, let him hear what the Spirit saith unto the churches.** (Rev 2:29) Notice two things here. First, Christians are to pay attention to and be guided by the Holy Spirit. Second, our Lord's admonitions were not to the Church singular, (i.e. the Catholic Church), but to the independent Churches making up the visible Body of Christ on earth. Nor was a single letter addressed to the bishop of Rome as it would have been had Christ established the office of the pope.

That the churches in Apostolic times and immediately thereafter were independent of each other and existed in small groups is further evidenced in Paul's various epistles. Seven different times Paul addresses greetings to named individuals in whose houses the church assembled and worshiped. Those named individuals are: Priscilla and Aquila twice (Rom 16:3, 5 and 1 Cor 16:19), Chloe (1 Cor

1:11), Stephanos (1 Cor 16:15), Nymphas (Col 4:15), Onesiphorus (2 Tim 1:16), and Archippus. (Philemon 1:2)

In the 10th century, largely because of Rome's insistence that the bishop of Rome—the pope—was the absolute Christ-appointed head of Christendom, the eastern Christian churches (Eastern Orthodox) split from Rome and have remained a separate entity to this day. Prior to that time, though Rome and Constantinople jockeyed continually for supremacy, representatives from both eastern and western churches had attended all of the convocations and councils. But thereafter, and since then, the western churches under Rome have held their councils and the eastern churches have held theirs. As a result, the eastern churches do not subscribe to the doctrines of the papacy, infallibility, nor the Assumption of Mary bodily into heaven.

For half a century I believed that Peter was the "Rock" upon which Christ built His church. I believed that he was the first pope and that the papacy was traceable all the way back to the time of the Apostles. I believed that doctrines such as the Immaculate Conception, Papal Infallibility, Mary's Assumption, etc., were from old time; and I never questioned their Biblical validity. I believed that the Catholic Church was established on Pentecost and was the one and only true church. In all of this I was terribly wrong; terribly mistaken, totally deceived by nuns, priests, and scholastics who were, themselves, deceived. Had I died during those years, my soul would have been condemned to hell for all eternity, for I was not "born again." (Cf. Joh 3:3) I did not know that my awful sins had been expiated on Calvary; that I could not atone for a single one myself here on earth, or after death in a purgatorial fire.

I was not indwelt by the Holy Spirit, and knew not the warning in the book of Romans: ***"Now if any man have not the Spirit of Christ, he is none of his."*** (Rom 8:9) There are millions of Catholics whose souls are in the same jeopardy mine was during those years I believed the doctrines and commandments of men. And they are just as ignorant of God's precious Word as I was. But they don't have to remain ignorant. The holy Bible is the most available book in all the world. Its message of salvation is easily grasped; no interpreter required. All it takes is a desire to know what God says instead of what men say. Catholics who are intimidated by fears they will be excommunicated for going against Rome's dictates really have nothing to fear. The pope is a great imposter; his infallibility is a fantasy; and if the Apostle Peter were to return tomorrow and be told of Rome's teachings about himself, he most likely would tear his tunic and cry out 'Nay, nay, brethren! I am but a man of like passions with you!"

Of a certainty Peter would vehemently deny being given the gift of infallibility, recalling how the first thing he did after Christ's ascension was disobey what he had been told to do. *"And, behold, I send the promise of my Father upon you: but tarry ye in the city of Jerusalem, until ye be endued with power from on high."* (Luke 24:29) The Apostles were to take **NO** action of any kind until Our Lord's promise of the Holy Spirit had been fulfilled. They were to wait. Period. Just before His ascension, Jesus reiterated the promise: *"...ye shall be baptized with the Holy Ghost not many days hence.* (Acts 1:5) *"But ye shall receive power, after that the Holy Ghost is come upon you: and ye shall be witnesses unto me both in Jerusalem, and in all Judaea, and in Samaria, and unto the uttermost part of the earth."* (Acts 1:8)

Instead of merely waiting for the power of the Holy Spirit as Christ had instructed, Peter spearheaded the election of Mathias to replace the traitor Judas Iscariot. Had Peter been infallible, there is little likelihood he would have acted contrary to what Jesus had ordered. Inasmuch as God allowed the appointment of Mathias, we conclude that he became a 13th Apostle, because Saul of Tarsus—Paul—was God's choice to be the 12th Apostle, replacing Judas Iscariot. It is a "given" that the Holy Spirit would not have allowed an "infallible" Peter to err as he did.

Rome claims Peter was the first pope, and on him Jesus founded His church. Does history, the early church writings, and the Word of God substantiate these claims? No; emphatically, no. Peter was not a pope or even a bishop of Rome. He was not the foundation "rock" on which Christ was to build His church. And, he was not infallible. None of the men claiming to be Peter's successors have been, either. Moreover, Rome, Catholicism's headquarters, is not the "eternal city," as the faithful have been led to believe. Jerusalem enjoys that singular honor. (Rev 21:1)

Before leaving this subject of Peter's alleged selection by Christ to head His church, the following Scripture begs a rational explanation from the Catholic theologians who feel "so sorry" for those of us who believe God's Word instead of tradition-bound Vatican rhetoric. *"And the night following the Lord stood by him, and said, Be of good cheer, Paul for as thou hast testified of me in Jerusalem, so must thou bear witness also at Rome.* (Acts 23:11) If Peter was **a** bishop, or **the** bishop, of Rome—God's choice to lead His church—why assign the job of witnessing at Rome to the Apostle Paul? Let's face it, Peter was no slouch as a preacher. His "track record" in Jerusalem, Samaria, Caesarea,—wherever he preached—was every bit as good as Paul's. Why would Peter have needed Paul's help? The answer, or course, is that Peter was every bit as effective as Paul;

he just wasn't the one God chose to plant the fellowship at Rome. Paul was not a pope. Neither was Peter. All who have claimed that title were, and are, THE GREAT IMPOSTERS.

4

The Money Machinery

"...make not my Father's house an house of merchandise."

(John 2:16)

The Church that Jesus left on earth when He ascended into heaven consisted of 11 Apostles and 109 disciples. On Pentecost Sunday, this group was empowered by the Holy Spirit to witness for Christ in Jerusalem, Judea, Samaria, and "the uttermost part of the earth." (Acts 1:8) That they succeeded in their mission beyond the most optimistic imaginings is verified by the ten often severe persecutions that the young church endured, the last of which ended with the death of the emperor Diocletion in 305 A.D.

From the time of the Apostles the Church was challenged by numerous heresies and sects. But its greatest challenge came in the last quarter of the 4th century when the emperor Theodosius decreed that Christianity was to be the state religion of the Roman Empire. Prior to that edict, the fledgling Church had been in the world but not of it. By forcing the populace to become Christians, Theodosius assured that from then on the world would be ever more deeply entrenched in the Church. As unrepentant, unconverted heathen flooded into the churches, long-established pagan beliefs and customs came along with them. Then, as the Roman monarchial system of government was embraced by the emerging Roman Catholic Church, the paganizing of Christendom first was accepted, then perpetuated by church councils and popes. Such popular Roman Catholic "staples" as incense, votive lights, candles, holy water, statues, vestments, holy days, feast days, processions, blessings, etc., all are of pagan origin, according to Catholic cardinal John Newman. Temples of pagan deities became churches. Pagan beliefs about celibacy, self-flagellation, auricular confession, the hereafter, etc., were, among others, introduced and absorbed. Christianity has largely recovered. Catholicism has not.

In the preceding chapters we have seen Rome's declared disregard of God's Word as the one and only source of doctrine. We have observed this disregard in action in the proclamation of the various unscriptural Marian dogmas, and the equally unsupported, unscriptural office of the pope. In this chapter, three more of Rome's doctrines will be subjected to the light of God's Word and the crucible of history. These—in the order they will be dealt with—are Purgatory/Temporal Punishment, Mortal/Venial Sin, and Indulgences. Together, they have been a productive part of Rome's "Money Machinery" since long before the Protestant Reformation caused curtailment of some of the abuses surrounding them. These doctrines have contributed greatly to the coffers of Rome spilling over with riches. Tragically, placing one's faith in them won't produce sanctification, only vain hopes and probable eternal condemnation.

PURGATORY.

It is of **pagan origin**, found in the false religions of Babylon, Egypt, Greece and Rome. There is no valid Scriptural support for it; in fact it contradicts the Biblical doctrine of justification by faith. It is an object of both fear and vain hope to Catholics who must believe in it under pain of sin. Fear of its tortures and the unknown length of time after death they must be suffered; vain hope that it will purify them for reception of a heavenly reward. Biblically, it is missing from the Gospel preached by the Apostles, and historically, it is not found in the documents left by the Apostles immediate successors. In sum, it is another heresy of Catholicism, a major contributor to Rome's steady drift into apostasy.

Its pains, we were told, are more excruciating than the pains of hell. St. Cyril (AD 827-869) said that one day in its fire would be far worse than all the pain suffered by all the people of the world since the time of Adam. (We should have asked our teachers how on earth he knew that.) Only there, said the dear nuns, in the horrible fire of Purgatory, could we **expiate** the temporal punishment due for sins committed against a holy God. And once there the poor sinner is helpless to help him or herself shorten its duration. A doctor of the Roman Catholic Church, Robert Bellarmine, taught that for some the pains of Purgatory may last—literally—until the day of judgment. For others, hundreds of years of temporal punishment may be required. These teachings from my childhood engendered a willingness, even a hunger, to believe anything that promised an escape from or a shortening of the time in Purgatory. Therefore, indulgences became the "spoonful of sugar" that made the "medicine" of Purgatory easier to swallow.

Those teachings from my childhood continue to exist as Catholic doctrine today, so a Catholic's only hope of avoiding the purgatorial fire is to be martyred for the faith, (not very likely in present-day America) or to gain what is called a plenary (full) indulgence at the time of death. That's why it's so prevalent among the Catholic faithful, to believe that if heaven is to be achieved at all, it will be through the purgatorial fire. But is there, in fact, a place, a state or a condition in which temporal punishment for sin is administered? A place where the sufferer, unable to help himself or herself, must rely on the efforts of living souls to merit the shortening or total cancellation of time spent there? And is there such a thing as temporal punishment to begin with? Rome's **teachings** appear on pages 268-69 of the 1994 Catholic Catechism"

> "**All who die in God's grace and friendship, but still *imperfectly purified*, are indeed assured of their eternal salvation; but after death they undergo purification, so as to achieve the holiness necessary to enter the joy of heaven.**"

It is Rome, not the Word of God, that says believers saved by God's grace are "imperfectly purified" at the time of death. The hottest fires of a Purgatory suffered for all eternity could not purify a single sinner to the state of holiness freely received the moment faith in Christ as Savior is expressed. *"For he hath made him to be sin for us, who knew no sin; that we might be made the righteousness of God in him."* (2 Cor 5:21)

There is no greater righteousness known than the righteousness of God. It is a righteousness that needs no purification. Believers are clothed in it the moment they become born again, literally born of God's seed, adopted as children into His family. *"Whosoever is born of God doth not commit sin; for his* (God's) *seed remaineth in him: and he cannot sin, because he is born of God."* (I John 3:9) The righteousness received by faith in Christ—the new nature—cannot be stained by sin; therefore requires no purification. The sins, past, present and future, committed by the old nature already have been judged, already have been paid for on Calvary's cross. *"But he (our Lord) was wounded for our transgressions, he was bruised for our iniquities: the chastisement of our peace was upon him; and with his stripes we are healed."* (Isa 53:5) Not only did Jesus pay the sin debt we pile up in a lifetime, He accepted the purifying punishment—the divine chastisement we deserved—that bought our peace with a Holy God.

By what Christ did, and not by any penances or purgation on our part, we literally are "healed"—made healthy, clean and acceptable to God. In His sight, thanks to Jesus, we are without spot or blemish and have no need of after-death purification. By faith in our Lord's atoning sacrifice, Jesus comes to live inside us, and we take up residence "in Him." This is regeneration, and the Scriptures tell us: *"Therefore if any man be in Christ, he is a new creature: old things are passed away; behold, all things are become new."* (2 Cor 5:17)

It is the new nature that is "in Christ" and cannot be stained by sin. (How could the old nature that continues to commit sin be "in Christ" the sinless One?) The old nature is reckoned dead, for the words "passed away" are translated from the Greek word ***parerchomai***, which means to perish, to die. This is in keeping with the Scripture repeated twice in Ezekiel: *"The soul that sinneth, it shall die."* (Eze 18:14, 20) The old nature dies by faith in Jesus. The new nature abides in Him, and is the nature that survives into eternity, completely righteous, completely redeemed, acceptable for everlasting fellowship with a holy God. But Rome does not believe any of this though it is clearly stated in dozens of Scriptures, a few of which already have been presented. Rome's rejection of what the Word of God makes so very clear is necessitated by the fact that Purgatory and temporal punishment, along with sin and indulgences, are important revenue producers. They must be retained even in the face of Biblical proofs and truths that directly contradict them. That this is true beyond the shadow of a doubt finds confirmation in the following from page 268 of the 1994 Catholic Catechism.

> "The Church gives the name Purgatory to the final purification of the elect, which is entirely different from the punishment of the damned. The Church *formulated her doctrine* of faith on Purgatory especially at the Councils of Florence and Trent. The tradition of the Church, by reference to certain texts of Scripture, speaks of a cleansing fire."

In Paul's second letter to Timothy we read: *"All scripture is given by inspiration of God, and is profitable for doctrine for reproof, for correction, for instruction in righteousness: that the man of God may be perfect, thoroughly furnished unto all good works."* (2 Tim 3:16, 17) When the words translated "perfect" and "thoroughly furnished" are studied in the Greek, the meaning is clear that Scripture alone should be the basis for all doctrine. But Rome charges ahead unfazed, admitting that the Purgatory doctrine is a **formulation of two church councils**, then citing church **tradition** that certain Scriptural texts speak of a "cleansing fire." These Scriptures, (1 Cor 3:15, 1 Pet 1:7) obviously, are meant to support what two councils decided, but neither of the cited verses has any relevance whatever to Purgatory or temporal punishment.

"If any man's work shall be burned, he shall suffer loss: but he himself shall be saved; yet so as by fire." (1 Cor 3:15) This verse taken out of context certainly could be considered a Scriptural affirmation of Purgatory. But it is out of context. When the Scriptures preceding it are viewed it is instantly apparent that Paul is relating events having nothing whatever to do with a place of purgation. Instead, he is pointing out that the believer's works done on behalf of Christ will be subjected on judgment day to a fiery test to determine whether they merit rewards. *"Every man's work shall be made manifest: for the (judgment) day shall declare it, because it shall be revealed by fire; and the fire shall try every man's work of what sort it is. If any man's work abide which he hath built thereupon, he shall receive a reward. If any man's work shall be burned, he shall suffer loss: but he himself shall be saved; yet so as by fire."* (1 Cor 3:13-15) These Scriptures have nothing whatever to do with Purgatory; only the value of works done on behalf of Christ **after** regeneration. The judgment of these works takes place **after** the saved soul already has been admitted to heaven by faith in Christ Jesus.

The other cited Scripture reads: *"That the trial of your faith being much more precious than of gold that perisheth, though it be tried with fire might be found unto praise and honour and glory at the appearing of Jesus Christ:"* (1 Pet 1:7) No help there, either. This citation is even less applicable than the other, for it speaks of a **trial** of one's faith **occurring during the believer's lifetime**; that is, before the coming of our Lord. There will be no trial of anyone's faith after death. It's either received or rejected here on earth. The decision made here determines where eternity will be spent. What Peter is referring to in the cited verse is the persecution of believer's that already had begun as he was writing the letter. Thus, two Scriptural references cited, two Scriptural references rejected as support for the Purgatory Rome invented, then confirmed via two church councils.

Those, however, aren't the only Scriptures Rome cites to support Purgatory and temporal punishment; there are a few others, and they certainly warrant an objective look. The first is found in the Sermon on the Mount related in the Gospel of Matthew. *"Agree with thine adversary quickly, whiles thou art in the way with him; lest at any time the adversary deliver thee to the judge, and the judge deliver thee to the officer, and thou be cast into prison. Verily I say unto thee, Thou shalt by no means come out thence, till thou hast paid the uttermost farthing."* (Mat 5:25, 26) The last seven words—*"till thou hast paid the uttermost farthing"*—don't dovetail with Rome's Purgatory doctrine that says the sinner suffering there is unable to help him or herself. It cannot apply to the damned in hell, either, because they're there for eternity. One must conclude then that this Scripture simply conveys the most expedient way to deal with human conflicts.

The entire chapter has to do with exemplary behavior, doing right things that please God. Verses 1-12—the Beatitudes—are a composite of Godly virtues every individual should strive for. Verses 13-16 are an admonition to conduct oneself in a way that gives a good example to others thereby causing the Father to be glorified. Verses 17-20 are a reminder that the Mosaic Law is not being abrogated. Verses 21, 22 deal with the proper attitude toward anger. Verses 23, 24 dictate the proper reaction to a spiritual brother that has been wronged. In the cited verses—25 and 26—Jesus counsels the sure way to avoid legal troubles by prompt admission of wrongdoing and immediate restitution where it is called for.

There is not a single parable in the entire chapter; no allegory, either. Surely to those who know and trust Him, God is not an adversary that must be agreed with in the way. He's both our Father and Savior. He's also our Judge, and our Advocate, our attorney, as it were. As believers, the debt we owed to the Father has been paid in full by our Lord. Once we have received Jesus as our Savior we don't have to spend a single minute in "prison." A debt owed to man, however, is a whole different matter. It's got to be paid in full right down to the last "farthing." No mercy. No grace. Pay up or else.

Another Scripture verse cited as "proof" for Purgatory appears in chapter 12 of the same Gospel. ***"And whosoever speaketh a word against the Son of man, it shall be forgiven him: but whosoever speaketh against the Holy Ghost, it shall not be forgiven him, neither in this world, neither in the world to come."*** (Mat 12:32) Rome's interpretation of this Scripture seems to be verbalized in the following Catechism entry attributed to Gregory I who was bishop of Rome AD 590-604.

> **"As for certain lesser faults, we must believe that,** *before the Final Judgment* **there is a purifying fire. He who is truth says that whoever utters blasphemy against the Holy Spirit will be pardoned neither in this age nor in the age to come. From this sentence we understand that certain offenses can be forgiven in this age, but certain others in the age to come."**

It is obvious Gregory believed, and Rome concurs, that the **"age to come"** is not really an age at all, but is eternity. This must be the case because of his reference to "purifying fire" preceding the "Final Judgment." It also seems apparent he believed that, besides purification, Purgatory brought forgiveness of sin as well, which is really stretching it. Of course, there is coming on this earth another age, one that Rome seemingly does not believe in, and about which the Catholic faithful never are informed. It is the Millennium of Christ's rule on earth, clearly described in the Book of Revelation. During this thousand-year "age" there will be sin and there will be the forgiveness of sin. But there will be no forgiveness of the blasphemy of God's Holy Spirit. As regards forgiveness of sin after death, the following Scripture gives us God's decision on that matter. ***"And as it is appointed unto men once to die, but after this the judgment."*** (Heb 9:27) Forgiveness of all sin except blasphemy of the Holy Spirit in the Millennial age, yes; forgiveness of sin after death, never!

Another of Rome's Catechism "proofs" for Purgatory is taken from II Maccabees, one of the Apocryphal books rejected both by the Hebrews who set the Old Testament canon, and by the early church fathers who compiled the New Testament canon. As was previously noted, the Council of Trent **added all the rejected books** to the Catholic Bible in the sixteenth century. It was one of many efforts undertaken to defeat the Reformation movement. Since that time, Rome arrogantly calls the spurious added books "Sacred Scripture" as will be noted in this next entry from page 269 of the 1994 Catechism.

> **"This teaching (Purgatory) is also based on the *practice of prayer for the dead* already mentioned in Sacred Scripture: 'Therefore I (Judas Maccabeus) made atonement for the dead, that they might be *delivered from their sin*."**

The Catechism entry doesn't include the complete episode taken from II Maccabees, but the Catholic Good News Bible does. From that latter publication we quote the following:

> **"He (Judas Maccabeus) also took up a collection from all his men, totaling about four pounds of silver, and sent it to Jerusalem to provide for a sin offering. Judas did this noble thing because he believed in the resurrection from the dead. If he had not believed that the dead would be raised, it would have been foolish and useless to pray for them. In his firm and devout conviction that all of God's faithful people would receive a wonderful reward, Judas made provision for a sin offering to *set free from their sin* those who had died."**

Apparently, the faithful are to conclude from this that temporal punishment and Purgatory are real because **Judas Maccabeus believed** a "sin offering" made for the dead would "free them from their sin." Not purify them for entry into heaven, mind you, but free them from their sin. It's hard to believe this is a key "Scriptural passage" Rome cites as proof for its temporal punishment/Purgatory doctrine. But it is, and it's as full of holes as a good Swiss cheese. The first problem is with the men for whom the "offering" was to be made. After the battle in which they died, it was discovered that they were **idolaters.** Every last one of them was carrying in his tunic an idol, a figurine of a false god. The Word of God leaves no doubt whatsoever as to the eternal destination of idolaters. And all the "sin offerings" in the world won't do them any good; won't release them from the torment of hell.

The second problem is with the uniqueness of Judas Maccabeus' belief. From the time of Abraham, resurrection of the body was a given. But nowhere in the Old or the New Testament do we read of offerings being made to **set dead people free from their sin.** Only in this book—rejected by the Hebrews and the early Church—is such a belief recorded. The third problem is Rome trying to make a case for the "practice" of prayer for the dead out of this one cited example from a formerly rejected Apocryphal book. To base a doctrine even partially on such evidence is nothing short of absurd.

The Jews in general did believe in the resurrection of the body. *"Thy dead men shall live, together with my dead body shall they arise. Awake and sing, ye that dwell in dust: for thy dew is as the dew of herbs, and the earth shall cast out the dead."* (Isa 26:19) And in the Book of Daniel we read the following: *"And many of them that sleep in the dust of the earth shall awake, some to everlasting life, and some to shame and everlasting contempt."* (Dan 12:2) There is evidence they also believed in an after-death abode (Hebrew: sh@'owl), translated at various times as the "grave," the "pit," and "hell." It was a place of punishment and no return for the wicked. *"I made the nations to shake at the sound of his fall, when I cast him down to hell with them that descend into the pit:"* (Eze 31:16)

It was a "holding" place of peace for the redeemed. *"Behold therefore, I will gather thee unto thy fathers, and thou shalt be gathered into thy grave in peace;"* (2 Ki 22:20) That the redeemed would one day be released from there also was well known. *"But God will redeem my soul from the power of the grave: for he shall receive me."* (Psa 49:15) And another from Hosea: *"I will ransom them from the power of the grave; I will redeem them from death: O death, I will be thy plagues; O grave, I will be thy destruction:"* (Hos 13:14) But a place after death **for the forgiveness of sins** was not known to the Jews. Judas Maccabeus seems to have been the inventor of it. The closest the Jews ever came to a doctrine of Purgatory derives from a concept arising about 200 BC. At that time they came to believe that God judges people according to their deeds—their works—and that loved ones should pray for God to have mercy on the souls of their deceased.

To complete the study of Rome's evidence for the existence of temporal punishment and Purgatory, two more quotes from page 269 of the 1994 Catechism are worth noting.

> **"From the beginning the church has honored the memory of the dead and offered prayers in suffrage for them, above all the eucharist sacrifice, (the Mass) so that, thus purified they may attain the beatific vision of God. The church also commends** *almsgiving* **and** *works* **of penance undertaken on behalf of the dead."**

More than likely the phrase "from the beginning" is meant to convey the impression that prayers and the "Eucharistic sacrifice" (the Mass) have been offered for the dead ever since the earliest days of the Christian Church. But that is at least 400 years away from the truth. Both prayers for the dead and the Mass with its transubstantiated communion wafer are products of the Roman Catholic religion whose emergence from Apostolic Christianity dates to the fifth century. Note in the above that almsgiving and indulgences are two suggested ways of helping to free the dead from Purgatory. And since the term "Eucharistic sacrifice" refers to the Mass, and Masses require a stipend for the priest, one gets a clear picture of Rome's Money Machinery in operation. Another interesting Catechism quote Rome advances as proof for the existence of Purgatory is attributed to John Chrysostom writing early in the 5th century:

> **"Let us help and commemorate them** (the dead). **If Job's Sons were purified by their father's sacrifice, why would we doubt that our offerings for the dead bring them some consolation? Let us not hesitate to help those who have died and to offer our prayers for them."**

Rome long ago elevated Chrysostom to the title of Saint of the Church. But if the above is any indication of how well he understood the Word of God, he must have been mortified when he stood before the Lord Jesus. The sacrifices Job offered for his sons were offered while they **were still alive.** *"And it was so, when* *the days of their feasting were gone about, that Job sent and sanctified them, and rose up early in the morning, and offered burnt offerings according to the number of them all: for Job said, It may be that my sons have sinned, and cursed God in their hearts. Thus did Job continually."* (Job 1:5) Secondly, we have no confirmation in the Word of God that because of Job's sacrifices his sons were "purified" as assumed by Chrysostom. The Bible implies that they were more interested in good times than in God times. While they were *"eating and drinking wine in their eldest brother's house,"* (Job 1:18) they and Job's daughters perished together in the Satan-generated tornado. There is no record given in the rest of the book that Job offered sacrifices for his deceased children. All good reasons to conclude that offerings for the dead have no value at all.

Justin Martyr, (AD 100-165) in his First Apology, a document in defense of Christian faith and practices, states quite clearly that the early Church had nothing to do with offerings and sacrifices to and for the dead. Rome loves to quote Justin Martyr, thereby conveying the impression that he was a "Catholic" saint. But the following is not one of the Justin Martyr quotes you will find posted in the Vatican.

> "And this is the sole accusation you bring against us, that we do not reverence the same gods as you do, *nor offer to the dead* libations and the savour of fat, and crowns for their statues, *and SACRIFICES."*

Catholic priests who are challenged regarding the reality of temporal punishment and Purgatory are noted for presenting hypothetical situations that are supposed to "prove" beyond a shadow of a doubt the soundness of this doctrine. For example: **"Two men,"** says the priest, **"Arrive at the end of their natural lives. The first man has lived an exemplary life of service to God and his fellow man ever since the day of his baptism as an infant. He has met all of the required conditions for gaining a deathbed plenary indulgence and is therefore taken directly into the presence of God. The second man lived a life of sin and degradation, and only in the final months of his life, as he faced certain death, did he convert to faith in God. Certainly this second man is not fit to go directly into God's presence, so there must be a place of purgation in which he can be purified from his sinful life."** Sounds reasonable, but Catholic priests don't know the Word of God. As a matter of fact they must swear before being ordained that they will never even question Rome's directives and interpretations regarding the divine Scriptures.

He who created all things, and knows all things, is never without an answer in His Word for the heresies and erroneous teachings of well-meaning but uninformed individuals and sects. Here from the Gospel of Matthew is God's response to the priest's hypothetical situation.

"For the kingdom of heaven is like unto a man that is an householder, which went out early in the morning to hire labourers into his vineyard. And when he had agreed with the labourers for a penny a day, he sent them into his vineyard. And he went out about the third hour, and saw others standing idle in the marketplace, And said unto them; Go ye also into the vineyard, and whatsoever is right I will give you. And Again he went out about the sixth and ninth hour, and did likewise. And about the eleventh hour he went out, and found others standing idle, and saith unto them, Why stand ye here all the day idle? They say unto him, Because no man hath hired us. He saith unto them, Go ye also into the vineyard; and whatsoever is right, that shall ye receive. So when even was come, the lord of the vineyard saith unto his steward, Call the labourers, and give them their hire, beginning from the last unto the first. And when they came that were hired about the eleventh hour, they received every man a penny. But when the first came, they supposed that they should have received more; and they likewise received every man a penny. And when they had received it, they murmured against the goodman of the house, Saying, these last have wrought but one hour, and thou hast made them equal unto us, which have borne the burden and heat of the day. But he answered one of them, and said, Friend, I do thee no wrong: didst not thou agree with me for a penny? Take that thine is, and go thy way: I will give unto this last, even as unto thee. Is it not lawful for me to do what I will with mine own? Is thine eye evil, because I am good. So the last shall be first, and the first last: for many be called, but few chosen. (Matt 20: 1-16)

There is no Purgatory and no temporal punishment to be suffered there. God has made the rules, not Rome. Heaven is the gift whether it is received early or late in life; whether it is received by a supposedly exemplary individual or a degenerate. *"For by GRACE are you saved through FAITH and that not of yourselves; it is the GIFT of God, not of works lest anyone should boast."* (Eph 2:8, 9) Man may think it unfair that the degenerate and the saintly receive the same gift, but the Kingdom is God's, and the sacrifice Christ's, and decisions regarding the disbursement of blessings theirs and theirs alone.

The Apostle Peter recognized the magnitude of God's love and grace when he wrote, *"…if the righteous scarcely be saved where shall the ungodly and the sinner appear?"* (1Pet 4:18) Not one of us—not the best of us—is worth saving.

In the sight of a holy God the saintliest among us has the appearance of a pile of filthy rags (Isa 64:6). And all the imagined purgatorial fires in all eternity would not be hot enough to make us pure in God's eyes. What it takes is not time in Purgatory, but a transaction made in this life. By faith in the shed blood of our Lord Jesus to be the propitiation for our sins, we trade Him our filthy sinfulness, and in return He clothes us with His holy righteousness. It's a completely unfair trade, our sins for Christ's righteousness. But that's exactly what God's grace is—Jesus getting what HE DID NOT deserve; us NOT getting what we DO deserve. For all who die clothed in His righteousness nothing else is needed to make them acceptable in His kingdom.

After reviewing what easily could be termed Rome's non-evidence for the existence of Purgatory, it becomes clear there really is no such place, state, or condition. Nowhere in the Scriptures does one find the Purgatory doctrine corroborated. It was not a belief embraced by the early Church. It wasn't even an article of the Roman Catholic religion until the infamous Council of Trent ratified it in the sixteenth century. Yet Rome has the effrontery to pronounce a curse upon all who deny her temporal punishment/Purgatory doctrine in the following Canon #30 from that Council's 6th Session:

> **"If anyone shall say that after the reception of the grace of justification, to every penitent sinner the guilt is so remitted and the penalty of eternal punishment so blotted out that no penalty of temporal punishment remains to be discharged either in this world or in the *world to come in Purgatory* before the entrance to the kingdom of heaven can be opened: let him be anathema (cursed.).**

To which curse the Word of God replies: ***"Who is he that condemneth? It is Christ that died, yea rather, that is risen again, who is even at the right hand of God, who also maketh intercession for us."*** (Rom 8:34) How a church that has so much trouble "rightly dividing the Word of God" can justify pronouncing curses on individuals not in agreement with its doctrines is beyond me. The curse quoted above again assumes that the world to come is eternity for that is where Purgatory supposedly is located. Earlier it was pointed out that Gregory I drew the same conclusion from Matthew 12:32 which reads: ***"....but whosoever speaketh against the Holy Ghost, it shall not be forgiven him, neither in this world, neither in the world to come."*** But the world to come that is mentioned several times in the New Testament is not eternity. As was pointed out earlier, it is the Millennial Kingdom to be established immediately after the seven-year tribulation period called "Jacob's Trouble." Our Lord Himself will sit on the throne of David, ruling here on earth for a thousand years in accordance with the prophecy of Revelation chapter 20. That Rome ignores these Scriptures does not in any way negate them.

"And he (an angel) *laid hold on the dragon, that old serpent, which is the Devil, and Satan, and bound him a thousand years, And cast him into the bottomless pit, and shut him up, and set a seal upon him, that he should deceive the nations no more, till the thousand years should be fulfilled: and after that he must be loosed a little season. And I saw thrones, and they sat upon them, and judgment was given unto them: and I saw the souls of them that were beheaded for the witness of Jesus, and for the word of God, and which had not worshipped the beast, neither his image, neither had received his mark upon their foreheads, or in their hands; and they lived and reigned with Christ a thousand years.* (Rev 20:2-4)

Obviously Rome has a real problem understanding what the "world to come" refers to. But an even bigger problem is Rome's position with respect to the justification of sinners. In the curse pronounced by the Council of Trent and quoted above, Rome stands in direct opposition to the Christian doctrine of justification by faith. (*sola fide*) Because she **must have temporal punishment** in order to have a place—Purgatory—for its administration, she curses all who believe that Jesus paid it all. She originates thereby a whole different Gospel than the one preached by the Apostles and their successors.

But God's Word does not lie. It is forever settled in heaven. It tells us that all who receive the Lord Jesus by faith in His sacrifice become a temple of the Holy Spirit. (1 Cor 3:16) It says that we have been anointed and sealed by God, bearing in our hearts the Holy Spirit's guarantee. (2 Cor 1:21, 22) The mystery hidden through the ages is now made known—Christ Himself living inside all who come to Him by faith. (Col 1:27) He, it is, who became sin for us in order that we can be clothed in His righteousness. (2 Cor 5:21) In Hebrews we are told: *"He is able also to save them to the uttermost that come unto God by him, seeing he ever liveth to make intercession for them."* (Heb 7:25) The Greek word translated "uttermost" in that comforting Scripture is ***panteles***. It means completely, totally, nothing left undone. When Christ saves us we are cleared of all guilt, excused from all afterlife punishment, sealed inside the divine righteousness for all eternity. Nothing is left for us to do but praise God for His love and mercy and obey His Word. In this life—although saved by God's grace—we will suffer the consequences of our sins, but there is nothing in God's Word that says we will be punished for them in eternity if we have trusted Jesus for our salvation.

During my years as a Catholic, I never really understood "born again" or the indwelling of the Holy Spirit. These were not taught. Today, however, I think a good question for the Catholic theologians is what happens to the Holy Spirit when a person dies and goes to Purgatory? Does Christ who indwells the believer through His Holy Spirit burn with the individual until he or she is purified? Or, contrary to what we read in Scripture, does the Spirit abandon the soul at the moment it departs the body? And why in 2 Cor 5:8, would God tells us that absent from the body means being with the Lord, if it's not true? Or, was Jesus just spoofing when He promised: ***"In my Father's house are many mansions: if it were not so, I would have told you. I go to prepare a place for you And if I go and prepare a place for you, I will come again and receive you unto myself that where I am, there ye may be also.*** (John 14:2, 3) Jesus is not in an invented Purgatory. His abode is heaven. He prepares a place there—a mansion—for all who trust in Him and Him alone for forgiveness and cleansing from all sins. Where He is, believers will also be.

In his classic work "The Two Babylons," Alexander Hislop traces belief in an afterlife place of purification through suffering all the way back to Babylon. He points out that every pagan religion **"…leaves hope after death for sinners who, at the time of their departure, were consciously unfit for the abodes of the blest."** Such individuals supposedly went to a place of purgatorial purification, the pains of which made their souls **"meet for final beatitude."**

The ancient Greek philosopher, Plato, (BC 428-348) projected a hereafter where all eventually could enjoy celestial peace. However, those deserving punishment as a result of evils done in their lives had to undergo a time of painful purging in a subterranean place of punition. Ancient Egypt's pagan religion also included belief in a purgatorial place of purification, as did the religion of pagan Rome at the time of Christ. Historically, "Sacrum Purgatorium" was a celebrated feast day of purification in pagan Rome. (Common to all civilizations adhering to a belief in an afterlife state of purgatorial purification was priestly extortion of monies and valuables in exchange for prayers and activities on behalf of the dead who were said to be suffering there. It is doubtful, however, that any of those ancient societies ever achieved the level of expertise in extracting monies for the dead that has been reached by the Roman Catholic church.)

One of the questions the Catholic faithful never ask is this: If there is a Purgatory where dead believers expiate the temporal punishment due for their sins, why did our Lord Jesus have to be beaten, crowned with thorns, spit on and nailed to a cross 'til dead? Why not just let every sinner burn in purgatory until all their sins have been atoned for? If man is able by a purgatorial fire to be made fit for entrance into heaven, and if the "works" of others still alive can "pay" part or all of an individual's temporal punishment debt, then the sacrifice on Calvary of the very Son of the Most High God was a horrible travesty. The answers, of course, based entirely on God's Word, are 1) there is no such place as Purgatory, 2) only faith in Jesus cancels sin debts, and 3) there is no fire hot enough or of sufficient duration to make a sinner fit to experience the presence of God. It was the finished work of Jesus on Calvary's cruel cross that made believers worthy of heaven, minus nothing, plus nothing, no cleansing fires needed.

One of the thieves crucified with the Lord Jesus asked to be remembered when Jesus came into His kingdom. Jesus said: "***Today shalt thou be with me in paradise.***" (Luke 23:43) Our Lord did not say "Some day after you expiate your sins in Purgatory you will be…etc." In the story of Lazarus, the beggar, and the rich man, Jesus told us Lazarus was in the "Bosom of Abraham," not in the fires of Purgatory. Paul tells us in 2 Corinthians 5:8 that being absent from the body will mean being with the Lord. And according to 1 Thessalonians 4:15-18 millions of believers are going to miss Purgatory at the same time when Jesus comes in the air for His Church. Unfortunately Catholics are not familiar with these Words of God:

"For this we say unto you BY THE WORD OF THE LORD, that we which are alive and remain unto the coming of the Lord shall not precede them which are asleep. For the Lord Himself shall descend from heaven with a shout, with the voice of the archangel, and with the trump of God; and the dead in Christ shall rise first; then we which are alive and remain shall be caught up together with them in the clouds, to meet the Lord in the air; AND SO SHALL WE EVER BE WITH THE LORD. (1 Thes 4:14-18)

I have dear relatives who have been so brainwashed with Catholic heresy that they believe fully all they have been taught in spite of what the Holy Word of God says. So settled are they in their faith that they will say, "I don't care what the Bible says. That's not what the Catholic Church teaches." Can you imagine standing before the one Who **IS** the **LOGOS**—the very **LIVING WORD**—and making such a rash statement? It may be that Jesus will point to Psalm 138:2: *"…For Thou hast MAGNIFIED THY WORD ABOVE ALL THY NAME."* To anyone so unfortunate there will be no Purgatory in which to "get it right," only the unending torment of hell.

It's really very sad how Catholics for the most part don't know—or even care to know—the Word of God, much less believe and trust it above all that man says or commands. They look forward after death to unspecified days, weeks, months or years in a place of excruciating pain that doesn't even exist. They give hard earned monies to societies and causes that promise to pray for their suffering souls in a place that's only a myth. They hope that their stay in this mythical place will be short, while at the same time ignoring all of the beautiful promises God has made to comfort and assure them.

"For God hath not appointed us to wrath, but to obtain salvation by Our Lord Jesus Christ." (1Th 5:9)

"Giving thanks unto the Father Who hath delivered us from the power of darkness, and hath translated us into the Kingdom of His dear Son; in whom we have redemption through His blood, even the forgiveness of sins." (Col 1:12-14)

"But God who is rich in mercy toward us, for His great love wherewith He loved us….Even when we were dead in sins hath quickened us together with Christ, (by grace are ye saved); and hath raised us up together and made us to sit together in heavenly places in Christ Jesus." (Eph 2:4-6)

"Therefore being justified by FAITH, we have PEACE with God through our Lord Jesus Christ." (Rom 5:1) The word translated 'justified" means cleared forever of all guilt; freed entirely from the deserved punishment.

"There is therefore now NO CONDEMNATION to them which are in Christ Jesus, who walk not after the flesh but after the Spirit." (Rom 8:1)

The Word of God tells us that *"…precious in the sight of the Lord is the death of His saints"* (Psalm 116:15) Why is that? So He can consign them to excruciating fire torture till they pay the debt they owe Him for their sins? Ridiculous! Jesus was made sin for us—in our stead—so that we could be *"made the righteousness of GOD in HIM."* (2 Cor 5:21) If as believers, who have placed our faith in Christ, we POSSESS THE VERY RIGHTEOUSNESS OF GOD, what further purification is needed to enter heaven? Who is as righteous as God? The pope? Hardly.

In John's First Epistle, we are told: *"But if we walk in the light, as He is in the light, we have fellowship one with another, and THE BLOOD OF JESUS CLEANSETH US FROM ALL SIN."* (I John 1:7) That is why Jesus was beaten, crowned with thorns, spit upon and nailed to a cross until dead. Through His shed blood our sins are wiped out; we are then presented to the Father spotless and without blemish, free from guilt and the punishment sin demands. Will Rome say purgatorial fire is superior to the precious blood of God's Son?

Purgatory is a colossal hoax perpetrated by greedy men to separate people from their money and keep them bound to an apostate church. Purgatory is a doctrine of fear. It exploits man's dread of pain and his affection for loved ones. Worst of all, it is a dangerous doctrine of false hope, deceiving people who have not experienced the new birth into believing that it will make them fit for heaven, when the Word of God says they are bound for hell. By combining Purgatory with its false teachings about sin and indulgences, Rome has been able to extort great wealth from the faithful while at the same time binding them to an apostate church. Purgatory is an invention of man. There is no Scriptural or historical support for it. Catholics need to be told.

MORTAL/VENIAL SIN.

When the light of God's Word is focused on Roman Catholic teachings about sin it quickly becomes apparent that something is amiss with this doctrine also. God's Word says, *"the wages of sin is death."* (Rom 6:23) No distinction is made as to the gravity or triviality of the sin, so **ALL** sin in the eyes of the Creator has damnation as its result. Rome has a different slant.

The Catholic child of my day was taught that venial sins are "little" sins—telling a lie, stealing a pencil, disobeying your mother—that sort of thing. Mortal sin, on the other hand, was really serious stuff—murder, adultery, robbery, missing mass on Sunday or holy days, eating meat on Friday, reading the King James Bible—things like that. We learned that venial sins weren't bad enough to get us cast into hell if we died with them on our soul. We weren't even required to enumerate them to the priest in the confessional box. But mortal sins—they were the really bad ones. If you died with one on your soul you went straight to hell and that was that.

Because of their gravity and potential for instant damnation, confession was not put off when a mortal sin had been committed. Unconfessed, it could kill your soul. So the confessional boxes were busy every Saturday afternoon and evening as the faithful flocked to unburden their souls of those "killer" sins. Venial sins, however, because they were so little and insignificant, weren't accompanied with similar remorse and concern. It was better not to commit them, of course, because you would have to pay for them in Purgatory. But if all one had to confess was venial sins they were not likely to be seen entering and leaving the confessional box.

The teachings from my childhood remain in effect today as a study of the 1994 edition of the Catholic Catechism quickly reveals. A section entitled *"The Gravity of Sin: Mortal And Venial Sin"* beginning on page 454, reiterates the fact that sins are evaluated according to their seriousness. Unconfessed mortal sins bring eternal damnation, while venial sin only:

> "....weakens charity; it manifests a disordered affection for created goods; it impedes the soul's progress in the exercise of the virtues and the practice of the moral good; IT MERITS TEMPORAL PUNISHMENT." (Emphasis mine.)

I consider that statement about venial sin to be one of the most repugnant of all Rome's repugnant statements. Not a word or a reference is there in it about its offensiveness to a pure, holy God. The focus is entirely on how venial sin affects the perpetrator, not how it hurts the God who died on a cross because all sin is ugly. Amazing! And the Baltimore Catechism—Lesson six—confirms Rome's callous viewpoint.

> 53. Q. How many kinds of actual sin are there?
> A. There are two kinds of actual sin-mortal and venial.
> 54. Q. What is mortal sin?
> A. Mortal sin is a grievous offense against *the law* of God.
> 57. Q. What is venial sin?
> A. Venial sin is a slight offense against *the law of God* in matters of less importance; or in matters of great importance it is an offense committed without sufficient reflection or full consent of the will.
> 58. Q. Which are the effects of venial sin?
> A. The effects of venial sin are the lessening of the love of God in our heart, *making us less worthy* of His help, and the weakening of the power to resist mortal sin.

What an incredible statement! First of all, no one sins against a **law**. We **break** laws, but we **sin against** the all-holy **God** of creation. Second of all, the soul worthy of God's help has never been born. *"...none is good, save one, that is, God."* (Luke 18:19) The most trivial sin makes every one of us a black sinner in the eyes of a holy God and worthy of nothing but eternity in hell. Adam and Eve committed a single sin of disobedience—what Rome would consider a "slight" offense—but that "slight" offense brought pain, suffering, physical and spiritual death upon all mankind. *"Wherefore, as by one man sin entered into the world, and death by sin; and so death passed upon all men, for that all have sinned."* (Rom 5:12) *"As it is written, There is none righteous, no, not one. There is none that understandeth, there is none that seeketh after God."* (Rom 3:10, 11) Moreover, any love of God that's in our hearts is not there because we're so great and wonderful: *"We love him, because he first loved us."* (1 John 4:19) And **that** love we have for Him actually came from Him as well, put there by the Spirit that indwells each believer: *"...the love of God is shed abroad in our hearts by the Holy Ghost which is given unto us."* (Rom 5:5)

Were it not for God's grace, His unconditional love for us, not a soul would ever pass through the pearly gates.

So it bears repeating that ALL sin—whether great or small in our eyes—is mortal sin in God's eyes. "Venial sin" is not in His vocabulary. And Scripture has numerous examples that prove it. God's judgment of sin in the Bible shows absolutely no distinction between what would be considered trivial and what the Catholic Catechism would call mortal sin.

Lot, the nephew of Abraham, who committed incest with his two daughters (Gen 19:36)—mortal sins according to Rome—obviously was not consigned to hell for them because he is referred to as a just (saved) man by the Apostle Peter. (2 Pet 2:7) Lot's wife, on the other hand, lost her life (Gen 19:26) for disobeying the angel's instructions not to look back. In His physical judgments at least, it appears God doesn't base His decisions on the degree of gravity of the sins judged.

It is true that many of the grave sins committed by the children of Israel were to be punished by stoning, others by banishment from the congregation. But two of Aaron's sons lost their lives simply for putting the wrong incense in their censors. (Num 3:4) One of Judah's sons—Onan—lost his life (Gen 38:9, 10) for refusing to raise up seed to his brother. At Jericho, Achan disobeyed God's command not to take any of the spoil. He did. And God judged his sin by 1) permitting the children of Israel to suffer defeat in battle at the hands of the citizens of Ai, and 2) by executing not only Achan himself, but his entire family. (Josh 7:24, 25)

Moses was told to **speak** to a rock in the wilderness and God would pour out water for the chronically complaining children of Israel. Angered by his charges, Moses **struck** the rock instead, (Num 20:11) seemed to take credit for bringing forth the water, and, as punishment for his sin, never set foot in the Promised Land. The nation of Israel's first king—Saul—on two occasions ignored specific orders from the Lord. (I Sam 13:9, 15:9) He lost his mind, his kingship and eventually his life. (1 Sam 3 1:4)

The first time King David tried to carry the Ark of the Covenant up to Jerusalem, a man named Uzzah reached out his hand to steady the Ark when it was in danger of falling. He died on the spot. (2 Sam 6:6, 7) Only Levites were permitted to touch the Ark. Uzzah wasn't a Levite. He paid with his life for a "little" sin. David committed some really despicable sins that resulted in absolute disaster for three of his sons. But his last one, a seemingly insignificant sin of ego, caused the death of 70,000 of his subjects from a God-sent pestilence of punishment. (2 Sam 24:15) Samson, second last of those who Judged Israel prior to establishment of the monarchy, committed many "grave" carnal sins in his life. But for the "little" sin of revealing his identity as a "Nazarite," (Jdgs 16:17) he lost first his hair, (Jdgs 16:19) then his sight, (Jdgs 16:21) finally his life. (Jdgs 16:30) Is he in hell? No, Hebrews chapter eleven counts him among the elect of the Lord. (Heb 11:32)

From these Old Testament examples it is apparent that **ALL** sin, small or great, is ugly and offensive to a pure, holy God. Finite, sinful man is tolerant of so-called "slight" sins. God tolerates **NO** sin. In the New Testament a husband and wife—Ananias and Sapphira—lied to Peter about the amount of money they received for a piece of land they had sold. Both died on the spot though about three hours apart. (Act 5:5, 10) As was stated earlier, in instances where God's judgment has been visible in the physical world there appears to be no distinction with respect to the gravity of the sin or sins, and the severity of judgment.

When the New Testament is consulted for proof that God views sin as mortal or venial only one Scripture can be found that even remotely suggests such a thing. Chapter 19 in the Gospel of John contains the account of our Lord's appearance before Pilate in which Jesus says: ***"Thou couldest have no power at all against Me, except it were given thee from above; therefore he that delivered Me unto thee hath the greater sin."*** (John 19:11) By classifying the sin of Judas as "greater" or more serious in God's eyes than Pilate's sin, was Jesus implying that Pilate's sin was more acceptable than that of Judas? No way! No sin is acceptable to God. Certainly He views murder as a more serious offense than petty theft. But to conclude that murder blackens the soul while petty theft does not; to conclude that murder deserves eternal damnation but petty theft does not, is to misunderstand entirely the holiness and purity of God. If, as the Scriptures relate in Isaiah 64:6, all our righteousnesses are as filthy rags in the sight of God, then we must realize that what we consider to be a miniscule sin blackens the soul just like a grievous sin, and makes it unfit for fellowship with a holy God. There may be varying shades of black in God's eyes, but ALL sin, whether we consider it small or great, colors the soul some shade of black, making it unacceptable to a holy God, and unfit for heaven.

Once when Jesus was teaching in the Temple (Cf. John 8) His enemies, the religious Jews, brought in a woman taken in adultery saying that she should—according to the Mosaic Law—be stoned to death. Jesus said: ***"He that is without sin among you let him first cast a stone at her."*** (John 8:7) In this exchange our Lord made no distinction between the sins of her accusers and the woman's "mortal" sin of adultery. Later in the same chapter, Jesus says: ***"I said therefore unto you that ye shall die in your sins: for if ye BELIEVE NOT***

THAT I AM HE, ye shall die in your sins." (John 8:24) Again no classification of their sins as mortal or venial; but a definite inference that dying in one's sins—whether "serious" or otherwise—results from rejecting Christ as Savior, and has eternal damnation as its reward.

In the Sermon On the Mount related in Chapters 5-7 of Matthew's Gospel, Our Lord speaks about a wide variety of sins without ever classifying them as mortal or venial. But in Matthew 5:29, 30, Jesus clearly reveals that the wages of sin is eternal damnation. This is repeated in the Book of Romans. ***"For the wages of sin is death..."*** (Rom 6:23) Not mortal sin. Not venial sin. Just....sin. The Book of James 2:9, 10 tells us that having respect of persons is sinful, but not whether it is mortal or venial. It also says that keeping the whole (Mosaic) law except in one point makes us as guilty as if we broke every commandment. 1 John says, ***"All unrighteousness is sin."*** (1 John 5:17). But is "unrighteousness" a mortal or a venial sin? From James: ***"But now ye rejoice in your boastings; all such rejoicing is evil."*** (Jas 4:16) Are we to believe that bragging a little is a mortal or a venial sin? James again: ***"Therefore to him that knoweth to do good and doeth it not, to him it is sin."*** (Jas 4:17) No classification. Just sin.

Luke's Gospel contains our Lord's response to people who seem to have thought themselves more righteous than others. He said: ***"Suppose ye that these Galilaeans were sinners above all the Galilaeans, because they suffered such things? I tell you, Nay: but, except ye repent ye shall all likewise perish. Or those eighteen upon whom the Tower in Siolam fell, and slew them, think ye that they were sinners above all men that dwelt at Jerusalem? I tell you, Nay: but except ye repent ye shall all likewise perish."*** (Luke 13:1-5) From this we conclude that repentance and faith in Jesus—not the degree of sin—is what is of greatest importance to God. Old Testament. New Testament. Sin is sin whether we call it grievous or minor. And God hates it. He is Holy, Pure, Light. Sin is darkness. **ANY** sin. And because "All our righteousnesses are as filthy rags" (Isa 64:6) we cannot of ourselves—through our most devout efforts, or the hottest fire of a Purgatory—pay for a single one of our sins. No, not even the littlest white lie or the theft of a sweet from the cookie jar. It required the precious blood of Jesus, ***"as of a lamb without spot or blemish"*** (1 Pet 1:19) shed on Calvary's cruel cross to be ***"the propitiation for our sins, and not for our sins only but for the sins of the whole world."*** (1 John 2:2) Every sin we have committed, every sin we will in the future commit, was paid for in full on Calvary. But to obtain forgiveness of our sins and freedom from the guilt that accompanies them, we must accept God's free gift of faith in the finished work of Our Lord, placing our complete trust for salvation in Him. As He gave up the Ghost on the cross

He exclaimed, ***"It is finished!"*** (John 19:30) The work of redemption was complete. Nothing done by any Pope, church, saint, or individual can add to Christ's work.

This brief study of sin as found in the Word of God thoroughly obviates the Catholic dogma of mortal and venial sin. So why is it taught? Because without it there would be absolutely no need for a place called Purgatory. No other reason makes sense. By classifying certain sins as venial—not fatal to the soul—but requiring temporal punishment after death, the need for a place of purgation is established. Thereafter, the ability of the living to help the dead to escape this place with prayers and ALMS is put forth and like magic the church coffers begin to swell. Following are excerpts from the 79th Tract of Bishop Usher (1581-1656) regarding how Rome says souls suffering in Purgatory can be helped by those who are still alive:

> **"By suffrages are meant, co-operations of the living with the dead; prayers, masses and works, such as ALMS, pilgrimages, fastings, &c. These aids which individuals can supply, ALMS, prayers, &c, only avail when offered by GOOD persons; for he who is not accepted himself, cannot do acceptable service for another. Moreover these aids may be directed either to the benefit of all souls in Purgatory indiscriminately, or specially to the benefit of a certain soul in particular."**

Thus, the real purpose of classifying sins is to involve living Catholics in activities on behalf of the dead; and, of course, in pursuit of ways to shorten their own time in the purgatorial fire. Most of these activities—works, if you prefer—include the expenditure of money for Masses, for sacramentals, for support of societies who specialize in getting souls released from Purgatory, etc. A second purpose is to bind the faithful to the church by the fear that without their works deceased loved ones, or they themselves, will never gain release from the purgatorial torment. And that is where "indulgences"—the third aspect of Rome's cunning marketing program—fits in.

INDULGENCES.

To strengthen the bond between the living and the "suffering" dead another doctrine—that of Indulgences—was made an article of the Catholic faith in the 16th century. The Council of Trent confirmed the indulgence dogma in its 25th and last session, December 4, 1563.

> "Whereas the power of conferring Indulgences was granted by Christ to the Church; and she has, even in the most ancient times, used the said power, delivered unto her of God; the sacred holy Synod teaches, and enjoins, that the use of indulgences, for the Christian people most salutary, and approved by the authority of sacred Councils, is to be retained in the Church; and it condemns with anathema those who either assert that they are useless; or who deny that there is in the Church the power of granting them."

The Council of Trent was convened on December 13, 1545, just 28 years after Martin Luther initiated the Reformation. It was comprised of 25 sessions spread over 18 years. Its sole purpose was to counteract the spread of the Reformation. Decrees issued by the so-called "sacred Synod" included a listing of the books of the Old and New Testaments, adding for the first time the spurious books known as the Apocrypha. As previously noted, these had been rejected both by the Jews and by the early Church fathers who 1) agreed with the Jews as to the canon of the Old Testament and 2) settled on the 27 books of the New Testament.

Among the many other decrees issued were those confirming the doctrines of Purgatory, mortal and venial sin and indulgences. It was the abuse of this last mentioned doctrine—indulgences—that motivated Luther's actions and brought about the beginning of the Reformation in the first place. Catholic theologians, defending Rome's claim that Christ Himself authorized the distribution of indulgences, fall back again on the binding and loosing argument that has been dealt with previously. Just as it had nothing to do with granting the Church authority to alter the Gospel, it has nothing to do with the granting of indulgences. For the simplest of reasons imaginable—**indulgences are not needed**! I Repeat. There is absolutely no need or place in Christianity for indulgences!

It is Christ's sacrifice on Calvary, His precious shed blood, which *"CLEANSETH us from ALL SIN."* (1 John 1:7) By our faith in Christ—itself a free, unmerited and undeserved **GIFT**—we receive the complete *"washing of regeneration"* (Tit 3:5) and the indwelling of Christ Himself in the form of His Holy Spirit. So, who needs anything more? Who needs these inventions Rome calls "indulgences?" Not born again Christians. Not those saved by God's mercy and grace.

But they've been "sold" to the Catholic faithful through a really great marketing job, one that has produced riches far beyond those of Solomon. It has three key elements: 1) invent a need for punishment after death. Call it temporal punishment and say it is necessary for the purging of unconfessed and unexpiated venial sins. 2) invent a place in which this temporal punishment can be administered. Pagan religions already had such a place; they called it purgatory. Great descriptive name; keep it. 3) invent a way the living can make provision for their own release after death and for the release of loved ones who have preceded them in death. Call this way indulgences, and be sure the living understand that a few bucks here and a few bucks there are the best way to obtain them. Claim that God is the source of this program, and top off everything by cursing any and all who say they're "useless," or deny Rome's authority to force belief in them on the faithful.

When, as a little shaver, I misbehaved, I was assigned by my mother to spend an hour on a very hard chair facing that place in our dining room where two walls came together. Those reflective hours did absolutely nothing to atone for my misdemeanors. They were forgiven and I'm sure forgotten each time when mother's voice announced, "Okay, you can get down now." What that "temporal punishment" accomplished was twofold. First, it confirmed that what I had done was not acceptable behavior; it was "sin." Secondly, it developed in me an early warning system that alerted my self-control center when it was about to be tested.

In the early days of the Church, severe penances sometimes were assigned to Christians whose sinful behavior brought an invocation of Church discipline. These fulfilled the exact same purpose as that hard chair facing the corner of our dining room. They made the miscreant aware of the seriousness of the sin or sins committed, and impressed upon him or her the importance of exercising self control when faced with future temptations. They did not in any way pay for, or purify from, the sins committed. Only Christ's shed blood could do that.

Occasionally these penances were reduced, sometimes even commuted entirely, because of the sinner's depth of remorse and willingness to repent. Rome can call such reductions or total cancellations of assigned penances indulgences all day long if they choose to, but they in no way even resembled the indulgences Luther abhorred and acted to eliminate. Early Church penances were assigned with the objective of improving one's Christian walk. But, once an individual has died there is no way, no opportunity, and no valid reason, to improve one's future behavior. The unregenerate sinner is in hell from which there is no escape. The saved sinner is in heaven, justified, sanctified, and glorified by our Lord's finished work on Calvary.

During the years I was a Catholic I believed the party line about indulgences, primarily because I believed in Purgatory and God's requirement of temporal punishment for my venial sins. But I never ceased to be confused by them. One work was good for 300 days of indulgence while another was good for 150 days.

A Plenary was supposed to wipe out all temporal punishment. You could apply it to yourself, or you could gain it for someone in Purgatory. Indulgences gained for yourself went into some kind of bank in heaven to be withdrawn when you died and began your suffering in Purgatory. Indulgences gained for someone already in Purgatory—say an indulgence worth 300 days—reduced the designated soul's time there by that many days.

It never occurred to me, or any of my peers, that eternity is timeless. There are no clocks there or calendars, either. Eternity is void of seconds, minutes, hours, or days. Jesus told the religious Jews: ***"Verily, verily, I say unto you, before Abraham was, I am."*** (John 8:5 8) Before the children of Israel had marched the first time around Jericho, or blown the first trumpet: ***"...the LORD said unto Joshua, See, I have given into thine hand Jericho and the king thereof, and the mighty men of valor."*** (Josh 6:2) Eternity seems to be a present-tense dimension in which such words as "days," or "years" are without meaning. There is no measurement of time there.

The above notwithstanding, there were, it seemed to me, an almost endless number of ways to gain indulgences, but by far the most popular was to pay the priest to "say" Masses for deceased loved ones. Through these, indulgences supposedly were earned and applied toward release from Purgatory of the deceased person(s). Another very popular way was to send money to one of the many convents or monasteries that specialized in praying for folks who were presumed to be in Purgatory. And, many Catholics, in their wills, left large sums of money to those kinds of ministries to be sure prayers and Masses would be offered up for their release from Purgatory after death. This practice continues popular in today's Catholic Church.

In His beautiful Sermon on the Mount, one of the many subjects Jesus dealt with was man's inclination to seek praise and honor from his peers, and material possessions for his own comfort. This while presuming to serve the Lord. He admonished His listeners as follows: ***"Lay not up for yourselves treasures upon earth, where moth and rust doth corrupt, and where thieves break through and steal: But lay up for yourselves treasures in heaven, where neither moth nor rust doth corrupt, and where thieves do not break through nor steal For where your treasure is, there will your heart be also.*** (Mat 6:19-21) Were these "treasures" the Lord referred to the "indulgences" of Roman Catholicism? No, for the same reason previously stated—there is no need, nor is there a place, for indulgences in Christianity. Christ's sacrifice more than sufficed for all who trust their salvation to His shed blood. The "treasures" our Lord referred to are the good works done in His name after salvation, for which the believer will receive rewards (crowns) in eternity. (Mat 25:34-36; 1 Cor 3:12-15)

One of the most difficult aspects of the indulgences-for-souls matter is the uncertainty about who exactly is in Purgatory. A soul you believe to be there might well be gone on to heaven, released by a Plenary Indulgence gained for him or her by another living loved one. Or as a lifetime wearer of the Scapular medal, that soul you thought was in Purgatory could already be in heaven, released by Mary, Christ's mother, who allegedly descends into Purgatory the Saturday after the death of each Scapular medal wearer to release him or her. Or, the individual may not have gone to Purgatory at all, but to hell because of an unconfessed mortal sin on the soul at the time of death. Confusion reigned, and continues to reign. Not even the pope can say who is in Rome's mythical Purgatory at any given time, a fact that keeps the money flowing in without end.

In my childhood, another very troubling thing about indulgences, temporal punishment, and Purgatory was the absence of any guidelines regarding the number of days punishment attached to each unconfessed, unexpiated sin. Some examples. If I lied to mother, was that worth one day or 100 days in Purgatory? If I bought candy with the money she gave me to drop in the collection box, was that worth one day or 100 days in Purgatory? If I copied Sarah Jane's answers on a written test, was cheating that way worth one day or 100 days in Purgatory? And, how about the use of profanity, idle gossiping, failing to tell the clerk she gave me five dollars too much change from my purchases? How many days in the "fire" did each of those offenses warrant?

There were no answers then. There are none now. Only God knows we were told. But a young person gets to figuring. If I live to be fifty-years-old and I commit an average of 3,650 venial sins every year (10 a day) that's a total of 182,500 venial sins in a lifetime. If each sin only requires an average of two days in the "fire" I can expect to spend 1000 years in purgatory. Frightening! My only hope was to gain more days indulgences than the required days of temporal punishment, but there was no way to know the unknown. This of course is the dilemma facing every Catholic soul. Because they trust what Rome says instead of what God in His Bible says, they are held captive by beliefs in things that don't even exist. In the 1994 Catholic Catechism the subject of indulgences is covered beginning on page 370. A few quotations from there deserve some attention. Example one:

> **"An indulgence is a remission before God of the temporal punishment due to sins whose guilt has already been forgiven, which the faithful**

Christian who is duly disposed gains under certain prescribed conditions through the action of the church which, as the minister of redemption, dispenses and applies with authority the treasury of the satisfactions of Christ and the saints."

A study of that lengthy definition yields several observations as follows. First of all, you can't have remission of something that doesn't exist. Temporal punishment is an invention of Rome. It is not found in God's Word. The only "remission" referred to in the Bible is found in Hebrews: *"Without shedding of blood is no remission"...of sins*, not temporal punishment. (Heb 9:22) Secondly, saying punishment still must be suffered after the "guilt has already been forgiven" is just plain stupid. Who ever heard of a court case in which a "not guilty" verdict resulted in a prison sentence for the vindicated defendant? "Not guilty" means FREE—FREE from the punishment reserved for, and deserved by, the "guilty." Rome can huff and puff and curse and condemn, but they cannot change the Gospel. On Calvary's cross, Jesus assumed our sin-guilt and suffered all of the punishment our sins deserved. The moment we trust Him and what He did for us, we are declared "not guilty" and set free from punishment of any kind in eternity.

Thirdly, the minister of redemption by virtue of His sacrifice on Calvary is the Lord Jesus, not Rome or the Roman Catholic Church. He said, *"I am the way, the truth and the Life; no man comes to the Father but by me* (John 14:5) In Acts 2:47 we read: *"...And the LORD added to the Church daily such as should be saved."* Paul understood the church's mission was to preach the Gospel. *"Who then is Paul, and who is Apollos, but MINISTERS by whom ye believed, even as the LORD GAVE to every man? I have PLANTED; Apollos WATERED; but GOD GAVE THE INCREASE.* (1Cor 3:5, 6) It is God and God alone who is the minister of redemption. The mission of the churches is to *"...be witnesses unto me both in Jerusalem, and in all Judaea, and in Samaria, and unto the uttermost part of the earth."* (Acts 1:8) As witnesses for Christ, churches are to *"...teach all nations, baptizing them....teaching them to observe all things whatsoever I have commanded you."* (Matt 28:19, 20) God is the redeemer. Churches are the messengers. Moreover, redemption of believers is a completed work, one that is not aided by Rome's supposed "dispensing" of indulgences from some mythical "treasury." In the Catechism entry quoted above, reference is made to a "treasury of the SATISFACTIONS of Christ AND HIS SAINTS." Lesson 21 of the Baltimore Catechism provides additional details regarding this unscriptural claim.

236. Q. How does the Church by means of Indulgences remit the temporal punishment due to sin?
A. The Church by means of Indulgences remits the temporal punishment due to sin by applying to us the merits of Jesus Christ, and the superabundant satisfactions of the Blessed Virgin Mary and of the saints; which merits and satisfactions are its spiritual treasury.

It is to be understood from these Catechisms that individuals designated as "saints" by Rome have added to the "merits" of Jesus "merits" of their own, accumulated during their holy lives on earth. These "merits" along with the "merits" of our Lord supposedly comprise a "treasury" from which Rome dispenses remissions in part or in full of the temporal punishment due for sin. In other words, what Jesus couldn't do by Himself, is done when the merits of His sinful creations are added in. Once again, there is no support in the Word of God for the existence of such a "treasury," nor is there any indication that Mary and the "saints" have contributed any "merits and satisfactions" to our Lord's redemptive work. On the contrary, Isaiah 64:6 says ALL of us are UNCLEAN. And the good works—the righteousnesses—that so impress us are, in the sight of God, *"...as filthy rags."* In Luke 17:10, Jesus calls the best of us *"...unprofitable servants"* who have simply done what we were supposed to do. In Romans we read: *"For all have sinned, and come short of the glory of God; Being justified freely by his grace through the redemption that is in Christ Jesus:"* (Rom 3:23, 24) If ALL have come short of the glory of God, how could anyone contribute anything to the redemptive work of Our Lord? He became sin for us believers to give us HIS RIGHTEOUSNESS. (2 Cor 5:21) We have no righteousness of our own, and neither did Mary or any of Rome's canonized "saints."

But Rome is very devious. They coin words like "temporal punishment," "venial/mortal sin," "indulgences," etc., and claim they are part of the "Tradition" that must be given equal reverence with Scripture. They use words like "treasury" and "satisfactions" and never explain why they're not found in God's Word. Sadly, the Catholic faithful place so much trust in what Rome says that they never consult the Word of God for confirmation of Catholic teachings. Following is more from the 1994 Catechism on the doctrine of indulgences.

> "To understand this doctrine (indulgences) and practice of the church, it is necessary to understand that sin has a double consequence. Grave sin deprives us of communion with God and therefore makes us incapable of eternal life, the privation of which is called the 'eternal punishment' of sin. On the other hand every sin, even venial, entails an unhealthy attachment to creatures, which must be purified either here on earth or after

death in the state called Purgatory. This purification frees one from what is called the 'temporal punishment of sin'.

From this, the faithful must believe that sin has a double consequence, contradicting the Word of God which says it has but one consequence, *"the wages of sin* (any sin) *is death."* (Rom 6:23) They also are to believe that an "unhealthy attachment to creatures" has to be "purged" either here or in a "state" called Purgatory. But God's Word says that **IT IS THE BLOOD OF JESUS** that cleanses us from ALL sin. Nothing else can or does. No purgatorial fire. No indulgences.

Now, look at that Catechism statement again. It is at once both ludicrous and blasphemous. Who needs to be purified from "an unhealthy attachment to creatures" after they are dead? Ludicrous! Or, how can indulgences—gained by one's self while alive or, after death, by other sinners on one's behalf—remit the punishment due for sin when the precious blood of Jesus apparently cannot? That's blasphemy! It's a different Gospel! Man-made and deadly to the most devout trusting soul. Catholics need to be told.

Indulgences, Purgatory, mortal/venial sin, temporal punishment, all are inventions of the Roman Catholic Church. None is mentioned anywhere in the Bible. However, afterlife places of punition are found in all of the ancient pagan religions. Acceptance, then, of Purgatory and the other doctrines is dependent entirely on Rome's say-so, and not on what God says in **HIS** book. This is the lot of the Catholic faithful who must accept doctrine after doctrine after doctrine without regard to whether or not there is Biblical support for them. As James, the Lord's brother said, *"brethren this ought not to be."* (Jas 3:10) Purgatory, degrees of sin, temporal punishment, indulgences—none found in God's Word—are creations of sinful men. Together they have for centuries produced enormous wealth for the Vatican as the faithful have dipped into their pockets to provide "offerings" that activate the "machinery" needed to deliver souls out of a fire that doesn't exist.

By the 16 century the "sale" of Rome's phony indulgences had become so common, and the promises made to those "buying" them so preposterous, that true men of God no longer could close their eyes to such abuses. Martin Luther led the way, followed shortly thereafter by the Roman Catholic rulers of Germany who petitioned the pope for a redress of grievances growing out of the abuse of indulgences. These are established historical facts that never change, and can be studied in depth elsewhere. Unfortunately, Rome's teachings with respect to Purgatory, sin and indulgences, never change, either. The Magisterium is still scaring the faithful with Purgatory, still blaspheming the Holy Spirit with temporal punishment, still "selling" indulgences through purgatorial societies, "offerings" for Masses, scapular medals, rosaries, relics, perpetual help ministries, etc.

It is an undeniable fact that the Roman Catholic Church of the 21st century continues in its apostate practice of, *"teaching for doctrines the commandments of men."* (Mat 15:9; Mark 7:7) Only by its insistence, (and the laity's acceptance), that "Tradition" is equivalent to the Word of God in matters of faith and morals is Rome able to project a semblance of credibility. That nearly one billion souls are deceived by such heresies is a tragedy of unspeakable proportions. That so few of that number are, like the Bereans of Paul's day, (Act 17:11) interested in comparing Catholic doctrine to the crystal-clear truths of Scripture, is a manifestation of the spiritual captivity in which the members of this cult find themselves. Only that kind of spiritual bondage can account for Catholics remaining faithful to this wicked, deceitful, apostate church.

We who are born again Christians, saved by the merciful grace of God and the sacrifice of our Lord, can have an impact on the lives of those Catholics we come in contact with, if we will place their names on our daily prayer list, and ask our heavenly Father to lead them into the Truth of His divine Word.

5

The Seven Dwarf Syndrome

"Not by works of righteousness which we have done, but according to his mercy he saved us, by the washing of regeneration, and renewing of the Holy Ghost;" (Titus 3:5.)

"Hi-ho, hi-ho, it's off to work we go…" So sang the seven dwarfs in the classic animated movie of long ago—"Snow White and The Seven Dwarfs." How applicable is that song to the Roman Catholic who begins at an early age to work his or her way to the salvation that the Word of God tells us is a free gift. To assist the Catholic faithful in this lifelong pursuit Rome has conceived many unique ways such as novenas, rosaries, indulgences, benedictions, stations of the cross, the "sacrifice of the Mass," just a whole host of ways to work one's way to glory. Some of these works are voluntary, others are mandatory. Several are said to be absolutely essential to the individual's salvation. Catholicism, then, is a religion of works, not grace. Faith is placed—not in Christ's finished work on Calvary—but in one's own works as the means and the method to earn salvation. Chief among these works Catholics are enjoined to do are what Rome has called "the sacraments." What they are, what they are said to do, and how they fare by comparison with God's Word, will be the subject of this chapter.

Catholic parochial schools of my era (the '30s and '40s) taught the seven sacraments as follows: 1) **Baptism**, 2) **Confirmation**, 3) **Penance**, 4) **Holy Communion**, 5) **Matrimony**, 6) **Holy Orders** and 7) **Extreme Unction**. Since then there have been changes in the alleged effects of Baptism and Confirmation, and the last one—Extreme Unction—has been replaced by "**The Anointing of the Sick**." In our religion classes as grade-schoolers great emphasis was placed on learning what graces each sacrament imparted and the rigidly prescribed preparations for their reception. The chart shown here is a compilation of information from the Baltimore Catechism. It provides a quick-reference as to the name, the primary purpose or effect of each sacrament and whether it is considered essential to salvation or merely voluntary.

SACRAMENT	PRIMARY PURPOSE/EFFECT	MANDATORY
Baptism	Removes original sin; gives Holy Spirit	YES
Confirmation	Reinforces Holy Spirit	NO
Penance	Oral Confession—Absolves from sin	YES
Eucharist (Communion)	Body & Blood of Christ received	YES
Matrimony	Marriage Vows—priest blesses	NO
Holy Orders	Ordination to the priesthood	NO
Extreme Unction	Confession, Communion, grace to die	NO

Looking at the chart, it is at once apparent that Catholic teachings about the sacraments do not line up with the Word of God. For instance, we search the Scriptures for something called the "original sin" that Catholic baptism allegedly removes; and we come up empty. We see that the Holy Spirit supposedly is "conferred" at a different time from a person's declaration of faith. We see oral (auricular) confession absolving from sin rather than faith in Christ's Calvary sacrifice. We see the body and blood of our Lord supposedly being ingested rather than the memorial bread and wine of the Last Supper. We see the exchange of marriage vows becoming a ritual supposedly laden with blessings for the uniting parties.

We see that some of these "works" are absolutely necessary for gaining eternal life, and Catholic teaching states that all of them have been instituted by our Lord. Here, again, Rome makes a mockery of the Word of God, now twisting it, now ignoring it, always subordinating it to so-called Tradition and the decrees of popes and councils. Following is a brief synopsis of things we know from the Bible about each of Rome's sacraments, and some of the key questions and problems surrounding them.

BAPTISM.

From the three synoptic Gospels we know that Jesus began His public life by submitting to the baptism of John in the River Jordan. (Mat 3:13; Mark 1:9; Luke 3:21) Being sinless, our Lord had no need for confession of sins or repentance. So His purpose must have been at least twofold; 1) to be publicly identified as the "Beloved Son" in whom God was "well pleased," 2) to endorse faith and repentance, in place of animal sacrifice, as God's new way to deal with sins. We also know that at the end of His earthly ministry He gave His Apostles the great commission to teach and baptize throughout the world. But we do not have a Biblical record of our Lord saying, or even inferring, that eternal life depends upon being baptized. Nor that the "original sin" of Adam is purged through baptism. It is fair, then, to ask what words of Jesus prove baptism is a must for eternal life; and where do we find that "original sin" is removed by it?

CONFIRMATION.

From the book of Acts, we know that the infilling of the Holy Spirit was experienced by the disciples of Jesus on the first Pentecost. This, of course, is comparable to Rome's sacraments of Baptism and Confirmation. But on Pentecost, the Holy Spirit came spontaneously, not as a result of any ritual or ceremony. And elsewhere in the Book of Acts, indwelling of the Holy Spirit accompanied the believer's expression of faith. Next question: How did receipt of the Holy Spirit become separated from the moment of regeneration? When and why did the Holy Spirit stop indwelling believers upon confession of their faith in Jesus?

PENANCE.

With respect to Rome's sacrament of Penance, there is no record in the Gospels that Our Lord ever uttered this word. In fact, there is no Greek word in the entire New Testament that can be ***correctly*** translated "penance." There are three Greek words, however, that ***always mean*** "repentance" or "repent," which is the word our Lord used in Matthew 4:17. Those Greek words are, ***metamelomai, metanoeo***, and ***metanoia***, and their meaning is far removed from penance, which infers atonement or reparation. Beyond that, Christ in His earthly ministry never at any time ordered or even intimated that forgiveness of sins would depend upon their being confessed aloud to another human being. Where, then, in the Bible is found Rome's justification for the confessional box and the sacrament of Penance? When did God stop denying eternal life to believer's who confess their sins directly to Him (Cf. 1 John 1:9; Acts 8:22) and not to a Catholic priest?

EUCHARIST:

Holy Communion. There is no record in the Bible that the last supper bread and wine turned into human flesh and blood. After blessing the elements Jesus referred to the wine, not as His blood, but as "the fruit of the vine." (Mat 26:29; Mark 14:25; Luke 22:18) At Cana, however, the water Jesus changed into wine actually became wine. In First Corinthians 11:26, the bread is always called "bread," and the wine is always called the "cup." Therefore on what Scriptural basis can the bread and wine of the Lord's Supper be said to become the physical body and blood of Christ? And how can one receive in Communion Him who supposedly already indwells one's soul?

MATRIMONY.

The union of a man and woman for the purpose of companionship and procreation was ordained by God on the sixth day of creation, not by our Lord during His earthly ministry. It has existed ever since as the natural and most ideal state in which the mutual love of a man and woman is expressed and perpetuated. In His earthly ministry our Lord attended a marriage on one occasion, spoke of it on another occasion as a permanent bond that man should not ***"put asunder."*** On what words of Christ, or other Scriptural grounds, has this coming together of two people been elevated by Rome to the status of a sacrament imparting special "graces"?

HOLY ORDERS.

By His death on Calvary Christ eliminated the Levitical priesthood. He did away with animal sacrifices by the sacrifice of Himself. He became the only High Priest, and His Word says ALL who place their faith for salvation in Him become "priests" offering up ***"spiritual sacrifices acceptable to God"*** through Him. (2 Pet 2:5; 2:9) Where in Scripture do we find Our Lord Jesus inserting another higher priesthood over the priesthood of believers He originally set up?

ANOINTING THE SICK. (Extreme Unction)

Jesus performed many miraculous healings in His earthly ministry, and in the Book of James, His half-brother, His Word counsels the sick among us to ***"call for the ELDERS of the church"*** (Jas 5:14) to pray and anoint the sick one with oil. Where in Scripture are we told that this prayer and anointing must be performed by **one individual** invested with special spiritual powers?

It's readily seen from the foregoing that Catholicism's seven sacraments are an amalgamation of Biblical acts and occurrences, given a mystical spin, and so planned as to require administration by the Catholic clergy, and **ONLY** by the Catholic clergy. They are a mixture of the real and the surreal. In the final analysis they are merely "works" in which the faithful participate on the promise that they either are gaining salvation through them, or they're accumulating for themselves graces supposedly imparted by the various rituals and ceremonies. Historically, they are not found as taught by Rome until long after the ten persecutions of Christendom had ceased early in the 4th century. Of note as well is the fact that the seven sacraments listed in the chart shown earlier were not confirmed as such by the Roman Catholic Church until the 11th century. That's a long time after the Apostles and the apostolic Church. And, whether they are taken individually or as a whole, the sacraments seriously conflict with what the Bible teaches about law, grace, works and justification. On page 292 of the 800-page 1994 Catholic Catechism, the faithful are told:

> **"The church affirms that for believers the sacraments of the New Covenant are necessary for salvation."**

But if that's true then the Word of God is false. Salvation occurs when we become justified (guiltless) in the eyes of a holy God. The Scriptures tell us we are *"…justified freely by his grace through the redemption that is in Christ."* (Rom 3:24) Our justification, first of all, is free. Second, it is unmerited, a gift from a God who loves us. *"Therefore we conclude that a man is justified by faith without the deeds* (works) *of the law."* (Rom 3:28) Third, our justification results from faith that Christ's sacrifice wiped out our guilt, did what our own works could never do. *"Knowing that a man is not justified by the works of the law, but by the faith of Jesus Christ, even we have believed in Jesus Christ, that we might be justified by the faith of Christ, and not by the works of the law: for by the works of the law shall no flesh be justified."* (Gal 2:16) The Law of Moses in the Old Testament included an extensive list of "works" the children of Israel were required to do. But these could not justify them, and neither can the sacraments (works) justify Catholics.

The long list of sins we have "written on the tablets of our lives" were nailed with Jesus to Calvary's cross. *"And you hath he quickened together with him, having forgiven you all trespasses; Blotting out the handwriting of ordinances that was against us, which was contrary to us, and took it out of the way, nailing it to his cross;"* (Col 2:13,14) Catholics are not any more able to keep the "Law" than the worst pagan, so all the sacraments (works) they participate in leave them looking like "filthy rags" (Isa 64:6) in God's holy eyes.

"Not by works of righteousness which we have done, but according to his mercy he saved us, by the washing of regeneration, and renewing of the Holy Ghost;" (Tit 3:5) Rome deceives the laity with the promise that salvation can be gained or contributed to by participation in the sacraments and other "works." The faithful, then, are lured into a false sense of security, placing their trust in rites and rituals rather than in a personal relationship with Jesus, who, through

His Holy Spirit, comes to live in each true believer's heart. Says the 1994 Catechism on page 293:

> **"The visible rites…signify and *make present* the graces proper to each sacrament. They** (the rites) **bear fruit in those who receive them with the required dispositions."**

When this statement is digested, we see that two kinds of "works" are involved with each sacrament. First, one must work to meet the conditions (dispositions) dictated by Rome for participation in the sacrament. Then one must actually perform his or her role in the execution of it. Take as an example, the adult who is to be baptized by a Catholic priest. He or she first must undergo a lengthy period of instruction in the church's numerous articles of faith, rules, rites, and traditions. That's the first work. The second work comes when the actual baptism takes place. These combinations of "works" allegedly *"make present"* certain graces peculiar to each sacrament. Ostensibly, the moment these various rituals and ceremonies are begun, heaven responds with an outpouring of blessings (graces) exactly matching what Rome says the particular sacrament provides.

In the quick-reference chart at the beginning of this chapter, removal of the stain of original sin and reception of the Holy Spirit are listed as the chief purposes/effects of Catholic Baptism. When I was a child educated in Catholic parochial schools, however, the Baltimore Catechism presented information of a substantially contradictory nature.

> **Q. What is Baptism?**
> **A. Baptism is a Sacrament which cleanses us from original sin, makes us Christians, children of God, and heirs of heaven.**

No mention there at all of the Holy Spirit being conferred. This sort of thing absolutely confounds me! In chapter three we saw that infallibility of the pope was **NOT** a doctrine one day, **WAS** a doctrine the next. Here, we have exactly the same situation. Just a couple of generations past, the Holy Spirit was **NOT** received in Catholic Baptism, but **IS** received in Catholic baptism today. In my childhood it was the sacrament of Confirmation that conferred the Holy Spirit. Today it's Baptism.

Who are these people that claim such total control over God? Telling Him when, where, how, to whom, and under what conditions He is to send His Holy Spirit? Then changing all the directions anytime they please. Dictating to the sovereign God of the universe the exact words, phrases, and ceremonies to which He must respond; and exactly what His response must be. Ordering Him to condemn any and all who oppose such utter silliness. I wonder today how I could have been so blind so long. How I could have blandly accepted this kind of foolishness without becoming indignant, without being inspired to look elsewhere for spiritual fulfillment. But I just went along with the crowd; and millions of Catholics today are doing the same thing. If you know a Catholic, pray that he or she will find grace with God.

Right up to the time of Vatican II in the 60's, many Catholics never received the Sacrament of Confirmation, (it was not mandatory) so, had Confirmation in those days actually conferred the Holy Spirit, lots of the faithful went through life without the indwelling Jesus promised to all believers. The truth, of course, is that the only Catholics who ever have, or ever will have, experienced the indwelling of the Holy Spirit, are those who have been born again by simple faith in, and total dependence on, Our Lord's expiating sacrifice for remission of sins and eternal life.

Since Vatican II, Catholic Baptism's alleged effects have been expanded to include the removal of all sins—mortal and venial as well as original—and, as previously seen, the conferring of the Holy Spirit. Of course, none of this can be found in the Bible, yet Rome loves to promulgate the belief that Catholicism's rituals are merely an extension of those practiced by the early church. Not surprisingly, that never quite jibes with history; and in the case of Baptism it is really a long way from the truth.

We see in the New Testament that baptism followed—usually at once—the convert's profession of faith and indwelling by the Holy Spirit. The baptismal act itself involved a brief immersion in water and was symbolic of the convert's rejection of the old life and commitment to the new life in Christ. (Acts 8:36-39; Acts 10:44-48; Acts 16:30-34) It identified the convert as one of Christ's disciples. Compared to this simple early church ritual the Catholic baptismal ceremony is a circus. The elements include a priest, a white garment on the individual being baptized, a godmother and a godfather, one or more *exorcisms*, two kinds of anointing oil, blessed water, salt, a candle, the sign of the cross, the laying on of hands and many formula prayers and blessings. According to the Catechism entry cited above, these elements, combined in the baptismal ceremony, **"activate"** and **"make present"** the graces that free the soul from "original" and all other sin, confer the Holy Spirit, and produce a new Catholic. All of this and more comprises the Catholic sacrament of Baptism, the first of the "works" Rome says **MUST** be experienced for salvation. But symbolism and rituals do not produce saved Christians if the Word of God is to be believed. Salvation is not in the

Scriptures denied to the unbaptized. Nor is the indwelling of the Holy Spirit dependent upon a dip in the river or some water trickled over the forehead. And where in the Bible do we find converts required to have godparents before they could be baptized?

On Calvary, as Christ suffered the punishment and death we deserve, a thief *"confessed with his mouth the Lord Jesus,"* and *"believed in his heart"* (Rom 10:9, 10) that our Lord would be raised from the dead. Speaking to the second thief who had berated the Lord, the first thief, the justified thief, said: *"Dost not thou fear God…we indeed justly…receive the due reward of our deeds: but this man hath done nothing amiss. And he said unto Jesus, remember me when thou comest into thy kingdom."* (Luke 23:40-42) It is the man's confession of faith in Christ—not the water of baptism—that brought remission of his sins and enabled our Lord to say: *"Verily I say unto thee, Today shalt thou be with me in paradise."* (Luke 23:43)

The Bible does not tell us, nor does it infer, that the 120 who were indwelt and filled by the Holy Spirit on the first Pentecost had previously submitted to John's baptism. It was, in fact, John the Baptist who made the following statement: *"I indeed baptize you with water unto repentance. but he that cometh after me is mightier than I, whose shoes I am not worthy to bear: he shall baptize you with the Holy Ghost and with fire."* (Mat 3:11) This is the baptism—the Holy Spirit baptism—that takes place spontaneously at the moment a new child of God embraces Christ as Savior and Lord. It is not brought about by the will or works of the believer, but by the will of God. Water baptism merely confirms what has taken place at that miraculous moment when sins past, present, and future are remitted, the gift of everlasting life is imputed to the believer, and adoption as a son or daughter of God is eternalized.

In the Old Testament there is no record that the Hebrews had to be baptized. As part of the Law, the men had to be circumcised, and all—both men and women—had to keep holy the Sabbath Day. But under the Law, they also had to offer the blood and the immolation of innocent animals in order to have their sins forgiven—not paid for, mind you,—forgiven. The Old Testament was attested to by the death and bloodshed of animals. The New Testament that obviated the Old, was attested to in the precious blood of Christ. Thus was ended the dispensation of "works," through which no one could be justified, and in its place was begun the dispensation of Grace in which everyone is justified who claims Jesus as his or her surrogate.

Nevertheless, Rome insists water baptism is absolutely essential for salvation, it supposedly being the only way to get rid of original sin staining the soul. But where on earth did this so-called original sin come from? We know that Adam and Eve committed the first human sin, and that all who are descendents of theirs have inherited the inclination to do evil. But nowhere in the Word of God can be found even one passage saying we have Adam's sin on our soul at the moment we are born. The nearest anyone can get to that belief is found in two Psalms of David: 1) *"Behold, I was shapen in iniquity; and in sin did my mother conceive me."* (Psa 5 1:5) And, 2) *"The wicked are estranged from the womb: they go astray as soon as they be born, speaking lies."* (Psa 58:3) In the first cited verse, the sin was not David's but his parent's, and in the second, the "wicked" referred to are "estranged" as soon as they are born, but not while in the womb.

Although no Scriptures exist that say sin stains the soul inside the womb, there are passages indicating infants are born **free of all sin** including the original sin of our first parents. When David sinned with Bathsheba while she was the wife of Uriah, the Hittite, a child was conceived which lived only a short time after it was born. Upon its death, David speaks as follows: *"...While the child was yet alive, I fasted and wept: for I said, who can tell whether GOD will be gracious to me, that the child may live? But now he is dead, wherefore should I fast? can I bring him back again? I shall go to him but he shall not return to me."* (2 Sam 12:22, 23) David, one of God's greatest prophets, knew the infant was in heaven; that upon his own death they would be reunited.

But according to Catholic teaching in my childhood, original sin on the child's soul would have prevented his entrance into heaven. In those days, Rome said the unbaptized infant went to a place called "Limbo," a place of eternal happiness but lacking the presence of God. Today, however, there is no Limbo in Catholic teachings, another case of Rome "patching-up" past doctrines by "patching-in" new ones. Today, the unbaptized infant who dies is consigned by "Mother church" to the mercies of God. (Cf. 1994 Catechism, pg. 321) However, unbaptized adults, according to Rome, can't go to heaven, so they must go to hell. There is no third option in eternity.

In speaking of the twins—Jacob and Esau—who were in Rebecca's womb, (Gen 25:24) Paul says: *"For the children being not yet born, neither having done any good or evil that the purpose of God according to election might stand, not of works, but of him that calleth; etc."* (Rom 9:11) The twins Rebecca was to bring into the world had to be sinless if they had done neither "any good or evil" while in her womb. Sin is a volitional act. One chooses to do wrong, to do evil, to rebel against the wishes of a holy God. Babies, infants, are incapable of volitional acts and are, therefore, unable to commit sin. When His Apostles sought to deny little children access to Him, our Lord said, *"Suffer lit-*

tle children, and forbid them not, to come unto me: for of such is the kingdom of heaven." (Mat 19:14) It is not likely that our Lord, knowing little children are stained with sin of any kind, would say of them, *"of such is the kingdom of heaven."* And how can Rome teach that the soul of every descendent of Adam bears Adam's sin when the Word of God says otherwise? *"The fathers shall not be put to death for the children, neither shall the children be put to death for the fathers: every man shall be put to death for his own sin."* (Deu 24:16) *"The son shall not bear the iniquity of the father neither shall the father bear the iniquity of the son."* (Eze 18:20)

Contrary to Catholic teaching, then, and perfectly in line with the Word of God, we have inherited not Adam's sin but Adam's knowledge of good and evil, and his acquired proclivity toward the latter. An infant—a pre-volitional child—can be thought of as a pure white sheet of paper on which nothing has been written. But above it, suspended between the paper and the light of God, are three translucent letters—S-I-N. As God's light shines through them, these cast their shadow upon the pure white paper. On the day the child attains volitional power it is constrained by its inherited nature to fill in the shadow letters with a black crayon, thus staining the paper, putting itself to an eternal death by its own hand. There is no baptismal water, oil, candle, or salt capable of removing that black stain. By choice (free will) an individual puts it there. By choice God in His mercy removes it and all subsequent stains as well, but only when the individual—by choice—places his or her faith in the shed blood of Jesus as the one, the only, the complete cleansing agent.

Or, consider the infant—the pre-volitional child—as carrying in his spirit at birth an invisible genetic virus that must have—and can only propagate in—darkness. So long as the child remains in the light of innocence the virus can not infect and make sick. But its very presence within the child's being constrains toward the darkness. On the day the power of volition is attained, the child hastens to depart the light, plunges into the darkness, and is infected unto spiritual death. Once again, the baptismal water merely wets the victim. What cures him or her, what restores to purity fit for fellowship with God in His kingdom, is the shed blood of Christ Jesus our Lord, not baptismal water.

Complete healing occurs at the moment the individual trusts—and asks—Christ to cure him or her spiritually through forgiveness of sins and cleansing from all unrighteousness. Since the 5th century it has been common practice in the Roman Catholic church to baptize babies shortly after birth. I, myself, was baptized at St Matthew Catholic church, (Norwood, Ohio), in early February, 1930, less than a month after I was born. Fifty-three years later I again was baptized, this time by immersion in water, and within a few months of being "born from above" by the wonderful grace of Jesus. When Rome baptizes infants who are sinless and have not yet the capacity to commit sin, there really is nothing removed from the child's soul for there is nothing there to be removed. What Rome **IS** doing is adding to its membership and its treasury, for there is always an offering" of money made to the officiating priest either by the parents, the godparents, or both. Thereafter, the baptized child is told he or she is a Catholic, and "once a Catholic, always a Catholic."

Worse than that, the infant who has been baptized grows up believing that the first step in working his or her way to salvation is an accomplished fact, when there is but a single step to be taken—faith and trust in Christ Jesus as Savior and Lord. *"...if thou shalt confess with thy mouth the Lord Jesus, and shalt believe in thine heart that God hath raised him from the dead, thou shalt be saved. For with the heart man believeth unto righteousness; and with the mouth confession is made unto salvation. For the scripture saith, WHOSOEVER believeth on him shall not be ashamed.*" (Rom 10: 9-11) Being saved, having one's sins remitted and their punishment cancelled, is not brought about by being dunked in water, anointed with oil, exorcised, candled, salted or prayed over by another sinful human being. *"The just shall live by his faith."* (Hab 2:4) *"...whosoever shall call upon the name of the Lord shall be saved."* (Rom 10:13) Faith in Christ's finished work and the act of calling upon Him, of asking Him for salvation, is the one sure way—the only way—to possess salvation. Thereafter, the "new creature in Christ" is indwelt by our Lord's Holy Spirit, given a new direction away from sin and toward the divine, encouraged at the proper time to publicly declare submission to Christ through water baptism.

Adults being baptized into the Catholic religion are led to believe that the lengthy, complicated ritual culminating in sprinkling or dunking forces a sovereign, holy God to swab away the filth of both original and committed sin, send down His Holy Spirit, and permanently mark the individual as a Roman Catholic. But God is not a genie. He is not at the beck and call of Rome's clerics. In truth, except a person already has been "born again" in accordance with **God's rules** the Catholic baptismal ritual is just an expensive, time-consuming way to get oily and wet.

"Verily, verily, I say unto thee, Except a man be born of water and of the Spirit, he cannot enter into the kingdom of God." (John 3:5) With these words, says the Catholic Catechism, Jesus instituted the sacrament of Baptism. But our Lord was not talking to Nicodemus about being baptized. He was talking to him about being reborn through faith in Christ as the propitiation for sin

promised in Isaiah 53. ***"The wind bloweth where it listeth, and thou hearest the sound thereof, but canst not tell whence it cometh, and whither it goeth: so is every one that is born of the Spirit."*** (John 3:8). Jesus is not speaking here or in the previous Scripture of anything physical. He is describing the spiritual change that accompanies the new birth. Regeneration through faith in Christ is not physically visible, but the presence of the Holy Spirit in one's life produces a noticeable, a visible change in lifestyle.

Thus, the water our Lord speaks of in John 3:5 is not physical water, but rather the *"living water"* of John, chapter four. To the lost Samaritan woman at Jacob's well in Sychar, Jesus said ***"If thou knewest the gift of God, and who it is that saith to thee, Give me to drink; thou wouldest have asked of him, and he would have given thee living water.*** (John 4:10) ***"Whosoever drinketh of the water that I shall give him shall never thirst; but the water that I shall give him shall be in him a well of water springing up into everlasting life."*** (John 4:14) What we understand, then, is that the "water" of regeneration is not physical but spiritual, and has nothing to do with baptism which is subsequent to, and publicly affirms, the new birth.

Certainly, our Lord endorsed baptism as a physical acknowledgment of the spiritual born-again experience. But it is a real "stretch" to say He instituted what John the Baptist and other Jews before him were advocating as evidence of a commitment to forsake sin. Furthermore, nothing that Jesus did or said can justify believing that water baptism has power to remit sin and confer the Holy Spirit. It is merely an external expression of an internal change, done in obedience to our Lord's Great Commission: ***"Go ye therefore, and teach all nations, baptizing them in the name of the Father, and of the Son, and of the Holy Ghost: Teaching them to observe all things whatsoever I have commanded you: and, lo, I am with you alway, even unto the end of the world."*** (Mat 28:19, 20)

The Apostles, the disciples, and all who have since been called, first were to do the "teaching" that brings about repentance and regenerative faith in Christ. Then was to come baptism, symbolic of the new birth that has taken place, and finally, more teaching to develop the neophyte believer into a mature worker for the Lord. Catholic Baptism does not—cannot—do what Rome says. It is simply a very involved "work," falsely masquerading as a vehicle that delivers from sin, something only Jesus can do—and does—when we put our faith in Him. It is not necessary for one's salvation and, in fact, can in no way contribute anything to the spiritual work done in the believer's heart by faith in Jesus.

Catholic baptism as taught by Rome, and Christian baptism as taught by God's Word, are acres apart, distinctly different. For instance, Catholic Baptism **precedes** the indwelling of the Holy Spirit. Christian baptism **follows** the Spirit's indwelling. Catholic Baptism purportedly remits sin. Christian baptism celebrates the previously-granted remission of sins. Catholic Baptism is a sacramental **"work"** necessary for salvation. Christian baptism is an act of faith in the finished "work" of Christ on Calvary. Catholic Baptism is the first step toward salvation. Christian baptism is the last step affirming regeneration has taken place. Catholic Baptism is **HOW** to be "born again." Christian baptism is **FOR** the already "born again." Catholic Baptism is for infants as well as rational individuals. Christian baptism is for believers only. Catholic Baptism is a sprinkling of the head. Christian baptism is total immersion.

Can Catholic Baptism save? No. Can it take away sin? No. Can it confer the Holy Spirit? No. Was Catholic Baptism instituted by Christ? No. Was Catholic Baptism as currently taught by Rome practiced in the early Church? No. Was baptism of infants a practice of the apostolic church? No. Can a Catholic who was baptized in infancy achieve salvation? **NO**. Salvation is not achieved, earned, merited, or purchased. It is the **FREE GIFT** of a loving God, secured for any and all who believe, by the once-for-all, once-for-all-time, sacrifice of His only begotten Son. Baptism—Catholic or Christian—won't save anyone. Faith in Christ will! ONLY faith in Christ will.

The second of the three Sacraments Rome has declared absolutely necessary for the soul's justification is "Penance." That is, the oral confession of one's sins to a priest and the priest's granting of forgiveness through absolution and the assignment of a "penance" (read that, "work") to the one confessing. The Catholic faithful are bound under penalty of sin to confess at least once every year, but are encouraged to participate much more often, once a month for example. In the previous chapter it was pointed out that the so-called "mortal" sins, the grave sins, are the ones that must be enumerated to the priest, while the so-called "venial" sins, the "lesser" sins, need not be confessed at all. However, all sin—even the unconfessed venials—supposedly are washed away by the priest's absolution, thereby restoring the sinner to a state of acceptance in the eyes of God. Catholics accept all this without making a peep, but anyone expecting to find an account in the Scriptures of this Catholic Sacrament will most assuredly be disappointed, for not even the word "penance" itself can be found there. Yet it is for a very good reason that Rome has chosen that name for this particular "work." On page 366 of the 1994 Catechism will be found the following information:

> "…Absolution takes away sin, but it does not remedy all the disorders sin has caused. Raised up from sin, the sinner must still recover his full spiritual health by *doing something more* to make amends for the sin: he must make *satisfaction for* or *expiate* his sins. This satisfaction is also called *penance*."

Once more Rome indicates that the "Catholic Jesus" is not sufficient in and of Himself to have cancelled our sin debt completely, freeing us from all responsibility to pay for them or to be punished in eternity for them. According to Rome, the sinner's "recovery" from sin requires **making satisfaction** for or **expiating** his or her sins. So, the above citation is clear proof why the name "Penance" has been given to this particular "work." And for sure, a "work" it is. In the Sacrament of Penance, the Catholic first examines his or her conscience to ascertain the nature and number of mortal sins committed. The individual then enters the "confessional," a structure that accommodates the priest in an enclosed center section flanked on each side by totally dark curtained spaces for the use of those confessing. When the person kneels down inside one of the curtained spaces, the priest opens a small door that enables communication between himself and the penitent. The penitent then says something like "Bless me Father for I have sinned; it's been x-number of weeks or months since my last confession." Thereafter the mortal sins are identified to the priest and enumerated. If the priest has no questions or advice, he assigns a penance to be performed by the sinner who then must recite an "act of contrition." Thereupon the priest gives "absolution," indicating the confessed sins are forgiven. The sinner then leaves the confessional, performs the assigned penance and—presto/chango—is back in the state of sanctifying grace, supposedly freed from the "death penalty" of mortal sin, but not yet fit for fellowship with God in heaven. Only Purgatory will accomplish that says the Vatican.

This doctrine of "auricular confession" is the same age as the doctrine of transubstantiation which is covered later in this chapter. Both were decreed in 1215 A.D. by the Fourth Lateran Council convened and dominated by the Innocent III of Inquisition fame. Prior to that time auricular confession was practiced but not required under penalty of sin. Justification for its inception supposedly is found in Matthew 16:19—the binding and loosing Scriptures previously dealt with—and John 20:23 which reads as follows: ***"Whose soever sins ye remit, they are remitted unto them; and whose soever sins ye retain, they are retained."*** Rather than rehash the whole binding/loosing/forgiving matter all over again, the reader is directed to study the various examples cited in chapter 3. Rome says the Scriptures they cite support institution of the sacrament they've named "Penance." They conveniently ignore everything in God's Word that is counter to their teachings. Some examples are in order.

Our blessed Lord forgave a Samaritan woman who never verbalized a single sin to Him. (John 4) He did the same to a woman caught in the very act of adultery. (John 8) A palsied man was forgiven of his sins—and then healed of his infirmity—without having uttered a word. (Mark 2) A young woman with an alabaster box of expensive perfume also had her unconfessed sins forgiven. (Mat 26; Mar 14) A sinful Publican by the name of Levi never, as far as we know, confessed his sins. Christ made him an apostle. We know him by the name of Matthew. (Mark 2; Mat 9) If, as Rome claims, the sacrament of Penance was instituted by Christ, our Lord didn't observe what He Himself had originated.

We have no record that Peter ever confessed his sins of denial to our Lord, but we know he was forgiven. The one person who confessed his sin to the priests was not forgiven. He ended up a suicide named Judas Iscariot. Thomas, called Didymus, never confessed his sin of unbelief. He simply cried *"My Lord and My God!"* (John 20:28) The lovable little guy named Zacchaeus in Luke 19 repented and was saved, but he never verbalized a single sin to the Lord Jesus and the Lord Jesus never required him to do so. Jesus, who came to call sinners to repentance, is not a very good example for Rome's doctrine of auricular confession—the Sacrament of Penance. And neither are the men who became His witnesses.

On the first Pentecost the 3000 converts to Christianity were told to repent, believe and be baptized. Not a word was said about confessing their sins to an Apostle before or after their conversion. When the former sorcerer named Simon tried to buy from Peter the power to confer the Holy Spirit, Peter did not "hear" his confession. Instead he recommended that Simon pray directly to God for the needed forgiveness. (Acts 8:20-22) Acts Chapter 15 is known as the "Council-of-Jerusalem" chapter. It is the chapter in which James, the Lord's brother, (not Peter as Rome would have us believe) proposes how the newly converted gentile Christians of Antioch, Syria, and Cilicia should be counseled regarding a proper Christian lifestyle. When the entire council ratified the proposal James had put forth, Judas and Silas, along with Paul and Barnabas, carried word to those Christians that they should *"…abstain from meats (foods) offered to idols, and from blood, and from things strangled, and from fornication; from which if ye keep yourselves, ye shall do well."* (Acts 15:29) This was welcomed with great joy, for they were thus "loosed" from the necessity of being circumcised. But just as important from our standpoint, not one word was said to them about "going to confession" or "eating the body and drinking the blood of Christ." Based on Rome's teachings, those souls could not have gone to heaven.

In 1 Corinthians 5:1-7, the man who was in a sinful relationship with his father's wife was required to repent (which he did), but there is not a single word that he was instructed to "go to confession," or to do "penance." In all honesty, if anyone can be said to have instituted a Sacrament in which an individual confesses sins orally it would be John the Baptist. In Matthew we read: ***"Then went out to him (John) Jerusalem and all Judaea, and all the region round about Jordan, and were baptized of him in Jordan, CONFESSING THEIR SINS."*** (Mat 3:5, 6) John, though, was not a priest and could not administer "absolution." So the people confessing were merely acknowledging their sins **publicly** before God.

Our Lord instructed the Apostle John to write letters to seven Asian churches in Chapters two and three of the Book of The Revelation. Not once were the churches admonished to confess their sins to priests. They weren't even warned to do penance. Rather, they were told to repent—change their ways and return to a proper Christian walk. Penance is a word that means self chastisement for the purpose of atoning, making amends, or making reparation. That is the work our Lord did on our behalf on Calvary, thereby liberating us from having to do so. Repentance, on the other hand, means changing one's mind and priorities from the direction of sin to the direction of the divine. Rome seems unable or unwilling to acknowledge the difference. In their Rome-approved bibles they have a compulsion to mistranslate as "penance" the three Greek words that always mean "repent" or "repentance."

In the early letters of Church leaders where the Christian manner of worship is described, there is nothing mentioned about a Sacrament called "Penance," or "priests" who "heard confessions," and administered "absolution." Biblically, we have God's Word that the sin question was dealt with once and for all time on the cross at Calvary. By our Lord's one-time sacrifice the past, present and future sins of every believer received adequate atonement. No "penance" assigned to a sinner by a priest can add to that Calvary atonement. But what about sins believers commit following their born-again experience?

Two things. First, sins committed after a genuine salvation has been experienced break our fellowship with the Lord but not our standing as redeemed souls. For example, David's grave sins of adultery and homicide broke his fellowship with God, but he remained a redeemed soul by virtue of his faith in God and His "Anointed." Second, the Word of God tells us what we **REALLY SHOULD DO ABOUT THOSE SINS**, and what it tells us has nothing to do with a Sacrament called "Penance," or a priest granting "absolution." In John's First Epistle, we are told: ***"If we say that we have no sin, we deceive ourselves, and the truth is not*** *in us. If we confess our sins He is faithful and just to forgive us our sins, and to cleanse us from all unrighteousness."* (I John 1:9) There were no Catholic "priests" when John by the power of the Holy Spirit wrote those instructions. There is no requirement of "absolution" mentioned; no indication that the confession of our sins involves a third party. Why?

At the exact moment our Lord bowed His precious head on Calvary's cruel cross and "gave up the ghost" the huge thick veil that separated the Holy Place in the Temple from the Holy of Holies was ripped apart from top to bottom—from heaven to earth—signifying the end of the Levitical priesthood and the dispensation of "works." No longer was there to be a go-between separating man from his Creator. From that moment on the Levitical priesthood offering up sacrifices to obtain forgiveness for sin was obsolete. Jesus was the last sacrifice, the ultimate sacrifice. Thereafter, man was given the awesome privilege of coming boldly and directly into the "holiest place of all," the very throne of God Himself, to confess sins and seek renewed fellowship, to obtain mercy and favor in matters dear to our heart, or to bring our offerings of praise and worship. We the believers became the New Covenant priesthood.

To any dear Catholic who may be reading this, that torn Temple veil is—of all proofs—the ultimate proof that God has set an open door before you. In two of His Revelation letters to the Asian churches, Jesus declared His "hatred" of the deeds and the doctrine of the Nicolaitanes—those who would impose a priesthood between Him and His flock. Therefore, no earthly "priest" has His approval to stand guard at the door. No pope has His approval to decree conditions of admittance. No programs of works are necessary to fit you for entrance.

The "Door" is Jesus. (John 10:7) And by your faith in Him and your trust that He alone is the *"Way, the Truth, and the life,"* (John 14:6), you are admitted into God's kingdom, your sins are forgiven and you are adopted forever into His family, never again to be counted a castaway. *"All that the Father giveth me shall come to me; and him that cometh to me I will in no wise cast out."* (John 6:37) Thereafter, when you sin, you confess them directly to the King—no go-between is required; no waiting till the confessional box is open. God's confessional box is always open. Its location is wherever you kneel in genuine repentance and agree with HIM that you have sinned. Oh, that every Catholic would come to trust God's sweet Word and not the words of men who seek to keep them captive and uninformed. *"Cursed be the man that trusteth in man."* (Jer 17:5)

In any discussion or analysis of the Roman Catholic doctrine of Penance, not to be overlooked is the awful toll taken on the pitiful men—the Catholic priests—who must listen time after time after time to sinful men and women admit to the vilest deeds, the most perverse practices, the ugliest thoughts and activities imaginable. God never meant for His children to be exposed to such filth in their service to Him. He who is pure, holy and without sin can hear the vile things we sinners do without being inclined to evil. But the priest—a sinner and vile person himself—cannot be fed a steady diet of such garbage without experiencing evil, evil effects. No wonder, then, that so many priests become alcoholics, homosexuals, pedophiles, and adulterers. Their lifestyle of enforced celibacy is, for most, utterly unnatural to begin with, and when you add to it the burden of listening to the fleshy sins of men and women, the mixture is poisonous and frequently leads to defilement. Many a Catholic diocese in America will be reeling for years from the turn-of-the-century priesthood scandals that made front-page news all over the world.

We read in the news or hear in the media of vicious, perverted, evil things men and women do and we are appalled. The priest hears that kind of ugly stuff every time he steps into the confessional box. For this reason, alone, Catholics ought to question the validity of this sacrament, realizing that a holy, loving God would never condemn any of His children to a lifetime of ingesting such filth. **"For it is a shame even to speak of those things which are done of them in secret."** (Eph 5:12) The Word of God says the things done by mankind in secret are so evil they should not even be talked about, and certainly, therefore, not listened to.

Charles Chiniquy, a 19th century priest who left the Roman Catholic Church because of its numerous deceptions and doctrinal aberrations, exposed the widespread wickedness and licentiousness indulged in both by priests and their female penitents in his book entitled, *"The Priest, the Woman and the Confessional."* It is a shocking first-hand account of the awful consequences suffered by both priests and their penitents from a sacrament Rome says is a "must" for an individual's salvation.

In answer to the questions posed early in the chapter—where in the Bible do we find Rome's justification for the confessional box and the sacrament of Penance; and when did God start denying forgiveness of sins to those who confess directly to him—Scripture does not support confession to a priest, and God has never denied forgiveness to a repentant sinner who comes to Him confessing his or her iniquities. David confessed his grave sins directly to God. So did Daniel, Nehemiah, Joshua, Isaiah, etc. God forgave them all; redeemed them all, and is **"no respecter of persons."** (Acts 10:34). He does the same for all who come to Him.

Controversy surrounding oral, or auricular, confession has been going on for centuries and continues unabated to the present day. But, it is as nothing compared to that which has accompanied the sacrament of Holy Communion (Eucharist) since the thirteenth century when the doctrine of transubstantiation was made an article of faith by Innocent III at the Fourth Lateran Council. By transubstantiation is meant that the bread and wine of the "Lord's Supper" is changed into the physical flesh and blood of our Lord Jesus. Participants, then, supposedly eat the literal flesh of Jesus and literally drink His blood. This is the third of the sacraments designated by Rome as absolutely essential for salvation. It is the highlight of Catholicism's chief form of worship—the Mass. A brief history of him who proclaimed it a doctrine follows.

The pontificate of Innocent III was from AD 1198 to 1216. During those years he claimed for himself the titles of "Vicar of Christ," "Vicar of God," "Supreme Sovereign over the Church and the World." One of his declarations stated that, "All things on earth and in heaven and in hell are subject to the Vicar of Christ." From this he claimed the right and the power to raise up or depose kings and princes. During his reign, rulers of Germany, France, England and Byzantia, obeyed his will, and in effect turned over to Rome complete control of Europe and the Middle East in temporal as well as spiritual matters.

Using indulgences as a motivator, Innocent III initiated the fourth crusade that destroyed the Byzantine **CHRISTIAN** cities of Zara (1202), and Constantinople (1204). History reports thousands of the Eastern Church Christians were tortured and murdered. Churches were vandalized and priceless treasures shattered or stolen. Under Innocent III the rift between the eastern and western branches of Christendom was permanently established. The second crusade he authorized was successful in exterminating the Albigenses, a Christian sect in Western Europe who denied papal authority and advocated Scripture only as the rule of faith. They were massacred as heretics. *"Yea, the time cometh that whosoever killeth you will think that he doeth God service."* (John 16:2)

He was the first pope to publicly advocate papal infallibility. He condemned the Magna Carta that brought the populace deliverance from oppression by royalty in England. It was Innocent III who founded the villainous Inquisition that murdered dissenting Christians for the next six hundred years, accounting for more bloodshed than all the wars of the past millennium. One is constrained to wonder how the man claiming to be infallible, and Vicar of Christ on earth, could advocate and condone the killing of "heretics" when Our Lord said: *"….Love your enemies, bless them that curse you, do good to them that hate you, and pray for them which despitefully use you, and persecute you; That ye may be the children of your Father which is in heaven: for he maketh his sun to rise on the evil and on the good, and sendeth rain on the just and on the unjust."* (Mat 5:44, 45) In the garden of Gesthemene, the Bible tells us, when the Jews came to arrest Jesus, one who was with our Lord cut off the ear of a servant of the High priest. He was instantly rebuked by Jesus who said: *"Put up again thy sword into his place: for all they that take the sword shall perish with the sword."* (Mat 26:52) Innocent III could hardly be called an humble emulator of the Lord Jesus, a "vicar" of the Christ who, in Isaiah 9:6, is called the Prince of Peace.

Besides decreeing transubstantiation, and auricular (oral) confession, he was the first pope to forbid publishing God's Word in any but the Latin language. Since only the most advantaged classes in those days could read Latin, Innocent III effectively kept the Holy Scriptures away from the rank and file of his day. This, then, was the pope who decreed that the bread and the wine of the Lord's Supper become Christ's physical flesh and blood during the celebration of the Mass. To give credence to this doctrine Catholic apologetics rely heavily on: 1.) the Last Supper accounts related in the Gospels; 2.) the sixth chapter of the Gospel of John; and 3.) a 2nd century letter explaining the Christian mode of worship.

At this point it is well to remember that prior to the year AD 1215 there was no doctrine of transubstantiation. Until then the Eucharist—from a Greek word meaning "thanksgiving"—was a central part of the worship service. But the elements of bread and wine were not declared to be the physical body and blood of our Lord. So, when the 2nd century letter to the Roman emperor, Antoninus Pius, is cited as evidence for this doctrine, we need to have a look at it. Following is the section from that letter which deals with the Eucharist:

> **"Then someone brings bread and a cup of water and wine mixed together to *him who presides* over the brethren. He takes them and offers praise and glory to the Father of the universe, through the name of the Son and of the Holy Spirit and for a considerable time he gives thanks that we have been judged worthy of these gifts. When he has concluded the prayers and thanksgivings, all present give voice to an acclamation by saying Amen. When he who presides has given thanks and the people have responded, those whom we call deacons give to those present the 'eucharisted' bread, wine and water and take them to those who are absent."**

In the foregoing, note the absence of the title "priest" for the one "who presides." Note also that the "deacons" are—in the second century—performing the same function as they were appointed to do in Acts, chapter six. Thirdly, the "Eucharisted" bread, wine, and water are not referred to as the physical body and blood of Christ, but to bread, wine, and water. So, where in the above can one find any reference to the changing of the bread and water/wine mixture into the flesh and blood of our Lord? As evidence for the doctrine of transubstantiation, the letter is a total failure; is in fact a much better proof that the early Church most definitely did not consider the bread and wine to be the physical body and blood of Jesus.

When the Scriptures Rome cites as proof for transubstantiation are consulted, they must be approached with this question in mind: when Jesus left us the Lord's Supper was it to be a **memorial service** reminding us of His sacrifice, or was it to be an actual **reenactment** of His crucifixion and death on Calvary's cross? The answer to that question will determine the validity or the fallacy of transubstantiation.

In the 26th chapter of Matthew we read: *"And as they were eating, Jesus took bread, and blessed it, and brake it, and gave it to the disciples, and said: 'Take, eat; this is My body.' And He took the cup, and gave thanks, and gave it to them, saying, 'Drink ye all of it; For this is My blood of the new testament, which is shed for many for the remission of sins. But I say unto you, I will not drink henceforth of THIS FRUIT OF THE VINE until that day when I drink it new with you in My Father's kingdom.'"* (Mat 26:26-29)

In Mark, chapter 14 we read: *"And as they did eat, Jesus took bread, and blessed, and brake it, and gave to them, and said: 'Take, eat, this is My body.' And He took the cup, and when He had given thanks, He gave it to them: and they all drank of it. And He said unto them, 'This is my blood of the new testament which is shed for many. Verily I say unto you, I will drink no more the FRUIT OF THE VINE until that day that I drink it new in the kingdom of heaven.'"* (Mark 14:22-25)

In Luke, chapter 22 we read: *"And He said unto them, 'With desire I have desired to eat this passover with you before I suffer: For I say unto you I will not any more eat thereof, until it be fulfilled in the kingdom of God.' And He took the cup, and gave thanks, and said, 'Take this and divide it among yourselves: For I say unto you, I will not drink of the FRUIT OF THE VINE until the kingdom of God shall come.' And He took bread, and gave thanks, and brake it, and gave unto them, saying, 'This is my body which is given for you: this DO IN REMEMBRANCE OF ME.' Likewise also the cup after supper, saying, 'This cup is the testament in My blood, which is shed for you.'"* (Luke 22:15-19)

Turning to chapter 11 of 1 Corinthians, we read: *"For I have received of the Lord that which also I delivered unto you, that the Lord Jesus the same night in which he was betrayed took bread: and when He had given thanks, He brake it, and said, 'Take, eat: this is My body, which is broken for you: this DO IN REMEMBRANCE OF ME.' After the same manner also He took the cup when He had supped, saying, 'This cup is the new testament in My blood: this do ye, as oft as ye drink it, IN REMEMBRANCE OF ME.' For as often as ye eat THIS BREAD, AND DRINK THIS CUP ye do shew the Lord's death till He come."* (1Cor 11:23-26)

Logic dictates that if it can be established that Jesus was using either of the elements—either the bread or the wine—symbolically, and not as His physical self, then we can be certain that both elements were symbolic of His coming sacrifice. Notice in each of the Gospels that our Lord speaks of drinking the FRUIT OF THE VINE with the disciples at a future time in His Father's kingdom, the kingdom of heaven or the kingdom of God, all of which are the same place. In Matthew's Gospel the pronoun **"THIS"** leaves no doubt whatsoever of the fact Christ was referring to the very same wine He had given the disciples to drink; the exact same wine He had said was His blood of the New Testament. If, in fact, the very blood of Jesus was in that cup then our Lord was promising to drink His own blood with the disciples at that expected future meeting. There is simply no other way of interpreting Christ's words if the wine in that cup had become His precious blood.

Besides being grossly offensive, the idea of Jesus drinking His own blood along with His disciples makes no sense at all, especially when we recall that the Jews were forbidden to consume blood. *" For the life of the flesh is in the blood: and I have given it to you upon the altar to make an atonement for your souls: for it is the blood that maketh an atonement for the soul. Therefore I said unto the children of Israel, No soul of you shall eat blood, neither shall any stranger that sojourneth among you eat blood."* (Lev 17:11.12)

Rome claims that partaking of the body and blood of Jesus in Communion is spiritual food for the sinful soul. Jesus was, is and always will be, sinless. He is not in need of spiritual food. He—in His holy Word—**IS THE SPIRITUAL FOOD**. There is absolutely no need for Him to eat His own body or drink His own blood. There is only one possible conclusion that can be drawn from Christ's promise to drink of THIS FRUIT OF THE VINE with His apostles at some future time. The wine in the cup at that last supper was wine. It was symbolic of the Blood Jesus would shortly shed on Calvary. But it was not blood. Moreover, if the wine was symbolic the bread certainly was as well.

Once it is understood that the elements of bread and wine were merely symbols of Christ's body and blood, there is no further possibility that what 1 Corinthians calls the "Lord's Supper" was to be an actual reenactment of Christ's crucifixion and death on Calvary. In Luke's Gospel and 1 Corinthians the Lord commanded that what He had done at the Passover repast was to be done **IN REMEMBRANCE** of Him. Paul, who had received his doctrine directly from Jesus, certainly understood that the Lord's Supper was to be a memorial service. *"For as often as ye eat this BREAD, and drink this CUP* (WINE), *ye do SHEW* (declare) *THE LORD'S DEATH until He come."* (1 Co 11:26) Paul DID NOT SAY, "...as often as you eat this BODY and drink this BLOOD."

Go back briefly to Exodus. When our Lord freed the Jews from their Egyptian bondage, He decreed on the very night of liberation that a feast was to be observed in every Jewish home whose door posts and lintels were marked with the blood of a sacrificial animal. Once out of Egypt, God commanded the nation of Israel to remember that great night of liberation by observing a feast called the "Passover" at the same time every year throughout their generations. The feast was a memorial service not a reenactment; no Egyptian first-born were slain each year. The sword of the Angel of the Lord remained in its scabbard. Thus, in the Old Testament it was the Passover feast that reminded the Jews how God in His love freed them.

Now, consider our Lord's words at the last supper. He said a new testament was on the way. It was to be initiated on Calvary's cruel cross. His perfect, sinless body was to be "broken" by the crushing weight of the whole world's sins. At the same time all of those horrible, scarlet sins were to be made white as snow in the fountain of His precious blood as it flowed and dripped from his dying form. The new freedom—this time for all mankind—was freedom from sin's eternal consequences. Atonement in the Old Testament had required the sacrifice of many innocent creatures. That would be done away with on the following day. The new atonement, the final and complete atonement, would be accomplished with a single sacrifice of the One Who CREATED all things. And a new feast would replace the memorial feast observed in the old covenant, the one which was about to be done away with. It would be called the Lord's Supper. It would not be a reenactment of Christ's sacrifice, but a service memorializing it. It would be ever a reminder to us how great was the cost of our freedom from the fires of hell.

But Rome goes to any length to defend its heresies. As further proof that what the disciples were given at the last supper was the physical body and the physical blood of our Lord, the sixth chapter of the Book of John is invoked. This, of course, is the great "Bread of Life" chapter, one of the most beautiful in the entire Bible. It begins with our Lord feeding the 5,000, later calming a stormy Sea of Galilee that was trying to swamp His Apostles, and finally preaching the Gospel in the synagogue of Capernaum to those whom He had fed the previous day on the other side of the sea. They, when they had found Jesus, wanted to know how He had gotten across the sea. In response, our Lord identified their lust for food as the reason they were looking for Him. He then admonished them to seek after the **food that lasts unto everlasting life**, food they could get only from Him, not physical but **spiritual** food.

When the people wanted proof, Our Lord said, among other things: *"I am the bread of life; he that cometh to Me shall never hunger; and he that believeth on Me shall never thirst."* (John 6:35) Later Jesus said; *"Verily, verily, I say unto you, He that believeth on Me HATH everlasting life. I am that bread of life."* (John 6:47, 48) *"...I am the living bread which came down from heaven: if any man eat of this bread, he shall live forever; and the bread that I will give is My flesh which I will give for the life of the world."* (John 6:51) At these words, the people became restive; accepting Christ's words as literal brought on serious doubts, perhaps even disgust. *"Verily, verily, I say unto you, except ye eat the flesh of the Son of man, and drink His blood, ye have no life in you. Whoso eateth My flesh and drinketh My blood, hath eternal life; and I will raise him up at the last day."* (John 6:53) *"This is that bread which came down from heaven: not as your fathers did eat manna, and are dead: he that eateth of this bread shall live forever."* (John 6:58) When it was obvious to our Lord that the Jews were offended by the idea of literally eating His flesh and drinking His blood, He said: *"It is the SPIRIT that quickeneth; the FLESH profiteth nothing: the words that I speak unto you, they are SPIRIT, and they are life."* (John 6:63)

The key to a proper understanding of our Lord's words is found in His promise that all who **COME** to Him and all who **BELIEVE** in Him shall never hunger, never thirst. The analogy is quite simple. **COMING** to Jesus is the spiritual act of eating His flesh. **BELIEVING** in Him is the spiritual act of drinking His blood. Thereafter the Holy Spirit takes over and everlasting life is assured. Assured because Jesus also said: *"All that the Father giveth Me shall COME to Me; and him that cometh to Me I will in no wise cast out."* (John 6:37) Rome is adamant, however. Catholic apologetics insists that Christ's words are to be taken literally. We must literally eat His flesh and drink His blood. This we can only do by participating in the sacrament of the Eucharist (Holy Communion) where the elements of bread and wine allegedly are transformed by the priest into the physical body and blood of Jesus. By doing so we become part of the reenactment of our Lord's sacrifice on Calvary's cross. He dies again an unbloody death, and we live spiritually because we have physically eaten His flesh and drunk His blood.

The Catholic faithful, sad to say, never question this. The Catholic Church teaches it; they believe it, and that settles it. They live in a Biblical never-never land that strips them of all desire for truth. They are never moved, nor are they able, to ask the hard questions. Hard questions such as this: In chapter 4 of John's Gospel, the **living water** Jesus promised in verse 10 to the Samaritan woman at the well, is it physical water that springs up inside the believer? Wouldn't the believer be drowned by such? And in John 7:3-8, the rivers of **living water** flowing out of the believer's belly, is that really physical water? Wouldn't such an individual create serious flooding problems for himself and others?

As always, Rome ignores these and any other Scriptures that cast doubt upon their teachings. But the Scriptures are there; and the hard questions. Is Jesus a physical **DOOR**? He said *"I am the DOOR."* (John 10:7). Is He on hinges, opening and closing to admit or block entrance into the SHEEPFOLD? And, is heaven really a sheepfold? Or, this: Is Our Lord the sun? He said *"I am the LIGHT of the world."* (John 8:12). Is He physical light? Did he glow brightly as he trod the earth? Again; is Jesus a physical shepherd? He said *"I am the good shepherd, and know my sheep, and am known of mine.* "(John 10:14) There is not one indication in the Bible or secular literature that Jesus ever kept a herd of sheep. Are those who follow Jesus physical sheep? Not human beings, but real honest-to-goodness rams and ewes, and lambs? Perhaps He was a **VINE**. He said *"I am the VINE, you are the BRANCHES."* (John 15:51) Do you look and feel like a branch? Insisting on a literal translation in only one of a dozen or more related places is known as Biblical smorgasbord. Rome is an expert at it.

The Jews were forbidden by the Mosaic laws to ingest blood. And the idea of dining on human flesh would have been revolting to them. When Christ spoke of the necessity to eat His flesh and drink His blood, the Jews to whom the mysteries of the kingdom remained hidden were repulsed and departed. His disciples, to whom it was given *"to know the mysteries of the Kingdom,"* (Matt. 13:11) understood that Our Lord was **SPIRITUAL** food and drink. That's why they didn't bolt for the door at the last supper when Jesus said: *"Take, eat, this is my body."*

In the 1994 Catholic Catechism Rome's teachings about the Eucharist are abhorrent to anyone whom our blessed Lord has saved by grace through His excruciating passion and crucifixion. On page 356 this is taught:

> "As sacrifice, the Eucharist is also offered *in reparation* for the sins of the living and the dead and to obtain spiritual or temporal benefits from God."

What an affront to our precious Savior! He alone made reparation for mankind's sins by undergoing suffering so intense that He cried out *"My God, my God, why hast though forsaken me!"* (Mat 27:46: Mark 15:34) To suggest that there are sins of living and dead for which reparation still must be made is to blaspheme the Holy Spirit who gave us God's Word. And teaching that a sinful human being—a priest—by uttering the words "This is my body, this is my blood" can bring Christ down from heaven and up from the dead, is more blasphemy. *"But the righteousness which is of faith speaketh on this wise, Say not in thine heart, Who shall ascend into heaven? (that is, to bring Christ down from above:) Or, Who shall descend into the deep? (that is, to bring up Christ again from the dead.)"* (Rom 10:6, 7) No priest, no words that he speaks, can or will cause Jesus to leave His place at the right hand of the Father to inhabit a wafer of unleavened bread and a cup of water/wine. He already is present through His Holy Spirit in the **temple of each believer's body**. So, with all the verbal coverings removed, Rome's Eucharist teaching has Jesus coming in Communion to where He should already be present by *"the righteousness of faith."* (Rom 10:6) Foolishness. Confusion. Blasphemy.

As is the case with the other doctrines we have compared to the Word of God, the Catholic doctrine of transubstantiation is man-made; is unsupported by the divine Scriptures, and was not an article of faith in the early Church. It did not, in fact, become an article of faith until the 13th century, declared to be a "must-believe" dogma by the founder of the murderous Inquisition. It is simply one more "damnable" heresy binding unsuspecting men and women to an apostate church.

As a youth indoctrinated with Catholic teachings, I never questioned how Jesus came into me through the Communion wafer, but His presence lasted only a matter of minutes, just until shortly after the wafer had dissolved in my mouth. Had I been indwelt by Christ's Holy Spirit in those days, I am certain I would have been constrained to ask the nuns and priests the following question: how can Jesus come to me in Communion when he already indwells me in the person of His Holy Spirit? To any dear Catholics reading this I strongly urge turning to the Gospel of John, chapter 16. There you will read why this question is critical to the doctrine of the Eucharist.

"Nevertheless I tell you the truth; It is expedient for you that I go away: for if I go not away, the Comforter will not come unto you but if I depart, I will send him unto you." (John 16:7) Unless an individual is indwelt by Christ's Holy Spirit, that person has not been born again and cannot see the kingdom of heaven. (Cf. John 3:3) In the cited Scripture, Jesus reveals that His physical presence on earth prevents His Holy Spirit from indwelling believers. He says that only after He has departed this world can His Holy Spirit abide in the hearts of His flock. I do not know why this is so, only that it must be so because Jesus said it. If, therefore, Catholics receive the indwelling of Christ's Holy Spirit in Baptism, as Rome teaches, they cannot be receiving His physical presence in the Communion wafer, as well. It works out like this: If His Holy Spirit is **in the person**, His physical presence **is not in the Communion** (wafer) **host.** If His physical presence is in the Communion host, His Holy Spirit is not in the person, for—by His own declaration—His physical presence and His Holy Spirit will not be in the same place at the same time. Catholics need to know.

For more than 800 years, it was only Catholicism's priests who ingested both the wafer and the wine during the "sacrifice" of the Mass. The laity received only the wafer, which, according to the church's teaching, contained both the flesh and the blood of the Lord Jesus. Since Vatican Council II in the 60's, however, Catholics have the option of taking both the wafer and the wine, or just the wafer as in the past. More Catholic confusion. If Christ's body and blood both are contained in the Communion wafer, the host, what is the purpose of the priest saying over the chalice of wine, "This is my blood?" And how does the blood get into the wafer when the priest only says over it, "This is my body?" Shouldn't he say, "This is my body and my blood?" I never wondered when I was a Roman Catholic. I do now. And Catholics should.

In keeping with its established practice of "patching up" old doctrines as well as "patching in" new ones, Rome has given the sacrament of Confirmation a facelift since my childhood. Back then, it was the sacrament that allegedly **conferred** the Holy Spirit. Today it merely **enriches** "with a special strength of the Holy Spirit." From the engine, as it were, to the caboose in just a couple of generations. Back then, the Holy Spirit supposedly was received for the **first time** when the bishop (priests can't administer Confirmation) laid his hand on **each head** and said "Receive ye the Holy Spirit." Today it's simply the "…completion of baptismal grace," as the bishop extends his hands over all the recipients at once and says a prayer that includes the words, "Send your Holy Spirit **upon** them."

As justification for including this ritual among the Sacraments, the 1994 Catechism again resorts to biblical smorgasbord. Quoting from page 326:

> "**From that time on** (the first Pentecost) **the apostles, in fulfillment of Christ's will, imparted to the newly baptized** *by the laying on of hands* **the gift of the Spirit that completes the grace of baptism.**"

But the Scriptures do not tell us that the Apostles laid hands on the 3000 Pentecost Sunday converts in order to impart the Holy Spirit to them. The Scriptures do not tell us that hands were laid on the 120 in the upper room who were indwelt and filled with the Holy Ghost earlier that same day. The Scriptures do not tell us that Peter, allegedly the first bishop, laid hands on the Roman Centurion, Cornelius, and his household in order to impart the Holy Ghost. " *While Peter yet spake these words, the Holy Ghost fell on all them which heard the word. And they of the circumcision which believed were astonished, as many as came with Peter, because that on the Gentiles also was poured out the gift of the Holy Ghost.*" (Acts 10:44, 45) The Catechism statement, then, does not jibe with the Word of God. From the Catholic Encyclopedia section on the Sacrament of Confirmation we read:

> "**Before the time of Tertullian the Fathers do not make any explicit mention of confirmation as distinct from baptism.**"

That voluminous publication places much stock on the writings of Tertullian regarding the Confirmation matter, but it should be noted first that Tertullian was a leading Montanist, and second, that he is two centuries removed from the apostolic church. Montanism, as reported in chapter 1, was declared a heresy by the apostolic church. And before Tertullian's time—the 3rd century—no Church fathers have anything to say about a rite called Confirmation. Quoting again from the Catholic Encyclopedia:

> "**The Sacrament of Confirmation is a striking instance of the** *development of doctrine* **and ritual in the Church....we must not expect to find there** (in the Scriptures) **an exact description of the ceremony as at present performed, or a complete solution to the various theological questions....**"

In fact, **all** of the Catholic Sacraments are a "striking instance of the development of doctrine and ritual in the church." With respect to Confirmation, even the infamous Council of Trent, so positive in its many decrees, injunctions, and condemnations, had little to say about it; could not even declare it to be instituted by Christ. And a 1907 declaration emanating from the church's Office of the Inquisition included the following admission:

> "There is *no proof* that the rite of the Sacrament of Confirmation was employed by the Apostles; the formal distinction, therefore, between the two Sacraments, Baptism and Confirmation, *does not belong to* the *history of Christianity.*"

Certainly there were occasions in the Book of Acts when the Holy Spirit was received following the imposition of hands by the Apostles. Careful attention to those episodes, though, reveal that the converts had not been given the whole Gospel that included information about the indwelling of our Lord's Holy Spirit. A further very serious sticking point is the absence in Scripture or the apostolic Church of converts requiring a sponsor in order to be so gifted, something that is mandatory for participation in the Catholic ritual of Confirmation.

In my estimation, Scripture itself presents the most serious challenge to Catholicism's "patched-up" sacrament of Confirmation in which the Holy Ghost—allegedly received in Baptism—is merely "strengthened" in the individual. As He was teaching His followers the importance of persistence in prayer, Jesus made this wonderful promise: *"If ye then, being evil, know how to give good gifts unto your children: how much more shall your heavenly Father give the Holy Spirit to them that ask him?"* (Luke 11:13) Born again Christians don't need a sponsor or hands laid on them and oil rubbed on their foreheads to receive more Holy Spirit power. By the words of Christ Himself, that power is theirs for the asking from the all-powerful Father in heaven. No wonder, as the Catholic Encyclopedia states:

> "Even some Catholics…have admitted that confirmation 'has not any visible sign or ceremony ordained of God.'"

As mentioned earlier, on only a couple of occasions in the Book of Acts was the Holy Spirit given after the laying on of hands. In each case the recipients were not in possession of the complete Gospel message. And the one example of already indwelt believers receiving increased Holy Spirit power (Acts 4:31) shows it resulted from reverent corporate prayer, not from any ritual of oil anointing and laying on of hands.

Confirmation is a striking example of INVENTED DOCTRINE, as are all the other sacraments. Biblically there was no ceremony involved when the Holy Spirit came upon the 120 upper room inhabitants on the first Pentecost. There was no ceremony when the Holy Spirit came upon the household of Cornelius while Peter was still preaching. In cases where the Holy Spirit was given following the laying on of hands, no "works" were required, just a comprehension of the complete Gospel message. A loving, merciful God in heaven confers His Holy Spirit on every sinner who comes to believe and trust His blessed Son for the forgiveness of sins and everlasting life. It is the assigned task of God's Church to proclaim the message of salvation. It is God Himself that *"giveth the increase."* (I Cor 3:7,8) It is God that gives the Holy Spirit freely to all who believe, and without requiring the recipient to meet certain man-made criteria.

That "various theological questions" have arisen with regard to Confirmation is not in the least surprising. Biblically there is no support for it. It never should have been. It is a source of great sorrow to me that most Catholic people with whom I have come in contact over the years are as lacking as I was in the Holy Spirit's influence and power. They—as was I—were baptized in infancy and confirmed at the age of 8 or 9. They never received the Lord Jesus through a profession of faith in His finished work on Calvary. They never trusted Him and Him alone for remission of their sins and eternal life. So they never have been "born again," and thereafter indwelt by God's Holy Spirit. They—as was I—are going through life without any Holy Spirit power to resist temptation and sin. But the greatest tragedy of all is that they are lost and on their way to hell. For the Word of God says: *"Now if any man have not the Spirit of Christ, he is none of His."* (Rom 8:9) Amen. Confirmation is one more "dead works" that does nothing more than promise what it cannot deliver. Its only result is to bond the Catholic more tightly to a church gone wrong, a church unwilling to go right.

In the case of what Rome has called the sacrament of Matrimony, it is again obvious that man—not God—has been busy turning an ancient, quite simple rite into an elaborate "work" that is supposed to impart special benefits to the participants. On Page 414 of the 1994 Catholic Catechism we read the following:

> **"The Sacrament of matrimony...*gives* spouses the *grace* to love each other with the love with which Christ has loved His Church; the grace of the**

> sacrament thus *perfects* the human love of the spouses, *strengthens* their indissoluble unity, and *sanctifies* them on the way to eternal life."

Here, once again, we find Rome attributing to a visible ceremony results that can only accrue to the man and woman who have a personal, dependent relationship with the Father and Jesus. It is a fact that the couple having a holy **vertical** relationship with God can expect nothing but blessings and joy in their **horizontal** relationship with each other. It is God, as the center of a Christian marriage, who empowers a man and woman to love each other with the sacrificial, *"agape"* kind of love Jesus has for us. No ceremony, no ritual, no words mouthed by a priest can do what only the Lord can do, and does, in a Christian marriage. To claim that a rite, a ritual, "sanctifies" a couple "on the way to eternal life," is as futile and empty as it is crass and arrogant. No saved individual is "on his or her way to eternal life." He or she **HAS** eternal life the moment of professed faith in Christ Jesus as Savior. (Cf. 1 John 5:13) Moreover, rites and rituals invented by sinful men do not "give grace." God, and only God, gives grace. From the famous Baltimore Catechism, more specious claims:

> A. The effects of the Sacrament of Matrimony are:
> 1. To sanctify the love of husband and wife;
> 2. To give them grace to bear with each other's weaknesses;
> 3. To enable them to bring up their children in the fear and love of God.

Once again, the indwelling of the Holy Spirit is ignored, and the assurance of a successful marriage is attributed to a "work" designated by Rome as the sacrament of Matrimony. But it is a sad fact of history and of our modern day as well, that the exchange of vows between a man and a woman in the presence of a Catholic priest is no guarantee of a permanent relationship. Unless the union is anchored by a mutual love and trust in Christ Jesus as Savior and Lord, its chances for survival until "death do us part" are slim indeed, as the incidence of divorce among Catholics clearly attests. It is redundant to keep repeating that works do not convey spiritual power. But it is necessary to do so, for it is the indwelling Holy Spirit from whom the power necessary for mutual, lasting love and respect in a marriage is derived. Without that Holy Spirit relationship two people are more likely than not to experience marital difficulties culminating in divorce.

Our Lord hates divorce. Nothing in the Bible is any clearer than that. But when unregenerate young people go before a priest to exchange marriage vows they are powerless—without the indwelling of the Holy Spirit—to order their lives according to Biblical principles. And, though Rome may scream "foul," the fact is that most Catholic youth, trained up in the Catholic religion, are not regenerated, are not "born again," do not have the Holy Spirit living in their hearts. The throne of grace is in heaven, not in the ritual of a marriage ceremony or any other sacrament for that matter. Leading the faithful to believe that they will receive graces from mere ritualistic "works" is comparable to helping them commit suicide. Catholic Matrimony is no grace-giver. It legally unites the couple, and that is all it does. Any other teaching is pure heresy.

Similar problems of an even more serious nature are encountered when the Catholic sacrament of Holy Orders is studied. Rome says that by this so-called sacrament is conferred the office of "priest" and only those who have received this sacrament are empowered to perform priestly duties. These include "saying Mass," "hearing confessions," changing bread and wine into Christ's body and blood, anointing the sick, and administering the sacraments of Baptism and Matrimony. According to the 1994 Catholic Catechism:

> **"The sacrament of Holy Orders communicates a *'sacred power'* which is none other than that *of Christ*...Through that sacrament priests by the anointing of the Holy Spirit are signed with a special character and are so configured to Christ the priest in such a way that they are able to act in the person of Christ the head."**

How very sad it is that the Catholic faithful accept such heresy without question. But it is because they are taught religion—Catholic religion—and not Biblical Christianity, that they trade the free gift offered to them by our Lord for bondage to a priesthood that was done away with on the hill Golgotha two millennia past. But even without a sound knowledge of the Scriptures, Catholics should be very disturbed by Rome's claims for this particular ritual of making "priests," for those claims are nothing short of astounding.

To even suggest that a wicked, sinful human being can be, through an elaborate man-made ritual, empowered "to act in the person of Christ," Himself, is a blasphemy of unspeakable proportions. To teach that this "works" program called "Holy Orders" confers the "sacred power" of our Lord upon a depraved, corrupt creation of His is itself the most damning evidence of man's arrogant, rebellious nature. ***"The heart is deceitful above all things, and desperately wicked: who can know it?"*** (Jer 17:9) It is no wonder that Jesus hated the deeds and the doctrine of the Nicolaitanes who sought to impose a priesthood on His young Church. Certainly He foresaw the days ahead when sinful men would claim to possess His sacred power and the authority to act in His person, and, thereafter, teach for doctrine the commandments of men.

Rome insists that it alone has been given the Scriptures; that it alone has the authority to interpret them to the faithful. Yet there is nothing anywhere in the Word of God that justifies the Catholic teaching about Holy Orders. It is an entirely man-made, man-motivated, man-exalting doctrine. The ritual conveys no special powers; it was not instituted by Christ, and God's blessings are not showered upon those who are initiated into its cult. History records the infamous, the vile, acts committed by priests, bishops, cardinals and popes down through the ages. These give eloquent testimony to the fallacy of Rome's claims for its clergy. But its claims continue, and the faithful believe them. Here, in reference to the elevation of priests to the office of bishop, is what the 1994 Catechism has to say:

> "Episcopal consecration confers, together with the office of sanctifying, also the offices of teaching and ruling....in fact....by the imposition of hands and through the words of the consecration, the grace of the Holy Spirit is given and a sacred character is impressed in such wise that Bishops, in an eminent and visible manner, *take the place of Christ Himself* teacher, shepherd, and priest, and act as His representative. By virtue, therefore, of the Holy Spirit who has been given to them bishops have been constituted true and authentic teachers of the faith and have been made pontiffs and pastors."

Teachings such as the foregoing are largely responsible for the Catholic faithful believing that it is the clergy—not the members—who are indwelt by the Holy Spirit. Every believer, at the moment of expressed faith in Christ, is indwelt by God's Holy Spirit. And nothing in Scripture can be found to support the claim that bishops are the ones who have been given this privilege, or given it in greater measure.

The Apostle Peter referred to himself as an "elder" not as one who was taking "the place" of Christ Himself. He admonished those who would come after him not to "lord" it over the flock of God. At Lystra, when the Lyaconians wanted to worship Paul and Barnabas as gods, the two men were horrified. Their reaction is recorded in the Book of Acts as follows: *"...when the apostles, Barnabas and Paul, heard of, they rent their clothes, and ran in among the people, crying out and saying, Sirs, why do ye these things? We also are men of like passions with you and preach unto you that ye should turn from these vanities unto the living God, which made heaven, and earth, and the sea, and all things that are therein."* (Acts 14:14,15)

There is no hierarchy placed between believers and the Father in heaven in the entire New Testament. We the believers are the "priests" of the New Covenant. ***"Ye also, as lively stones, are built up a spiritual house, an holy priesthood to offer up spiritual sacrifices, acceptable to God by Jesus Christ."*** (1 Pe 2:5) A few verses later, we read: ***"...ye are a chosen generation, a royal priesthood an holy nation, a peculiar people; that ye should shew forth the praises of him who hath called you out of darkness into his marvellous light."*** (1 Pe 2:9) Peter, himself a Jew, knew the Levitical priesthood was ended.

The Apostle, Paul, who was NOT ORDAINED by the other Apostles but was directly called and ordained by God Himself, would write in the Book of Romans: ***"I beseech you therefore, brethren, by the mercies of God, that ye present your bodies a living sacrifice, holy, acceptable unto God, which is your reasonable service."*** (Rom 12:1) As priests of the New Covenant, we believers are constrained by the Word of God to conduct ourselves in such a way—by the power of the indwelling Holy Spirit—that we become living sacrifices pleasing to the God who has forgiven our sins and granted us eternal life. Moreover, we are not to consider ourselves in any way superior to others. ***"For I say, through the grace given unto me, to every man that is among you, not to think of himself more highly than he ought to think; but to think soberly, according as God hath dealt to every man the measure of faith.*** (Rom 12:3) Every believer, repeat, every believer, has been given the measure of saving faith that fits him or her for fellowship with God. **No one is more saved than another**. Therefore, no one is more of a New Covenant "priest" than another, no matter what Rome claims and teaches.

Catholic apologetics thrives on compound-complex sentences composed of high-sounding words and phrases aimed—it seems—at impressing rather than informing the reader. Unfortunately, theirs are the words of sinful men, and when the Word of God is consulted, how pretentious they are shown to be, and how misleading. Scripture gives us the true, Christ-given mission of His Church, beginning with elimination of an ordained priesthood. ***"And the veil of the Temple was rent in two from the top to the bottom."*** (Mark 15:38) **Priesthood done away with!**

"Go ye into all the world and PREACH the gospel to every creature." (Mark 16:15) **MISSION: PREACH**. *"Go ye therefore, and TEACH all nations, BAPTIZING them in the name of the Father, and of the Son, and of the Holy Ghost: TEACHING them to observe all things whatsoever I have commanded you..."* (Matt 28:19,20) **MISSION: TEACH, BAPTIZE**. *"...that repentance and remission of sins should be PREACHED in His* (Christ's)

name among all nations. (Luke 24:47) **MISSION: PREACH.** *"....ye shall receive power, after that the Holy Ghost is come upon you: and ye shall be WITNESSES unto Me both in Jerusalem and in all Judaea, and in Samaria, and unto the uttermost part of the earth."* (Acts 1:8) **MISSION: WITNESS.**

Earlier it was pointed out that destruction of the Temple veil at the moment of our Lord's death signified the end of the Levitical priesthood. In the Old Covenant, the Priests acted as the go between for the people with the most-high God. They performed the daily sacrifices, prepared and immolated the various sin, transgression, peace and free-will burnt offerings. They attended to matters of the Tabernacle in the wilderness and the Temple when it was constructed in Jerusalem. They kept the candles lit in the Holiest Place, attended to the Showbread, burned incense, and so forth. Once a year the High Priest entered the Holy of Holies to make atonement for himself and the entire nation of Israel. When the Temple veil was ripped from top to bottom the need for the daily sacrifice, the yearly atonement, and all the other Old Testament sacrifices came to an end. The old Temple was obviated. The new temple was in men's hearts, Christ Himself taking up residence there.

By His death on the cross, our Lord fulfilled God's requirement of justice completely and for all time. No other sacrifice ever would be required. The offices of priest and high priest were no longer needed. Christ became the High Priest, the go-between, the intercessor, the mediator between God and men. A totally new order was needed. The Church established by Jesus was to **PREACH**, and to **TEACH**, and to **BAPTIZE**, and to be His **WITNESSES**. Thus, the early Church had no priests, no Masses, no transubstantiation, no confessionals, no sacraments at all. The mission of that Church was to spread the Gospel, not to subordinate the believers; not to dabble in the temporal matters of the state; not to build itself into a dictatorship. The titles with which the early Christians were familiar included bishop, deacon, elder and presbyter. There were no Christian priests. Bishops, elders and presbyters were equivalent to pastors. They led the worship services, preached, taught and baptized. Deacons were the workers. All were WITNESSES to the FACT of Christ's death and resurrection. No one "lorded" it over the brethren.

It is worthy of notice that the Catholic church of today ecumenizes with a wide variety of diverse denominations, including several that are a far way from Christian. The pope has been known to join "prayer" assemblages that included Hindus, Bhudists, Zoroastrians, Shintoists, and Muslims as well as other "liberal" Christian denominations. No harsh criticism of their beliefs ever is heard from Rome. But of those who hold strictly to the doctrines presented in the Word of

God, Rome has only derision and disdain. "Fundamentalists" are to be shunned; their beliefs to be ridiculed. Such public attacks on those who hold to the truth and preeminence of God's Word can only be attributed to the appealing simplicity of the original, true Christian message. To wit: Jesus was the sinless Son of God. His death on Calvary's cross atoned completely for the world's sins. His resurrection from the dead is assurance that His sacrifice satisfied God's justice. All who believe this, repent, and place their hope of salvation in Christ's atoning death have forgiveness of their sins, receive the indwelling of the Holy Spirit, and are assured of eternal life in heaven.

Such a fundamental doctrine—devoid of sacraments, indulgences, catechisms, popes, etc.—is a very real threat to a complex religion like Catholicism. And the Word of God supports the "fundamentalist" position over that of Rome. *"But I fear, lest by any means, as the serpent beguiled Eve through his subtilty, so your minds should be corrupted from the SIMPLICITY THAT IS IN CHRIST."* (2 Cor 11:3) And in the Epistle to the Galatians: *"I marvel that you are so soon removed from Him that called you into the Grace of Christ unto another gospel: which is not another; but there be some that trouble you, and would pervert the Gospel of Christ. But though we, or an angel from heaven, preach any other gospel unto you than that which we have preached unto you, let him be accursed."* (Gal 1:6-8) What gospel did Paul preach? The preceding paragraph is an accurate synopsis of it; Catholicism is a perversion of it. The roots, the very foundation, of the Catholic Church, were in the simple faith of the early Church. To understand how Catholicism has evolved into the complex, apostate church of the 21st century requires a brief look into the history of Christianity. And that will be done in the next chapter.

Before leaving the subject of the Catholic sacraments, and specifically the sacrament of Holy Orders, attention is directed to what our Lord Himself left to the Church that He established. In Ephesians we read: *"And He gave some apostles; and some, prophets (read preachers), and some, evangelists; and some, pastors and teachers; For the perfecting of the saints, for the work of the ministry, for the edifying of the body of Christ.* (Eph 4:11, 12) It is our Lord Himself Who calls men to the ministry and empowers them to preach, to teach, to evangelize and to shepherd His flock. Just as He chose the 120 in the upper room on that first Pentecost to "get the ball rolling" as it were; just as He chose Paul to carry His message to the gentiles, so He chooses men today to carry the simple message of the only true gospel to the uttermost part of the earth. That man has complicated the message of salvation is a manifestation of his sinful inclination to be his own God, making his own rules and imposing them on others. In the Church

Jesus established, WITNESSING—spreading the good news of God's provision for the saving of mankind—was its commission.

The daily sacrifice of the old covenant requiring the services of a Levitical priest was eliminated. And the only sacrifice required in the new covenant is found in Romans 12:1, quoted before and repeated here. *"I beseech you therefore, brethren, by the mercies of God, that ye present your bodies a living sacrifice, holy, acceptable unto God, which is your reasonable service."* Reasonable, indeed; considering the sacrifice of our Lord that atoned for our every sin and gives us the blessed hope of eternal bliss. Just how much of a sacrifice is it for us to—as Paul said—keep our *"bodies under"* (1 Cor 9:27) and thereby glorify our Savior?

The final sacrament of the Catholic church—once called Extreme Unction—is the Anointing of the Sick. Until recently this sacrament was only available to those who were sick unto death. To them came the priest to hear their confession, bring them the Communion wafer and anoint them with oil for their trip into eternity. Today, the sacrament is comprised of the same exact elements, but it is available to all who are seriously ill or at death's door. Originally it could be received only once in the same illness. Today it can be received often by the seriously ill. The Epistle of James encourages those who are sick to: *"…call for the ELDERS of the Church; and let them pray over him, anointing him with oil in the name of the Lord: and the prayer of faith shall save the sick, and the Lord shall raise him up; and if he have committed sins, they shall be forgiven him."* (Jas 5:14,15).

Here again, Rome ignores the Word of God and substitutes its own version of what Scripture directs. The Bible says the sick are to call for "the elders" of the Church, not for a single individual who supposedly has an "in" with God. The very Scripture the Catholic apologists love to quote so much is the very scripture that here pertains and is patently ignored. *"Verily I say unto you, whatsoever ye shall bind upon earth shall be bound in heaven; and whatsoever ye shall loose on earth shall be loosed in heaven: Again I say unto you; That if two of you shall agree on earth as touching anything that they shall ask, it shall be done for them of my Father Which is in heaven. For where TWO OR THREE are gathered together in My Name, there am I in the midst of them."* (Mat 18:18-20) When the elders—the proven devout faithful "prayer warriors" of a Bible-directed Church—are called to pray over and anoint the sick miraculous things have been known to happen. Cancers have disappeared to the confounding of physicians. People at death's door have been raised up. But when they haven't recovered, they have gone on to be eternally with the Jesus in whose blessed sacrifice they trusted for redemption.

Certainly to the faithful Catholics who accept as truth the various doctrines disseminated by Rome, the sacrament known as the Anointing of the Sick will be a source of great comfort during serious or terminal illnesses. But what a tragedy for those who have not experienced the new birth; those to whom our Lord's words *"You must be born again"* are unknown and not experienced. The unregenerate soul—no matter how moral, no matter how devout and sincere—cannot enter the Kingdom of heaven. That's not this writer's opinion. That is the Word of God. Catholics trusting in sacraments to gain them favor with God and a place in heaven are horribly deceived, desperately disillusioned, and in dire jeopardy of losing their souls.

It has been pointed out previously that good works are the RESULT of regeneration and not the way to obtain it. *"The just shall live by his faith"* (Hab 2:4), not because of, or by, his works. The Catholic sacraments as taught and as practiced are at the best self-serving good works; at their worst they are a great delusion that will condemn for all eternity the souls of those who rely on them for salvation. No Catholic with whom I have ever had contact believes that salvation is a free gift from God and can be received without participating in a single Catholic sacrament. So thoroughly indoctrinated are they with the heretical doctrine of sacraments for salvation they will not accept God's Word over the words of mere men. *"For by grace are ye saved through faith, and that not of yourselves; it is the GIFT of God, not of works lest any man should boast."* (Eph 2:8, 9)

To any dear Catholic soul who may be reading this book, I am constrained to keep repeating the fact that salvation is a GIFT. Yes, a completely FREE GIFT. You don't have to work for it. You CAN'T work for it. You receive it by FAITH in Christ's finished work on Calvary. He did the work FOR you. It is HIS love, not your good works, that assures salvation. *"For God so loved the world, that He GAVE His only begotten Son, that WHOSOEVER believeth in Him should not perish, but have everlasting life.* (John 3:16) Prior to that, He had told Nicodemus: *"...Verily, I say unto thee, Except a man be born again, he cannot see the kingdom of God."* (John 3:3)

The good news is you can be born again this very minute! How? Admit you are a sinner unable by any good works or sacraments to save yourself. Believe that Jesus atoned for every one of your past, present and future sins on Calvary's cross. Understand that nothing you do can atone for even one of your sins. Ask Him to forgive you those sins and empower you to repent of the lifestyle that has come between Him and yourself. Then call upon Jesus to save your soul and grant you eternal life. ***"For WHOSOEVER shall call upon the name of the Lord shall be saved"*** (Rom 10:13) How wonderful it would be for every dear Catholic who devoutly desires eternal life to take those simple steps into the Kingdom of God!

As this study of the Catholic sacraments comes to a close, the following brief comments are offered as both general and specific "points to remember." 1) Sacraments are "works." God's Word tells us works are the result of regeneration and not the means by which it is obtained or graces gained. 2) Sacraments as taught by Rome are supposed to "confer" a whole list of great benefits on the recipients. No justification for this belief can be found in God's Word. The effect of this teaching is to focus the recipient's attention on self-gain rather than on exalting Jesus. 3) Rome teaches that Baptism is absolutely essential for salvation. This conflicts with God's Word. The thief on the cross was not baptized. None of the Old Testament saints were baptized. From Scripture we can't even be sure Mary, our Lord's mother, ever was baptized. 4) Baptism as originally taught by Rome only removed "original sin" from the soul. But according to God's Word, we inherit from Adam a "sin nature" not the original sin itself. 5) Baptism as taught by Rome today, not only removes "original sin" but also confers the Holy Spirit. According to God's Word, the Holy Spirit indwells the believer at the very moment of belief in the merits of Christ Jesus. In the Bible, baptism is the visible act representing death, burial and resurrection of the believer into the regenerated life, 6) Confirmation as taught by Rome, originally conferred the Holy Spirit. In today's changed capacity it merely "enriches" the recipient with the Holy Spirit. Confirmation is not taught in the Bible. 7) Bread and wine, as taught by Rome, are transformed by the words of a priest into the physical body and blood of the Lord Jesus Christ. This is a prime example of twisting Scriptures to fit a doctrine. Jesus changed ordinary water into real wine. At the Passover meal He could have changed the wine into real blood. He didn't. The bread and wine at the Passover meal merely signified the sacrifice that would be made the following day, and became the elements of a memorial that would be celebrated as the "Lord's Supper" from that time forward. 8) Auricular confession as taught by Rome requires Catholics to confess verbally to a priest their serious sins so that they may receive forgiveness of them through a process called "absolution." There is no such teaching in the Bible. This was not a Catholic doctrine until 1215 AD. John's first epistle (I John 1:9) is the biblical way to confess and be forgiven. 9) Holy orders as taught by Rome confers upon men the power to take the place of Jesus and act as His surrogate in the performance of church offices. There is no such teaching in the Bible. The priesthood was eliminated by Calvary. Christ is now our High Priest. Sacrifices were eliminated by Calvary. All believers are "priests" and the only sacrifice we present is our bodies as a living sacrifice to the Lord. 10) Anointing of the sick as taught by Rome does not agree with what is ordained in the Word of God. "Elders" are to be called on to do the anointing and praying according to the Scriptures.

The object of the Catholic sacraments is to obtain benefits for self. From infancy, (Baptism) to the grave, (Anointing of the Sick) Rome has a program of works that appeals to one's selfish aims and desires, and locks an individual into Catholic church membership. None of these works have as their primary purpose the glorification of God, the exaltation of our Savior. For this reason they must be classified as "dead works" that do not lay up in heaven treasures for those who participate in them. Catholics who are relying on sacramental works to obtain salvation have the same chance of achieving it as the seven dwarfs had by the works that they performed. It's Jesus and only Jesus who's **"the Way, the Truth, the Life!"**

Sacramental rites and rituals do not "signify and make present" the grace needed for salvation. That grace is a free gift (Eph 2:8, 9) from a loving and merciful God who gave His only begotten Son (John 3:16) as the one and only source of redemption. Sacraments are simply more devilish distractions invented by sinful men to entrap and bond unsuspecting souls to a religion of works not grace. Sacraments have no saving power; only empty promises they can never fulfill. To those trusting Catholics who are depending on them for achieving salvation, may God grant a hunger to know and trust only His Word before it is eternally too late.

6

The Aposta-Seeds

"I am the Way, the Truth and the Life; no man comes to the Father but by Me."

(John 14:6)

When Catholicism as it exists in this the 21st century is viewed under the light of Biblical revelation and secular history, we wonder how it could have strayed so far from the original Church instituted by Christ. There was no pope back then, and no priesthood. There was no worship of Mary, the mother of Jesus; no "sacrifice of the Mass;" no transubstantiated bread and wine; no Purgatory; no indulgences; no sacraments. Baptism—by immersion—was for believers only, following a profession of faith that brought the indwelling of the Holy Spirit. Christ's Calvary sacrifice was memorialized and declared by participation in the "Lord's Supper." All believers were called saints, and there were no Catholics, just followers of Jesus known as "Christians." So, what went wrong? How did the doctrinal disaster of modern Roman Catholicism come about? Some of the answers to those questions are the subject of this chapter.

That the roots of Catholicism spring from the early Christian Church is a firmly established historical fact. But for the first five centuries after our Lord's resurrection and ascension there was no Catholic church as such. It was at Antioch that followers of "The Way" first were called Christians. (Acts 11:26) Thereafter all who embraced this new faith were so designated. It is true that Ignatius, (AD 67-110), bishop of Antioch, in a letter written to the Roman churches early in the second century referred to the Church as **"katholikos"** from which we get our English word "catholic." However in the Greek, **katholikos** does not designate a religious denomination. It means "universal." In his letter, Ignatius used **katholikos** to describe how the Christian Church had become universal in spite of Rome's sporadic attempts to crush it.

It is not until Augustine of Hippo, (AD 354-430) that we find the word "catholic" coming into common usage as an appellation for the Christian Church. History records the fact that Augustine's mother, Monica, prayed that he would become a "Catholic Christian." The point here is that the Catholic religion has proceeded from the Christian Church founded by Christ, and was not the original church, as clearly shown in chapter one.

In the early Church there were no denominations and no divided communities. Organization, if it could be called that, was a loose confederacy of local fellowships each headed by a bishop (pastor), or by an individual that Justin Martyr (AD 100-167) called "the president" in his description of a typical worship service of that time. After the office of bishop came the presbyters and the deacons. The latter appointed for service by the Jerusalem council in the Book of Acts, chapter six. It was these individuals who cared for the sick, looked after the widows and orphans, brought the blessed elements of bread and wine to the infirm. These offices—bishop, presbyter, and deacon—were known by other names including elder, president, director, etc., but the functions were the same. **There was no priesthood**. But even before the end of the first century, we know that efforts were underway to establish that office. In His Revelation letters to two of the Asian churches, those who even then were trying to establish a priesthood were called *"Nicolaitanes"* by Jesus. He said He "hated" their deeds and their doctrine, thereby condemning the future imposition of a clergy between Himself and His flock. APOSTA-SEED Number-One was the *"Nicolaitanes"* determination to recreate the office of priest that Christ's sacrifice had eliminated.

Very early on—within thirty years of our Lord's death, resurrection and ascension—certain men emerged whose acumen in the faith inspired other fellowships to look to them for counsel and doctrinal guidance. Until the end of the second century, remember, the New Testament that we have today was a collection of loose documents being circulated among the churches. It was quite natural, then, for newer converts in leadership positions to seek out for advice men—bishops—who had known the Apostles and been discipled by them. For example, Simeon, said to be our Lord's youngest brother, was bishop of Jerusalem until he was martyred by crucifixion in AD 107. Polycarp, (AD 69-156) bishop of Smyrna, had been a pupil of the Apostle, John, as were Ignatius, (AD?-ll0) and Papias, (AD 70-155) bishops of Antioch and Hierapolis respectively. As the various and quite numerous heresies of those early days circulated, these were the men younger, newer Christians turned to for instruction in the faith, a fact that in the long run had a deleterious effect. APOSTA-SEED Number-Two: bishops began assuming authority over other fellowships besides their own.

The first century Christian Church endured three persecutions under Nero, Domitian, and Trajan. In AD 70 the emperor Vespasian sent his successor Titus to the Holy Land where he destroyed Jerusalem and initiated the Jewish diaspora. This action served to disperse the new Christians as well, and the Gospel thereafter was carried all over the known world. With the destruction of Jerusalem, however, Rome began to emerge as the center of western Christianity simply because it was the capitol of the Roman Empire. With the rapid growth of the Church, this fact—that Rome was the head of the empire—became highly advantageous to bishops of Rome who began as early as the second century to claim for themselves preeminence over other bishops.

By his fallen nature, man respects his own ideas and opinions above all others, relishes power, loves to exercise control over others. Some will go to any lengths to achieve such goals. As early as the middle of the second century, for instance, Anicetus, bishop of Rome AD 154-158, tried imposing his will upon churches beyond his own jurisdiction. He attempted to have the Smyrna church change the date of its Easter celebration, but was soundly rebuked by Smyrna's famous bishop, Polycarp. Just one generation later, Victor, a bishop of Rome (AD 190-202) threatened to excommunicate the eastern churches for observing Easter on a date different than was observed in Rome. Polycrates who was bishop of Ephesus was not intimidated by Victor's threat; he ignored it. Irenaeus, bishop of Lugdunum, a western church, sharply renounced the ambitious Victor for meddling in Eastern Church matters that were none of his affair.

The Apostle Peter had never been considered a bishop of Rome (or a pope), until either the end of the second century or early in the third. At some point in that time period, what have been named the Pseudo Clementine Letters and Homilies made their appearance. These were the first of the fraudulent, forged documents Rome has used over the years to give credence to the office of the papacy. Included among the copious collection of documents was a letter allegedly written at Rome by Clemens Romanus to James, the Lord's brother, in Jerusalem. It is a forgery, possibly the work of a sect known as the Ebionites. In the letter, Peter is said to have been appointed by Christ to head His church, and as Peter's death was approaching, he is alleged to have appointed the writer, Clemens Romanus, to be his successor. Catholic sources have admitted that this forged, spurious, false document is the only evidence ever found connecting Peter with the office of bishop of Rome.

It was not known at the time that these documents were deliberate forgeries, so they became useful to bishops of Rome in their claims of supremacy. In the 3rd century, Calixtus, bishop of Rome AD 218-223, declared himself the successor to Peter by virtue of Matthew 16:18 which, said he, was authorization from Christ to be the sovereign ruler over all Christendom, eastern as well as western churches. For referring to himself as "bishop of bishops' he was called a usurper by the great Tertullian, bishop of Carthage. However, to use an old expression, "the fat was in the fire." APOSTA-SEED Number-Three: bishops of Rome militantly striving for Monarchial control of Christendom, supported in their claims by forged documents and misinterpreted Scripture.

It is worthy of note that of the first 55 recorded bishops of Rome, (called "popes" by the Roman Catholic church), extending from the end of the 1st century to almost the middle of the 6th century, all but four of them retained their own names. It was not until Felix IV, in AD 526 that it became common practice with bishops of Rome, (popes), to assume the names of predecessors and to identify themselves by the use of Roman numerals. The timing of this practice seems to coincide with the beginning of heavy emphasis on the importance within Christendom of "apostolic succession" as a determinant for identification of the so-called "true" Church.

At the same time certain ambitious bishops of Rome were attempting to seize control of all the churches, another seed of future church apostasy was being planted. Martyrdom became so honored and admired by Christians in the first three centuries that the tombs, possessions and especially the body parts of the martyrs became objects of veneration, and supposed sources of Holy Spirit power. This practice was a sharp departure from the Old Testament Scriptures, and was absent from the letters and documents that were being assembled into what we now know as the New Testament. But it served as the foundation for a whole set of "traditions" now cited as support for various Catholic dogmas. It led immediately to the introduction and veneration of statues, first in eastern, and subsequently in western Christendom. It was the forerunner of praying to deceased men and women of virtue instead of praying to the Father as Christ had instructed. APOSTA-SEED Number-Four: elevation of the martyred saints to a place of special honor and veneration.

In addition to ambitious bishops of Rome and a growing cult of relics and icons, a fifth seed of future Church apostasy was brought about by the Jews defamation of Mary the mother of Jesus. Judaism's contention that Mary was an unwed mother, and Jesus the product of an illicit relationship, brought to her defense those whose faith in her purity was so great that she became the "ever-virgin" before, during, and after Christ's birth. This unscriptural belief is thought by some to have originated with a sect of Jewish converts—the Nazarenes—who believed in Christ's divinity and virgin birth by the power of the Holy Spirit. In the Church of the first three centuries this myth of Mary's lifetime virginity attracted a minimum of attention. Only many hundreds of years later would that APOSTA-SEED Number-Five germinate into one of the key doctrines that identifies Roman Catholicism as the apostate church.

In the eastern branch of Christendom another early heresy about Mary was gaining adherents. Based on the fact that Christ had the natures both of God and man, eastern orthodoxy began referring to Mary as ***Theotokos***, a Greek word meaning "God bearer." This was aggressively opposed by those who said Mary was simply ***Christotokos***, the "Christ bearer." As early as the middle of the fifth century, this APOSTA-SEED Number-six would come to fruition in the acceptance of ***Theotokos*** by two church councils as the appropriate title for Mary.

The New Testament speaks of the penalties for sin, i.e. **"*The wages of sin is death*"** (Rom 6:23), and "***Whosoever was not found written in the book of life was cast into the lake of fire.***" (Rev 20:15) It preaches a message of repentance and forgiveness of sin, and encourages restitution for wrongdoing. But nowhere is found an instance of penitential works being performed to atone for sin. In the early church, believers who sinned and then sought restoration to the fellowship sometimes received from the church exceedingly severe penances. These were an invention of the churches themselves, and not biblically based. It is most likely that the purpose of such stiff penances was to bring home to the sinner the seriousness of sinning against a Holy God and the need for true repentance—that is, a turning away from sin and a turning toward the ways of the Lord. But the result produced in later centuries was an erroneous belief that such penances were a form of "payment" for sins committed. APOSTA-SEED Number-Seven: penances being thought necessary to fully satisfy for sin.

During the same first three centuries, the ideal of Christian perfection attracted certain individuals who, by voluntary celibacy and a self-imposed life of privation and suffering, sought to attain this ideal. In Matthew 19:12 our Lord said: "***...and there be eunuchs, which have made themselves eunuchs for the kingdom of heaven sake.***" He thus acknowledged that there were then, and would continue to be, individuals whose desire to please God would motivate them to forsake the worldly pleasures in a life of voluntary celibacy and self-denial. Monasticism was founded by such early Church idealists. But APOSTA-SEED Number-Eight, the seed of forced celibacy was sown by this movement.

Toward the end of the second century, some of the churches began teaching a doctrine of regeneration through baptism instead of the biblical believer's baptism. From this erroneous practice the baptism of infants evolved, and, at the same time, the door was opened to admit unregenerate individuals into church fellowships through water immersion. Collateral to this practice came disagreement within the church over the forgiveness of sins committed after baptism. One faction said sins committed after baptism could be confessed and forgiven. The other faction said sins committed after baptism could not be forgiven. Some churches insisted on baptizing only believers and on re-baptizing believers who were baptized as infants. These came to be known as Ana-Baptists, (re-baptizers). APOSTA-SEED Number-Nine: baptism becoming the vehicle rather than the visible sign of regeneration.

These that have been enumerated were by no means the sum of the total of the APOSTA-SEEDS sown in the early centuries of the Christian church. Converts from pagan religions, for instance, brought with them belief in a place after death where partly good, partly bad people could be purged of the bad and made fit for a place of bliss. By the middle ages this had grown to a belief in Purgatory. Another example, sinners who had been assigned severe penances occasionally, for one reason or other, had their penances reduced or entirely remitted. The forerunner, obviously, to the doctrine of indulgences. Fasting and dietary beliefs of the Judaizers began reappearing, and prayer beads from ancient pagan religions were introduced.

That these errant conditions and practices were occurring in early Christianity is an unfortunate fact of history. But the formation of a sound biblically based theology had to wait until all 27 "pieces" of the New Testament had been assembled into a single unit, and that didn't happen until the end of the second century. What is hard to understand, though, is how every one of the errant beliefs listed found their way into accepted "Tradition" of the Roman Catholic Church. That Catholicism has elevated this body of tradition to a position of equality with the Holy Scriptures is unconscionable. Be that as it may, by the close of the third century, the seeds of future apostasy had been sown by the "enemy" and needed only a proper climate in which to germinate and grow. That favorable climate was not long in coming.

Diocletian, Roman Emperor from AD 284-305, established a tetrarchy to rule the vast territories under Roman control. There were two having the title, Augustus—himself and Maximian—and two Caesars—Constantius and Galerius. Each had responsibility for a section of the empire. History records that Galerius, angered by the progress of Christianity within the still-pagan empire, and inflamed by the imprudent actions of certain congregants—i.e. the building of a Christian church directly across from Diocletian's palace in Nicomedia—convinced Diocletion to initiate a violent persecution of Christendom. It was the tenth, the last, and perhaps the most severe persecution of all, but it failed in its attempt to wipe out Christianity. It lasted for a decade during which Diocletian and Maximian both abdicated. In the midst of an ensuing power struggle, Galerius, who inspired the persecution, himself tired of it and ordered its cessation in AD 311 just a short time before his death.

Constantine the Great, son of Constantius, and Maxentius, son of Maximian, along with Licinius, a protege of Galerius, emerged as the three strong men surviving the dissolution of Diocletion's tetrarchy. At the Milvian Bridge outside Rome in AD 312, Constantine defeated Maxentius who lost his life by drowning in his flight to escape his conquerors. That left only Licinius as Constantine's rival for total control of the empire. A brief alliance of Constantine and Licinius resulted in the famous Edict of Milan (AD 313), which, for the first time established freedom of religion throughout the Roman Empire. Christianity was at last granted the liberty to worship without fear of reprisals and to openly proselytize. Though still a minority, Christendom was greatly benefited by the fact that Constantine, who emerged as emperor, declared himself to be a Christian and thereafter exerted a powerful influence over the churches.

He it was who convoked a Church-wide council—Nicaea—in AD 325 to deal with the Arian heresy that denied Christ's divinity, teaching that He was a created being. Constantine took to himself the title Pontifex Maximus, (Chief Priest) and assumed control of the Christian Church. He directed all of the activities and approved all of the decisions emanating from the Council of Nicaea. Before Constantine, Christendom was in the world but not of the world. It was Constantine who brought the world into Christendom and provided the climate that enabled the seeds of apostasy to germinate and grow.

At the time of that first Nicaean Council there were 1800 bishoprics in the Roman Empire. However only 318 bishops were in attendance at the Council sessions that ratified the first formal statement of Christian beliefs. Called the Nicene Creed, this document more than any other, was responsible for giving Christianity a new name—the Catholic Church. In one of the Creed's last four articles of faith the following statement was ratified: "We believe in one holy catholic and apostolic Church." The word catholic was not capitalized indicating it was meant to declare the universality of the church, and not to change its Christ-honoring name. But once the Creed found its way into general acceptance, the universal or catholic characteristic of the church emerged as its most identifiable feature. By the time Augustine became bishop of Hippo, Africa, in AD 395 or 396 the Church was sometimes referred to as the Catholic Christian church. By the seventh century it had become simply the Catholic Church. As divisions in liturgy and administration grew between the eastern and western branches of the Church, the western church became known as the Roman Catholic Church and the eastern branch as the Eastern Orthodox church.

Not only in name was the Church established by Jesus beginning to change, to drift slowly away from its foundation, but in its organization as well, for it began—first in the western branch and much later in the eastern branch—to pattern itself after the political structure of the Roman Empire. When Constantine moved the capitol of the empire from Rome to Byzantium in AD 330 and named it Constantinople, the bishop of Rome emerged as the strongest force in the western branch of the church. At the Council of Sardica, held in the middle of the 4th century and attended only by bishops of the western churches, the bishop of Rome was recognized as the supreme bishop to whom all other bishops were to be subject. Thus was begun in the church's western branch the change from a loose confederacy of local independent bodies of believers, into an amalgamation of connected bodies under the authority and control of a single dictator—a monarch—eventually the individual now called the pope.

The eastern branch of Christendom did not accept the Council of Sardica's decision awarding such far-reaching power to the bishop of Rome. Instead, the bishops of Constantinople, Antioch, Jerusalem and Alexandria in the east shared equal authority with each other and were responsible individually for their own areas. But when the empire divided at the end of the fourth century, and with the increasing preeminence of the bishop of Rome, the patriarchs (as they were called) of Antioch, Jerusalem and Alexandria came to acknowledge the bishop of Constantinople as the supreme head of the eastern branch. By the middle of the fifth century when the Council of Chalcedon (AD 451) simply confirmed their preeminence, Christendom was headed by two monarchs—the bishop of Rome in the west and the patriarch of Constantinople in the east. This most serious departure from biblical principles—the establishment of centralized authorities—was solidly in place, though still vehemently opposed, by the end of the sixth century.

Our Lord had wanted a unified church ruled from heaven by Himself, and guided by the Holy Spirit-inspired Scriptures. It was to be a spiritual body with Him as its head. Its concern was to be the souls of mankind and proclamation of the Gospel message to the four corners of the globe. It was to be separated from the temporal encumbrances of governments, existing within whatever political configuration happened to be in place, and obedient to civil authorities and laws. But with the establishment of Rome in the west and Constantinople in the east as the centers of church authority; with temporal rulers making or interfering with ecclesiastical organization and decisions, the church as it existed for the first 400 years was ended and the path to apostasy firmly staked out.

Bickering between east and west over organizational and ecclesiastical matters flourished from late in the third century until the final severance of relations that occurred in AD 1054. But because this manuscript is primarily concerned with the heresies and apostasy of the Roman Catholic church, further accounts of developments in the eastern branch must be left in the annals of history.

By the end of the fourth century, Christianity had been established as the official religion of the Roman Empire, this through the auspices of the emperor Theodocious (AD 347-395) and the result was an absolute disaster for Christendom. The church and the empire became a unified force. Unregenerate pagans found it expedient to become members of a church. The 27 books of the New Testament had been accepted as Holy Scripture, but were unavailable to the rank and file. Emperors became involved in church matters and bishops of Rome began to inject themselves into, and exercise influence in, matters of state.

Believers' baptism as practiced by the apostolic church became the baptism of regeneration. In the apostolic church baptism always followed the profession of faith and the indwelling of the Holy Spirit. Conversion—salvation—came first, then baptism as the public expression of repentance and entrance into the Body of Christ. But with the establishment of Christianity as the state religion baptism became the instrument of salvation, not the expression of it. This resulted in a rapidly expanding church, but one suddenly filled with unregenerate individuals.

Compounding the error, the practice of baptizing babies became common practice as the church sought—at the expense of sound, biblical doctrine—to assure its perpetuation. Whereas a strong centralized authority in possession of the complete New and Old Testaments could have directed Christendom into purely biblical paths, it fell instead into a pattern of accommodating early errant beliefs and practices as well as acceptance of paganized and Judaic rites and ceremonies. As the power of the bishop of Rome grew so grew the incidence of invented doctrines based on these early, errant, APOSTA-SEEDS. What amazes is the fact that most of the spurious doctrines that Rome condoned early on—though practiced on a limited scale—were not formalized until the middle ages or later.

The Lord's Supper in the early church was not shared by catechumens (aspirant converts) or individuals who were under severe penances. They were dismissed before baptized believers partook of the blessed elements. In the Latin churches, they departed when a deacon announced ***"ite missa est,"***—"you are dismissed." Thus, the first part of Christian worship services became known as the ***"missa,"*** while the last part that included the Lord's Supper was called the ***"missa fidelium,"***—service of the faithful. As the Roman Catholic Church evolved from original Christianity, drifting farther and farther from its roots, the entire worship service acquired the name "Mass." However, it took about 800 years before the Mass was changed from a communal meal into a complex drama, and transubstantiation was decreed.

A Roman poet—Virgil (BC 70-19)—had refined an ancient idea that there are three different states after death into which souls are consigned. The first, a place of happiness for good people. The second, a place of torment for bad people, and the third, a place where partly good, partly bad people could purge out the bad and eventually qualify for the place of happiness. This idea was brought into the church by pagan converts and by the fifth century believers were praying for those who had died but probably weren't good enough to make heaven on the first try. Worse yet, the veneration of martyrs evolved into worship of them by virtue of the fact that they were being prayed to by believers and trusted to respond favorably to those prayers. In the Scriptures all believers are referred to as "saints," but by the 6th century the Catholic Church was applying it only to dead believers who had lived exemplary lives. About the same time, it became popular in Catholic circles to precede prayer and worship by making the "sign of the cross." This is done by touching the forehead, breast, left shoulder and right shoulder in that order while saying the words, "In the name of the Father, the Son, and the Holy Ghost, amen."

It is well to remember that the 27 books of the New Testament had been assembled in their entirety at least as early as the last third of the second century. They had been accepted in the church as the New Testament canon by the end of the third century, (before Catholicism) and certainly were available at least to the bishops of that era. This must be true because Diocletion ordered the destruction of all Bibles as well as all Christians when he began his persecution of the church at the end of the third century. Moreover, Constantine the Great, early in the fourth century directed Eusebius to produce fifty complete Old and New Testament Bibles for him for his own use and distribution. This, history reveals, was accomplished in a remarkably short time. It is quite obvious, then, that as heretical practices and beliefs infiltrated the Church, the Word of God was not being consulted, nor was the guidance of the Holy Spirit being sought.

From history one must conclude that the quest for power and authority, both ecclesiastical and temporal, was of far greater importance to the Catholic Church hierarchy than riding herd on theology to assure compliance with God's holy Word. For instance, Leo I who was bishop of Rome in the middle of the fifth century (460-461) claimed to be "primate of all bishops," this by divine selection and appointment. So obsessed was he to have this claim validated that he took the time to convince Emperor Valentinian III to support him with a formal declaration of imperial recognition. Thereafter, Leo identified himself as the "Lord of the Whole Church." He supported a "papacy" exclusively occupied by bishops of Rome having universal authority. He it was who first advocated putting heretics to death, thereby ignoring our Lord's admonition that His followers should *"love your enemies."* (Mat 5:44.) Leo's ultimate blasphemy was the declaration that resistance to his authority was a guarantee of condemnation to an eternity in hell.

Soon after Leo I, the Western Roman Empire crumbled, (AD 476) and bishops of Rome were freed from the influence of a central civil authority. Out of the chaos that resulted with the fragmentation of the west into many small barbarian fiefdoms, subsequent "popes" were successful in forming advantageous alliances that enabled them to emerge in the dark ages as the most powerful force in the west. But not powerful enough, or perhaps not interested enough, to get the western church back on a purely biblical footing. Simony—the sale and purchase of bishoprics for large sums of money—flourished as greater powers accrued to those having the title bishop.

Early in the dark ages, an exemplary bishop of Rome, Gregory I, occupied the seat from AD 590-604. Surprisingly, although he had in actuality all of the power and authority others before and after him claimed for the bishop of Rome, he himself staunchly resisted being referred to as "Universal Bishop." When the patriarch of Constantinople applied that title to himself, Gregory said the man was "vicious" and "haughty." Nevertheless, he was immersed more in temporal matters than in those having to do with proper doctrine. It was his influence with the Lombards, the Goths and other petty kings of the time that produced the only stability Europe experienced in his day. With great zeal he attempted to correct the organizational abuses the Catholic church already was suffering. He tried in vain to eliminate simony, but did succeed in getting rid of some bishops who had purchased their office or otherwise were unfit to rule.

However, even a great man like Gregory I could not reverse the doctrinal slide of the Catholic Church into heresy and the apostasy of today. In utter disregard of the numerous cultures into which Christianity had spread, and the variety of languages spoken, the seventh century witnessed the establishment of all Catholic worship in the Latin language. That pretty well eliminated spontaneous prayer and worship on the part of the faithful and had the effect of solidifying the sharp delineation between clergy and laity. In that same seventh century the practice of permitting sinners who had been given rather harsh penances to abrogate part or all of their penance by fasting, or by the donation of valuables (read that money) to the church became popular and these abrogations became known as "indulgences." In the very next century—the eighth—belief in a real Purgatory grew in popularity, as did the worship of Mary and the "saints." The quest for and reverence of relics that had invaded the early church experienced a revival in the eighth century, and to this day every Catholic church altar contains the relics of some saint or other, and the sale of relics to the faithful remains a source of church revenue.

It was in that same century—the 8th—that the bishop of Rome, the pope as he had come to be called, became a temporal king as well as monarch of the Roman Catholic Church. Stephen II bishop of Rome, (AD 752-75 7) convinced Pepin, father of the great Charlmagne, to attack the Lombards who controlled Italy. Pepin did so, defeated them, and donated their lands—all of central Italy—to the pope. His son Charlmagne, King of the Franks and grandson of Charles Martel, confirmed the gift of Rome and central Italy to the papacy. Thus was born the temporal kingdom of the popes historically known as the Papal States. For one thousand years thereafter, Roman Catholic popes ruled and warred just like any other earthly monarch. As a reward to the great Charlmagne for confirming the papacy to be a temporal monarchy, Leo III (AD 795-816) conferred upon him the title of Roman Emperor—head of the Holy Roman Empire.

Many there were in that ninth century who still resisted the bishop of Rome's claim to have authority over the entire church. So, quite conveniently for the ambitious bishops of Rome, there came to light, in AD 857, a book containing a collection of forged documents now known as "The Isidorian Decretals." Included in them was a section called "The Donation of Constantine," The effect of these false documents was confirmation of the supremacy of the bishop of Rome, supposedly dating back to the time of Constantine the Great. Early bishops and councils were alleged to have acknowledged the divine right of the bishop of Rome to be Christendom's supreme leader. Furthermore, Constantine the Great was alleged to have granted "pope" Sylvester, (AD 314-335) the rule and authority over all the world's bishops.

Nicholas I, bishop of Rome (AD 858-867) was the first pope to wear a crown. He claimed that the Isidorian Decretals had been buried in the Roman Catholic church's archives from way back in ancient times. He attested to their authenticity and greatly benefited from them, as did his successors. According to the section entitled "The Donation of Constantine," pope Sylvester had miraculously healed the emperor of leprosy and converted him to Christianity. So grateful was Constantine that he granted to Sylvester, and his successors, supreme authority over the entire church, its bishops, its faith and its worship. In addition, Sylvester allegedly was granted supreme temporal power over Rome and the entire Western Roman Empire. (It is worthy of note however, that "pope" Sylvester was not present at the first Council of Nicaea, (AD 325) the one convoked and controlled by Constantine the Great.

The Isidorian Decretals and the Donation of Constantine, combined with the forged Pseudo Clementine Letters and Homilies of the second or third century, made it appear that the Papacy had been an established office from antiquity, endowed with supreme temporal as well as ecclesiastical authority. At the time, and for several centuries thereafter, the documents were accepted as authentic by both the supporters and the opponents of a monarchial church government. It was the revelation of these documents and their acceptance as genuine that enabled the papacy to solidify its claims to both spiritual and temporal supremacy, and to enforce those claims throughout the middle ages. After the 9th century the office of the pope has never again been in danger of revocation, not even following discovery of the forged nature of the evidence that placed it beyond opposition. By the 12th century the most powerful and the most feared man on earth was the bishop of Rome—the Pope. Kings feared him and did his bidding. He himself was king of the Papal States.

"Ye are of your father the devil, and the lusts of your father ye will do. He was a murderer from the beginning, and abode not in the truth, because there is no truth in him. When he speaketh a lie, he speaketh of his own: for he is a liar, and the father of it (John 8:44) The Isidorian Decretals, the Donation of Constantine, obviously were "not of God." They were forgeries, (read that, deceptions, lies, falsehoods) made some time between AD 750 and 800 by several Frankish authors. First exposed in the fifteenth century by Lorenzo Valla, they were confirmed as forgeries in the seventeenth century by David Blondel. They were acknowledged thereafter by the Catholic Church to be forgeries, false, spurious, just as the Pseudo Clementine Letters of the third century that had supported Papal claims made in that earlier era. At least 40 falsifications were found in letters allegedly written by "popes' Sylvester and Gregory I.

Thus, all claims for Peter as the first pope, and all claims for the papal office itself, have been based on falsehood and deception. And way back in the time of Calixtus, bishop of Rome (AD 218-223), when he claimed for himself supremacy over the church based on Matthew 16:18, the great Tertullian knew he was dishonestly interpreting God's Word. He called him a would-be usurper. During my Catholic years—as a student first, and later as an adult—none of this information ever was brought to my attention. I am afraid now that even if I had learned these things, the very thorough brainwashing I'd been subjected to in my youth would have caused me to disbelieve that my church could ever have been involved in such nefarious activities. But it was. And the apostate condition of the Catholic Church in our day is in great measure the result of it.

Nicholas I, who vouched for the integrity of the spurious documents and was the first to benefit from them, knew of a certainty they were forgeries because he stated they had been kept in the Catholic church archives from antiquity, a claim he absolutely knew to be untrue. How many of his successors were aware of the deception remains a mystery. This same papacy whose existence has been justified by such God-dishonoring mendacity is the very authority responsible for ordering or approving all of the following:

1. **Meatless Fridays under penalty of mortal sin. AD 998**
2. **Blessing water into "holy water." AD 1000**
3. **Reciting the Rosary—a pagan practice. AD 1090**
4. **Masses for the dead FOR MONEY. AD 1100**
5. **Priests forbidden to marry; celibate for life. AD 1123**
6. **Indulgences sold for MONEY. AD 1190**
7. **Initiated, supported the INQUISITION AD 1200-1800**
8. **Decreed TRANSUBSTANTIATION. AD 1215**
9. **Decreed AURICULAR CONFESSION. AD 1215**
10. **Catholic Church declared the true church. AD 1303**
11. **PURGATORY real—MONEY frees souls. AD1438**
12. **TRADITION EQUAL TO SCRIPTURE AD 1545**
13. **Salvation by WORKS. AD 1545**
14. **APOCRYPHA (spurious) added to Bible. AD 1563**
15. **Massacre of Huguenot Protestants on St Bartholomew's Day AD 1572**
16. **Decreed IMMACULATE CONCEPTION. AD 1854**

17. **Decreed PAPAL INFALLIBILITY. AD 1870**

18. **Decreed ASSUMPTION OF MARY. AD 1950**

19. **Decreed Queendom of Mary. 1965**

In addition to the heretical, extra-biblical doctrines introduced into the Roman Catholic Church under the auspices of an illegal papacy that has conferred infallibility upon itself, there is the long history of papal animosity toward God's Word—the Bible. As pointed out in a previous chapter, the Catholic Catechism claims that the Catholic Church, as the one and only true church, has been entrusted with the Scriptures and exercises sole authority over their interpretation. Yet as far back as the reign of Gregory VII (Hildebrand, AD 1073-1085) Rome has attempted to keep the Scriptures out of the hands of the faithful. Innocent III (1198-1216), Gregory IX (1227-1241), Paul IV (1555-1559), Clement XI (1700-1721), Leo XII (1821-1829), Pius VIII (1829-1830), Gregory XVI (1831-1846) and Pius IX (1846-1878) all were popes who sought to limit or, in one way or another, deny the reading of God's Word by the Catholic faithful.

This animosity toward the Word of God continues to this day, for even the Catholic priests—in an oath taken before ordination—give up their personal freedom to interpret the Scriptures, promising to abide by whatever meaning Rome extracts from them. The path to the apostasy of the Roman Catholic Church has been marked by the incorporation over the centuries of numerous heresies not biblically supported. But the single most crucial step in the direction of apostasy—the most damaging departure from the Word of God—has been the concentration of power, the concentration of authority, in the hands of a mere man called "the pope," and his associates. Jesus never meant that to be. The Scriptures make that very clear. *"Ye also, as lively stones, are built up a spiritual house, an holy priesthood to offer up spiritual sacrifices, acceptable to God by Jesus Christ."* (1 Pet 2:5) *"But ye are a chosen generation, a royal priesthood an holy nation, a peculiar people; that ye should shew forth the praises of him who hath called you out of darkness into his marvellous light;"* (1Pet 2:9) *"I beseech you therefore, brethren, by the mercies of God, that ye present your bodies a living sacrifice holy, acceptable unto God, which is your reasonable service."* (Rom 12:1)

In Our Lord's plan, all believers were—and still are—meant to be "priests," offering our bodies willingly as sacrifices to God along with the praises of our lips. No pope was needed. Only the Holy Scriptures, carried to the faithful by pastors and preachers. Only the guidance and teaching of the indwelling Holy Spirit.

Only the immersion in water to express publicly our trust in Jesus and His acceptance of us into the Body of Christ. Only the confession—privately and directly to God—of our sins committed after conversion. Only the celebration of the Lord's Supper to memorialize and proclaim Christ's death until His return. Only the love of one another to show ourselves His disciples. No frills. No ostentation. No sacraments. No rosaries, scapulars or miraculous medals. No Purgatory. No indulgences. No votive candles in front of statues. No statues. No monarch. No hierarchy at all.

Any church, religion, or individual human being who forsakes, twists, adds to or takes from the Holy Word of God can go just one way—into heresy and apostasy. The seeds of the same were planted long ago in the very early days of Christianity. Scriptures misunderstood, misinterpreted, ignored, or perhaps unknown, gave rise to man-made traditions, commandments and organization, all in opposition to God's Word. The Roman Catholic Church could have and should have led the way back to biblical Christianity. Instead, Rome adopted and fostered—even initiated—false doctrines that make it the apostate church of today. Moreover, in spite of what the Catholic Church teaches and commands, all it takes to become a child of the living God is to acknowledge one's sinfulness and the holiness of God, request and accept His forgiveness of one's sins, repent—that is turn away from one's past lifestyle—then trust the Lord Jesus to keep His promise of indwelling by His Holy Spirit and eternal life in His presence.

As I write this manuscript it is my understanding that Pope Pius IX (AD 1846-1878) is being considered by the Roman Catholic curia for elevation to the status of "saint of the church." A brief history of his pontificate will enable you to make your own decision as to this man's worthiness for such a high—though spiritually bankrupt—honor. Pius IX is the pope who unilaterally proclaimed the Immaculate Conception of Mary to be a must-believe doctrine. He it was who a few years later declared that popes are infallible when speaking about matters of faith and morals. He declared it acceptable to suppress heresy and heretics by force. *"But I say unto you, Love your enemies, bless them that curse you, do good to them that hate you, and pray for them which despitefully use you, and persecute you."* (Mat 5:44) He condemned the separation of church and state, commanding Catholics to obey the pope over civil authorities. *"Submit yourselves to every ordinance of man for the Lord's sake: whether it be to the king, as supreme; Or unto governors, as unto them that are sent by him for the punishment of evildoers, and for the praise of them that do well For so is the will of God, that with well doing ye may put to silence the ignorance of foolish men:"* (1 Pet 2:13) Pius IX denounced freedom of conscience, worship, speech and the press. He condemned Bible Societies. **"Heaven and earth shall pass away, but my words shall not pass away."** (Mat 24:35) **"So then faith cometh by hearing, and hearing by the word of God.** (Rom 10:17) **"Verily, verily, I say unto you, He that heareth my word and believeth on him that sent me, hath everlasting life, and shall not come into condemnation; but is passed from death unto life."** (John 5:24) He it was who proclaimed Protestantism to be "no form of the Christian religion," and he declared that "Every dogma of the Roman Catholic church has been dictated by Christ through His vice regents (read that popes) on earth." But none of the Catholic dogmas are supported in God's holy Word which carries the following admonition: **"For I testify unto every man that heareth the words of the prophecy of this book, If any man shall add unto these things, God shall add unto him the plagues that are written in this book."** (Rev 22:18)

According to 19th century priest, Charles Chiniquy, Pius IX was a notorious violator of his vow of celibacy. In chapter 11 of his book, *"The Priest, the Woman, and the Confessional,"* Chiniquy says visitors to Rome in his day would be shown the two beautiful daughters Pius IX sired with two of his mistresses. He adds that the names of five other mistresses—three of them nuns and all from Pius IX's days as a priest and bishop—were well known to Italian Catholics.

The seeds of apostasy were sown early on. The evolution of apostolic Christianity into the Roman Catholic Church, following the reign of Constantine the Great, watered and nourished those seeds into the fruit of today's full fledged apostasy. It is an apostasy that denies the Jesus of Scripture, teaching in His place a Jesus who failed in His assigned mission; a Jesus who is—in our day—still occupied with the work of redemption, and shares with others His advocacy with the Father. How sad for the millions of Roman Catholics, past and present, who have and are placing their trust for eternal life on the words of men—the commandments and promises of men—rather than on the sweet Words of the King of Glory.

"Come unto me, all ye that labour and are heavy laden, and I will give you rest." (Mat 11:28) Our Lord told us to come to Him, not to a priest or a pope. He said we would find rest in Him, not in religion or the commandments of men. **"Take my yoke upon you, and learn of me; for I am meek and lowly in heart: and ye shall find rest unto your souls."** (Mat 11:29) The pope wears a jeweled crown. Jesus wore a crown of thorns. The pope lives opulently in a palace. Jesus **"had not where to lay His head."** (Mat 8:20) The pope is attended by a battery of servants. Jesus came as a servant to do His Father's will. (Mat 12:18)

The pope looks down upon his subjects from a majestic throne. Jesus looked down upon sinners from an old rugged cross. Of the two, which is "meek," and "lowly in heart?" *"For my yoke is easy, and my burden is light."* (Mat 11: 30) The pope has bound upon the faithful a heavy yoke of works that cannot bring salvation. Our Lord's yoke is simple requiring nothing more than faith in His sacrifice, trust in His promises, obedience to His Word.

"The kingdom of heaven is likened unto a man which sowed good seed in his field: But while men slept, his enemy came and sowed tares among the wheat, and went his way." (Mat 13:25) Early on Satan sought destruction of Christ's legacy through direct attack—persecution. When this strategy failed, he found a better way—subterfuge. With great effectiveness, he sowed the seeds of apostasy in a Christendom that was in its infancy and vulnerable to "doctrines of devils." (1 Tim 4:1) Catholicism—the Roman Catholic Church—is the shameful result.

7

The Sacrifice That Isn't

"But this man, after He had offered one sacrifice for sins forever, sat down on the right hand of God." (Heb 10:12)

Nowhere else is the conflict between Roman Catholic doctrine and the Word of God as readily apparent and as severely pronounced as in the so-called "Holy Sacrifice of the Mass." In the liturgy of Catholicism the Mass is the central element of worship. It is called a "sacrifice" because during the course of it, our Lord supposedly is offered up anew. He is, as it were, sacrificed again in a re-presentation of His death on Calvary's cross. And, since there are nearly a billion adherents of the Roman Catholic religion, this sacrificing of Himself goes on twenty four hours a day as Masses are conducted all around the globe. It is very likely that every minute of the 1440 minutes in a day, Christ—according to Roman Catholic doctrine—is being offered up literally on dozens of altars.

I am not at all sure that the majority of Catholics understand what the Mass really is all about. I know that as a youth raised and educated in the religion I could not have explained to anyone the real essence of the Mass. To me it was what you went to on Sunday and Holy Days as commanded by the church. (It is a mortal sin to deliberately miss Mass on Sunday or Holy Days.) It was conducted as follows: The priest, assisted by one or more acolytes (I was one of the latter) said and read a lot of prayers. He blessed the congregation several times with the words ***"dominus vobiscum"*** which translated means "The Lord be with you." (Latin was the language of the Mass in those days.) At a part known as the "Offeratory" he filled a gold cup called a "chalice" with wine and water; then said prayers over the cup and a round white wafer about two inches in diameter called a "host." The wafer lay on a gold metal plate—a "paten".

Shortly after reciting aloud the "Pater Noster"—Latin for the "Our Father"—he leaned over the host and said ***"Hoc est enim corpus meum,"***—"Truly, this is my body." These words supposedly changed the host into the physical flesh of Jesus. Then he leaned over the cup filled with the wine/water mixture and said

"Hic est enim calix sanguinis mei,"—"Truly, this cup is my blood." These words supposedly changed the wine/water mix into the physical blood of Jesus. He lifted both the host and the cup up over his head for the people to see. Shortly thereafter he consumed the host—Christ's alleged body—and drank the wine—Christ's alleged blood.

Then he unlocked a little cubicle in the middle of the altar called a "tabernacle," and took out a large, covered, gold cup called a "ciborium." It was filled with dozens of hosts, much smaller than the one he had consumed. These, through the words of "consecration" spoken by the priest, were supposed also to have become the flesh of Jesus. As he was removing the ciborium cover, people began filing out of their pews, coming to kneel at the altar railing. The priest then proceeded to pass out to each person at the railing one of the little hosts, placing it gently on the person's extended tongue. As he did so he whispered each time, **"Corpus Christi,"**—"Body of Christ." (Since Vatican II, congregants have the choice of receiving the host only or both the host and the wine; and in America, English is now the language of the Mass.) People who received one of the little round hosts believed they had received the actual body of Jesus under the appearance of bread. They went back to their pews to pray and reverently contemplate this great mystery that brought Jesus physically into their mortal bodies. In a matter of maybe a whole minute, the little host had dissolved in the mouth—we were forbidden to chew it—and had entered the alimentary canal on its way to being digested.

The rest of the service took about six or seven minutes at the most. The priest put the ciborium with the hosts back in the tabernacle and locked it up. He said a few more prayers, washed the wine chalice and shined the paten, then turned to the people and said **"Ite Missa est,"** which in English means, "You are dismissed." Apparently the presence of Jesus inside the folks who had received communion was also ended, for the congregation filed out and went their way, satisfied that they had complied with the church's command to attend Mass once a week on Sunday. Jesus had come inside them for a few minutes, but now they were back to themselves alone and could proceed with their lives. I am convinced that 8 out of 10 Catholics from my era would agree that the foregoing is a pretty accurate synopsis of the Holy Sacrifice of the Mass as performed in those days. However, not one of them would have believed that Christ's Calvary sacrifice, His suffering and death on Golgotha' s rocky hill, had just taken place all over again before their very eyes. But that, in fact, is exactly what the Roman Catholic

Church teaches. The 1994 Catechism says on page 335 the Mass is called The Holy Sacrifice...

> "...because it makes PRESENT the one sacrifice of Christ the Savior...and it COMPLETES and SURPASSES all the sacrifices of the Old Testament." (Emphasis mine.)

Inasmuch as Christ's "one sacrifice" entailed His physical death, and in the Mass that same sacrifice allegedly is "present"—actually happening all over again—then the sole purpose of the Mass, it seems, is to "slay" the Lord Jesus anew. All of the Old Testament sacrifices demanded the death of the victim or destruction of the oblation offered. Therefore, inasmuch as the Mass is said to "complete" and even "surpass" all the Old Testament sacrifices, surely it slays the Lord Jesus all over again. Well, not exactly. Catholic theology says, YES, the Mass is a Holy Sacrifice, but NO, the victim—Jesus—is not slain. His real flesh and His real blood, under the appearance of bread and wine, are consumed by both the priest and the congregants, but He is not slain. The Holy Sacrifice of the Mass, then, is the SACRIFICE THAT ISN'T. Are you just a bit confused? Read what is stated in the Baltimore Catechism about the Mass:

> 263. Q. What is the Mass?
> A. The Mass is the unbloody sacrifice of the body and blood of Christ.
> 264. Q. What is a sacrifice?
> A. A sacrifice is the offering of an object by a priest to God alone, and the *consuming of it* to acknowledge that He is the Creator and Lord of all things.
> 265. Q. Is the Mass the same sacrifice as that of the Cross?
> A. The Mass is the same sacrifice as that of the Cross.
> 266. Q. How is the Mass the same sacrifice as that of the Cross?
> A. The Mass is the same sacrifice as that of the Cross because the offering and the priest are the same—Christ our Blessed Lord; and the ends for which the sacrifice of the Mass is offered are the same as those of the sacrifice of the Cross.
> 268. Q. Is there any difference between the sacrifice of the Cross and the sacrifice of the Mass?
> A. Yes; the manner in which the sacrifice is offered is different. On the Cross Christ really shed His blood and was really slain; in the Mass there is no real shedding of blood nor real death, because Christ can die no more; but the sacrifice of the Mass, through the separate consecration of the bread and the wine, represents His death on the Cross.

This information tells us that the mass is exactly the same sacrifice as our Lord's sacrifice on Calvary, except that it's not exactly the same because it's an unbloody sacrifice; and it really isn't a sacrifice, either, because the victim—although fully consumed—is not put to death. This kind of hocus-pocus is unworthy of the loving God who gave His only begotten Son to be punched, kicked, beaten and nailed to a cross for our justification. Stripped of Rome's verbal trickery and trappings, the Catholic Mass is nothing more than an elaborate ceremony constructed around what was the Lord's Supper—a communal meal—in the early church. It is the flashy vehicle that carries the faithful to consumption of some unleavened bread and fermented wine that they have been told was turned into the actual flesh and blood of Christ. Moreover, the claims made for the Mass and the Eucharist are a Scriptural disaster. On Catechism page 336 we read that the Mass is:

"the liturgy in which the mystery of salvation is accomplished…"

The mystery of salvation—that is, the atonement for the sins of the whole world—was accomplished by Jesus on Calvary's cross. Our Lord said: *"It is finished!"* (John 19:30) Nothing that Jesus came to do was left undone. *"I have glorified thee on the earth: I have finished the work which thou gayest me to do."* (John 17:4) The mystery of salvation—man's reconciliation to God through Christ's death on the cross—was completed at Calvary, never to be repeated again. The mystery of salvation is not a work in progress. It's a finished work; the liturgy of the Catholic Mass is not accomplishing it. Faith and faith alone in Christ's one-time, never-to-be-repeated sacrifice personalizes the mystery to each and every believer: *"To whom God would make known what is the riches of the glory of this mystery among the Gentiles; which is Christ in you, the hope of glory."* (Col 1:27)

Believers need not attend Mass to receive the Lord Jesus. He indwells them through His Holy Spirit at the very moment He is embraced as Lord and Savior. He remains in them—not for a few minutes—but for life. *"Know ye not that ye are the temple of God, and that the Spirit of God dwelleth in you?"* (1Co 3:16) It has been said before, and it definitely bears repeating often that the Catholic Jesus is not the Jesus of the Bible. The Catholic Jesus has left "works" for the Catholic Church and its members to do. Going to Mass every Sunday and holy day of obligation is one of the works they must do till "the mystery of salvation is accomplished." What a blessing it is to serve the Jesus of the Bible who left nothing to be done but to believe and trust in Him.

Over the ages, Rome has become expert at making claims. They dress them up in compound-complex sentences to give them an authoritative ring, then throw in an apparent endorsement from an early-church saint for an air of authenticity. An excellent example of this is found on page 339 of the 1994 Catechism where it is claimed that the "Eucharistic celebration"—read that the Mass—is about the same today as it was in the second century church.

> **"From that time** (of the apostles) **on down to our own day the celebration of the Eucharist has been continued so that today we encounter it everywhere in the Church with the '***same fundamental structure.***' As early as the second century we have the witness of St. Justin Martyr (c.100-165) for the basic lines of the order of the Eucharistic celebration. They *have stayed the same* until our own day for all the great liturgical families."**

Rome cites as support for these claims a letter written by Justin Martyr to emperor Antoninus Pius in the middle of the second century. In it he describes the Christian worship service of that period. Following is a synopsis of what that letter relates.

The worship of the early church was simply a gathering together in one place of believers from both the city and the suburbs. The first order of business was readings from the "memoirs" of the Apostles who had been with Jesus. (These memoirs became our New Testament.) Then came more readings, these from the Old Testament, usually the Prophets. Following the readings, the "president" of the gathering gave what today we call a "sermon." Then came a period of prayer in which all in the group participated. Greetings and fellowship came next, followed by the celebration of the Lord's Supper. In this early Church celebration, someone provided bread and a mixture of water and wine. Prayers of praise and thanksgiving for God's generosity and soul-saving grace then were offered up by the president, after which the group partook of the bread and wine,(not the body and blood) and those called deacons took some to the believers not able to be present.

In Justin Martyr's description of an early church service a lot is missing that Rome includes in the Mass of the 21st century. There is no mention of a "Mass." There is no mention of a "priest." There is no mention of the bread and wine/water mix changing into the actual body and blood of our Lord. There is no mention of a "sacrifice." There is no mention of sins being forgiven by the act of eating the bread and drinking the wine. There is no mention of special garments worn by the person presiding. There is no indication participants believed their "Eucharistic celebration" contributed in any way to the work of redemption that was completed by Christ on Calvary. So how can Rome conclude that today's Mass has STAYED THE SAME in its FUNDAMENTAL STRUCTURE as the worship service in which the early Christians engaged? Such nonsense! And Rome gets away with it because the faithful are too cowed or too lazy to investigate.

These kinds of claims are no more and no less than vain attempts by Rome apologists to revise history; to give the Catholic Church an appearance of antiquity. The importance of this to Rome cannot be over emphasized. As seen in chapter 1, without evidence that it is the one true church founded by Christ, with roots extending all the way back into the first century and the days of the Apostles, the Roman Catholic Church is just one more denomination making empty claims of preeminence over all other denominations. But any comparison of the Roman Catholic Mass of today with the worship service of early Christians shows them to be about as similar as a jellyfish and a giraffe.

According to the Didache, an early second century chronicle of—among other things—church practices, the observance of the Lord's Supper was a fellowship meal memorializing Christ's Calvary sacrifice. The elements of bread and wine were part of a thanksgiving celebration and came to be known as the Eucharist from the Greek word, eucharistia, which means "thanksgiving." In those first centuries of Christianity, long before it evolved into the Roman Catholic Church, participants in the Lord's Supper considered it both a remembrance and a preview; a remembrance of Christ's death, and a preview of the heavenly banquet awaiting all believers.

The whole mood of early Christian participation in the Lord's Supper was one of joy, as if they were already sitting down with Our Lord at the soon-expected Marriage Supper of the Lamb. (Rev 19:9) At no time was this joyful event considered a "sacrifice," nor were the elements of bread and wine considered to be the actual flesh and blood of the Lord Jesus. It was not until the middle ages, after the emergence of Roman Catholicism, that the transubstantiation doctrine was decreed.

In actuality, the present day Catholic Mass is a product of evolution occurring through several centuries. John Knox, sixteenth century preacher of the Gospel and leader of the Reformation in Scotland, attributed its existence in his day to the influence and additions of four different popes spanning several centuries. Sixtus III, bishop of Rome AD 432-440, is credited with the establishment within basilicas of the "altar" where the elements of bread and wine were blessed. These were not stone altars initially, but merely wooden tables. (The original basilicas were meeting halls and had no altars.) Felix IV, (AD 526-530) set the altar aside as a holy place to be used exclusively for blessing the Eucharistic elements prior to distribution and consumption. His successor, Boniface II (AD 530-532) came up with altar coverings—now three linen cloths—and then Gregory I (AD 590-604) in his early 7th century reforms added the candles, tabernacle for the blessed elements, and the vestments worn by priests. These, however, were simply cosmetic changes, and it is safe to say that the original celebration of the Lord's Supper as a communal meal survived at least into the eighth century. In his "**Compact History of the Catholic Church**," author Alan Schreck claims the Mass did not change from a communal meal into a drama until the 12th century. This is plausible when it is remembered that the doctrine of transubstantiation was not decreed until the fourth Lateran Council in AD 1215.

A woefully small number of Catholics actually "read" the Word of God. Therefore they have no idea how extensively their religion has been influenced by Old Testament Jewish customs and rituals. For example, the Jewish temple had an altar on which the sacrifices were immolated. Every Catholic Church has an altar for carrying out the "sacrifice." The temple sacrifices were performed by priests. The Catholic Mass is conducted by a priest. The Jewish priests were adorned with special garments. The garments worn by the Catholic priests are almost identical to those worn by the Jews. The Jewish temple had a tabernacle—the Holy of Holies—where God dwelt above the Mercy Seat and the Ark of the Testimony. This area was off limits except to the high priest who was permitted to enter once each year. The tabernacle in the Catholic Church contains the hosts that supposedly have been turned into the body of Jesus. It is supposedly the place where God dwells. Only the priest has access to this Holy of Holies. It is off limits to the laity. The temple had candelabra, so does the Catholic Church. The temple had a Mercy Seat; the Catholic Church has the New Covenant equivalent, a crucifix. To deny that Judaism has had a profound influence on Catholicism is to ignore history.

Even the Lord's Supper as celebrated by the early church succumbed to the influence of the Judaizers, evolving—from a simple, easily understood commemoration of our Blessed Lord's sacrifice, and a joy-filled preview of the Marriage Supper of the Lamb—into an elaborate, alleged re-sacrifice of our Savior, that really isn't a sacrifice at all because the victim is not slain. This so-called "unbloody sacrifice" purports, among other things...

"To perpetuate the sacrifice of the cross throughout the ages."

That claim appears on page 334 of the 1994 Catechism. But what is the purpose of "perpetuating Christ's sacrifice throughout the ages"? The Scriptures over which Rome claims exclusive interpretive authority are quite emphatic in their affirmation that Jesus "paid it all." He left nothing undone. And gave us His own assurance of this when, on Calvary's cross, He exclaimed, *"It is FINISHED!"* Not so, say the great minds of the Roman Church. Quoting again from their own book—the Catechism, page 343:

"...as often as the sacrifice of the cross (the Mass)**...is celebrated on the altar, the WORK OF OUR REDEMPTION IS CARRIED OUT."**

Just as the Catholic faithful never can be sure of their own personal salvation, their church can never be assured that the "work of redemption" is a completed work, accomplished once and for all by our Lord on Calvary's cross. Else, why this daily carrying out the "work of redemption"? And, for heaven's sake, how many more years of thousands upon thousands of Masses every day will it take to complete the work of redemption to Rome's satisfaction? Confusion reigns.

"For God is not the author of confusion, but of peace, as in all churches of the saints." (1Co 14:33) On the one hand Rome says we have been redeemed by Christ's sacrifice. On the other hand Rome says redemption is an ongoing, daily—many times daily—work in progress. Which is it? It cannot be both. Either our Lord did it or it's still being done. One, or the other. Either He died once, or He has to keep offering Himself up. Either Christ paid our sin debt on Calvary or He has to keep paying daily for our sins, and will be required to do so until the last Mass is ended.

As a Catholic, this incredible contradiction never came to my attention. Like all "good" Catholics, I accepted the Mass as our form of worship and never questioned the rationale behind it. The "Holy Sacrifice of the mass" was a phrase to me. Whether redemption was complete, or an ongoing program, never occurred to me because I was "working" my way to heaven. But the Word of God is very clear on the matter: *"Who* (Jesus) *needeth not daily as those high priests, to offer up sacrifice, first for his own sins, and then for the people's: for this he did once when he offered up himself."* (Heb 7:27) *"Neither by the blood of goats and calves, but by his own blood he* (Jesus) *entered in once into the holy place, having obtained eternal redemption for us."* (Heb 9:12) *"So Christ was once offered to bear the sins of many; and unto them that look for him shall he appear the second time without sin unto salvation."* (Heb 9:28)

More Confusion *"If we confess our sins, he is faithful and just to forgive us our sins, and to cleanse us from all unrighteousness."* (l John 1:9) In the early Church, celebration of the Lord's Supper was a memorial of Christ's sacrifice and not a sacrifice in itself. It was a truly joyful acknowledgement that Jesus had secured for us on Calvary the forgiveness of our sins; it was not considered a vehicle for conveying that forgiveness. But Rome's replacement for the Lord's Supper—the Mass—claims to be a sacrifice, a means of unity with Jesus, and a vehicle conveying the forgiveness of sins. The "sacrifice" occurs when the bread and wine, supposedly turned by the priest into the actual body and blood of Christ, is consumed by the priest and then distributed for consumption to the congregants. This consumption of the elements, supposedly brings about the CLEANSING of their sins. Read Rome's teaching from Catechism page 351.

> **"Holy Communion separates us from sin. The body of Christ we receive in Holy Communion** (the sacrifice) **is 'given up for us,' and the blood we drink 'shed for the many for the forgiveness of sins.' For this reason the Eucharist cannot** *unite us to Christ* **without at the same time** *cleansing us from past sins* **and preserving us from future sins."** (Emphasis mine.)

As a trusting Catholic I never would have questioned the above. As a born again Christian I must. How, I want to know, can ingesting a little round wafer unite me to the One Who already lives inside of me twenty-four hours of every day? *"Know ye not that ye are the temple of God, and that the Spirit of God dwelleth in you?"* (1 Co 3:16) When our Lord was preparing His Apostles for His departure, this is what He promised them: *"I will pray the Father, and he shall give you another Comforter, that he may abide with you for ever Even the Spirit of truth; whom the world cannot receive, because it seeth him not, neither knoweth him: but ye know him; for he dwelleth with you and shall be IN you. I will not leave you comfortless: I will come to you.*" (John 14:16-18)

Something is radically wrong here. The Word of God tells us that the Holy Spirit (of Jesus) indwells us at the moment we come to trust Christ as our Savior. *"For by one Spirit are we all baptized into one body, whether we be Jews or Gentiles, whether we be bond or free; and have been all made to drink into one Spirit.*" (1 Co 12:13) Scripture also tells us that the indwelling of the Holy Spirit is THE MARK of the child of God *"But ye are not in the flesh, but in the Spirit, if so be that the Spirit of God dwell in you. Now if any man have not the Spirit of Christ, he is none of his."* (Rom 8:9) But the Holy Spirit was not to be given until after our Lord's ascension into heaven, until after His physical departure from earth. *"Nevertheless I tell you the truth; It is expedient for you that I go away: for if I go not away the Comforter will not come unto you; but if I depart, I will send him unto you."* (John 16:7)

Rome says Jesus is physically present in the elements of bread and wine; that these actually are the physical body and blood of Jesus. The Bible says the physical presence of Jesus is in heaven; that He is sitting at the right hand of the Father. (Heb 1:3, 8:1) Rome says that those who receive Communion are united with Christ and are cleansed from past sins. The Bible says a true child of God is INDWELT by the Holy Spirit of Christ, (Rom 8:9) and that the physical presence of Jesus and the spiritual presence of His Holy Spirit will not occur at the same time on earth. (John 16:7.) Contradicting its own teachings about the sacrament of Penance, Rome says cleansing from sins is the natural result of uniting with Christ in communion. The Bible says cleansing from sin results when we acknowledge them in confession directly to God. (I John 1:9) Rome says the Mass is a reenactment of our Lord's sacrifice, and at the same time, it's a memorial of that sacrifice. (Unexplained, is how something happening in the present is a memorial of itself.) The Bible says Christ's sacrifice was a one-time event, (Heb 9:12) and the Lord's Supper is a memorial only, a proclamation of our Lord's death until His return. (l Cor 11:26) These are critical differences in Catholic and Biblical doctrines. There is no way to reconcile them.

In a comparison of what Rome says versus what God's divine Word says, only one conclusion is possible—the "Holy Sacrifice of the Mass" is no sacrifice at all. It's an elaborate charade performed by men who have no more power to "speak" Jesus into a bit of unleavened bread or a cup of wine than Satan does. Scripture says through the Lord's Supper we are to ***"show the Lord's death till He come.*** (I Cor 11:26) It does not tell us that He comes, and keeps coming, every time some mere mortal dons some fancy clothing and intones words that Jesus spoke prior to His one-time-only Calvary sacrifice.

The Catholic Mass is a stage play put on by deceived actors for a misled audience. And it is adaptable to virtually any purpose. In one case, Christ is "sacrificed" in a marriage ceremony; in another, He is "sacrificed" at someone's death. He is "sacrificed" to get souls out of a Purgatory that doesn't exist, or for someone's own personal intentions. Only rarely, is He **not** "sacrificed" for money. For the Catholic faithful, attending Mass and receiving communion are merely a couple of the "dead works" referred to in Hebrews 6:1. They are meaningless; may even be the ultimate cause of eternal punishment in hell. How can I, myself a former Catholic, be so sure of this? My assurance—and the assurance for any interested practicing Catholic—is contained in the precious Word of God that Rome has tried so diligently to keep away from its faithful.

In the Old Testament, before Christ's blood was shed to expiate the sins of the whole world, the Levitical priests had to offer a daily sacrifice for their own sins and the sins of the nation of Israel. But the coming of our Lord, the promised Messiah, did away with the Old Testament and established a new one. *"And for this cause he is the mediator of the new testament, that by means of death, for the redemption of the transgressions that were under the first testament, they which are called might receive the promise of eternal inheritance."* (Heb 9:15) By our Lord's death on Calvary the first thing done away with was the daily sacrifice and the need for men set apart as priests to offer it. The blood of goats and bulls and calves shed in those Old Testament sacrifices was merely a foreshadowing of the ultimate sacrifice—Jesus—who was to eliminate once and for all man's efforts to "save" himself. *"Neither by the blood of goats and calves, but by his own blood he entered in ONCE into the holy place, having obtained eternal redemption for us."* (Heb 9:12) Obviously, redemption is NOT a work in progress. As the perfect *"Lamb of God which taketh away the sin of the world,"* (John 1:29) our Lord by His willing sacrifice settled the sin matter for all time. He would not have to do it again—ever.

"For Christ is not entered into the holy places made with hands, which are the figures of the true; but into heaven itself, now to appear in the presence of God for us: Nor yet that he should offer himself often as the high priest entereth into the holy place every year with blood of others; For then must he often have suffered since the foundation of the world: but now in the end of the world hath he appeared to put away sin by the sacrifice of himself. And as it is appointed unto men once to die, but after this the judgment: So Christ was ONCE offered to bear the sins of many; and unto them that look for him shall he appear the second time without sin unto salvation." (Heb 9:24-28) Obviously, He is not being offered daily as Rome claims.

All sin was to be judged in Christ through a single once-for-ever-sacrifice, willingly endured by our Lord. *"Then said he,* (Jesus) *Lo, I come to do thy will, O God. He taketh away the first, that he may establish the second. By the which will we are sanctified through the offering of the body of Jesus Christ ONCE for all."* (Heb 10:9, 10) When Rome declares that Christ is offered again and again in Mass after Mass, God's holy Word is blasphemed by the very crowd that claims the exclusive right of interpreting it. *"But this man,* (Jesus) *after he had offered ONE sacrifice for sins FOR EVER sat down on the right hand of God."* (Heb 10:12) *"For by ONE offering he hath perfected FOR EVER them that are sanctified."* (Heb 10:14) *"Now where remission of these* (sins) *is, there is no more offering for sin.* (Heb 10:18)

In the Old Testament, the Jews were to commemorate their deliverance from slavery in the land of Egypt by celebrating the Passover sacrifice and meal each year. Although today's orthodox Jews continue to observe the Passover, our Lord's death ushered in a new covenant, and a new way for it to be commemorated. The Lord's Supper as it is called in the Bible was instituted by Jesus to "proclaim" His death, His one-time sacrifice, until He comes again, first to gather His church out of the world, and then to rule the world from Jerusalem for 1000 years. The Word of God is crystal clear regarding our Lord's sacrifice. He did it once. Took willingly on Himself the sin of the entire world from creation to the end-time immolation. *"For he* (the Father) **hath made him** (Jesus) *to be sin for us, who knew no sin; that we might be made the righteousness of God in him."* (2 Co 5:21) And more than 700 years before our Lord was born:

"All we like sheep have gone astray; we have turned every one to his own way; and the LORD hath laid on him the iniquity of us all." (Isa 53:6) The world's sin—every bit of it—was judged in our Lord on the cross of Calvary, never to be judged again in those who claim Him as their Savior. Let Rome proclaim in the most eloquent words imaginable that Christ is sacrificed anew in the Mass, it will not change the Word of God. And the Word of God says only one perfect sacrifice was needed; our Lord was that perfect sacrifice, and no man saying words over a wafer and a cup will bring Him down from heaven to be offered again in order that the already completed works of redemption "might be carried on."

It is not necessary for the born-again Christian to participate in Catholic "Communion" to unite for a few short minutes with Jesus. The Lord Jesus Himself lives inside every true believer every day of his or her life. No wafer, no "works," on the part of a believer can in any way increase the unity that occurs the moment faith is placed in Christ as Savior and Lord. And no wafer has the power to cleanse from sin. The believer's acknowledgement of iniquity directly and privately to God assures forgiveness and cleansing from all unrighteousness. (I John 1:9.) Jesus is not in the wafer—the host—the Catholic priest prays over during the Mass. That's not our Lord's body, nor is the cup of wine His precious blood.

When the priest, before consuming them, elevates first the host and then the wine for the congregation to worship, Rome is saying: "Look, here is Christ!" But following is what our Lord said during His earthly ministry: *"Then if any man shall say unto you, lo, here is Christ, or there; believe it not. For there shall arise false Christs, and false prophets, and shall shew great signs and wonders; insomuch that, if it were possible, they shall deceive the very elect. Behold, I have told you before. Wherefore, if they shall say unto you, Behold, he is in the desert; go not forth: behold, he is in the secret chambers; believe it not."* (Mat 24:23-26) Our blessed Lord is in heaven, awaiting the time He will come in the air to catch up His church to the celestial glory. (1Th 4:17) He is not in the wafer, (host) nor is He in the wine. He is not in the "secret chambers" of the Catholic Church tabernacles. He is only in the hearts of true believers everywhere.

The host (wafer) is a false Christ. Popes who have declared themselves "Vicars of Christ" on earth are false prophets. Rome is the apostate church preaching a man-made Gospel not found in the precious, unchanging, infallible Word of God. The office of "priest" was done away with when the Temple veil was rent from top to bottom at the moment of Christ's death. To all the wonderful, sincere people who are entrapped by Catholic heresies—not the least of which is the "Holy Sacrifice of the Mass"—the Word of God entreats them as follows: **"Wherefore come out from among them, and be ye separate, saith the Lord, and touch not the unclean thing and I will receive you."** (2Co 6:17) Because it is an icon—a false Jesus—the host, the wafer, of the Catholic Mass is an unclean thing. Those who bow to it, touch it, receive it into their bodies are engaging in a serious act of idolatry.

Paul said that he had persecuted Christ's people out of sheer ignorance. As a former Catholic who worshiped the host, ingested it, bowed to it, all out of sheer ignorance, I am convinced that the faithful Catholics of today are as deceived and misled as I was. They are ignorant of the irrelevance of the Mass; the blasphemous nature of a scrap of unleavened bread that remains a scrap of unleavened no matter how many times a powerless man says over it "This truly is my body." One of the great and continuing prayer needs for all born-again Christians to put on their list is that more and more Catholics who are serious about the eternal destiny of their souls come out from that apostate church into the glorious light of the Word of God. In it they will find that the Mass is no reenactment of Christ's sacrifice, for it lacks the illegal trial, the screams of the crowd, "Crucify Him! Crucify Him!" There is no heartless scourging, no piercing crown of thorns, no heavy old rugged cross, no rusty nails driven through healing hands and weary feet. The soldiers gambling for His meager vestments are missing; so are the religious hecklers and the lost thief challenging Him to come down from the cross. The saved thief is not there, either, nor are the sweet words of our Savior, **"This day shalt thou be with me in Paradise,"** followed shortly by, **"IT IS FINISHED!"** There can be no reenactment of such a selfless, loving sacrifice. Nor is there any need for one found in the Word of God.

It—the Word of God alone—changes not. It is forever settled in heaven. It is **"the Sword of the Spirit."** (Eph 6:17.) Catholics who never read and trust God's

Word are lacking the only offensive weapon we have been given to effectively witness for Christ and successfully repel the false doctrines that promise what only Jesus can deliver. But more than that, without reading and trusting God's Word, Catholics are lacking the ***"whole armor of God,"*** (Eph 6:13-17) with which believers are equipped to defend themselves against man's ever present antagonists—the world, the flesh, and the devil. God help our unsuspecting, unregenerated, hopelessly lost, Catholic friends who are staking their souls on Masses, Communions, and other works rather than the precious blood of Christ Jesus our Lord as revealed in the divine Scriptures.

8

The Apparition Addiction

"Beloved, believe not every spirit, but try the spirits whether they are of God: because many false prophets are gone out into the world." (1 John 4:1)

An age-old saying has it that "Seeing is believing." There's another more recent that says "What you see is what you get." But magicians using sleight-of-hand have for many years proved such expressions are a good bit less than accurate. Just when you think you know under which shell the pea is, the trickster lifts it up and the pea is not there. It's deception, pure and simple, and it's as old as the human race. The fruit looked so good to Eve, as if it would not only taste great, but contained exactly what would make her as beautiful and wise as God. She ate it, gave some to Adam, and here we are.

Lot's eyes told him the well-watered plains of Jordan were the perfect spot to settle down. He ended up in one of the worst messes you can imagine. Samson's eyes told him Delilah was not only lovely to look upon, but could be trusted as well. He ended up blind…and dead. The Jews' eyes saw in Jesus an ordinary man instead of the conqueror they were expecting. They turned Him over to Pilate and have missed the blessings of Christianity ever since. Military leaders have learned that vehicles, personnel and targets can be hidden from the naked eye simply by painting them the mottled colors of their environment. What is seen, is not what's really there.

Because our eyes are the primary organ through which we ingest information, we tend to believe that what we are seeing is…exactly what we are seeing. That's why the magician—by simple misdirection—is able so easily to deceive us. It's also the reason why Satan, whom the Bible calls the father of liars, (John 8:44) is able to lead us into sin. Often what appears to us innocent enough, or attractive enough, or definitely worthwhile, is simply the camouflage behind which is behavior offensive to a holy God. Certainly the saying "If it looks good and feels good, do it!" has been inspired by that master deceiver of mankind. Of course, there is a good way to make sure our eyes are not being deceived, and that way is to keep our ears open at all times. In all spiritual matters especially—and secular ones as well—it is a good idea to remember the words of our Lord at the end of each letter to the Churches in Revelation: ***"He that hath an ear, let him hear what the Spirit saith unto the churches."*** (Rev 2:29) And, in order to hear what the Holy Spirit has to say, our one sure source is the Bible. ***"For the prophecy came not in old time by the will of man: but holy men of God spake as they were moved by the Holy Ghost.*** (2Pet 1:21)

In this chapter we will be looking into various Marian apparitions to determine whether such phenomena are of and from God, or of and from the devil. Since the Author of the Scriptures is the Holy Spirit we rest assured that the Word of God never lies, never deceives, and never contradicts itself. By consulting it we will be able to discern whether the Marian apparitions and the miracles associated with them, are to be accepted, or are to be declared deceptions of Satan that direct attention away from the one and only Savior of the World. We will be paying attention—not to what was seen by the visionaries—but to **what they heard**.

Didn't Juan Diego really see Mary at Guadalupe in 1531? Didn't she cause roses to bloom in December and leave her countenance impressed on Juan's serape? Didn't she tell him she was the mother of God? Although serious doubt exists about this episode's reality, let us accept it as does the Catholic Church. In December of 1531, says the legend, at Guadalupe outside of what is now Mexico City, Juan Diego, a peasant, saw an apparition that worked a couple of notable miracles and claimed to be the mother of God—*theotokos*. But was the apparition that of Mary, the mother of Jesus? Were the miracles performed by her? How can we learn the truth?

As we cover this subject of Marian apparitions and the miracles associated with them, we are going to be guided by truths, admonitions, and instructions found in the Bible. We will keep in the forefront of our mind, **a) Jesus is the Way, the Truth, and the Life; no one comes to the Father but by Him;** (Cf. John 14:6) **b) the work of redemption was completed on Calvary, and we in no way can contribute to that work, nor can anyone else alive or dead; c) salvation is by faith in Jesus Christ, by faith in him alone;** and, **d) Only God is to be the object of prayer and worship.**

Down through the centuries there have been literally hundreds of Marian apparitions reported, most recently in Georgia, New Jersey, and the former Yugoslavia. Moreover, the Marian apparitions seem to be addicted to Catholics—born again Christians never are visited—and Catholics most surely are addicted to the apparitions, as witnessed by the proliferation of books, articles, and devotions they have inspired. What we are setting out to discover in this chapter is whether the Marian apparitions are really Mary, the mother of Jesus, or satanic masquerades. The best place to start any investigation, of course, is in the Word of God

"...Son of man, take up a lamentation upon the king of Tyrus, and say unto him, Thus saith the Lord GOD; Thou sealest up the sum, full of wisdom, and perfect in beauty Thou hast been in Eden the garden of God; every precious stone was thy covering, the sardius, topaz, and the diamond, the beryl, the onyx, and the jasper, the sapphire, the emerald, and the carbuncle, and gold: the workmanship of thy tabrets and of thy pipes was prepared in thee in the day that thou wast created. Thou art the anointed cherub that covereth; and I have set thee so: thou wast upon the holy mountain of God; thou hast walked up and down in the midst of the stones of fire. Thou wast perfect in thy ways from the day that thou wast created, till iniquity was found in thee." (Eze 28:12-15)

In this passage from Ezekiel we have a description of our adversary—Satan—who was God's anointed cherub before his fall. Apparently he was the most beautiful of all the angels, for none other is described in the the Word of God as *"perfect in beauty."* His countenance combined the splendor of nine precious stones and the most precious of metals—gold. He was so beautiful, so radiant that he was appointed guardian of the very throne of God. Even when he sinned and was evicted from God's presence, he retained his radiance, for we read: *"And he* (Jesus) *said unto them, I beheld Satan as lightning fall from heaven."* (Luke 10:18) He not only has retained his radiance, but, like Gabriel and Michael, has the capacity to assume a human appearance. *"For such are false apostles, deceitful workers, transforming themselves into the apostles of Christ. And no marvel; for Satan himself is transformed into an angel of light."* (2 Cor 11:13,14) Lastly, we are told that angels are sexless: *"For in the resurrection they neither marry, nor are given in marriage, but are as the angels of God in heaven."* (Mat 22:30) From this last it is apparent that Satan can assume either a male or female appearance.

These Scripture verses enable us to do what police artists do—draw a composite of Satan the deceiver. When we do, what we see is not a gargoyle-like figure with horns, a tail and a pitchfork, but a radiant, glowing male or female creature of surpassing beauty. Moreover, when we consult the Scriptures, we find that God—for His own purposes—grants to Satan great powers. In the case of Job, God allowed Satan to, a) motivate humans on two occasions to perform murderous acts; b) bring fire (perhaps lightning) down from heaven; c) produce a killer tornado; and d) smite Job from head to toe with painful boils. In Luke 13, Satan had a woman "bound" for 18 years by a "spirit of infirmity," (Luke 13:11-16) and in Exodus, Pharaoh's magicians with their "enchantments"—read that "Satanic powers"—were able to produce serpents out of their rods, cause water to become blood, and bring up frogs out of the river. (Exo 7:12; 7:22; 8:7)

In the Scripture from Ezekiel previously cited, one other characteristic of Satan is most notable, and that is the fullness of wisdom God created in him. Certainly his sin and continual rebellion against a holy God have perverted that wisdom. But his innate brilliance gives rise to a unique craftiness, a cunning, a duplicity far beyond what an ordinary mortal mind can comprehend. He is without scruples; will resort to the vilest schemes in his ongoing efforts to defeat his Creator and gain the seat he covets in the *"sides of the north."* (Isa 14:13) That he had the audacity to tempt the very God who created him attests to his boldness and dedication to evil.

A highly effective weapon of deception in his arsenal is the half-truth, which, in the final analysis is always a falsehood. For example, in Eden, he told Eve they would not surely die, but would become as God knowing both good and evil. Of course they did not die at once physically, and they did immediately recognize the evil of what they had done. So in these respects, Satan told the truth. Hidden from her was the seriousness of disobedience to God's command and the resultant consequences. Thus the entire temptation was a lie. In today's society, this tactic of Satan has found perfection, especially in the advertising profession. In TV and print ads, for example, young people are shown having a good time drinking some company's beer. Yep, folks can have a good time drinking beer. What is not shown is the debauchery beer drinking often leads to and the misery it engenders. In other ads, the pleasures of a costly trip abroad are featured with the invitation to enjoy now and pay later. What is not shown is the chaos resulting from the "pay-later" aspect when a job is lost or sickness strikes. In assessing the validity of Marian apparitions this proclivity of Satan to deal in half-truths also must be considered.

As we read and study the Word of God, eventually we come to the conclusion that the entire 66 books point to a single personality—the Lord Jesus Christ. From Genesis to Revelation He and He alone is what it's all about. He creates. He conserves. He promises. He calls out. He chastises. He redeems. He judges. All of the other personalities we encounter are merely the supporting cast. It is God in the person of Jesus who occupies the lead role from the alpha of Genesis to the omega of Revelation. That this is true was clearly revealed by Jesus to His

Apostles before His crucifixion. *"But when the Comforter is come, whom I will send unto you from the Father, even the Spirit of truth, which proceedeth from the Father, he shall testify of me:* (John 15:26). In the very next chapter, the same point is emphasized. *"He shall glorify me for he shall receive of mine, and shall shew it unto you. All things that the Father hath are mine: therefore said I, that he shall take of mine, and shall shew it unto you.* (John 16:14, 15) This fact, also, that all things point to and exalt Jesus, will receive special attention in our study of the Marian apparitions.

In constructing a proper background of Biblical facts that will permit an objective analysis of the apparitions, a few missing boards still need to be nailed in place. It is the truth that there is but one Gospel, the Gospel given to and preached by Paul the Apostle. *"But though we, or an angel from heaven preach any other gospel unto you than that which we have preached unto you, let him be accursed. As we said before, so say I now again, if any man preach any other gospel unto you than that ye have received, let him be accursed."* (Gal 1:8, 9) It also is true that we have been living in the "last time" ever since the apostolic era ended. *"Little children, it is the last time: and as ye have heard that antichrist shall come, even now are there many antichrists; whereby we know that it is the last time."* (1 John 2:18) The "last time" will be marked by the deception of false preaching, false doctrine and imposters working great signs and miracles. *"For there shall arise false Christs, and false prophets, and shall shew great signs and wonders: insomuch that, if it were possible, they shall deceive the very elect."* (Mat 24:24) With these words of our Lord Jesus from his prophetic "Olivet Discourse" we have completed a foolproof Biblical backdrop against which to project several famous Marian apparitions that are highly endorsed by the Roman Catholic Church.

Following is a summary of things we will be considering in order to decide the validity or the fraudulence of the apparitions and miracles covered in this chapter. If the ones studied are determined to be fraudulent, we can safely conclude all others are likewise fraudulent.

1. What a person sees may not be what the person believes he/she sees.

2. Only Jesus is the Way to the Father; no other mediator or way exists.

3. He (Jesus) completed the work of redemption. No other works needed.

4. Salvation is by faith in Jesus alone; works of any kind can't help.

5. Only God is to be worshiped. Prayer (worship) to another is a no-no.

6. Satan can assume human form as male or female and appear beautiful.

7. God—for His purposes—sometimes grants Satan preternatural powers.

8. Satan was created full of wisdom. He is brilliant, cunning, unscrupulous.

9. Satan is a master of half-truths, and doctored facts.

10. If someone other than Jesus is exalted it is not of or from God.

11. There is ONE ONLY Gospel. It is found in God's Word.

12. The "last time" is right now, and will be marked by deceivers working great miracles.

GUADALUPE.

Earlier we posed these questions: "Didn't Juan Diego really see Mary at Guadalupe in 1531? Didn't she cause roses to bloom in December and leave her countenance impressed on Juan's serape?" The answer to the first is "No." The answer to the others is "yes." Juan Diego, who has now been declared a "saint" of the Roman Catholic Church, reportedly saw an apparition on the 9th and 12th of December, 1531, but it was not Mary the mother of Jesus. However, the apparition did perform the two mentioned miracles, assuming the entire legend is true. Following is a synopsis—from Catholic sources—of the words spoken by the apparition to Juan Diego.

> "Know for certain that I am the *perfect and perpetual Virgin Mary, Mother of the true God*...here I will show and offer all my love, my compassion, my help and protection to the people. I am your merciful mother, the mother of all who love me, of those who cry to me, of those who have confidence in me. Here I will hear their weeping and their sorrows...their necessities and misfortunes...listen and let it penetrate your heart...do not be troubled or weighed down with grief. Do not fear any illness or vexation, anxiety or pain. Am I not here who am your mother? Are you not under *my* shadow and *protection*? Am I not your FOUNTAIN OF LIFE? Are you not in the folds of my mantle? In the crossing of my arms? Is there anything else you need?"

In chapter two we learned from the Word of God that Mary had four sons, the half-brothers of Jesus, and at least two daughters, His half-sisters. The brothers on several occasions actually are named in the Scriptures. In the same chapter, we saw that Mary was the mother of Jesus the man, cannot by any stretch of the imagination be the mother of God who is an eternal, uncreated being. We learned that only Jesus was perfect; that there was none greater than John the Baptist of persons born in the normal way. John was not perfect, so Mary was not perfect, either, since both had normal conceptions.

Mary the mother of Jesus who is in glory with the Lord knows she was not perfect, and, by her own admission, needed a Savior. (Luke 1:47) She knows she had other children after Christ's birth; and knows she is not the mother of God. Had the apparition seen by Juan Diego been Mary she would not have lied about herself. She would not have made the claims she did which are a usurpation of the powers and attributes possessed only by God Himself. Had the apparition seen by Juan Diego been Mary she would have exalted the Lord Jesus Christ (background point #10) and proclaimed Him to be Juan's "fountain of life." (John 4:14) That the miracles—assuming they really happened—were notable works cannot be denied. But our Lord warned us that such wonders (background point #12) would almost deceive even the elect—that is, those who have been saved by their faith in Christ. Satan is in the business of deflecting attention and honor away from Jesus, setting up false gods and alternate paths to salvation. Had Juan Diego's bishop known and believed God's Word; had he not been taken in by the erroneous fables about Mary that Rome embraced and fostered, he would have instantly spotted the hand of Satan in the Juan Diego episodes. He didn't and it is believed that over 7000 poor peasants were converted to Catholicism as a result of the Guadalupe apparition.

Today, Rome counts Mexico a Catholic country; its patron is "Our Lady of Guadalupe," honored with a huge basilica and shrine on the outskirts of Mexico City. Mexicans pray not to Jesus but to "the Lady." Healings that have occurred periodically at the shrine are attributed to Mary not to our Lord. And most assuredly not to Satan. Missionaries seeking to bring the true Gospel to Mexico are condemned by Catholic officials and their evangelistic efforts criticized, opposed, often frustrated. Through the Guadalupe apparitions, Satan has successfully led an entire country into the apostate church. Where the Word of God is not the preeminent guiding force in all matters of faith, morals and doctrine, it is open season for Satan to deceive and destroy.

PROUILLE, FRANCE, AD 1208.

More than 300 years before Guadalupe, an apparition said to be Mary occurred in the small town of Prouille, France, to a Spanish clergyman named Domingo de Guzman. Today, he is a "saint" of the Catholic Church—St Dominic, founder of the Order of Friar Monks, otherwise called the Dominicans. Guzman was in France preaching against the Albigensians—also known as Cathari—a Bible-believing sect considered heretics by Rome, and eventually slaughtered at the direction of pope Innocent III. As Catholic tradition has it, Mary appeared to Guzman while he was praying in chapel one day, and gave him the Rosary that has become the Catholic laity's number-one form of prayer. Guzman was urged by the apparition to **preach the Rosary to all people** as a remedy against heresy and sin. (Violation of background points 2, 4, 11.) In His commission to the Apostles before His ascension into heaven, Our Lord is thus quoted. *"Go ye therefore, and teach all nations, baptizing them in the name of the Father, and of the Son, and of the Holy Ghost: Teaching them to observe all things whatsoever I have commanded and, lo, I am with you alway, even unto the end of the world."* (Mat 28:19, 20)

Where in the Bible do we read that Mary the mother of Jesus was given the authority to countermand a direct order given by her Lord and Savior? At what point since His ascension into heaven did our Lord decide that it was more important that the Rosary be preached as a remedy for heresy and sin, rather than the Gospel of salvation? A million Rosaries can't save a single soul, but it is a diabolically clever way to demean the Gospel and take the people's eyes off the only One who can forgive sins and grant eternal life. Listen to the incredible promises made by the apparition (no, it was definitely not Mary) to those who recite the Rosary:

1. **Whoever shall faithfully SERVE ME by the recitation of the rosary shall receive signal graces.**

2. **I promise MY SPECIAL PROTECTION and the greatest graces to all those who shall recite the rosary.**

3. **The rosary shall be a powerful ARMOR AGAINST HELL; it will destroy vice, decrease sin, defeat heresies.**

4. **It will cause virtue and good works to flourish; it will obtain for souls the abundant mercy of God; it will withdraw the heart of men from the love of the world and its vanities, and will lift them to the**

desire of eternal things. Oh, that souls would sanctify themselves by this means.

5. The soul which recommends itself to me by recitation of the rosary, **SHALL NOT PERISH.**

6. Whoever shall recite the rosary devoutly, applying himself to the consideration of its sacred mysteries shall never be conquered by misfortune. God will not chastise him in His justice, he shall not perish by an unprovided death; if he be just he shall remain in the grace of God, and **BECOME WORTHY OF ETERNAL LIFE.**

7. Whoever shall have a true devotion for the rosary shall not die **WITHOUT THE SACRAMENTS** of the (Catholic) **Church.**

8. Those who are faithful to recite the rosary shall have during their life and at their death the light of God and the plentitude of His graces; at the moment of death they shall participate in the **MERITS OF THE SAINTS** in Paradise.

9. I shall **DELIVER FROM PURGATORY** those who have been devoted to the rosary.

10. The faithful children of the rosary shall merit a high degree of glory in heaven.

11. You shall **OBTAIN ALL YOU ASK** of me by the recitation of the rosary.

12. All those who propagate the holy rosary shall be aided by me in their necessities.

13. I have obtained from my divine Son that all the advocates of the rosary shall have for **INTERCESSORS** the **ENTIRE CELESTIAL COURT** during their life and at the hour of death.

14. All who recite the rosary are my son, and brothers of my only Son Jesus Christ.

15. **Devotion of my rosary is a great sign of predestination.** (All emphasis mine.)

There is so much heresy and deception in the above it simply could not have come from the one who has been called "blessed." And it certainly is not from

God for it is a totally different Gospel from that preached by Paul and the other Apostles. In promises #1 and #2, Jesus, not Mary, is the source of all grace; and Mary has no power whatever to protect. In promise #3, it is the "whole armor of God" (Eph 6:11, 13) that protects against evil, and only after the millennial rule of Jesus will vice be destroyed, sin, heresy and death cast into the Lake of fire. (Rev 20:14) Promise #5 is downright blasphemy. Faith in Jesus, not rosaries, assures salvation. *"For God so loved the world, that he gave his only begotten Son, that whosoever believeth in him should not perish, but have everlasting life."* (John 3:16)

More blasphemy in promise #6. No one is **worthy** of eternal life; no one becomes worthy by works such as saying rosaries. Eternal life is a gift from God to those who believe in and trust our Lord for salvation. *"For by grace are ye saved through faith and that not of yourselves: it is the gift of God: Not of works lest any man should boast."* (Eph 2:8, 9) To promise #7, I can only repeat the sacraments are man-made dead works. What is needed at the hour of death is faith in the promises of the Lord Jesus, not Roman Catholic heresy. Promises #8 and #9 are Catholic doctrine not Biblical doctrine. There is no such thing as the "merits of saints in Paradise." The holiest person who ever lived, got to heaven entirely on the merits of Christ's death on Calvary, not on anything he or she did in life. As for Purgatory, it's an invention of Rome. Mary, who was NOT a Catholic—she was Jewish—would have known nothing of it.

Promise #10 is so dangerous it makes me shudder. Devotion to the rosary not only won't assure one a high place in heaven, it will guarantee an eternity in hell. *"And they said, Believe on the Lord Jesus Christ, and thou shalt be saved, and thy house."* (Acts 16:31) How many times does the Bible have to say salvation is by faith in Jesus Christ and only by faith in Jesus Christ before Rome will believe it, and teach it, and preach it? As to promise #11, reciting the rosary may motivate Satan to give a person what they request, for he has that power. (Mat 4:9) But reciting the rosary will get no hearing from the Lord. *"And whatsoever ye shall ask in my name that will I do, that the Father may be glorified in the Son. If ye shall ask any thing in my name I will do it."* (John 14:13, 14)

Promise #13 is a repetition of heretical Catholic doctrine and #14 is another very serious blasphemy. *"But as many as received him to them gave he power to become the sons of God even to them that believe on his name."* (John 1:12) *"...whosoever shall do the will of my Father which is in heaven, the same is my brother, and sister and mother."* (Mat 12:50) As believing sons of God—not as sons of an apparition—we become brothers of the man Christ Jesus and joint heirs (Rom 8:17) with him of heaven and all its bliss. The only assurance to be gained from Promise #15 is that eternity will be spent in the lake of fire.

The more one delves into the various Marian apparitions, the more one realizes there is a common thread that ties them all together. The most obvious is the fact that all of them expound **Catholic doctrines** never to be found in God's Word. Since Scripture doesn't contradict itself, this fact alone supports the conclusion that the apparitions and their attendant miracles are satanically inspired, definitely not from heaven. Moreover, when one studies Catholic doctrines and compares them with God's Word, it is easy to conclude that Satan's objectives are best served by doing everything he can to promote the Catholic religion and its myriad dead works. Examination of the promises made for devotion to, and reciting of, the rosary in the light of what the Bible says, shows beyond the shadow of a doubt that whatever or whoever appeared to the monk, Domingo de Guzman, it was absolutely NOT Mary the mother of Jesus.

CAMBRIDGE, ENGLAND, AD 1251.

On July 16 of the year 1251, a monk named Simon Stock reported that Mary the mother of Jesus appeared to him and gave him a brown woolen scapular to be worn henceforth by the Carmelite order of friars. She is purported to have told him the following:

> **"Take, beloved son this scapular of thy order as a badge of my confraternity and for thee and all Carmelites a special sign of grace; whoever dies in this garment, will not suffer everlasting fire. It is the SIGN OF SALVATION, a safeguard in dangers, a pledge of peace and of the covenant."**

We are told that prior to the apparition, the Carmelites were experiencing serious problems; that Simon Stock prayed for deliverance from them, and that after the apparition the problems ceased. Here again we have promises made by an apparition that not only don't line up with the Word of God, but seriously contradict it. (Background points 2, 3, 4, 11.) Our Lord Jesus was beaten to a pulp, crowned with thorns, hanged from nails on a cross until dead that we might have the forgiveness of our sins, eternal life in heaven, salvation. Why would His heavenly Father have allowed His only begotten son to experience such inhumane torture if 1200 years later he intended to grant salvation to all who wear a brown woolen scapular throughout their lives?

"Forasmuch as ye know that ye were not redeemed with corruptible things, as silver and gold, (or brown woolen scapulars) *from your vain conversation*

received by tradition from your fathers; But with the precious blood of Christ as of a lamb without blemish and without spot": (1 Pet 1:18, 19) Such promises as those allegedly made to Simon Stock are satanic, deceiving individuals into a false sense of soul-security. There is only one Gospel and one Savior. Brown scapulars don't qualify. Faith and trust in Jesus Christ and in Him alone provides soul-security for the lost sinner.

As further proof that the apparition seen by Simon Stock was not Mary the mother of Jesus, an additional promise is alleged to have been made. It is called by Rome the "Sabbatine Privilege." It applies to all who, after being "invested" in the brown scapular, wear it faithfully throughout their lives. To these applies the promise that the ones who go to Purgatory when they die will be escorted out of the purgatorial fire by Mary no later than the first Saturday after their death. But, there is no Purgatory. It is a man-made doctrine not found in the Word of God. It is a doctrine of pagan origin, showing once again that the "rulers of the darkness of this world," are committed to promoting the apostate Catholic religion. If only devout Catholics would believe God's promises and come out from among them! When Rome fosters belief among the faithful that a couple pieces of brown wool suspended on strings that fit over the neck are a passport to salvation, a grave sin is committed and the blood of souls lost because of such foolishness is on the heads of all in authority there. The apparition seen by Simon Stock was not Mary the mother of Jesus.

AGREDA, SPAIN 17TH CENTURY.

A Franciscan nun—Maria de Agreda (1602-1665)—claimed to have had so many private apparitions and visions of Mary the mother of Jesus, and of God Himself, that she was able to write eight books having the coverall title of "The Mystical City of God." In it is set forth the life of the Blessed Virgin, from her alleged Immaculate Conception to her crowning as queen of heaven. In its unabridged form "The Mystical City of God"—a pseudonym for the Blessed Virgin—contains 2676 pages, and sells for $65. The abridged version contains 794 pages and 59 chapters. It sells for $17.95 or $18.50 in Catholic bookstores. The book has been "acclaimed by popes, cardinals, bishops and theologians" as "one of the greatest Catholic books ever."

The book is called the Blessed Virgin's autobiography because, supposedly, both Mary and God, via countless mystical visions, provided the information it contains. Included in the voluminous text are such things as the meaning of the Apocalypse, (Catholic version of the Revelation) Lucifer's sin and fall, where hell is located, the death of Mary's parents, (who are not mentioned in the Bible) how

Mary and Joseph became betrothed, etc. It relates that Mary never appeared to be more than 33-years-old, never ate meat, just fruits and vegetables, (Joseph was the meat eater) and the little child Jesus—just by His presence—caused healings and exorcisms of evil spirits.

Rome's Congregation of the Inquisition condemned the book August 4, 1681. The "infallible" pope at the time, Innocent XI, forbade the reading of it. Several popes thereafter followed suit. At the end of the 17th century 102 out of 152 commission members appointed to render a decision on the book condemned it for a long list of reasons including its "scandalous assertions." In our day, however, it is considered one of the "greatest Catholic books ever." As a matter of fact, in April of 1929 Pius XI, another "infallible" pope, declared:

"We grant the apostolic benediction to all readers and promoters of The Mystical City of God."

Publications of the book available today all carry an official Imprimatur of the church meaning it contains nothing contradictory to Catholic teachings and doctrines.

As a Catholic child educated in the parochial school system, I, and my peers, accepted the various Marian teachings as divine truth. We never questioned where the myriad teachings originated, or whether they were biblical. We accepted that Mary's parents were named Anne and Joachim. We accepted that Joseph was the patron of a happy death because both Jesus and Mary were with him when he died. We accepted Mary's alleged perpetual virginity, bodily assumption into heaven, crowning as queen of heaven, everything. I now realize that much of what we were taught about Mary came from or was profoundly influenced by "The Mystical City of God," which itself appears to have been heavily influenced by the 13th century theologian, John Duns Scotus, also of the Franciscan order. (Refer to Chapter 3.)

In retrospect, I deeply regret having devoted so many years to a religion that is so disdainful of the Bible, and so dedicated to the exaltation of our Lord's earthly mother. If ever there was a prayer need it is this: that Catholics who have been hoodwinked into accepting as divine truth the heresies of Rome will be granted the grace to extricate themselves and be born again before it is everlasting too late; and that God in His mercy and love will open their eyes to His holy Word, enabling them at last to understand and accept the one and only true Gospel of Jesus Christ.

That wonderful, easily understood gospel is nowhere to be found in "The Mystical City of God." Since escaping from Catholicism I have been shocked over and over by Rome's disregard for God's precious Word, and the arrogance to claim sovereign authority over its interpretation. But "The Mystical City of God" goes far beyond shocking. It is better described as nauseating in the extreme. From the first chapter of the first book, entitled *"Why God Revealed The Life Of Mary In These Our Times,"* to the final chapter of book 8, entitled *"The Coronation Of The Mother Of God,"* this work is a fountain spewing heresy after heresy, and is in fact a shameless polemic for the propagation of false Roman Catholic doctrines. The entire work deals with "faith and morals" about which "infallible" popes allegedly can never err. Yet several popes declared the book taboo, while others have enthusiastically endorsed it. So much for papal infallibility.

Ever wondered why God created heaven and earth? Maria de Agreda says she was given the following reason by the apparition:

> **"...God determined to create a locality and an abode, where the incarnate Word (Jesus) and His mother (Mary) should converse and dwell. For them primarily did He create the heaven and earth with its stars and elements and all that is contained in them."**

Imagine that. God created the entire universe just for Jesus and His earthly (created) mother. But God's Word that lies not gives an entirely different reason. **"Thou art worthy, O Lord, to receive glory and honour and power: for thou hast created all things, and FOR THY PLEASURE they are and were created.** (Rev 4:11) No indication there that God gave any consideration to Mary the mother of Jesus when He set about to create. Moreover, the Bible tells us in numerous Scriptures that the Word (Jesus) was Himself the instrument of creation. **"In the beginning was the Word and the Word was with God, and the Word was God"** (John 1:1) **"All things were made by him and without him was not any thing made that was made."** (John 1:3) **"And the Word was made flesh, and dwelt among us, (and we beheld his glory, the glory as of the only begotten of the Father,) full of grace and truth."** (John 1:14)

More from chapter 1 of book 1. Maria de Agreda relates:

> **"I saw a great and mysterious sign in heaven; I saw a Woman, a most beautiful Lady and Queen, crowned with the stars, clothed with the sun, and the moon was at her feet. (Apoc. 12:1). The holy angels spoke to me: 'This is that blessed woman whom saint John saw in the Apocalypse and**

in whom are enclosed, deposited and sealed up the wonderful MYSTERIES OF THE REDEMPTION.'"

But the Bible contradicts the "holy angels." The woman in Revelation 12:1 is not Mary but the nation of Israel. And the mysteries of redemption were never "enclosed, deposited, or sealed up" in Mary. They were openly preached on Pentecost and have been openly preached ever since. *"Even the mystery which hath been hid from ages and from generations, but now is made manifest to his saints; To whom God would make known what is the riches of the glory of this mystery among the Gentiles; which is Christ in you, the hope of glory."* (Col 1:26, 27) The God of heaven was to come and take up residence within the heart of believing men. *"And they said, Believe on the Lord Jesus Christ, and thou shalt be saved, and thy house."* (Acts 16:31) Faith in Christ was salvation's seal. *"For God so loved the world, that he gave his only begotten Son, that whosoever believeth in him should not perish, but have everlasting life."* (John 3:16)

Thanks be to God, the mysteries of Redemption are not hidden in Mary or anyone else. They have been revealed so that all—even devout Catholics—can trust Christ for salvation and be indwelt by His Holy Spirit. In the "vision" related above the apparition used traditional "Catholic" terms—Apocalypse instead of the Revelation, and "saint" John instead of the Apostle John. It has always been Catholic teaching that the woman depicted in chapter 12:1 of the Revelation is Mary. But the context of the chapter shows the woman to be the nation of Israel. (Refer to Chapter 2—The Goddess Man Has Made.) In relating the episode when Gabriel appeared to Mary announcing her selection to be the mother of the Savior, Maria de Agreda reports that Mary replied as follows:

"How shall this happen, that I conceive and bear, since I know not, NOR CAN KNOW MAN?"

Note the **flagrant addition** to God's Word of the phrase "nor can know." Here's what the Bible says: *"Then said Mary unto the angel, how shall this be, seeing I know not a man?"* (Luke 1:34) The reason for the addition is to accommodate the man-made ever-virgin doctrine of Catholicism made popular by John Duns Scotus, Franciscan monk of the 13th century. Mary is supposed—according to Agreda—to have taken a lifetime vow of chastity with the approval of God. Thus she was never to "know" man. But the Bible says Mary the mother of Jesus also was the mother of four other sons who are specifically named and at least two daughters who are not named. (Mat 13:55) The apparition quite obviously gave Maria de Agreda information that contradicts the Word of God.

In the 3rd chapter of Book 7, M. de Agreda relates events attendant to Mary's first and only reception of "Communion" from the hands of the Apostle Peter. We read:

> **"The Apostle (Peter) partook himself of the SACRAMENT** (Roman Catholic word) **and communicated it to the eleven Apostles as Most Holy Mary had instructed him. Thereupon, at the hands of St. Peter, the heavenly Mother partook of it, while the celestial spirits then present attended with ineffable reverence. She returned to her place,** (Catholics go forward to an altar to receive the host) **and was entirely transformed and elevated, completely absorbed in this divine conflagration of the love of her most holy Son, whom She had now received bodily. She remained in a trance, elevated from the floor; but the holy angels shielded Her somewhat from view according to Her own wish. If the Lord (Jesus) had not found this way of remaining with Her in the sacramental species,** (Roman Catholic phrase) **He would have come down from the right hand of the Father to the world in order to render companionship to His mother while she sojourned with His Church.**

But the Bible says our Lord will remain at the Father's right hand until a specific time in the future. *"The LORD said unto my Lord, Sit thou at my right hand, until I make thine enemies thy footstool"* (Psa 110:1) It is to be doubted that anything could—or can—cause Jesus to leave the right hand of the Father until the time appointed. *"But this man, after he had offered one sacrifice for sins for ever, sat down on the right hand of God; From henceforth expecting till his enemies be made his footstool."* (Heb 10:12, 13) Furthermore, Mary already had Jesus living inside her in the form of his Holy Spirit received on Pentecost; and in the apostolic church, believers partook of the Lord's Supper, not of a Catholic "sacrament" called "Communion." Too, Peter and the eleven were scattered throughout the middle east and Asia proclaiming the Gospel, not playing church in Jerusalem. What an affront all this stuff is to the loving Jesus who all by Himself—and with no help from Mary or anyone else—purged the sins of the world on Calvary and then sat down at the right hand of the Father in heaven.

With respect to Mary's death and her alleged assumption into heaven, Maria de Agreda's apparition attributes the following words to our Lord Jesus:

> **"My flesh is her flesh; she cooperated with me** (a Catholic teaching) **in the works of redemption, hence I must raise Her, just as I rose from the dead, and this shall be at the same time and hour. For I wish to make Her like Me in all things."**

But the Bible says: *"For he made Him* (not Him and her) *to be sin for us, who knew no sin; that we might be made the righteousness of God in Him.* (2Co 5:21) Redemption was a one-man show. *"Forasmuch as ye know that ye were not redeemed with corruptible things, as silver and gold, from your vain conversation received by from your fathers; But with the precious blood of Christ as of a lamb without blemish and without spot:"* (1 Pet 1:18)

It was Adam alone who bore—and still bears—responsibility for bringing sin and death into the world. It was and is Christ alone who paid our ransom. *"...He was wounded for our transgressions, He was bruised for our iniquities: the chastisement of our peace was upon Him; and with His stripes we are healed. All we like sheep have gone astray; we have turned every one to his own way; and the LORD hath laid on Him* (not Him and her) *the iniquity of us all."* (Isa 53:5, 6) I don't believe for one minute that Our Lord Jesus uttered the words attributed to him above. Moreover, as shown in a previous chapter, Mary's Assumption is a man-made doctrine of Rome, unscriptural in every way, and one more reason why Catholicism is the apostate church.

Remember that this entire Maria de Agreda thing is supposed to have been given her by both Mary the mother of Jesus, and the Most High Majesty. All supposedly was given to her in a series of visions, apparitions and private revelations She states that she was ordered by them to write the book, which should have been entitled—not "The Mystical City of God"—but "New Gospel According To Mary." If that seems a bit judgmental, read on.

An episode that occurred a few days prior to our Lord's ascension into heaven supposedly was revealed to Maria de Agreda in a vision she describes as a meeting attended by the Blessed Trinity—Father, Son and Holy Spirit—by Mary the mother of Jesus, and by our Lord's Apostles. Following is what allegedly transpired.

> **"The Father then spoke to the blessed Mary saying: "My Daughter, to Thee do *I entrust the Church* founded by my Only begotten, the new law of grace He established in the world, and the people, which He redeemed: to Thee do I consign them all."**

Moments later, our Lord is alleged to have said the following:

> **"My most beloved Mother, I go to my Father and in my stead I shall leave Thee, and I charge Thee with the care of my Church; to Thee do I commend its children and my brethren, as the Father has consigned them to Me."**

This, of course is contradictory to another Catholic doctrine—that Christ left the Apostle Peter in charge and at the head of His Church. Obviously contradictions don't bother Rome, but I wonder, did Pius XI ever read this stuff? Shortly thereafter, the combined Trinity—Father, Son and Holy Spirit,—are reported to have said the following:

> **"This is the *Queen* of all created things in heaven and earth; She is the *Protectress of the Church*, the Mistress of creatures, the Mother of piety, the *Intercessor* of the faithful, the *Advocate* of sinners. In her are contained the *mysteries of our Omnipotence* for the salvation of mankind....whoever shall call upon her from his heart shall not perish; whoever shall obtain *her intercession* shall secure for himself *eternal life*."**

The foregoing constitutes an entirely new gospel having Mary—not the Lord Jesus—as the source of redemption and advocacy with the Father. Probably nowhere else will be found more damaging evidence against Rome's claim of papal infallibility. In 1681 a supposedly "infallible" pope—Innocent XI—condemned "The Mystical City of God" and forbade Catholics to read it. That it deals with the most serious matters of faith and morals cannot be denied. And popes, when they speak on matters of faith and morals, are said by Rome to be infallible. Yet in April of 1929, another "infallible" pope—Pius XI—issued the following declaration: **"We grant the apostolic benediction to all readers and promoters of "The Mystical City of God."**

The Gospel taught in the Word of God says only those who call upon the name of the Lord Jesus will be saved. (Rom 10:13) It says that whosoever believes in Jesus will not perish. (John 3:16) It says that He—Jesus—is our advocate with the Father. (1 John 2:1) To believe that the apparitions and visions seen by Maria de Agreda were of and from God, one must be satisfied that there are other ways to be saved than by faith in Christ who said: *"I am the way, the truth, and the life; no man comes to the Father but by me."* (John 14:6) But, of course, there is but one Gospel; all deviations carry the curse that's repeated here: *"But though we, or an angel from heaven, preach any other gospel unto you than that which we have preached unto you, let him be accursed As we said before, so say I now again, if any man preach any other gospel unto you than that ye have received, let him be accursed* (Gal 1:8, 9)

This new cursed "gospel" that received the papacy's "apostolic benediction" says calling on Mary and obtaining her intercession is assurance of eternal life. But the Holy Spirit wrote: *"For there is one God, and one mediator* (only one, not two) *between God and men, the man Christ Jesus."* (1Ti 2:5) And in another place He (the Holy Spirit) wrote: *"Wherefore he is able also to save them to the uttermost that come unto God by him* (not Him and her) *seeing he ever liveth to make intercession for them."* (Heb 7:25)

There is much more blatant heresy and blasphemy in the pages of "The Mystical City of God." For example, in keeping with man-made, false Catholic doctrine, the "Mary" apparition uses—at various times throughout the book—such recognizable Catholic terms as venial and mortal sin, Holy Father and Vicar of Christ in referring to Peter, the Mass, the sacraments, state of grace, Holy Communion, catechumens, the passion of Christ, etc. In one episode, the Marian apparition is supposed to have confided to M. de Agreda the following:

> "I may justly complain of men, that they load themselves with eternal damnation and refuse me the glory of saving their souls."

Mary the created earthly mother of Jesus, able to save souls? I challenge the Roman Catholic clergy, from the lowest priest to the pope in Rome, himself, to cite a single Scripture from the Word of God that confirms such a blasphemous claim. In another episode, the apparition says:

> "I have demonstrated *my ability to save all* by so many thousands of miracles, prodigies, and favors operated in behalf of those devoted to me."

Nowhere in Scripture does the Word of God grant Mary the "ability" to "save" anyone. In chapter 6 of Book 8, M. de Agreda has a vision in which Mary, kneeling at the feet of "Saint" John the Apostle, says:

> "Pardon, my son and my master, my not having fulfilled toward thee the duties of a mother as I ought and as the *Lord had commanded me* when from the cross He appointed thee as my son and me as thy mother."

Does Rome understand that **it's a sin to disobey a commandment of God**? Infallible popes who proclaim Mary as sinless from her conception to her "Assumption," also have endorsed this work in which **Mary admits to the sin** of disobeying what the Lord told her to do. Amazing. It was Adam's sin of ***disobedience*** that created this "veil of tears" to begin with.

Chapter 9 of Book 5 contains the description of a vision in which M. de Agreda sees Mary holding the baby Jesus, Who, though a mere infant, speaks intelligibly to "saint" Joseph as follows:

> "...**father I came from heaven upon this earth in order to be the light of the world, and in order to rescue it from darkness of sin; in order to seek and know my sheep as a good shepherd, to give them the nourishment of eternal life, teach them the way of heaven, open its gates which had been closed by their sins, etc.**"

To this, Joseph in the "profoundest humility," is supposed to have thanked the infant for calling him "father." But a passage in Luke's Gospel attributes the following to our Lord at the age of twelve: *"**And he** (Jesus) **said unto them, How is it that ye sought me? Wist ye not that I must be about my Father's business?**"* (Luke 2:49) Jesus had but one Father and He was not Joseph. Notice, too, the infant alleged to be Jesus, declares his purpose is to **"open heaven's gates,"** a notorious heresy of Catholicism which refuses to acknowledge Christ's payment in full of each believer's sin debt. According to Rome, Christ opened the gates so man could "work" his way through them.

The last chapter of the book relating the alleged crowning of Mary as Queen of heaven, earth, and hell, is probably the most offensively blasphemous communication I've ever read. The words attributed to a holy God who is "no respecter of persons" are simply disgusting. As the priceless crown is placed on Mary's head by "the three divine persons," a voice from the throne is heard saying to her:

> "My Beloved...our kingdom is thine...We give thee power, majesty and *sovereignty*...our own will shall be at thy disposal for the execution of thy wishes...thou shalt be the Empress and Mistress of the militant church...its *Protectress*, its *Advocate*, its *Mother* and *Teacher*...special *Patroness of the Catholic countries*...We make thee the *Depository* of our riches, the treasurer of our goods...nothing do we wish to be given to the world, which does not pass through thy hands."

God's rebuttal to this horrid blasphemy is found in Isaiah. ***"Thus saith the LORD the King of Israel, and his redeemer the LORD of hosts; I am the first, and I am the last; and beside me there is no God."*** (Isa 44:6) Or, Goddess, Empress, Protectress, Mistress, either.

Certainly by now there can be no doubt in anyone's mind regarding the real author of M. de Agreda's many apparitions, visions, and private revelations. What confounds more than anything else, however, is the fact that "infallible" popes have both condemned and positively endorsed this atrocious collection of blasphemies. In the middle of the 20th century, a new edition of "The Mystical City of God" was published with the following endorsement:

> **IMPRIMATUR**
> Santa Fe, New Mexico, February 9, 1949.
> I gladly give my "Imprimatur" as of today, to the new edition of the work, "The Mystical City of God" by Sister Mary of Jesus, to be reprinted from the original authorized Spanish Edition of the year 1902 without change, and already bearing the Imprimatur of His Excellency, Most Reverend H.J. Alerding, Bishop of Fort Wayne.
> +EDWIN V. BYRNE, D.D.

"But though we, or an angel from heaven, preach any other gospel unto you than that which we have preached unto you, let him be accursed. As we said before, so say I now again, if any man preach any other gospel unto you than that ye have received, let him be accursed." Gal 1:8, 9) Background point 11, there is only one Gospel. It's found in the Bible, not in "The Mystical City of God," and certainly not in the cult Catholicism has become.

God will not be served by further quotations from this fountain of heresy. What already has been presented is sufficient to prove once again that the forces which provided the material for Maria de Agreda's manuscript, through apparitions, visions, revelations, etc., were not of God or from God, but most assuredly were from Satan who—for seventeen centuries—has been actively promoting faith and trust in the Catholic religion, the apostate church.

LOURDES, FRANCE, AD 1858.

Perhaps the most famous and believed of all the Marian apparitions, are those which took place in the year 1858, beginning in February and culminating in July. Eighteen times an apparition allegedly appeared to a 14-year-old peasant girl, Bernadette Soubirous. When pressed for a description of the vision, Bernadette responded as follows:

> "She has the appearance of a young girl of sixteen or seventeen. She is dressed in a white robe, girdled at the waist with a blue ribbon which flows down all along her robe. She wears upon her head a veil which is also white; this veil gives just a glimpse of her hair and then falls down at the back below her waist. Her feet are bare but covered by the last folds of her robe except at the point where a yellow rose shines upon each of them. She holds on her right arm a rosary of white beads with a chain of gold shining like the two roses on her feet."

The appearances took place in a remote grotto some distance from Bernadette's humble home, and about the same distance from the little town of Lourdes. By the fourth or fifth appearance spectators had begun to attend the sightings, but the apparitions were visible only to Bernadette. What the spectators saw was a teenage girl who appeared each time to become entranced, her eyes fixed unflinchingly on a niche in the rocks of the place, her facial expressions changing periodically from smiles to frowns, occasionally even to tears. She seemed to be in conversation with someone, but no audible words issued from her lips. In her possession during each of the appearances was a candle for light in the pre-dawn of the winter mornings when most of the visits occurred, and a rosary which she said she and the "lady" prayed together.

(How odd that "Mary" would pray the following 50 times to "herself" with each recitation of the rosary: "Hail Mary full of grace, the Lord is with thee; blessed art thou amongst women, and blessed is the fruit of thy womb—Jesus. Holy Mary, mother of God, pray for us sinners, now and at the hour of our death, amen." Very strange, indeed.)

Unlike most of the other Marian apparitions this one was anything but verbose. Bernadette claimed the beautiful lady spoke not a word during the first appearance on February 11th, 1858. As the second appearance (Sunday, Feb. 14th) was in progress, Bernadette's brother, Antoine, in obedience to their worried mother, pulled the girl away from the grotto while she was still entranced. He reported that her eyes remained fixed a little bit in front and above her all the way to a landmark called the Savvy Mill. Only when they had arrived there did the expression of intense ecstasy on her face disappear, there to be replaced by her normal countenance.

The apparition's first words were spoken on the third appearance, Thursday, February 18th. Bernadette was told to be at the grotto every day for the next two weeks. The lady also said:

> "I do not promise to make you happy in this world, but in the next."

But the following day—Friday, February 19—the lady again was silent. During that appearance, however, Bernadette reported hearing loud, contentious, ANGRY VOICES coming up from the river URGING HER TO ESCAPE. Upon hearing the commotion, Bernadette related, the "lady" shifted her eyes in the direction of the voices that immediately "were seized with fear" and began at once to diminish. Shortly thereafter they ceased entirely. The apparition's promise to make Bernadette happy in the next life violates background point 10, and is a contradiction of Catholic teachings that we have been created to "know God, to love Him and to Serve Him in this life, and to be happy forever with **Him** in the next." (Baltimore Catechism, Lesson 1, question 6.)

The apparition gave Bernadette a private prayer during the next appearance, Saturday the 20th. From that day until her death Bernadette recited the prayer daily, but never revealed it to another person. The following day, Sunday, the girl was distressed during the vision by the look of abject sorrow on the lady's face. When she was asked the reason for her sadness the lady responded,

"Pray for the sinners."

By this time, crowds were assembling at the grotto each morning; reporters were implying that the whole thing was a scam, and her parents were fearful for the girl's sanity. She was forbidden to go to the grotto on Monday the 22nd; was ordered to go directly to school. On her way to school she said she came up against **"an invisible barrier (that) prevented me from passing."** Unable to comply with her parents' instructions she went to the grotto, but experienced no vision that day.

At the urging of a trusted relative, Bernadette's parents permitted her return to the grotto early the following morning—Tuesday, February 23rd. During this encounter, Bernadette was given three secrets by the apparition, secrets that were for Bernadette only, not to be shared with anyone else, not even her Confessor. Even at death's door, the girl never revealed the secrets. During the vision of the next day—Wednesday—the crowd observed Bernadette's usually rapt, ecstatic expression change to one of abject sadness; tears streamed down her cheeks, her arms fell limply to her sides. Turning from the niche in the rocks she faced the crowd and three times repeated the words **"Penitence, penitence, penitence!"** (Roman Catholic terms) The first of two "miracles" occured during the vision of Thursday, February 25th. While she was reciting her rosary, Bernadette was directed by the apparition in a serious but friendly voice:

> "Go, drink and wash in the fountain."

When Bernadette—seeking to comply—went in the wrong direction, she was called back and pointed to a spot below and to the left of the grotto. Bernadette relates that she saw no water there. Witnesses who were present say that the girl went one way, then another way, then went down on her knees and began scraping the ground with her hands. The spot she was scraping turned to a wet slimy mud as a little water released from the ground. Bernadette cupped her hands and ingested some of the muddy water, leading spectators to believe that the child was mad. When, later, Bernadette also ate some of the vegetation growing on the floor of the grotto, spectators were convinced of her mindless condition. But afterwards the girl reported the apparition had pointed to the grotto floor while directing her to:

> "Go, eat of the herbs you will find there."

(Would Mary, the mother of Jesus, have directed a young girl to ingest muddy water and eat grass?) Though the crowd of witnesses went away believing Bernadette had lost her mind, the little trickle of water from the ground where she had scraped became by the next day a notable stream, one that eventually became a small river, and continues still to flow. (Satan, "the god of this world" would have known an underground stream or spring was there.)

During the next vision on Saturday, February 27th, she was observed approaching the rock of the niche where the lady supposedly appeared, kissing the ground all along the way. This, she explained afterwards, was in compliance with the lady's instruction to

> "Go, and kiss the ground in penance for sinners."

Another familiar Catholic term—penance. But how would kissing the ground make reparation for sinners? Was Calvary a charade? Refer to background points 3 and 4. Later in the same episode, she was directed by the apparition to:

> "Go, and tell the priests to have a chapel built here."

With fear and trepidation, Bernadette, accompanied by a trusted relative, brought the apparition's request for a chapel to the local clergy where she was told to find out the "beautiful lady's" name. Thereafter during each subsequent encounter, Bernadette claimed to have asked the apparition to identify itself. Her request was studiously avoided, but with a smile, each time.

On Monday, March 1st, a friend gave Bernadette a rosary, asking her to have the beautiful lady bless it. During the vision, the apparition reportedly asked Bernadette what had happened to her own rosary. Bernadette held up the rosary she was using and said **"Here it is."** To this the apparition is alleged to have replied:

"You are wrong; this rosary is not yours."

The girl then realized she had mistakenly taken out the rosary given her by her friend. When she returned it to her pocket and held up her own rosary, the apparition is supposed to have said, smiling,

"Use those."

On the next day, Tuesday, she was told once again to tell the priests that she wished a chapel built, and on this occasion the apparition had added a second request:

"I wish people to come here in procession."

The encounter of Wednesday, March 4th, did not take place at its usual early morning time, but late in the day. The apparition is alleged to have explained her morning absence as follows:

"You did not see me this morning because there were some people there who wanted to see what you looked like in my presence. They were not worthy of this honor; they spent the night at the grotto and they dishonored it."

The following day, Thursday, after completing the recitation of her rosary in the apparition's presence, Bernadette could not lift her hand to make the sign of the cross that indicated she was finished. Afterwards she explained that the lady hadn't finished her prayer and until she made the sign of the cross (a Catholic practice) Bernadette was not able to do so. (This brief but significant loss of motor control is suggestive of a hypnotic condition or trance.)

Though the girl went often to the grotto after March 4th, it was not until Thursday, March 25 that the apparition appeared to her again. On this occasion, when asked for its name, Bernadette related the following:

> **"The lady was standing above the rose bush, in a position very similar to that shown on the miraculous medal.** (A Catholic sacramental) **At my third request, her face became very serious and she seemed to bow down in an attitude of humility. Then she joined her hands and raised them to her breast. She looked up to heaven. Then, slowly opening her hands and leaning towards me, she said to me in a voice vibrating with emotion: 'I am the Immaculate Conception.'"**

Subsequently, Bernadette saw the apparition on two other occasions, on the morning of Wednesday, April 7th, and for the last time on Friday, July 18th. Witnesses to her ecstatic trance during the April appearance were astounded when the candle she was holding became tipped in a manner that caused the flame to bear directly on her other hand. After her three-quarter-hour rhapsody ended it was discovered that her hand showed no sign of having been burned. Thus the Lourdes apparitions are known for the two miracles—the spring of water and the tipped candle. Rome declared the apparitions to be authentic and worthy of belief by the faithful in 1862. Since then the number of individuals visiting the shrine that was constructed there has continued to grow. Today official calculations set the number of visitors at nearly 5.5 million persons per year. Numerous healings over the years have been attributed to bathing in or drinking the Lourdes "holy" waters.

Although the words spoken by the Apparition were few and far between there was enough said for us to contradict Rome and declare the apparitions another deception of the devil. By declaring itself to be the Immaculate Conception, the apparition placed itself in direct opposition to the Word of God. *"**Wherefore, as by one man sin entered into the world, and death by sin; and so death passed upon all men, for that all have sinned.**"* (Rom 5:12) The Bible is crystal clear in its message that only the Lord Jesus was the perfect, sinless *"**Lamb of God.**"* (John 1:36) *"**For all have sinned and come short of the glory of God;**"* (Rom 3:23) And, *"**As it is written, There is none righteous, no, not one:**"* (Rom 3:10)

In the second chapter it was shown that the Immaculate Conception doctrine is not found or even inferred anywhere in God's Word; that the early Church fathers did not entertain or promote such a belief. The Apostle John, to whom Jesus on the cross entrusted the care of Mary, wrote five books of the Bible and never once mentioned Mary as having been specially conceived or her body assumed into heaven at her death. It is hard to believe that John wouldn't at least have mentioned such miraculous occurrences had they actually taken place. There is no support for the Assumption doctrine, and the only support for the Immaculate Conception is in a spurious document dating from the fourth century. A monk, John Duns Scotus resurrected the belief in the 13th century and the blasphemous "Mystical City of God" in the 17th century contributed much to its acceptance.

The strange coincidence of the Lourdes apparitions occurring less than four years after Pius IX declared the Immaculate Conception a Catholic article of faith probably was not a coincidence at all for there was much residual opposition to the pope's proclamation. Be assured that Satan is served by directing attention away from Christ our Savior, and would have been most anxious that the Immaculate Conception doctrine be perpetuated.

There are other impediments to the authenticity of the Lourdes apparitions, including it's endorsement of the rosary, its promise to make Bernadette happy in the next life, and its call for "penance, penance, penance!" which Bernadette repeated to the onlookers during the 8th appearance on February 24th. Mary the mother of Jesus knew nothing of the rosary, which in her lifetime would only have been associated with false religions of the orient. Had she been the vision seen by the girl she would have promised her happiness in the next life only through faith and trust in the Lord Jesus. (Background point 10) Lastly, had the apparition been that of Mary the mother of Jesus, she never would have used the term penance which is a Roman Catholic exclusive. In 66 books of the Bible the word penance appears not once. It is Rome's deliberate misinterpretation of Christ's command to repent. *"From that time Jesus began to preach, and to say, repent for the kingdom of heaven is at hand."* (Mat 4:17)

The Catholic Church loves that word penance for it entails works, and works is what the entire Roman Catholic religion is based on. The Biblical word repent seems to be completely absent from Rome's list of buzzwords. The Catholic faithful are taught that doing penitential works can make up for sinful behavior. But the good news is that repentance is a lot easier, and it's from God not from man. In repentance the responsibility to atone for sins is turned over to the Lord Jesus Christ. On the sinner's part, the mind is made up to turn away from sins while turning to Him for the grace and the power to forsake them. Trust in man-made Catholic schemes for salvation when forsaken, enable Catholics to begin placing their trust in the completed sacrifice of Christ Jesus our Lord. Truth is that ten thousand penances performed by the most devout Catholic will not buy God's pardon or cancel the punishment due for even one of the littlest sins ever committed. But a change of heart—repentance—and complete trust in Christ will free the filthiest sinner from having to pay for his or her own sins, and will open the hardest heart to be indwelt by the Holy Spirit of Jesus.

Besides the deliberate deception of the apparition itself, there is another dark side to the Lourdes experience that is not generally known. Recall if you will, the encounter of February 19th. During that episode Bernadette reported hearing loud contentious voices urging her to escape. The vision, she said, quelled the noise with a glance in the direction from which the voices were emanating. After the apparitions had ended, a young woman and a young man—on separate occasions—experienced unearthly voices coming from the grotto, voices that literally terrified them. And a youth who had left some companions to pray at the grotto for a few minutes saw a beautiful "lady" walking toward him with her hands and lower body concealed in a gray cloud-like substance. Said the boy after he calmed down, **"She fixed her great black eyes on me and seemed to wish to seize me. I thought at once it was the devil and I fled!"**

In the book of Luke, chapter 16, our Lord related the life and death experiences of two men, one lavishly rich but unnamed, the other a poor sore-infested beggar named Lazarus. Both died. Lazarus went to Abraham's bosom, the place where saved souls awaited Christ's sacrifice on Calvary. The rich man went to hell and was tormented. Seeing Abraham and Lazarus across a gulf separating the two places, the rich man asked Abraham to have Lazarus dip just the tip of his finger in water and come and cool his tongue for, as he said, *"I am tormented in this flame."* (Luke 16:24)

In responding to the rich man's plea, Abraham pointed out that the gulf separating them could not be traversed from either direction, which brought a response from the rich man that is the point of this example. Said he to Abraham: *"…I pray thee, therefore, father, that thou wouldest send him* (Lazarus) *to my father's house: For I have five brethren; that he may testify unto them, lest they also come into this place of torment."* (Luke 16:27, 28) Here, in the very words of our Lord is an example of a lost sinner's desire to warn loved ones still alive to avoid eternal life in such awful torment. Could the loud voices Bernadette heard urging her to escape have been lost souls trying to warn her about the real identity of the apparition? Was it Satan who with a mere glance intimidated the voices into silence? After the apparitions ended were the voices again raised in warning?

When we compare the Lourdes experiences to the unchanging, settled-in-heaven Word of God, we come away once more with the conviction that the whole thing was a monstrous hoax, once again aimed at promoting the Roman

Catholic religion. That there were a couple of miracles performed and have been healings attributed to the Lourdes waters has nothing whatever to do with the identity of the apparition. Our Lord, we remember, warned us that such great signs and wonders would be worked in the last days by the evil forces, (background point 12) that even the elect would come dangerously close to being deceived.

FATIMA. PORTUGAL, 1917.

As famous as the Lourdes apparitions of the 19th century were, the ones that occurred at Fatima, Portugal, early in the 20th century have become even more famous. Whereas the vision that appeared at Lourdes spoke rarely and verbalized but one request—that a chapel be built there in its name—the visions, yes, visions, (plural), of Fatima were extremely talkative and put forth many demands. Events actually began in the spring of 1916 with the appearance of an "angel" on three occasions to three Portuguese children—shepherds. Lucia dos Santos, aged 9, was the oldest; her cousins, Francisco and Jacinta Marto were aged 8 and 6 respectively. All three were of the Catholic religion. On the first appearance to the children, the "angel" reportedly said:

> **"Don't be afraid; I am the angel of peace. Pray with me."** Prostrating itself, the vision then prayed as follows: **"My God, I believe, I adore, and I love you! I beg pardon of you for those who do not believe, do not adore, do not hope and do not love you."**

He is alleged to have repeated this prayer three times, then, as the appearance ended, he instructed the children as follows:

> **"Pray thus; the hearts of Jesus and Mary are attentive to the voice of your supplications."**

At the second appearance in the summer of 1916, the "angel" directed the children to:

> **"Pray, pray a great deal. The hearts of Jesus and Mary have merciful designs on you. Offer prayers and sacrifices continually to the Most High. Make everything you do a sacrifice, and offer it as an act of REPARATION FOR THE SINS by which God is offended, and as a petition for the conversion of sinners. Bring peace to our country in this way....I am the guardian angel of Portugal. Accept and bear with submission all the**

sufferings the Lord will send you." (Compare this angel with the "prince" of the Kingdom of Persia, Daniel 10:13.)

Before going to the third appearance of the angel, I am compelled to comment on the above. The Bible says Jesus has merciful designs on all. *"For there is no respect of persons with God."* (Rom 2:11) He has no favorites, plays no favorites, wants everyone to be saved. He is the One *"Who will have all men to be saved, and to come unto the knowledge of the truth."* (l Tim 2:4) Moreover, even if an individual volunteered to be nailed to a cross as a sacrificial act for the reparation of sins, not even one little white lie would be atoned for in the eyes of a holy God. For two reasons. First, only one man in all of history qualified as the sinless, unblemished sacrifice that could satisfy the demands for justice of a holy God. His name was Jesus. Second. Every sin committed by every believer in every age from creation to the end of time, was fully and completely expiated by that same Jesus on Calvary's cross. It is obvious at once that the "guardian angel of Portugal"—a demonic "prince"—was sent by the god of this world, not by the holy God we serve. (Cf. Dan 10:13)

The "angel's" final appearance in the fall of 1916 was even more bizarre. He appeared to the children with a chalice that he suspended in the air. Above it there was a host. (Catholic term for the Communion wafer) Drops of blood fell from the host into the chalice. The "angel" prostrated himself on the ground and said

> **"Most Holy Trinity, Father, Son, Holy Spirit, I adore you profoundly and offer you the most precious body, blood, soul and divinity of Jesus Christ**—(who is) **present in all the tabernacles of the earth—in reparation for the outrages, sacrileges, and indifference with which He Himself is offended. And through the infinite merits of His most sacred heart, and of the immaculate heart of Mary, I beg of you the conversion of poor sinners."**

After repeating the above three times, the "angel" lifted up the host saying:

> **"Take and drink the body and blood of Jesus Christ, horribly insulted by ungrateful men.** *Make reparation* **for their crimes and console your God."**

He then gave the host to Lucia, the only one who had received her first Holy Communion. I am again constrained to offer the following commentary on the preceding blasphemy. *"But this man, after he had offered one sacrifice for sins for ever, sat down on the right hand of God; From henceforth expecting till his enemies be made his Footstool. For by one offering he hath perfected for ever them that are sanctified"* (Heb 10:12-14) Fifty-trillion people ingesting little round hosts will not make reparation for the theft of a half-chewed pencil. It is a denigration of Christ's selfless sacrifice to say or believe otherwise. Furthermore, as we have shown in previous chapters, Jesus is not present in those countless hosts stuffed in chalices and locked in the tabernacles of Catholic churches all over the world.

A further blasphemy is the imputation to Mary of any "merits" in the conversion of sinners. Christ did that all by Himself. He needed no help from His earthly mother or anyone else. (Background point 10) To have encouraged a child of nine to believe she could make reparation for sins by ingesting a host was criminal, and certainly not of or from the holy God who died for her sins. I am still astonished at the "angel's" suggestion that the all-sufficient, sovereign God needs to be "consoled."

As I have researched these various apparitions, and compared the things said with the Word of God, I've experienced a feeling of utter helplessness and frustration at the realization so many millions upon millions of souls have been led to believe these things are of God. I have wished for a way to tell the Catholic faithful all over the world that Jesus did it all. No one can add to what He did even by the most holy acts imaginable. And Mary, wonderful Mary, was so blessed; chosen by God to be the channel through which the Savior was to enter the world. A great servant was she. But not sinless and pure as Jesus. This sweet, humble creature who fulfilled her role—as did John the Baptist, Peter, the other Apostles, Paul, Silas, Stephen, Timothy, and all the rest—was a loving wife and mother who bore Joseph four natural sons and at least two daughters. Worthy is she of our great love and respect. But it is blasphemy of the Holy Spirit to exalt her to the level of God Himself as Rome has done with the help of the Marian apparitions. As for the Fatima apparitions themselves, they began occurring on May 13, 1917 with the "lady" floating down on a cloud, surrounded by a bright light and holding a rosary

"Don't be afraid. I won't hurt you,"

These were the first words attributed to "her." "She" then said "she" was from heaven; wanted the three children to come there on the 13th of each month for the next six months. 'She" told Lucia in, response to a question, that she would go to heaven. Jacinta and Francisco also would go to heaven but Francisco would have to say many **rosaries**. "She" told Lucia that of two girls who had died recently, one already was in heaven; the other would be in Purgatory (Catholic invention) until the end of the world. Then (here we go again) "she" asked the children the following question:

> "Do you wish to offer yourselves to God, to endure all the suffering He may please to send you, as an act of reparation for the sins by which He is offended, and to ask for the conversion of sinners?"

When the children said yes, "she" told them they would have to suffer much, but God's grace would be their comfort. Knowing how Jesus loved the little children, (Mat 19:14, Mark 10:14, Luke 18:16) my mind balks at the thought He would send His earthly mother to enlist three little kids, ages 9, 8, and 6, to suffer for the "reparation of sins" He already had atoned for, and to pray for the conversion of sinners.

On Wednesday, June 13th the second appearance occurred. Several dozen curious onlookers were with the three children as the cloud descended and hovered over a bush near where the children stood. In this encounter, the "lady" allegedly spoke as follows:

> "I want you to come on the 13th day of the next month and to pray the rosary every day and I want you to learn to read. Yes, I will take Francisco and Jacinta (to heaven) soon, but you (Lucia) must remain on earth for some time. Jesus wishes to use you to make me better known and loved. He wishes to establish in the world devotion to my immaculate heart."

Besides promoting recitation of the pagan-inspired Rosary, the apparition's claim that Jesus desired establishment of devotion to Mary is a serious contradiction of God's Word which says: *"I am the LORD: that is my name: and my glory will I not give to another neither my praise to graven images."* (Isa 42:8) Lucia then wanted to know if she would have to stay on earth all alone, to which the "lady" is reported to have replied:

> "No, my child, and would that make you suffer? Do not be disheartened. My immaculate heart will never abandon you, but will be your refuge and *the way that will lead you to God.*"

Two serious contradictions of God's Word are apparent here. First: ***"Let your conversation be without covetousness; and be content with such things as ye have: for he hath said, I will never leave thee, nor forsake thee."*** (Heb 13:5) God's Word says it is Jesus, not Mary or anyone else, who will never abandon the believer. And the second: ***"Jesus saith unto him, I am the way, the truth, and the life: no man cometh unto the Father, but by me."*** (John 14:6) There is one "way" to God, and it is not Mary the mother of Jesus. But, common to all of the Marian apparitions are claims such as the above that usurp God's promises and powers.

There were about 5000 spectators at the third appearance on Saturday, July 13th. During this encounter, the "lady" gave the children three "secrets." (Note that the Lourdes apparition had given Bernadette "three secrets," also.) Before the secrets, "she" repeated previous instructions to:

> **"…pray the rosary every day in honor of Our Lady of the Rosary, in order to obtain peace for the world and the end of the war for she alone can help."**

Then the "lady" promised that in October she would reveal her identity and perform a miracle…

> **"…so that everyone may see and believe."**

Several serious contradictions to God's Word are observed here. For one thing, praying to Mary (background point 5) is useless for two reasons. One, God has already established when peace will come, and who will bring it about: ***"And he shall judge among the nations, and shall rebuke many people: and they shall beat their swords into plowshares, and their spears into pruninghooks: nation shall not lift up sword against nation, neither shall they learn war any more."*** (Isa 2:4) Two, praying to Mary or anyone else is in opposition to our Lord's instructions to the Apostles to pray in His name to the Father. (John 14:13, 14.) (Background point #5)

Another contradiction is found in the phrase "she alone can help." Our Lord said nothing can be done if He is not in it. ***"…without me ye can do nothing."*** (John 15:5) The last contradiction is seen in the statement that a future miracle will cause everyone to believe. However, God's Word tells us that miracles don't guarantee belief. Christ worked many notable miracles during His earthly ministry and was crucified. Abraham told the rich man in hell that the greatest miracle of all would be to no avail if the Scriptures are not believed and observed. *"And he said unto him, If they hear not Moses and the prophets, neither will they be persuaded, though one rose from the dead."* (Luke 16:31) Though Jesus rose from the dead, billions refuse to believe.

During that third appearance Lucia was heard to say the "lady" wanted people to recite the rosary. Then, before disclosing the three secrets, the "lady" instructed the children as follows:

> **"Sacrifice yourselves for sinners and say often, especially when you make some sacrifice, 'O my Jesus, this is for the love of You, for the conversion of sinners, and in *reparation* for the offenses committed *against* the Immaculate Heart of *Mary*.'"**

(The alleged offenses committed against the "immaculate heart of Mary" are enumerated later.) The first "secret" given to the children was a vision of hell. The children were so frightened by it that subsequently they undertook the most severe sacrifices. (Would the gentle Mary have shown a sight of such unspeakable horror to three innocent little children?) After showing them the vision, the "lady" allegedly said:

> **"In order to save them,** (sinners) **God wishes to establish in the world devotion to my Immaculate Heart. If people do what I ask, many souls will be saved and there will be peace"** (Cf. Isa 42:8 and background point 10.)

Another contradiction of Scripture is apparent in the above. While on earth, our Lord said it was His purpose, and His alone, to save sinners. *"When Jesus heard it, he saith unto them, They that are whole have no need of the physician, but they that are sick: I came not to call the righteous, but sinners to repentance."* (Mar 2:17) *"For the Son of man is come to seek and to save that which was lost."* (Luke 19:10) Devotion to Mary's alleged "immaculate heart" has as much chance of saving someone's soul as a punctured inner-tube has of saving a drowning man.

The second secret given by the "lady" to the children was a prophecy that World War I would end, (no date given) but another worse one would come in the reign of Pius XI if people kept offending God. (Pius XII, not Pius XI, was the pope of WW II, and the Bible tells us people will be offending God till the end of time.) A "night illuminated by an unknown light" would announce the beginning of God's punishment of the world. He would use war, famine, persecution of the Church (Catholicism) and the Holy Father to accomplish His chastisement. However, the "lady" promised:

> "**To prevent it** (God's punishment) **I shall come to ask for the consecration of Russia to my Immaculate Heart, and the communion of reparation on the first Saturdays.**"

The "lady" promised that a positive response to "her" requests would assure the conversion of Russia (to Catholicism) and peace in the world. If not, many would be martyred, the pope would suffer much, nations would be destroyed. But in the end:

> "**My Immaculate Heart will triumph. The Holy Father will consecrate Russia to me; it will be converted (to Catholicism) and a certain period of peace will be granted to the world.**"

It is not likely that fulfilling the "lady's" requests then or now would produce peace in the world, for the Word of God says: *"I form the light, and create darkness: I MAKE PEACE and create evil: I the LORD do all these things."* (Isa 45:7) And, we know from God's Word there is a "Prince of Peace," (Isa 9:6) but nowhere in Scripture do we read about a princess or a queen of peace. Russia, consecrated by the papacy to Mary for almost a century now, remains unconverted to Catholicism, and world peace continues to elude us. *"The prophet which prophesieth of peace, when the word of the prophet shall come to pass, then shall the prophet be known, that the LORD hath truly sent him."* (Jer 28:9) Obviously the apparition was no prophet sent by God.

During this same appearance, the "lady" disclosed to the children a third "secret" which Lucia earmarked for opening in 1960, but was not revealed by Rome until the year 2000. The third "secret" is printed in its entirety later, and the reader will see why the popes were loathe to discuss its contents at all. Disclosure of the third secret ended the July apparition and the August 13th visitation didn't come about until the 19th because the authorities had taken the children into custody on the earlier date. The "lady's" message on the 19th was more prayer and sacrifice for sinners, and a promise to bring with her on the October 13th appearance, St Joseph, baby Jesus, and our Lord. The September 13th appearance brought another instruction to recite the rosary daily in order to obtain the end of the war.

On October 13th there were an estimated 70,000 people on hand to witness the miracle promised by the "lady" and to learn "her" identity. They were not disappointed.

> "I am the Lady of the Rosary, I have come to warn the faithful to amend their lives and ask for pardon for their sins. They must not offend our Lord any more, for He is already too grievously offended by the sins of men. People must say the rosary. Let them continue saying it every day. I would like a chapel built here in my honor; the war will end soon."

It didn't "end soon." It lasted another horrible 13 months. And when our Lord was asked by His Apostles, "teach us to pray," He did not instruct them to say, "Hail, Mary, full of grace." Rather said He, *"After this manner therefore pray ye: Our Father which art in heaven, Hallowed be thy name…etc."* (Mat 6:9) Would His blessed mother have ordered the faithful to disobey her Son by praying—not to the Father—but to herself? Such a possibility is no possibility at all!

Saturday, October 13, 1917, dawned with a relentless downpour that continued as the crowd gathered in the field where each of the apparitions had taken place. Some said the mud had become ankle-deep by the time Lucia cried out **"Put down your umbrellas, everyone!"** The rain stopped. The clouds began to dissolve and a silvery sun was seen. When, after finishing speaking to the children, the "lady" pointed to the sun, it began—according to eyewitness reports—to whirl and dance in the sky. Some said it changed colors and seemed to fall toward the earth, terrifying the crowd. This phenomenon supposedly was visible over a 600-square-mile area, but only reporters for the Portuguese press gave accounts of it. It was said to have lasted for about twelve minutes, during which time, the children were exposed to visions of Jesus, Joseph and Mary, and to Jesus carrying His cross. Thus ended the Fatima apparitions to the three children. But in alleged private appearances to Jacinta the 6-year-old, the, "lady" is credited with the following:

> A) "Our Lady can no longer uphold the arm of her divine Son which will strike the world. If people amend their lives, our Lord will even now save the world, but if they do not punishment will come." B) "If the government of a country leaves the church in peace and gives liberty to our holy religion, (Catholicism) it will be blessed by God." C) "Tell everybody that God gives graces through the Immaculate Heart of Mary. Tell them to ask graces from her, and that the heart of Jesus wishes to be venerated together with the Immaculate Heart of Mary. Ask them to plead for peace

from the Immaculate Heart of Mary, for *the Lord has confided the peace of the world to her."*

That the Catholic church endorses this kind of blasphemy is proof positive that it is the apostate church, teaching for doctrines a gospel far removed from that which was preached by Paul, Peter, John, et al. When the revelations to Jacinta are exposed to the light of Scripture, the influence of the "Father of Liars" is clearly visible. It is not an apparition, or even the real mother of Jesus, that holds back the arm of divine justice; rather it is God's own Holy Spirit. *"For the mystery of iniquity doth already work: only He* (the Holy Spirit) *who now letteth will let, until He be taken out of the way."* (2 Th 2:7) When Christ's Church is "caught up" out of the world, the Holy Spirit that indwells it will have been "taken out of the way" as well, permitting the arm of divine justice to fall upon a sin-wracked world.

With respect to the dispensation of graces, no third party is involved. Thanks to Calvary, all who believe may approach directly Him who is the dispenser of mercy, love and grace. *"Seeing then that we have a great high priest, that is passed into the heavens, Jesus the Son of God, let us hold fast our profession. For we have not an high priest which cannot be touched with the feeling of our infirmities; but was in all points tempted like as we are, yet without sin. Let us therefore come boldly unto the throne of grace that we may obtain mercy, and find grace to help in time of need."* (Heb 4:14-16)

Furthermore, the possibility of God "confiding" the peace of the world, or any other worldly matter, into the hands of someone other than Himself is nil and none. *"My righteousness is near; My salvation is gone forth, and mine arms shall judge the people; the isles shall wait upon me and on mine arm shall they trust."* (Isa 51:5) *"I am the LORD; that is my name; and my glory will I not give to another,"* (Isa 42:8) All that pertains to the world is for God's pleasure and for His sake alone. *"For mine own sake, even for mine own sake, will I do it, and I will not give my glory unto another.* (Isa 48:11) There is only one way and one who leads the way: *"Thus saith the LORD, thy Redeemer, the Holy One of Israel; I am the LORD thy God which teacheth thee to profit, which leadeth thee by the way that thou shouldest go."* (Isa 48:17)

The sun was back in its place. The mud had turned to dust. The 70,000 spectators had gone home. A great basilica to Our Lady of Fatima soon would be constructed there, to be visited each year by millions of pilgrims seeking her favor. But the Fatima saga was not quite over. On December 10th, while Lucia was praying in chapel, a vision appeared to her, a "lady" holding an infant. It was the child who spoke, saying:

> "Have pity on the heart of your most holy mother. It is covered with thorns, with which ungrateful men pierce it every moment, and there is no one to remove them with an *act of reparation.*"

It was then seen that the "lady" of the apparition was holding a heart encircled with sharp thorns. Then spoke the "lady" herself:

> "Behold my heart surrounded with thorns which ungrateful men place therein at every moment by their blasphemies and ingratitude. You at least try to console me. Announce in my name that I promise to help at the hour of death with the graces needed for salvation whoever on the first Saturday of five consecutive months shall: 1) confess and receive holy Communion; 2) recite five decades of the rosary; 3) keep me company for fifteen minutes while meditating on the fifteen mysteries of the rosary, with the intention of *making reparation to me.*"

We are told that reparation to Mary must be made to atone for the five ways people offend her Immaculate Heart These offenses are: 1. Attacks on Mary's Immaculate Conception. Scripture is the worst offender. *"For all have sinned, and come short of the glory of God."* (Rom 3:23) 2. Attacks against her perpetual virginity. Scripture is the worst offender. *"Is not this the carpenter's son? is not his mother called Mary? and his brethren, James, and Joses, and Simon, and Judas? And his sisters, are they not all with us?"* (Mat 13:55, 56) 3. Attacks on her divine maternity; refusal to accept her as mother of all mankind. Scripture is the worst offender. *"When Jesus therefore saw his mother, and the disciple standing by, whom he loved, he saith unto his mother, Woman behold thy son! Then saith he to the disciple, Behold thy mother And from that hour that disciple took her unto his own home."* (John 19:26, 27.) 4. For public attempts to make children indifferent, contemptuous, hateful of her. Scripture is the worst offender. *"Teaching them to observe all things whatsoever I have commanded you,"* (Mat 28:20) Note: No born-again Christian teaches hatred of Mary the mother of Jesus. 5. For insults of her sacred images. Scripture is the worst offender. *"Thou shalt not make unto thee any graven image, or any likeness of any thing that is in heaven above, or that is in the earth beneath, or that is in the water under the earth.* (Exo 20:4)

There are no thorns in the heart of Mary the mother of Jesus. All the thorns were in the crown that sinful man pounded into the blessed head of our Lord Jesus. There is no reparation to be made to Mary, nor even to Jesus. The one, only and complete reparation for every sin ever committed or still to be committed was expiated, propitiated, atoned for, paid for, taken out of the way, 2000 years ago on Christ's Calvary cross. For man to believe that he himself can atone for a single sin is a blasphemy of the Holy Spirit, and obviates the need for our blessed Lord's suffering and death. Not only is there none righteous, no not one, but what righteous acts we perform are not very sanitary in the eyes of a holy God. *"But we are all as an unclean thing, and all our righteousnesses are as filthy rags; and we all do fade as a leaf; and our iniquities, like the wind, have taken us away."* (Isa 64:6) Man's attempts to atone for his own sins is like trying to clean a window with an oily rag. The best of us, the most devout, is totally devoid of any true righteousness. That only comes from God through faith in Christ Jesus. *"For he hath made him to be sin for us who knew no sin; that we might be made the righteousness of God in him."* (2Co 5:21)

Like all of the other apparitions, Fatima was a repudiation of the Word of God. In the first appearance, if Francisco went to heaven when he died it was not because of the rosaries he said per instructions of the "lady." If he went to heaven it was through the merits of our Lord and Savior Christ Jesus. If he went to heaven it was because he truly believed in Jesus and His Calvary sacrifice. If he went to heaven it was because God imputed to him as a believer the sinless, righteousness of the Lord Jesus. For him to have depended on reciting the rosary for his salvation would have meant the eternal loss of his soul in hell. By referring to Purgatory during the first appearance, the apparition revealed its source to be from someone other than God. Purgatory is a Catholic invention unsupported by the Word of God and with no historical presence in the early Christian Church. That all of the apparitions from Guadalupe to Fatima continually confirmed critical sections of false Catholic doctrine is eloquent proof of an ongoing effort to convert souls to Catholicism, to turn them away from total reliance on the Word of God, to entangle them in performing works that cannot save them, and can ultimately turn them eternally into hell.

God's Word could not be clearer, could not be easier to understand. He will never—I said, never—promote devotion to any created being, including Mary His earthly mother. He will never—repeat, never—share His glory with a created being. His only begotten Son, suffered the agonies and infamy of Calvary to redeem mankind. No one, but no one, will be allowed to share in that act of infinite love, not Mary, not Moses, not Elijah or Daniel. No One! All of the innocent little children in the world could not by the most severe sacrifices, make reparation (atone) for even one sin. If they could there was no need for Jesus to have suffered. An apparition's promise to "never abandon" a soul and to be the "way" that leads to heaven is as worthy of trust as a candle is to heat a ten-room house. There is but one way to obtain salvation, and only one name given under heaven by which we can be saved. That name is not Mary, not Immaculate Conception, not Lady of the Rosary, not Immaculate Heart, not Mother of God. That name is **JESUS**, only begotten Son of the Most High God, Savior of all who will accept His free gift of faith.

Saying rosaries is not the way to peace, and only God is our source of help. *"the peace of God, which passeth all understanding, shall keep your hearts and minds through Christ Jesus."* (Phi 4:7) *"God is our refuge and strength, a very present help in trouble."* (Psa 46:1) To say as the apparition did during the July 13th appearance that God wants to establish devotion to some creature's "heart" in order to save sinners is an evil of such gigantic proportions as to never be forgiven in this life or the millennium to come. But then, Satan's hope of forgiveness died with his expulsion from heaven.

Moreover, the prophecy about the conversion of Russia through papal dedication to the apparition plus lots of rosaries is basically a collection of empty words. Before communism, before the Bolsheviks, Russia was already a predominantly Christian country. An estimated 80-million citizens were practicing their faith in the Russian Orthodox Church that was not and is not affiliated with Rome. The prophecy is more wishful thinking on Rome's part than anything else. How the Vatican would love to have control over the millions of Russian believers in Jesus. Conversion of Russia to the Roman Catholic Church is what the prophecy was all about, and it hasn't happened. Whether Rome's new policy of conquest through ecumenism succeeds in overcoming the hostility of the Russian Orthodox Church to Rome and the Vatican is in the hands of God, not the pope, the people saying rosaries, or an apparition spouting blasphemies.

That 70,000 people witnessed a dancing sun on October 13th, 1917, has nothing to do with the identity of the vision seen by the children in the various apparitions. For Satan has been permitted great powers by God. In Ephesians 2:2 he is called the *"prince of the power of the air,"* indicating his God-allowed control of that area above the surface of the earth. In John 12:31 our Lord called him the *"prince of this world,"* indicating his influence in all earthly matters. The book of Daniel revealed that Satan has "angels" assigned to influence proceedings in nations and cities. Jesus referred to the city of Pergamos as the place where *"Satan's seat is."* He also told us that in the last times the signs and wonders performed by the evil forces would nearly deceive the very elect—the saved of the Lord.

Early in this chapter it was noted that what is seen with the eyes may not be in accordance with what we hear with our ears. In the case of the "Marian" apparitions that I have researched, only a few of which are featured in this chapter, the reported supernatural beauty of the visions is more than offset by the evil words spoken. In all cases, honor and glory that rightly belongs to the Lord Jesus Christ is usurped and directed toward a created being. In all cases, Catholic false doctrines are expounded as true and God-given, rather than heresies originated by men. In all cases, man's works are validated as a means of gaining or influencing their salvation. In all cases, the Word of God is repudiated.

We can only conclude that the "Marian" apparitions—all of them—are a tool of Satan to leverage biblically illiterate souls into the Roman Catholic Church where their chance of being saved by the grace of God is sharply reduced, and in many cases, I fear, utterly eliminated. Finally, what are we to make of the third and last Fatima "secret"? Originally it was supposed to be made public in 1960. Three popes read it and hid it. At last—in response to intense public pressure—it was revealed in the year 2000 by John Paul II with a lengthy, rather weak attempt to give it credibility. As you read it remember it was given to the Fatima children in July, 1917 for disclosure in 1960.

> "…at the left of Our Lady and a little above, we saw an Angel with a flaming sword in his left hand; flashing, it gave out flames that looked as though they would set the world on fire; but they died out in contact with the splendor that Our Lady radiated towards him from her right hand: pointing to the earth with his right hand, the Angel cried out in a loud voice: 'Penance, Penance! Penance! And we saw—in an immense light that is God something similar to how people appear in a mirror when they pass in front of it—a Bishop dressed in white; we had the impression that it was the Holy Father. Other Bishops, Priests, men and women Religious, going up a steep mountain, at the top of which there was a big Cross of rough-hewn trunks as of a cork-tree with the bark; before reaching there the Holy Father passed through a big city half in ruins, and half trembling with halting step, afflicted with pain and sorrow, he prayed for the souls of the corpses he met on his way; having reached the top of the mountain, on his knees at the foot of the big Cross he was killed by a group of soldiers who fired bullets and arrows at him, and in the same way there died one after another the other Bishops, Priests, men and women Religious, and various lay people of different ranks and positions. Beneath the two arms of the Cross there were two Angels each with a crystal aspersorium in his hand, in which they gathered up the blood of the

Martyrs and with it sprinkled the souls that were making their way to God."

Of special note in the foregoing are the "corpses" met and prayed for along the pope's way, and the total annihilation of pope, bishops, priests, religious order members and the Catholic laity. Are the "corpses" those of all the imposters who—as popes—claimed sovereignty over the body of Christ down through the ages? Is the total annihilation pictured the end-time fate of the apostate Catholic Church?

From The Revelation of Jesus Christ to the Apostle John, we know that the "universal," apostate church of the end times will meet destruction at the hands of the ten powers allied with the anti Christ. (Rev 17:16-18) Satan is a Bible scholar without a human peer. He, of all creatures, is familiar with end-times prophecy. Even now he awaits his chance to indwell the man whose name expressed in numerals will be 666. This third secret given to the Fatima children makes sense only if it came from Satan, and is his understanding of the fate that will befall the Catholic church in the last 3-1/2 years of the great tribulation. In reading it, I sensed that the reason Rome withheld it from publication for more than forty years, was a nagging fear that it accurately portrays its end-times fall as the "Mystery Babylon" of Revelation.

Catholics who are taken in by the various Marian apparitions are to be pitied and prayed for. The more they place their faith and trust in the words the apparitions spoke, the farther they are carried away from biblical truth and a personal relationship with our Savior. That appears to be Satan's plan. Countless millions of souls are being directed to an eternity with him through these always blasphemous encounters. We who are saved by the matchless grace of God will not find a greater prayer need than the millions of lost Catholics who believe themselves to be safe in the arms of an apostate religion, while praying to a sweet, dead lady who neither hears their prayers nor possesses the power to answer them.

9

The Catechism Cataclysm

"For God is not the author of confusion, but of peace, as in all churches of the saints." (1Co 14:33)

There is probably nothing more indicative of the awful confusion that reigns among Roman Catholics than the typical answers one receives from even the most devout Catholics to the question "Are you saved?" Ask it to 100 of the faithful and the answer 100 times will be either "I'm a Catholic" or some variation of "I hope so." The first answer always is a gentle put-down of the questioner, a polite way of saying, "I belong to the only true religion founded by Christ." The second answer, and variations thereof, reveals the individual's dependence on works and the fear that serious sin at the hour of death will somehow negate them. Both responses, however, indicate how really confused Catholics are about salvation and how it is attained.

I was witnessing a while back to a Catholic lady who knew me when I shared her beliefs. During the conversation I asked her exactly how a Catholic gets to heaven. Not only did she not answer me, she became furious. She attacked me for having deserted the one true religion. I was instructed to keep my "heresy" to myself; she would not hear of it. But her heated negative reaction to a simple yet critical question concerning the eternal destiny of her soul is eloquent testimony to this sorry truth: most Catholics haven't a clue as to how one gets to heaven.

Somewhere in the back of the Catholic mind is the belief that being a Roman Catholic is the key qualification—the critical first step, as it were—in one's journey to a heavenly reward. But from that point on the path becomes so muddied by contradictory doctrines and teachings, so obscured by mandatory and voluntary works, as to leave the individual with no clear understanding of how one gets to heaven. As a result, the spiritual life of a great majority of Catholics is comprised of attending weekly Mass, going periodically to Confession and Communion, saying the rosary, and being "good." This, however, is certain: no one will make it to heaven who gives the answer "I'm a Catholic" or "I hope so" to the question "Are you saved?" Upon all who so answer, a holy God will pour out His wrath because they have not believed His Word. Some verses in Paul's second letter to the Corinthians are applicable to modern Catholics whose religion is infected with what I call the Contradiction Affliction, a malady that can be fatal to one's soul.

"But I fear, lest by any means, as the serpent beguiled Eve through his subtilty, so your minds should be corrupted from the simplicity that is in Christ. For if he that cometh (the Vatican) *preacheth another Jesus whom we have not preached, or if ye receive another spirit, which ye have not received, or another gospel which ye have not accepted, ye might well bear with him."* (2 Cor 11:3, 4)

It is a misfortune of disastrous proportions that modern Catholics do not realize the Jesus preached and taught by Rome is not the Jesus of the New Testament; not the Jesus preached by Paul and the early patriarchs. They do not realize that the spirit they have received is the spirit of religion, not the Holy Spirit of Jesus, nor that the gospel they believe is not the Gospel of our Lord Jesus Christ. These are soul-threatening facts—not because I say so—but because God says so in His Word. *"And to you who are troubled rest with us, when the Lord Jesus shall be revealed from heaven with his mighty angels, In flaming fire taking vengeance on them that know not God, and that obey not the gospel of our Lord Jesus Christ. Who shall be punished with everlasting destruction from the presence of the Lord, and from the glory of his power;"* (2Th 1:7-9)

What has been said before bears constant repetition: there is only one Gospel of our Lord Jesus Christ. It is simple, easily understood, a Gospel of grace, not works. Those who embrace it are gifted with eternal life in heaven. Those who don't, find their portion in the lake of fire. Catholics who say they believe in Jesus are very naive, for the Jesus they are taught to believe in is not the Jesus of the New Testament. It is little more than lip service that Rome gives to the Jesus of the Bible. Our Lord might well have been speaking of the pope and the college of cardinals when He said: *"Ye hypocrites, well did Esaias prophesy of you, saying, This people draweth nigh unto me with their mouth, and honoureth me with their lips; but their heart is far from me. But in vain they do worship me, teaching for doctrines the commandments of men."* (Mat 15:7-9)

The Jesus of Catholicism is denied the power to *"...save them to the uttermost that come unto God by him, seeing he ever liveth to make intercession for them."* (Heb 7:25) Rome grants Him the power to open heaven's gates, (Page 268 of the 1994 Catechism) but the faithful are required by penances, works such as sacraments in life, and by suffering in Purgatory afterwards, to expiate their own sins. Nor is the Jesus of Catholicism the only pure, sinless unblemished soul who ever lived. To Mary, Rome has granted sinlessness equal to that of her Creator. Mary, then, theoretically, was equally qualified to be the *"Lamb of God Who takes away the sin of the world,"* (John 1:29) since she, too, according to Rome, was sinless, without spot or blemish. Furthermore, Rome has assigned to Mary the titles "co-mediatrix" and "advocate." Therefore, the Jesus of Catholicism is not our one and only intercessor with the Father as the Bible teaches: *"My little children, these things write I unto you, that ye sin not. And if any man sin, we have an advocate with the Father, Jesus Christ the righteous:"* (1 John 2:1) *"For there is one God, and one mediator between God and men, the man Christ Jesus."* (1 Tim 2:5)

Still think the Jesus of Catholicism is the same as the Jesus of the New Testament? Think again. Rome's Jesus is not the sweet compassionate Jesus who told His Apostles: *"Suffer little children, and forbid them not, to come unto me: for of such is the kingdom of heaven."* (Mat 19:14) Nor is He the Jesus who said to the woman taken in adultery *"Neither do I condemn thee: go, and sin no more."* (John 8:11) Rome's Jesus is unapproachable and aloof. To move Him requires prayer to His earthly mother Mary or some other "saint" who has the Lord's ear. This, in opposition to what our Lord Himself said: *"If ye shall ask any thing in my name I will do it."* (John 14:14) Alfonse Liguori went so far as to say that if Jesus rejected him he would go immediately to Mary and she would assure his salvation. (I shudder at the thought that he faced Jesus an instant after he drew his last breath.) Since Rome fully endorsed the teachings of Liguori by elevating him to "saint of the church" status, the Catholic Jesus, quite obviously, is not the only one with the power to save. His earthly mother Mary has been granted the same power. But by Rome, not by God.

The Catholic Jesus is not the Jesus of Heb 1:3 *"Who being the brightness of his glory, and the express image of his person, and upholding all things by the word of his power, when he had by himself purged our sins, sat down on the right hand of the Majesty on high:"* Rome's Jesus must be sacrificed anew every day in every "Holy Sacrifice of the Mass" so that the "work of redemption may be carried on." Neither is the Catholic Jesus the immutable, unchanging Jesus of Scripture: *"Jesus Christ the same yesterday, and to day, and for ever."* (Heb 13:8) Over the years, the Catholic Jesus has departed from His original salvation plan as stated in John 14:6: *"Jesus saith unto him, I* (meaning Himself alone) *am the way, the truth, and the life: no man cometh unto the Father, but by me."* The Catholic Jesus allows Catholics to be saved in a variety of ways other than total trust in Himself. For example, persons who are invested in the scapular medal and wear it continually throughout their lives are guaranteed to be saved. Individuals devoted to praying the rosary are promised they won't "perish." Likewise individuals who go to Mass and Communion and say a rosary on five consecutive first Saturdays, or nine consecutive first Fridays, are assured of salvation. On and on.

Adding to the confusion, the Catholic Jesus does not—cannot—come to indwell the faithful in the person of His Holy Spirit, because He allegedly is received physically in the Communion elements. Our Lord told His disciples, *"It is expedient for you that I go away: for if I go not away, the Comforter will not come unto you; but if I depart, I will send him unto you."* (John 16:7) What this means is that Jesus will not be physically present in a host at the same time His spiritual presence is indwelling the bodies of believers.

Such is the Contradiction Affliction that besets Catholicism on all sides. And what a sickness it is! Doctrine after doctrine is contradicted by the Word of God. It is even true that Catholic doctrines and teachings having to do with establishment of the papacy, with the role of heavenly advocate, with prayer, the Holy Spirit, etc., are found to contradict each other in the 1994 Catechism, a spiritual cataclysm of disastrous proportions.

Not only is the Catholic Jesus different from the biblical Jesus, the Catholic gospel and the biblical Gospel bear very little resemblance to each other. Here are some prime examples of how contradictory they are to each other. *"These things have I written unto you that believe on the name of the Son of God; that ye may know that ye have eternal life and that ye may believe on the name of the Son of God."* (1 Joh 5:13) *"Verily, verily, I say unto you, He that heareth my word, and believeth on him that sent me, hath everlasting life and shall not come into condemnation; but is passed from death unto life."* (John 5:24)

These Scriptures tell us God wants us to know for sure that we are saved and even now are in possession of eternal life. But the Catholic gospel classifies personal certainty of salvation as the "mortal" sin of presumption, and pronounces a "curse" (anathema) upon all who believe what the Bible says. Incredibly, then, it is a mortal sin for a Catholic to believe what the Word of God teaches about the believer's eternal security. No wonder Catholics say, **"I don't care what the Bible says, it's not what the Catholic Church teaches."** They would be well served to start caring right now.

Catholics are taught that when the soul is free from mortal sin it is in what Rome calls "the state of sanctifying grace," and is, therefore, fit for a heavenly reward—after a stint in the purgatorial fires, of course. The flip side of that teaching, however, says the soul stained by mortal sin is unfit for heaven, is, in fact, condemned to hell if death occurs before confessional absolution is obtained. The Catholic can be saved one minute and in the next, condemned. This kind of doctrine results in the erroneous belief that each individual is responsible and able to save—or to lose—his or her own soul. But the Bible says you can't save yourself; only Jesus can do that. And once you've been saved by Him—"adopted" into His family—you haven't the power nor the authority to "lose" yourself, either. The Scriptures teach eternal security, whereas Catholic doctrine teaches lifetime insecurity. The Scriptures teach that once a person is "born again" he or she cannot be "unborn." Catholic doctrine teaches that you can have salvation one day and be condemned to hell the next. The Bible teaches that by faith we become adopted children of God and cannot be UN-adopted.

Rome says it makes no difference how you live or what you believe, one unconfessed mortal sin on your soul at the time of death zaps you into hell for all eternity. Rome should make available to the faithful signs that read: "DESTINATION UNKNOWN," for there is not a Catholic on earth who can say with absolute assurance, and without committing a grave sin: **"I'm definitely going to heaven when I die."**

The question suggested by the contradictions we've looked at is how can a Catholic know who or what to trust for salvation? Rome encourages prayer (a definite form of worship) to Mary, to saints, to angels, and almost as an afterthought, to the Father through our Lord Jesus. Mary is declared as sinless and pure as Jesus. She is credited with having participated with Christ in the act of redemption. Her intercession is considered far superior to that of our Lord by millions of Catholics who have more confidence in Mary to save them than they do in Jesus. Saints are said to have built in heaven a bank of graces by their meritorious lives on earth. These can be tapped into by the living faithful without going through Jesus or the Father. When you get right down to cases, why does the Catholic Church "gospel" include Jesus anyway?

Mortal and venial sins confessed to a priest are forgiven, but not paid for. Each sin carries a requirement of temporal punishment to be expiated by penances performed, indulgences gained, or purgatorial fires endured. No one has a clue as to how much temporal punishment is due for each of the myriad sins committed. Hence there is no telling how many indulgences are needed to offset and cancel out the temporal punishment. But each individual is responsible for his own temporal punishment and expiating it as well. Not much need for Jesus in Rome's "gospel."

Our Lord never gave us rosaries to recite, medals to wear or penances to perform. He never gave us novenas to say, stations of the cross to do, first Fridays or first Saturdays to observe. He never gave us mortal and venial sin, indulgences, Purgatory or temporal punishment. He never gave us popes or priests, hosts or monstrances, forced celibacy or litanies and processions. He never commanded us to observe certain days or seasons; never demanded that we atone for our own ugly sins. He never suggested that we pray to anyone other than the Father, and that through Himself. He never promised us anyone other than Himself would be our advocate with the Father in heaven. He never gave mankind a new mother as a replacement for Eve whom Adam called the "mother of all living." But Rome's "gospel" has given all of the above to the faithful, so who needs Jesus? If faith and trust in Him can't deliver a dying soul into heaven, if Purgatory is inevitable, what good is Jesus anyway?

Purgatory is such a major doctrine of Catholicism. But no one—not the pope himself—can be sure who goes there, how long they'll be there or when they are released. No one can be sure that the person they are praying to be released from Purgatory is even there, or ever was there. Nor can they know how many indulgences have to be gained, how many Masses have to be said, how many rosaries must be recited to obtain one soul's release. Confusion. What's worse, the soul in Purgatory can't help itself, has to depend entirely on the living to plead its cause before God. But wait. That in itself is contradictory! Rome teaches that what Jesus accomplished on Calvary wasn't sufficient to pay off a soul's sin debt. But once a soul is in Purgatory, an ordinary created being who is still alive can perform some Rome-inspired work that pays off the dead person's temporal punishment debt. Contradiction? Worse. Heresy! The apparition that appeared to three children at Fatima told Lucia that a girl recently deceased would be in Purgatory till the end of the world. Poor little girl, what Jesus did wasn't enough. And poor Jesus; Rome sure doesn't credit Him with much authority, power or influence.

Holy Communion is another source of contradiction and confusion. First of all, our Lord's physical presence—actual body and blood—is said to be contained in the host—the Communion wafer—and in the wine respectively. But until a few years ago the faithful only received the wafer. Many who have no taste for wine still only receive the wafer. Rome says that's okay. You've received the whole Jesus, body and blood, soul and divinity. But when the priest supposedly changes the wafer and the wine into Christ's body and blood, he only says, "This is my body" over the wafer. That raises some interesting questions. For one, how does the wafer—the host—become both the body and the blood of Christ except the priest says, "this is both my body and my blood"? For another, if the host—by the words "this is my body"—becomes both the body and the blood, what purpose is there in having a cup of wine and saying, "this is my blood" over it?

At the Last Supper described in the Bible, all of the Apostles partook of both the bread and the wine. In the apostolic church gatherings, participants in the reenactment of the Lord's Supper ingested both the bread and the wine, and both elements were carried by the deacons to the sick and infirm. The Council of Trent, however, determined that Christ is completely present—both His body and His blood—in either element, and pronounced a curse on those who say otherwise.

Still on the subject of Catholic Communion, the faithful who have been baptized since Vatican II allegedly receive the Holy Spirit in addition to being cleansed from "original sin." (Before Vatican II the Holy Spirit was conferred only in Confirmation.) Now the Bible tells us in a number of places that it's the Holy Spirit of Jesus who comes to live inside each and every believer. Previously it has been noted that our Lord told the Apostles the Comforter (Holy Spirit) could not come to them until He—Jesus—had ascended to heaven. Here's the contradiction. Jesus is physically present, they say, in the Communion wafer the faithful receive. But supposedly His Holy Spirit is already living inside each baptized person. So how can Jesus come to where He already is? Why would He tell the Apostles one thing, then permit Rome to promise what He said would not be done?

Another problem with respect to Catholic Communion arises if we allow that the host really is the physical body and blood of the Savior. That physical presence of Jesus within the faithful who receive the wafer lasts but a few minutes, then is gone until the next Communion. How can this be? In the digestive process food (the wafer) is broken down into nourishment and distributed to the body's blood, bones and tissue. With each reception of Communion, shouldn't the faithful be getting more and more of Jesus in their systems? Why would Jesus be physically present when He's ingested, then disappear when digestion begins? It seems to me His disappearance from the wafer before it's digested is as big a miracle as his inhabiting it in the first place. And here is the ultimate Communion contradiction, the wafer supposedly is physical food that provides spiritual strength and growth. But after hundreds—even thousands—of Communions Catholics can't even be sure if they're going to heaven or to hell.

One of the greatest areas of contradiction in the Roman Catholic religion is Rome's real, true position with respect to God's Word as recorded in the Bible. The following quotes from the 1994 Catechism serve to illustrate the point.

"God is the author of Sacred Scripture."
"God has said everything in His Word."

> "There will be no further Revelation.
> "The inspired books teach the truth.
> "God chose certain men....as true authors...they consigned to writing whatever He wanted written and no more."
> "The Son is His Father's definitive Word; so there will be no further Revelation after Him."

The foregoing lead one to believe that the Holy Scriptures have been given their rightful place of sovereignty over Roman Catholic doctrine. But Rome is never embarrassed by contradictions, not even when their apologists contradict themselves. Other quotes appearing elsewhere in the same 1994 Catechism are unabashed contradictions of all those listed above.

> "The Gospel was handed on in two ways: Orally by the Apostles. In writing by those Apostles (and their associates)"
> "This living transmission (Apostolic Succession), accomplished in the Holy Spirit, is called Tradition since it is distinct from Sacred Scripture.
> "Through Tradition the church in her doctrine life and worship perpetuates and transmits...all that she herself is, all that she believes.
> "The Church does not derive her certainty about all revealed truths from the holy Scriptures alone. Scripture and Tradition must be accepted and honored with equal sentiments of devotion and reverence."
> "The Magesterium is not superior to the Word of God, but is its servant. It teaches only what has been handed on to it."

Obviously Catholics don't read their own Catechism, much less the Word of God. If they did, they would notice that on the one hand the Word of God is said to be complete, the truth, final in its revelation. On the other hand is the blank check Rome calls "Tradition" which imputes an aura of antiquity to doctrines never known or practiced in the first five centuries of Christianity. A thorough review of the writings of the early Church patriarchs reveals a total absence of anything new or different from the Gospel contained in what we today know as the New Testament. In Book III of *"Irenaeus Against Heresies,"* written before AD 200, it appears that the Apostles passed on to the early churches nothing beyond the known Gospel, as the following entry confirms:

> "...if the Apostles...(knew of hidden mysteries)...they would have delivered them especially to those (bishops) to whom they were also committing the churches themselves."

Such Catholic doctrines as the priesthood, transubstantiation, the Immaculate Conception, Purgatory, indulgences, auricular confession, infallibility, sacraments, the Mass, etc. did not come from the early Church patriarchs. They were unknown to the Apostles, never preached by them, certainly not "handed on" by apostolic succession.

When Rome admits that its Magisterium is not superior to the Word of God, it speaks truth. When it says the Magisterium only teaches what has been "handed on to it" it also speaks truth. But what has been handed on to it traces back—not to the first, second, third or fourth centuries—but to the dark, the middle, and even the modern ages, as bishops of Rome (popes) have decreed man-made doctrines contradictory in every way to the Word of God. It sounds great to say of the Scriptures, "God has said everything in His Word," and "There will be no further revelation." See above. But to come right back and say there is an additional "living transmission" called "Tradition" that occupies a position of honor equal to that of God's Word is nothing short of absurd. Either God said everything in His Word or he didn't. One or the other, but not both. Either no further revelation has come to light or the Scriptures really weren't complete after all. The contradictions are obvious. Catholics need to be made aware of them.

For another example of Rome's true position with respect to the Scriptures we call attention to its stand on "Origins"—that is, the book of Genesis containing God's account of Creation. When we again consult the 1994 Catechism the following is what we find.

> "The *question* about the origins of the world and of man has been the object of many scientific studies which have splendidly *enriched* our *knowledge* of the *age and dimensions of the cosmos*, the *development of life forms* and the *appearance of man*. "Among all the Scriptural texts about creation, the first three chapters of Genesis occupy a unique place. From a literary standpoint, these texts may have had diverse sources. The *inspired authors…etc."*

How can Rome justify, and how can Catholics believe, that the "inspired Books teach the truth" when science so-called is credited by Rome with enriching our knowledge of the age of the cosmos, in direct opposition to God's Word? There is no *question* about origins among born again Christians. And there is nothing mythical, nothing allegorical, nothing mystifying about the first three or all fifty chapters of Genesis. It is a faithful historical account of the creation of the universe, our world, living organisms and mankind. The approximate age of the cosmos is easily calculated from the genealogies given in Genesis and confirmed in Chronicles. Together, these attest to a young universe, a young earth, not more than 7000 or 8000 years old. And there is an abundance of empirical scientific evidence to support this fact.

What "science so-called" has done is wrongly interpret geologic and fossil evidence to support an anti-God agenda that arose early in the nineteenth century. Moreover, whatever science so-called has had to say about the "development of life forms and the appearance of man" is completely obviated by Genesis 1:1-31. All life, man included, was created by God ex nihilo within a period of six twenty-four-hour days. Anything that says otherwise is false no matter how much phony evidence is cited. As for the "authors" of Genesis, their names were, Moses, Moses, and Moses, through the inspiration of the Holy Spirit. Jesus gave Moses the credit for compiling the books of the Law—the Pentateuch—and that should be good enough for Rome. *"And he* (Jesus) ***said unto them, These are the words which I spake unto you, while I was yet with you, that all things must be fulfilled, which were written in the Law of Moses and in the prophets, and in the psalms, concerning me."*** (Luke 24:44)

And so, in one part of the Catechism we read, "the inspired books teach the truth." But in another we read that science has "enriched our knowledge" about the development (not the creation) of life forms, and the appearance (not the creation) of man. In dealing with the subject of creation, the 1994 Catechism that must be considered a spiritual cataclysm, repeats again and again that God's account "expresses (the various actions) in symbolic language." It should be a source of abject fear to Catholics who read on page 95:

> "The Church, interpreting the *symbolism* of biblical language in an authentic way, in the light of the New Testament and Tradition teaches that our first parents, Adam and Eve, were constituted (not created?) in an original state of holiness and justice." (According to the Council of Trent.)

Catholics should be shouting, "What do you mean, **symbolism of biblical language**?" God's Word is clear, accurate, concise, and complete. Any symbolism found in the Creation chapters of Genesis has been put there by Rome, not the Holy Spirit who inspired Moses. And where did the Council of Trent get the idea Adam and Eve were "constituted" when Scripture says they were created. Who can accept such contradictions? There seems to be no end to them. In Chapter 3 we covered the fact that Rome has based its justification for the papacy heavily on a passage from the Gospel of Matthew which reads ***"And I say also unto thee,***

That thou art Peter, and upon this rock I will build my church; and the gates of hell shall not prevail against it." (Mat 16:18) Rome interprets this Scripture to mean that Jesus meant to build His Church on the rock of Peter. But—and here we go again—the Catholic Catechism contradicts its own doctrine. On page 106 of the 1994 edition the following appears:

> "Moved by the grace of the Holy Spirit and drawn by the Father, we believe in Jesus and confess: 'You are the Christ, the Son of the living God.' On the *rock* of this faith confessed by St. Peter, Christ built His Church.

Here, on page 106, the Catechism recognizes Peter's admission that Jesus was the promised Messiah—his statement of faith—as the true "petra" (foundation rock) on which our Lord intended to build His Church. But just 35 pages later—on page 141—rationale for the existence of the office of pope is stated as follows:

> "....Our Lord then declared to him (Peter): 'You are Peter, and on this rock I will build My Church....' Christ, the 'living stone,' thus assures His Church, *built on Peter*, of victory over the powers of death."

This kind of confusion should alert sincere Roman Catholics that Rome has not been trusted with the authority to determine how Holy Scriptures should be interpreted. It should alert them to Rome's determination to justify man-made doctrines without regard to what is in God's precious Word. On page 116 of the Catechism there appears another passage that contradicts what God has said in the Bible. We read:

> "...the Son of God became man, so that we might become God. The only begotten Son of God....assumed our nature, so that he....might make men gods."

Our Lord said He came to save that which was lost. He said He came to call sinners to repentance. He said He came to give us life, and to give it more abundantly. He said He exchanged our sins for His righteousness. But, He never said His purpose was to make us—created beings—into gods. Elsewhere in God's Word we are told believers become heirs to the Kingdom, and that God's love is manifested in our being called the *"sons of God."* (1 John 3:1.) We are only "adopted" children, however, adopted brothers and sisters of the MAN Christ

Jesus. (Gal 4:5; Eph 1:5) But that in no way makes us God or gods. Else God's Word would contradict itself, for we are told in Isaiah: ***"Ye are my witnesses, saith the LORD, and my servant whom I have chosen: that ye may know and believe me, and understand that I am he: before me there was no God formed, neither shall there be after me."*** (Isa 43:10) God is in the business of saving helpless sinners from the fires of hell through faith and trust in our Lord Jesus. Making created beings into gods is not His style. But how many biblically illiterate Catholics are misled into thinking they are going to be gods? Shades of the Mormons, who teach the same thing.

Here is even more contradiction. Rome has determined that Mary the mother of Jesus—contrary to what the Bible says—is co-mediatrix with the Lord Jesus. Through recitation of the rosary, scapular medals, first Saturday devotions, special prayers, etc., the faithful are urged to seek Mary's intercession on their behalf. In the Word of God we are told that there is but one mediator between God and man, and that one mediator is the man Christ Jesus. (I Tim 2:5) Though the 1994 Catechism promotes Mary as co-mediatrix with Jesus, it admits on page 249 that there really is only one mediator between God and men. We read:

"They (the saints in heaven) do not cease to intercede with the Father for us, as they proffer the merits which they acquired on earth through the *one mediator* between God and men, *Christ Jesus.*"

Way back on page 642, item #2674 includes the following:

"Jesus, the *only mediator* is the way of our prayer;"

The Catholic faithful are not stupid, only deceived, misled and misinformed. Because they do not read God's Word regularly and in the power of the Holy Spirit, they do not know that there is not one verse in the entire Bible suggesting that prayer be offered up to anyone but God Himself through our intercessor—our mediator—the Lord Jesus. They do not understand that neither Mary the mother of Jesus, nor any other holy, separated individual, is said in God's Word to have accumulated merits during their lives on earth that can be beneficial to those of us still alive. Hence, when the Catechism presents a passage like the one cited above, the Catholic faithful who sincerely desire salvation should be closing it for good and opening the Word of God. In His precious Word no duplicity is found, no confusion, and no contradictions such as are common in Catholicism. As a further example of how really serious Rome's contradiction affliction has become, there is another Catechism entry just three pages removed from the one recognizing Jesus as the lone mediator between God and men. On page 252 we read:

> "Taken up to heaven she (Mary) did not lay aside this saving office but by her manifold intercession continues to bring us the gifts of eternal salvation….Therefore the Blessed Virgin is invoked in the church under the title of *Advocate Helper, Benefactress* and *Mediatrix.*

Catholics are brainwashed. I know because I was one of them. For fifty-two years I was a blind follower who hadn't the faintest idea what God's Word contained. Not only was Mary not taken up bodily to heaven, a "saving office" occupied by Mary is not in the Word of God. She had no such office on earth to take with her to heaven. Her "intercession" is a relatively recent creation of Rome, and she has no say-so in awarding the "gifts of eternal salvation. On page 257, just five pages after appearance of the above entry, the Catholic Catechism contradicts itself again:

> "…our Lord Jesus Christ, the *only author* and liberal *giver* of salvation…etc."

For more than 1000 years, Christendom first, and then its successor, Catholicism, recognized that there is but one intercessor in heaven, and His name is Jesus, not Mary or St. So-and-So. *"My little children, these things write I unto you, that ye sin not. And if any man sin, we have an advocate with the Father, Jesus Christ the righteous:"* (1 John 2:1) The advocate we have with the Father is not subject to the decisions or declarations of an apostate church, whose supreme leader holds an office founded on fraud. It is God's Word, not the word of man, which tells us: *"For there is one God, and one mediator between God and men, the man Christ Jesus*; (1 Tim 2:5) The Catechism has it right on pages 249 and 257. The one mediator we have with the Father, and the only giver of salvation, is Jesus, not His earthly mother Mary. To teach otherwise, as is the case on page 252, is to teach heresy.

In previous chapters we have seen that Rome claims absolute right of interpretation over the Word of God. Even their priests, before being ordained, must take an oath that they will never ever interpret the Scriptures contrary to the consensus interpretations of the church hierarchy. But at least two contradictory entries in the 1994 Catechism lead one to question Rome's motives for insisting on such dictatorial control. From pages 286 and 298 in that order:

> "The Holy Spirit gives a spiritual understanding of the Word of God to those who read or hear it, according to the disposition of their hearts." "When the Holy Spirit awakens faith, He…gives an understanding of the Word of God etc"

These entries acknowledge the teaching ministry of the Holy Spirit as clearly set forth in a number of Scriptures. *"**But the anointing** (the Holy Spirit) **which ye have received of him abideth in you, and ye need not that any man teach you: but as the same anointing teacheth you of all things, and is truth, and is no lie, and even as it hath taught you, ye shall abide in him."*** (1 John 2:27) See also Col 3:16 and 2 Tim 2:15. Catholics never wonder why Rome insists on total control of Scriptural interpretation. Based on the above two entries in their own Catechism, they should.

To the careful observer, Rome's Contradiction Affliction became an epidemic following Vatican II (1962-65). The list of its canonical reversals is extensive. The "Communion fast" was done away with. Thereafter, communicants could eat and drink right up to the start of the Mass without it being considered a sin. The Mass that for over 1200 years had to be conducted in Latin could henceforth be conducted in the native language of the land. Compulsory Mass attendance was changed from Sunday only to Saturday or Sunday. For centuries, the faithful received only the wafer (the host) in Communion. The Council of Trent adamantly insisted that only the host, or wafer, be ingested, not the wine. After Vatican II both the host and the wine could be taken, but those who have no taste for wine could continue receiving only the host. Permission to touch the consecrated elements by other than clergy was permitted. The Friday fast from meat was eliminated. Henceforth Catholics could eat all the meat they wanted on Friday without it being considered a mortal sin.

Big changes also were made in several sacraments. Prior to Vatican II Catholic baptism did not claim to confer the Holy Spirit. After Vatican II, Rome claims Catholic baptism does now confer the Holy Spirit. Prior to Vatican II, the Holy Spirit was supposedly received in the sacrament of confirmation. After Vatican II the previously baptized individuals:

> "…are more perfectly bound to the church and are enriched with a special strength of the Holy Spirit."

That entry from page 326 contains an honest admission of the real reason for Catholic sacraments. Through them, the faithful are, **"more perfectly bound"** to the apostate Catholic Church. The sacraments are a crucial component of the

Vatican's Tradition Trap that binds the trusting faithful to Catholicism from the cradle to the grave. The cited entry also contains a serious untruth—that the Confirmation ritual confers a "special strength" of the Holy Spirit on those receiving it. Nowhere in God's Word can any such promise be found. What can be found are the words of Jesus telling His Apostles, (and us who have believed in Him through them) how to obtain more Holy Spirit strength and power. *"If ye then, being evil, know how to give good gifts unto your children: how much more shall your heavenly Father give the Holy Spirit to them that ask him?"* (Luke 11:13)

Another sacrament—Extreme Unction—was eliminated by Vatican II and replaced with the Anointing of The Sick. Before Vatican II Rome designated a place called "Limbo" as the eternal locus provided for unbaptized deceased infants. Since Vatican II, Limbo is no longer mentioned in polite Catholic circles. Rome's new teaching about infants who die with the stain of original sin on their souls is synopsized as follows on Catechism page 325.

> **"With respect to children who have died without Baptism, the liturgy of the church invites us to Trust in God's mercy and to pray for their salvation."**

Prayer for **salvation** of **any deceased person** is not Scriptural. *"And as it is appointed unto men once to die, but after this the judgment."* (Heb 9:27) It's all so demeaning to Catholics, this doctrinal turbulence that demands belief in one set of teachings one day and a completely opposite set the next. Baptism didn't confer the Holy Spirit one day, does confer Him the next. Confirmation did confer the Holy Spirit one day, doesn't confer Him the next. Deceased, unbaptized infants went to a place called Limbo one day, are entrusted to God's mercy the next because Limbo never existed. Catholics eating meat on Friday one week could go to hell for doing so, while the following Friday the same folks could eat six T-bone steaks without committing even a venial sin.

Imagine the dilemma you would have faced as a Catholic living in the 19th century. In 1853, the Bible you're reading (without the knowledge or consent of your pastor) says Mary, the mother of Jesus, and Joseph, her spouse, had a holy marriage that God blessed with four named sons and at least two daughters—the half brothers and sisters of our Lord. In 1854, however, Mary is declared to have been born without a sin nature and remained a sinless virgin from the cradle to the grave. As a result, the marriage of Mary and Joseph is declared a lifelong platonic relationship, clearly contradicting the Word of God, (I Cor 7:4, 5) In 1853,

Jesus has half brothers and sisters according to the Bible; in 1854 Rome says don't believe God's Word, they were merely close relatives of our Lord. And then comes the year 1870.

The Catechism you've been studying addresses accusations that have arisen regarding Catholic claims of infallibility. Right there in vivid black and white it says Rome makes no such claim; it's just a Protestant lie. The next morning a glaring headline on the local newspaper screams; "Popes Declared Infallible!" How can intelligent people accept those kinds of doctrinal reversals? How on earth can people explain or defend such contradictions? And why would God delay for eighteen centuries revealing that Mary was immaculately conceived, was a sinless virgin for life, and popes whose office He did not establish, are, nevertheless, infallible?

But, fast forward 80 years to 1950 and the decree that Mary's body did not decay but was assumed into heaven. Talk about having to scramble; that announcement caused Rome to sell Mary's tomb in Jerusalem to the Armenian church which continued operating it for pilgrims who came to see where Christ's mother was buried. Again, what possible purpose could God have had for taking over 1900 years to disclose the fact that Mary's remains were taken up to heaven? More Catechism contradictions. Page 265, item 1018:

> **"As a consequence of original sin, man must suffer bodily death, from which man *would have been immune* had he not sinned."**

But, according to Catholic doctrine, Mary the mother of Jesus was free from original sin and lived an absolutely sinless life. Rome acknowledges that she suffered "bodily death" by its proclamation of the Assumption of her corpse directly to heaven. Shouldn't she have been immune to death because of her sinlessness? Jesus voluntarily gave His life and indicated it could not have been taken from Him otherwise. But Mary just died. Like any other sinner. If item 1018 is a true statement—and it is—then a sinless Mary should still be alive. But she isn't. Contradiction.

Rome teaches that redemption is an ongoing effort. (Cf. Page 343, Item 1364.) It is carried out anew with the celebration of each "Holy Sacrifice of the Mass." Our Lord on the cross said it was a finished work, and the Catholic Catechism, in other places, contradicts itself by agreeing with Jesus. Page 664, Item 1403 says in part:

> "The petitions addressed to our Father, as distinct from the prayers of the old covenant, rely on the mystery of salvation, once for all, in Christ crucified and risen."

And on page 659, Item 2749, the following is stated:

"Jesus fulfilled the work of the Father completely. So which is it? An ongoing work, (page 343) an accomplished work, (page 664) or a work completely fulfilled? (page 659.) To a majority of Catholics, (me, too, when I was one) these kinds of contradictions are both unknown and unimportant. The faithful are simply too busy doing the things commanded by Rome, hoping that their end will be heaven…through the Purgatorial fire, of course.

Of all the astounding contradictions with which Rome has saddled itself since the sixth century, the ultimate contradiction dogging Catholicism is, without a doubt, the so-called "unbroken chain" of popes stretching all the way back to the Apostle Peter. It is a fine sounding phrase—"unbroken chain"—engendering visions of a continual procession of holy men robed in scarlet, wearing the jeweled crown and holding the scepter of authority allegedly conferred on Peter by Christ the Lord. Unfortunately for Rome, the papacy itself is a serious contradiction of the Word of God, as has been noted in previous chapters. And the so-called "unbroken chain" of popes is a Vatican Fairy Tale.

Unabashed as usual by history, Rome offers in support of this myth a lengthy list of popes—beginning with the non-pope, Peter—and for added authenticity supplies the dates of their reigns. This evidence, unquestioned by the typical Catholic, is sufficient to convince the faithful that the Roman Catholic Church is the one true and only church founded by Christ.

But for papal succession to be true as it is applied in Catholicism, the Bible and history should clearly record the existence of certain papal characteristics right from the time our Lord ascended into heaven, and His Holy Spirit indwelt the 120 occupants of the upper room on Pentecost. For example, we should find in the Bible, or at least in history, mention of the infallibility of the bishop of Rome—the Pope—the successor to St Peter. But nowhere in the Bible is there such a reference, and the word infallibility is never associated with any bishops in the early or even the medieval church. We can't even be sure there was only one bishop of Rome at a time, because bishops in the early days of Christianity were overseers of individual assemblies or churches.

The Greek word that translates "bishop" in English is "episkopos" and is defined as the superintendent, guardian, curator, elder, or overseer of a Christian church. From Paul's letter to the Romans we conclude there were many churches in Rome, each one surely headed by a bishop. In vain we search the Bible and the history of the early church for references to any bishop of Rome being called "infallible," the "Vicar of Christ," the "Universal or Supreme Bishop," or "Pontifex Maximus"—Supreme Priest. That last title which is applied to today's popes originally designated the highest priest in the pagan polytheistic religion of the Romans. It was assumed by Constantine when he became leader of Christendom after the last persecution, and has become one of the titles applied to the Roman pope since the middle ages.

From a distance of two millennia, Rome commands the faithful to believe that Peter was the first bishop of Rome and infallible. That he was succeeded in the year 67 AD by Linus, and Linus was succeeded by Anacletus in AD 76. But the early church fathers—Irenaeus, Tertullian and Jerome—who were only a century or so removed from the time of the Apostles could not agree on who came after—not Peter alone—but Peter AND Paul. And none of them referred to either Peter or Paul as anything but Apostles. Moreover in Book III of *"Irenaeus Against Heresies"* it is reported that the Apostles ordained lots of bishops who headed up lots of different churches and were equivalent to each other in authority. Irenaeus stated that the number of bishops succeeding the Apostles was so great as to prevent his listing all of them. Because Rome was the Capitol of the empire, he thereafter, listed only his understanding of the bishops of Rome that had come after the Apostles. In no way did he indicate that Peter or Paul had filled the office of bishop of any church in Rome or elsewhere. Nor did he indicate that Peter was in any way superior to the other Apostles including Paul.

From what Irenaeus wrote near the end of the second century it is obvious that the bishops of all the churches—not just the bishops of Rome—were considered, and were in fact, successors to all of the Apostles. For Rome in modern times to claim infallibility and a higher calling only for bishops of Rome is to propagate a serious falsehood, a deliberate deception. For 500-plus years after the Apostles, no bishop of Rome exercised supreme authority over the western branch of Christendom. No pope in all of history has exercised supreme authority over all of the churches that emerged from early Christendom. And this is critical: bishops of Rome for the first five centuries were elected by members of Roman churches only, and not by the cumulative Apostle-ordained bishops overseeing churches all over the Roman Empire. There was no College of Cardinals electing pontiffs until the middle ages. So, there was no concentration of "apostolic succession" in the bishops of Rome until a couple of hundred years after the forged, fraudulent, Pseudo Isidorean Decretals showed up at the end of the 9th century.

The non-existent unbroken chain matter is fraught with other problems also, problems Rome successfully hides from the Catholic faithful. Chief among these problems is the nasty skeleton in Rome's closet known as the "antipopes." These were men who occupied the office of pope at the same time it was occupied by one or more others having the same claim. Sometimes there were two men, sometimes three men claiming to be pope at the same time, each with the backing of loyal supporters. As expected, Catholic apologetics denies that there were two or more popes at certain times, citing as evidence for this the fact that there can be only one "infallible" pope at a time, only one successor at a time to the Apostle Peter. This, of course, is circular reasoning of the worst kind, and presupposes that Peter was the first pope, the first bishop of Rome. It assumes that he was endowed with the gift of infallibility, which he passed on only to bishops of Rome that the Vatican now says were his authentic heirs. The writings of Irenaeus previously cited give the lie to that presumption, but if they didn't, the antipope debacles that began in the third century (pre-Roman Catholicism) certainly do.

Historically there were at least 35 so-called antipopes; some accounts say the number actually is 39. In any case, an antipope was one who was elected, appointed, or self-proclaimed to be bishop of Rome, (Pope) simultaneously with one or more others claiming the same office. In compiling a list of the alleged successors to St Peter, it is Rome that has made the decision in each case as to which claimant of the office was in fact Peter's successor and which was the imposter. But the very fact that such situations existed—not once or twice, but at least 35 times—knocks the props completely out from under the unbroken chain claim. Especially when a goodly number of those designated antipopes by Rome had historically as good or better a claim to the subject office as the one said to have been the real bishop of Rome—the real Pope. A few examples will serve to illustrate the point.

Hippolytus, (AD 170-235)—designated a Saint of the Catholic church—is the first of the listed antipopes, having reigned as a bishop of Rome—a "papa" or pope—from AD 217-235. From 199 to 217 the bishop of Rome had been Zephyrinus whom Hippolytus accused of supporting the heresy that Father, Son and Holy Ghost were not three distinct persons in a single Godhead, but three names for a single personality. When Zephyrinus died in 217, he designated his clerk—Calixtus—to succeed him, and a faction that supported Zephyrinus duly elected Calixtus as his successor. But another faction elected Hippolytus. Thus, some of the Western Church claimed Calixtus and others of the Western Church claimed Hippolytus. The reign of Calixtus ended in 222 and Urban was elected by those who had supported Zephyrinus and Calixtus. His reign ended in 230 and the same faction then elected Pontian who reigned until 235. In that year, Hippolytus and Pontian, (both considered bishops of Rome—"popes"—by separate factions) were banished to the mines at Sardinia during a persecution by the Roman Emperor Maximinus. The two simultaneous bishops of Rome were reconciled there and both resigned in order that a single bishop of Rome—Anterus, (who was acceptable to both their followings)—could be elected to succeed them. Historically, it is a fact that the rites and liturgies employed by the third century churches in Rome were originated by Hippolytus, and one of his works—The Philosophumena—contended that the various heresies plaguing early Christendom all could be traced to pagan origins. So, who was rightful bishop of Rome from AD 217 to 235? Was it Hippolytus or the other three? From the distance of many centuries, how can Rome say which faction were the God-inspired electors? What if Rome is wrong and Hippolytus was the rightful bishop of Rome? What does that do to Rome's unbroken chain of popes?

It's so wonderful to be a born-again Christian with faith and trust placed exclusively in the Word of God and His promises, free from concerns about man-made inventions such as the papacy. The Apostles' true successors are all those who embrace the saving Gospel of Jesus Christ and carry the message to others.

In the fifth century another "double-pope" instance occurred as follows. Anastasius II, bishop of Rome AD 496-98, made conciliatory overtures toward the Eastern Church headed by the bishop of Constantinople. This action was met with severe resistance on the part of much of the Roman clergy. When Anastasius died, the clergy opposed to pacification of the Eastern Church elected Symmachus to succeed him. But another coalition of the Roman clergy that favored peace with the Eastern Church elected Laurentius to be the new Bishop of Rome. Both men were consecrated to that office on November 22, AD 498. What to do? Draw straws? Flip a coin? Hold a general election? Unable to settle the issue among themselves, the two factions turned for a decision to a completely secular and presumably impartial source—Theodoric The Great who was the Ostrogothic King at the time. Now we have a secular king deciding who is the real successor to the Apostle Peter, who is the Vicar of Christ on earth, who is the one blessed with 'infallibility." Amazing.

Theodoric picked Symmachus, and Laurentius became bishop of Nocera in Campania. But hold everything; that's not the end of the matter. Following a Roman Synod of AD 501, (the Palmary Synod by name) convoked by Theodoric, the king apparently decided he had made a mistake, for he brought back Laurentius who was then proclaimed to be the real true successor to Peter. Theodoric appears to have been content with the existence of two bishops of Rome reigning at the same time, but for the next four years war was waged between supporters of Symmachus and the Laurentians as each faction fought to have their man named the one true successor to Peter.

Sometime between AD 505 and 507, a Roman ambassador to the Ostrogothic king—Dioscorus—prevailed upon Theodoric to re-name Symmachus as exclusive bishop of Rome, which he did. So, Laurentius was turned out of Rome for the second and last time. Symmachus, originally elected by clergy who rebelled against the conciliatory actions of the previous "pope," is listed by the Catholic church as the true successor to Peter from AD 498-514. Laurentius is consigned to the junk heap of antipopes in spite of his election by clergy loyal to the philosophies of his predecessor. Oh, well.

It was noted previously that Dioscorus convinced Theodoric to change his mind a third time and rename Symmachus the true bishop of Rome. This is the same Dioscorus who, on or shortly after September 22, AD 530, was elected bishop of Rome (Pope) by 60 out of 67 of the Roman clergy The previous occupant, Felix IV, violating the procedure for selection of bishops of Rome, hand-picked his successor—Boniface II—who claimed the office immediately upon the demise of his benefactor. But the Roman clergy opposed the choice of Boniface and elected Dioscorus. Both men were consecrated simultaneously and once again, there were two men occupying the same office—Dioscorus the one with the stronger claim. Another horrible schism seemed in the offing, but less than a month later Dioscorus died and the appointment of Boniface by his predecessor was allowed to stand. Emerging as the winner was not enough for Boniface. He convened a Synod in December and had Dioscorus "anathematized" posthumously. Today Rome classifies Dioscorus as an antipope and Boniface, the **son of a priest**, as the true successor to Peter. The appointed one over the elected one.

History reveals that there was much political maneuvering and infighting that went on when the time for a new "pope" came along. Bribery, deception, violence, every imaginable dirty trick, often accompanied the quest for that coveted office which Rome points to as proof that it is the one true Church left on earth by our Lord Jesus Christ.

Constantine II—was elected Pope on July 5, AD 767 in a legitimate canonical election. Those who opposed his election took cover with the Lombards in southern Italy. The Lombard King, Desiderius, then sent troops to Rome. They deposed Constantine and murdered his brother, Duke Toto of Nepi, who had promoted his election. Desiderius, the last of the Lombard rulers, subsequently set up as Pope a monk named Philip. But he was rejected as well. A second election then was held on August 1, AD 768, resulting in the election of a Benedictine monk—Stephen—to the papal office. The Franks, who had not supported the valid election of Constantine, did support Stephen, and ordered Constantine to be blinded. A year later, Stephen convoked a Lateran Council that canonically ratified the deposition of the **validly elected** Constantine, who today is listed by Rome as an antipope.

All of the foregoing pale by comparison with the incredible events that transpired in an eight year period from AD 896 to 904. In that bloody and infamous span of time there were seven different popes and an antipope, thievery, immorality and, yes, even murder. Most bizarre of all was the posthumous trial by one pope of the corpse of a previous pope. Shame on Rome for pretending that such criminals as occupied the office of pope in those dark days were Vicars of Christ here on earth. Rather than list them as successors to Peter, their names should be expunged, and the memory of their deeds buried in the Kidron Valley.

The reign of Stephen VI began with his election in May of 896 and ended in July of 897 when a rebellion removed him from office. He was placed in prison where he died a month later—**strangled**. During the 14 months of his pontificate, however, one of the most bizarre trials ever recorded was staged. The defendant was a validly elected but deceased Pope—Formosus—whose decomposing body—in the grave since the previous year—was disinterred, dressed in papal attire and propped up in the papal throne. A deacon was pressed into service to answer for the dead corpse. His answers failed to placate the council. Formosus was convicted of all charges leveled against him. His election was declared invalid. His acts and decrees, including ordinations and appointments he had made, all were declared null and void. His index fingers and thumbs—the digits used to hold the consecrated Communion host—were severed from the body. The corpse then was stripped, cast first into a makeshift grave, later into the Tiber River. And Rome boasts about an unbroken papal chain. Subsequent "infallible" popes exonerated, condemned, exonerated and again condemned the deceased "infallible" Formosus.

Early in the tenth century Sergius III became pope. He took as his mistress a woman named Marozia. History says Marozia bore him a son who grew up to be pope John XI. Sergius III reigned until his death on April 14, AD 911. He is considered by Rome to have been a legitimate entity in the so-called unbroken chain of popes. The line between pope and antipope is so thin in many cases that it's anybody's guess who should be placed in the "unbroken" line. Briefly, some examples. Otto I The Great convened a synod in December AD 963 that deposed the sitting pope—John XII. Otto then got Leo VIII elected. When Otto left Rome John XII was brought back and Leo deposed. In May the following year John died and Benedict V was elected. But Otto came roaring back, forcefully disenfranchised Benedict V and returned Leo to the throne. Surely there was an antipope among that group of three. Rome lists all three as real "infallible" popes.

A Roman faction deposed the sitting pope—Benedict IX in January AD 1045. Sylvester III then was elected to replace him. But not for long. In February the supporters of Benedict threw Sylvester out and restored Benedict to the throne. But Benedict really didn't want to be pope after all. He sold the papacy to one Giovanni Graziano (no relation to Rocky) who got himself elected Gregory VI in May of AD 1045. At this juncture, Benedict did an about-face and tried to have Gregory deposed. Wrong move. The Holy Roman Emperor, Henry III, got involved and forced Gregory to convene a synod that deposed Benedict, Sylvester and Gregory and replaced them all with Clement II. In Rome's list of legitimate popes all of them are listed as follows:

POPE NUMBER	NAME	DATE REIGNED
146	Benedict	1032-1045
147	Sylvester III	1045
148	Benedict IX	1045
149	Gregory VI	1045-1046

From AD 1378 to 1417, a period known as the western schism, there were different popes or antipopes in Rome and Avignon, France, each supported by their own college of cardinals, each with a loyal following among the faithful. In that 39-year period, all of the following claimed to be pope at one time or other: Urban VI, Clement VII, Boniface IX, Benedict XIII, Innocent VII, Alexander V, John XXIII, and Gregory XII. The whole mess was cleared up when the Emperor Sigismund pressured John XXIII to convoke the Council of Constance in AD 1414. That august body deposed both John XXIII and Benedict XIII, got Gregory XII to resign and opened the way for election of Martin V.

Certainly it must have become obvious by now that Rome's claim that the papacy and the popes can be traced all the way back to Peter in an unbroken chain is nothing more than propaganda. Moreover, it is a pity that faithful Catholics are under the impression that men such as we have looked at were Vicars of Christ on earth, were infallible in their decrees, and models of virtue and holiness in their personal lives. Nothing, of course, could be farther from the truth. As previously noted, pope John XI was the illegitimate son of pope Sergius III. Pope Silverius was the illegitimate son of pope Hormisdas. Pope Innocent I was the illegitimate son of pope Anastasius. Bishop Damasus was sired by pope Theodore I. All of the following popes were sons of Catholic priests: Boniface, Felix II, Anastasius II, Agapitus, Marinus I, Gelasius, and John XV.

Pius II is reported to have said that Rome was "the only city run by bastards." He himself admitted fathering a couple of illegitimate children by different women. Pope Sixtus IV raised money by taxing first, Rome's numerous houses of prostitution, and second, the **mistresses** of Catholic clergymen. John XII was a mere 16 when he became pope. Maintained what amounted to a harem in the Lateran Palace. Was reported to have drunk a toast to Satan in the basilica of St. Peter. Boniface VIII had both a mother and daughter as mistresses at the same time. Rodrigo Borgia who became Alexander VI, had at least ten illegitimate children by various mistresses. His favorite, Vannozza Catanei, bore him Caesar and Lucretia, two Borgias who succeeded in establishing their own vile reputations. At age 58 he tired of Catanei and took as his mistress Giulia Farnese who was but 15-years old and recently married to another. Farnese wangled a promotion to cardinal for her brother—the "Petticoat Cardinal"—who became Paul III in AD 1534 and convened the infamous Council of Trent in 1545. According to ex-priest, Charles Chiniquy, Pius IX had two beautiful daughters from two of his mistresses. He is up for "canonization" as a saint of the Catholic Church.

Rome lists all of these men as legitimate "infallible" popes in the alleged unbroken chain stretching back to the non-pope Peter. But men who are not impeccable in their behavior could never in a million years be infallible in their judgments. What is of real significance, however, is not a list of so-called popes stretching in an alleged unbroken chain back to the time of the Apostles. Of real significance is the fact that **any list of any kind is an exercise in futility**, for Christ never instituted the priesthood, never built His church on Peter, never appointed Peter the supreme leader, never established the papacy. Just as Paul was called and empowered—not by ordination or laying on of hands by the eleven Apostles—but directly by God, so were and are the holy men down through the ages who have preached and taught the biblical Gospel of salvation.

Antipopes and wicked popes, contradictory doctrines and teachings, an exalted Mary and an aloof, ineffectual Jesus; rules and rites and ceremonies, sacraments, indulgences, Purgatory, and canonized saints; all are part and parcel of the confusion known as the Roman Catholic Church. Long ago it got off the Jesus track and into a labyrinth of heresies. Its preoccupation with temporal power and the wealth that accompanies it prevented the excision of wrong beliefs before they became set in the concrete of time and tradition.

Most tragically of all, at Trent in northern Italy, from 1545-1563, Rome spurned a golden opportunity to embrace the divinely inspired Scriptures as the sole source of doctrine and Gospel truth, choosing instead a path that is not illuminated by the unchanging, infallible Word of God. Thereafter, study of Scripture by the faithful, though recommended, has been discouraged under the pretense that only Rome has interpretive authority from the Lord, another blatant contradiction of the Scriptures. This is reminiscent of the religious hierarchy in our Lord's time, of whom Jesus said: *"For they bind heavy burdens and grievous to be borne, and lay them on men shoulders; but they themselves will not move them with one of their fingers."* (Mat 23:4) Without God's Word as the beacon to guide it, the Catholic Church exhibits *"...a form of godliness, but denies the power thereof."* (2Ti 3:5)

In this chapter many—but not all—of the contradictions afflicting Catholicism have been exposed. They and numerous others not cited are primarily responsible for the widespread inability of Catholics to explain exactly how one's heavenly reward is attained. How sad to realize most of them are unaware or don't care that there are no contradictions in the Word of God or the Gospel of salvation. Jesus is the Savior. There is no other. Faith is the key. Works don't work. And nothing has been added to, taken from, or changed in this glorious Gospel message since the day Christ was taken up to heaven. He said: *"I go to prepare a place for you. And if I go and prepare a place for you, I will come again, and receive you unto myself that where I am, there ye may be also."* (John 14:2, 3) To be where Jesus is is to be in heaven, not in Rome's invention—Purgatory.

Today, millions who claim allegiance to Catholicism are suffering the ravages of Rome's Contradiction Affliction, and are in mortal danger of eternal damnation because they are **not born again**. To any of them who are exposed to this manuscript, I apologize if I have seemed overly hard on and critical of Catholicism. My only explanation is that I've "been there" and it almost cost me the loss of my immortal soul.

In the next and final chapter of this work, the one Gospel of the Kingdom is fully explained in the hope that at least some Catholics will be able—when asked, "Are you saved?"—to answer: "Yes! I'm saved; saved by the blood of the Crucified ***ONE!***"

10

The Sword and the Lamp

"For ever, O LORD, thy word is settled in heaven." (Psa 119:89)

In spite of what the Catholic church teaches, (or any other religious group, for that matter) the Word of God—the Bible—asserts very clearly and very often that there is only one way to be redeemed, and that way is through faith in the precious shed blood of our Lord Jesus Christ. Making the nine first Fridays or the five first Saturdays will not do it. Wearing the scapular medal from the cradle to the grave will not do it. Praying rosaries and receiving sacraments, attending Mass, lighting votive candles, donating to charities, invoking the intercession of Mary, none of these will do it. Salvation cannot be earned or purchased. It is a free gift to be received purely by faith, an unshakable faith that Christ satisfied fully God's requirement that man's sins be paid for by the shedding of innocent blood. *"For the life of the flesh is in the blood: and I have given it to you upon the altar to make an atonement for your souls: for it is the blood that maketh an atonement for the soul."* (Lev 17:11)

It is extremely difficult for devout Catholics to grasp the twin facts that, a) Christ's innocent blood paid in full their total sin debt, and b) their own works or the works of others cannot in any way add to what Jesus has done. They are very much like the religious Jews that Paul encountered, and about whom he observed: *"Brethren, my heart's desire and prayer to God for Israel is, that they might be saved. For I bear them record that they have a zeal of God but not according to knowledge. For they being ignorant of God's righteousness, and going about to establish their own righteousness, have not submitted themselves unto the righteousness of God."* (Rom 10:1-3)

Devout Catholics have a "zeal for God," but they have been taught from childhood that salvation depends largely on what **they** do, not on what Jesus did. Going to Mass, receiving the various sacraments, praying the rosary, trying to live a moral life, these things are begun early in life and are firmly established habits by the time they become adults. But all these together are nothing more than vain attempts to achieve a righteousness the Bible tells us only comes from trusting Jesus. (2 Cor 5:21) Even the most devout have little Bible knowledge, so it is really hard for them to grasp a salvation message that says **"Jesus purchased it with His precious blood, and you can have it—by faith—free of charge."** In many instances, Scriptures with which they may be familiar have an entirely different meaning to them than God intended, or evangelical Christians understand. Such is the result of erroneous teachings they should—but never do—challenge or question.

For example, our Lord's admonition to Nicodemus: *"Verily, verily, I say unto thee, Except a man be born again, he cannot see the kingdom of God."* (John 3:3) To the Catholic, being born again takes place when one is baptized. Since most have been baptized as infants, they believe their "born-again" experience is behind them. It is a real challenge to make them understand that the new birth depends on **conscious choices** an infant is not able to make. As a result there are not many born-again Catholics indwelt by the Holy Spirit. This is the natural result of teachings such as the following taken from pages 195 and 196 of the 1994 Catechism:

> "From His (Christ's) **fullness, He poured out the Holy Spirit on the** *apostles* **and the** *church.*
> "**The Holy Spirit, whom Christ the head pours out on His members builds, animates, and sanctifies the church. She** (the church) **is the Holy Trinity's communion with men."**
> "**Through the church's sacraments Christ communicates His Holy and Sanctifying Spirit to the members of His body.**

There is a great chasm between the "pouring ON" and the "dwelling IN of God's Holy Spirit. Rome manifests a deep-seated aversion to this truth. So the faithful believe it was the church personified by the Apostles—not individual believers—into which Jesus "breathed" the Holy Spirit. (John 20:22) They trust the sacraments of the church to convey the Holy Spirit to them, rather than the independent act of Jesus who sends His Holy Spirit to INDWELL each and every believer at the moment faith is professed in Christ's atoning sacrifice. Foreign to them is the Scripture: *"Know ye not that ye are the temple of God, and that the Spirit of God dwelleth in you?"* (I Cor 3:16) When the indwelling of the Holy Spirit is not intimately associated with the new birth, it is virtually impossible to grasp what being born again really means. So, as far as most Catholics are concerned they were born again when they were baptized. Which means they are not born again.

In reviewing my own experience as a Catholic, I now realize that Catholics are not free. They are captive to a religious system that has educated them to believe what Rome wants believed and not to believe what Rome wants not believed. They are like new recruits in the military who are told when to get up, when to eat, how to dress, what to study, how to march, etc., and don't foul up or you'll end up in the stockade. When their beliefs are questioned, they cannot cite Scripture verses in support of them, so they resort to "That's not what the Catholic Church teaches." Many immediately go on the defensive when quotes from God's Word contradict those teachings. No Catholic I ever have witnessed to cites verses from the Catholic Catechisms to rebut excerpts from the Scriptures.

We are told twice in Proverbs: *"There is a way which seemeth right unto a man, but the end thereof are the ways of death."* (Pro 14:12, 16:25) Catholics have been indoctrinated with the conviction that the Catholic Church is the "Way" to heaven, (through Purgatory, of course) and are preconditioned by that belief to accept all the other "ways," (dogmas) the end result of which is eternal "death" in the lake of fire. What amazes me, a former Catholic, is how long I believed the Church was the "Way" to heaven, but never could have told anyone the "how" of getting there. Nor for even one minute was I confident I would even make it to Purgatory, much less heaven. The mortal sin doctrine gripped me with a fear that became at times almost overwhelming. As one whose feet ran to sin like iron to a magnet, I lived continually in a "what-if" state of terror. What if I die in mortal sin? What if I can't confess to a priest at the time of my death? What if?

There are no "what ifs" in Christianity. Jesus gave us every assurance of that. *"Then said Jesus to those Jews which believed on him, If ye continue in my word then are ye my disciples indeed; And ye shall know the truth and the truth shall make you free."* (John 8:31, 32) It is Truth that sets one free from doubts about one's eternal destiny, and that Truth is found only in the Word of God—the written Scriptures—not in decrees, declarations and dogmas dictated by what Rome has dubbed "Tradition."

Can Catholics be freed from the mind-control practiced by Rome? Well, I was. My wife was. Several of our friends have been. Many former priests and nuns have been, and several have written books like this. But liberation from Rome's spiritual bondage only can occur when our heavenly Father, in His mercy and Love, endows a Catholic with the desire to compare his or her beliefs with God's holy Word. *"No man can come to me, except the Father which hath sent me draw him: and I will raise him up at the last day. It is written in the prophets, And they shall be all taught of* (by) **God.** *Every man therefore that hath heard and hath learned of the Father cometh unto me."* (John 6:44, 45)

Catholics have a great chance to be liberated—and saved—when they are *"taught of* (by) *God"* through His Word, not the words of Rome. *"So then faith cometh by hearing, and hearing by the word of God."* (Rom 10:17) Saving faith, the faith that enables vile sinners to know they will spend eternity in heaven, comes not from the mouths of men, but from the lips of the Lord Jesus Himself. *"God who at sundry times and in divers manners spake in time past unto the fathers by the prophets, Hath in these last days spoken unto us by his Son, whom he hath appointed heir of all things, by whom also he made the worlds; Who being the brightness of his glory, and the express image of his person, and upholding all things by the word of his power, when he had by himself purged our sins sat down on the right hand of the Majesty on high."* (Heb 1:1-3)

Rome has its Catechisms, and they contain pieces of God's Word. But as with a jigsaw puzzle, unless all the pieces are there a whole picture cannot be produced. In the case of eternal life, having bits and pieces of God's Word is fatal, because there is no such thing as being half saved or partially saved. A person is either saved or lost. There is no middle ground. A Catholic has a great chance of being freed from Rome's bondage, then, when He or She begins to take God at His Word—all of His Word—without concern for Rome's opinion or interpretation. Some examples.

"For by grace are ye saved through faith and that not of yourselves: it is the gift of God not of works lest any man should boast. For we are his workmanship, created in Christ Jesus unto good works which God hath before ordained that we should walk in them." (Eph 2:8-10) The word "grace" here means the unmerited favor of God. The faith referred to is in Our Lord's once and for all sacrifice as full payment of our sin debt. Both the grace and the resulting faith are free gifts from God that can't be earned or influenced by any works a sinner does, or any sacraments a Catholic receives. Once the sinner has been newly "created in Christ"—born again—good works are the result. When this wonderful Scripture grabs hold of the open-minded Catholic's spirit, Rome's smokescreens begin to clear away.

The god of Catholicism is an "Indian-giver." He supposedly gives the "gift" of salvation to an individual in the state of "sanctifying grace," but takes it back when that "grace" is lost through "mortal" sin. To the Catholic, then, salvation really isn't a free gift at all as the Word of God states in Ephesians 2:8 and 9.

Rather, **salvation is a reward one earns by good behavior and good works, but forfeits for wrongdoing.** A true gift, on the other hand, is something freely given with no strings or conditions attached. And, once given, a true gift is never taken back. In the epistle to the Ephesian Christians, God says salvation is a true free gift that cannot be earned by good works, or lost by misbehavior. A Catholic who grasps this awesome truth is on the road to an appointment with the "new birth" and assurance of everlasting life with Jesus.

Catholic sacraments are some of the "works" ruled out by God's Word as producers of, or even contributors to, salvation. What's more, the sacraments really don't qualify as "good works" after one is saved, because Rome has decreed six out of the seven are only beneficial to the one who receives them. The good works done by saved sinners always are beneficial to others so that God may be glorified.

At a given point, the Catholic drawn to Jesus by the Father, confronts the fact that God's mercy—not sacraments received a thousand times—is what produces saving faith, and only because God's Word says so. *"Not by works of righteousness which we have done but according to his mercy he saved us, by the washing of regeneration, and renewing of the Holy Ghost."* (Tit 3:5) A thousand Communions cannot set a sinner free, only Jesus has that power. *"...this man, after he had offered one sacrifice for sins for ever sat down on the right hand of God; From henceforth expecting till his enemies be made his footstool. For by one offering he hath perfected for ever them that are sanctified."* (Heb 10:12-14) The saving power of our Lord is measured in "forevers," not in the minutes it takes for a scrap of bread to dissolve. The soul who is being drawn will see in that Scripture the death knell for the Catholic Mass which claims to offer Jesus anew each time it's celebrated.

One sacrifice, **one** offering, by **one** Man, for **all** believers, **for ever**. The Scriptures leave absolutely no room for the Catholic Mass. The Word of God exposes Rome's justification teachings as false and unacceptable. As a result of the once-for-all-forever-sacrifice, God says: *"their sins and iniquities will I remember no more. Now where remission of these is, there is no more offering for sin."* (Heb 10:17, 18) Yes, there is hope for Catholics to be freed from the influence of Rome. For once they fully understand the truth of the Scriptures; doubts about the veracity of what they have been taught become increasingly more difficult to shrug off. In my case, the mortal sin doctrine had me so bound up in abject fear I just knew I couldn't even make Purgatory. The Catholic who is similarly burdened will find real comfort in Scriptures like this: *"Being confident of this very thing, that he which hath begun a good work in you will perform it until the* *day of Jesus Christ."* (Phil 1:6) I don't have to "keep" myself saved. I am kept saved by the power and love of my Savior. (1 Pet 1:5)

Catholics are trying to "keep themselves" ready for eternity; but the born again Christian is kept by Jesus who "began" the good work of sanctification with the free gift of faith in His Calvary sacrifice. Paul, who called himself the "chief" of sinners said: *"for I know whom I have believed, and am persuaded that he is able to keep that which I have committed unto him against that day."* (2Tim 1:12) No sin can keep a born again Christian out of heaven. But placing one's trust in Catholicism rather than God's Word is guaranteed to bring eternal damnation. *"He that believeth on him is not condemned: but he that believeth not is condemned already, because he hath not believed in the name of the only begotten Son of God."* (John 3:18) And: *"Cursed be the man that trusteth in man."* (Jer 17:5)

Sin or the fear of it cannot have dominion over anyone who trusts his soul to Jesus instead of to religion. *"All that the Father giveth me shall come to me; and him that cometh to me I will in no wise cast out."* (John 6:37) There is no mortal or venial sin with God; all sin is abomination to Him. But the soul that comes to Jesus—though he or she sin at the very hour of death—will not be "cast out" because Jesus promised! And He keeps that promise through His Holy Spirit. *"That we should be to the praise of his glory, who first trusted in Christ. In whom* (Christ) *ye also trusted after that ye heard the word of truth, the gospel of your salvation in whom also after that ye believed ye were sealed with that holy Spirit of promise."* (Eph 1:12, 13) Every believer who comes to Jesus in faith is marked as eternally protected by the seal of the indwelling Holy Spirit. No sacraments needed; just faith.

Such comforting expectations and confidences no Catholic sacraments can provide. As a matter of fact, Rome has declared such confidence to be the grievous sin of "presumption." So the fortunate Catholic who comes to Jesus in faith can cease striving to be saved, spending time instead learning, then carrying out, God's will for his or her life. *"...the Lord is faithful, who shall stablish you, and keep you from evil."* (2Th 3:3)

Another troublesome doctrine for me when I was a Catholic was the matter of the so-called temporal punishment for sin. It was something you couldn't avoid. It seemed that, no matter what you did you couldn't escape punishment in Purgatory. You confessed your sins to the priest to obtain forgiveness; you did the penance he gave you; but the temporal punishment still had to be suffered. Catholics who have piled up the kind of sin debt I did, who are looking at more time in Purgatory than there ever will be time for, will be delighted with the wonderful promises in God's Word to our kind of people. *"As far as the east is from the west, so far hath he removed our transgressions from us."* (Psa 103:12) When God removes our sins from us they are gone forever, for the distance between east and west is infinite. God, who is the only absolutely just judge, does not declare us "not guilty" of our sin debt, then send us to prison to pay what our Lord Jesus already paid with His precious blood.

Moreover, God doesn't see or remember our forgiven sins, either. *"For I will be merciful to their unrighteousness, and their sins and their iniquities will I remember no more."* And… *"…thou hast in love to my soul delivered it from the pit of corruption: for thou hast cast all my sins behind thy back."* (Isa 38:17) The loving God who sent His only begotten Son to die in the place of every repentant sinner never looks behind Him. How, then, if our sins are out of His sight and out of His mind, fully paid for by Jesus, can there be such a thing as temporal punishment to be endured after death? *"For our conversation is in heaven from whence also we look for the Saviour, the Lord Jesus Christ:* (Phi 3:20) The word translated "conversation" has nothing to do with people talking; it means a "state," a "commonwealth," or a "country." That being the case, all believers are going to the "country" of heaven, not to the imagined Purgatory of Catholicism. The Apostle Peter said it this way: *"To an inheritance incorruptible, and undefiled, and that fadeth not away, reserved in heaven for you."* (1 Pet 1:4)

What an exciting revelation that is to any Catholic who is stuck on the treadmill of works, always running, but never getting a foot closer to the assurance of salvation. Heaven is an **inheritance** willed by God, as the result of Christ's sacrifice, to each and every soul who asks Jesus for forgiveness of sins and everlasting life. *"For as many as are led by the Spirit of God, they are the sons of God."* (Rom 8:14) Faith deposited—not in Holy Mother Church—but in Christ Jesus brings the Holy Spirit to indwell, to lead, and to permanently adopt the believer into the family of God. *"For ye have not received the spirit of bondage again to fear; but ye have received the Spirit of adoption whereby we cry, Abba, Father. The Spirit itself beareth witness with our spirit, that we are the children of God, And if children, then heirs; heirs of God and joint heirs with Christ; if so be that we suffer* (the world's rejection) *with him, that we may be also glorified together."* (Rom 8:15-17) As children of God—adopted for all eternity—believers look forward to a mansion in heaven, not temporal punishment in a non-existent place of purgation.

"In my Father's house are many mansions: if it were not so, I would have told you. I go to prepare a place for you. And if I go and prepare a place for

you, I will come again, and receive you unto myself; that where I am, there ye may be also." (John 14:2, 3) Where Jesus is is called heaven, the state of eternal bliss. For each believer in His atoning sacrifice, our dear Lord is preparing a mansion, not a fiery torture chamber. Unbeknownst to him or her, the Catholic's best friend is the Sword of The Lord, (Eph 6:17) which is the divine Word of God.

In my years as a Catholic I never once heard of a future event known as the "Rapture" of the church. This prophesied event is found in 1Thessalonians. And any Catholic who believes what the Word of God says is going to happen will subsequently understand the reason for Rome's uncharacteristic silence regarding this matter. *"For this we say unto you by the word of the Lord, that we which are alive and remain unto the coming of the Lord shall not prevent (precede) them which are asleep. For the Lord himself shall descend from heaven with a shout, with the voice of the archangel, and with the trump of God: and the dead in Christ shall rise first. Then we which are alive and remain shall be caught up together with them in the clouds, to meet the Lord in the air: and so shall we ever be with the Lord.* (I Thes 4:15-17) At a time unspecified, but certainly prior to the great tribulation prophesied in Daniel and the Revelation, our Lord will come in the clouds to "Rapture"—directly to heaven—all the born again believers alive at that time on earth. They will be "caught up" to meet Christ in the air and shall be ever with Him in heaven. THOUSANDS, PERHAPS MILLIONS, WILL MISS TEMPORAL PUNISHMENT IN THE ALLEGED FIRES OF PURGATORY!!!

Catholics to whom these "Rapture" Scriptures are totally new information, should be encouraged to ponder why a just God would punish in Purgatory souls who have died prior to this prophesied event, while allowing those who are "caught up" in the "Rapture" to avoid Purgatory and temporal punishment entirely. Also, after taking thousands or millions directly to heaven in the "Rapture," would a just God allow those previously deceased who are suffering in Purgatory to remain there? Either God is an unjust God, which He isn't, or temporal punishment and Purgatory are foolish inventions of foolish men, which they are. For good reason Rome chooses to ignore this prophesied event, directed to do so by Leo X in AD 1516. He said it this way:

> **"All preachers (priests) shall explain the Gospel according to the Fathers. They** *shall not* **explain futurity** (the Rapture) **or the times of antichrist."**

His directive notwithstanding, Leo X was not able to expunge the prophesied Rapture from the infallible Word of God. It's there. It's going to happen. And most Catholics will be left behind because they choose to place their faith in a religion of works rather than a free, grace-based trust in the shed blood of our Lord Jesus Christ. When witnessing to Catholics, it is critical that they receive a clear understanding of this fact: if **any** born again believers EVER will be taken directly to heaven, we can be confident that **all** born again believers ALWAYS have been, are being, and will continue to be, taken directly to heaven by a just and holy God! Obviously Leo X and all his successors realized that the Catholic inventions—Purgatory and temporal punishment—cannot exist next to 1 Thessalonians 4:15-17. Only by keeping the Bible away from Catholics and Catholics away from the Bible, has Rome been able to endow with plausibility the "Tradition" doctrines of Purgatory, mortal and venial sin, temporal punishment and indulgences.

The possibility of Catholics escaping from Rome's works-oriented trap increases a great deal if they can be made to understand the blood-atonement mandate set by God in the Garden of Eden. *"And when the woman saw that the tree was good for food, and that it was pleasant to the eyes, and a tree to be desired to make one wise, she took of the fruit thereof, and did eat, and gave also unto her husband with her; and he did eat. And the eyes of them both were opened, and they knew that they were naked; and they sewed fig leaves together and made themselves aprons."* (Gen 3:6, 7)

God's perfect creatures fell into sin, became knowledgeable of good and evil, tried to cover their nakedness, and failed. The fig leaf aprons may have been quite attractive and a very modest covering. But they were man's solution to the sin problem, not God's. Therefore, *"Unto Adam also and to his wife did the LORD God make coats of skins and clothed them."* (Gen 3:21) Innocent animal blood was shed by the Lord to obtain the skins needed for coats to cover their nakedness, which, in the Old Testament, is representative of sin. Thus it became a mandate of God right there in the Garden of Eden that innocent blood be shed as the covering for sin.

Catholic teachings have the faithful continually "sewing fig leaves together" to cover the nakedness of their sins. Say rosaries. Wear scapulars. Go to Mass. Go to Confession. Receive Communion. Do penance. Gain indulgences. Donate monies. Trust the pope, the bishops, the priests, the Catechism. All is in vain. Atonement is not found in any of those man-made works or teachings. All are unacceptable "fig leaves." Atonement is found in the shed blood of His only begotten Son. *"Neither by the blood of goats and calves, but by his* (our Lord's) *own blood he entered in once into the holy place, having obtained eternal redemption for us."* (Heb 9:12) Christ Jesus did not just "open the gates of heaven" as Catholics are led to believe. He "obtained eternal redemption for us" who are born again by faith in His Calvary sacrifice.

God called out the Children of Israel to be His chosen people. They had been enslaved in Egypt for over 400 years. During that time they had grown from Jacob (Israel) and his family of 70 people into a great nation numbering in the millions. Moses and his brother, Aaron, were assigned the task of dealing with Pharaoh, the Egyptian ruler, who steadfastly through nine different plagues refused to let the Children of Israel go. The tenth and final plague—the one that brought freedom from Egyptian slavery—is a graphic example of deliverance from sin and death through the shed blood of an innocent victim. Following are God's instructions to Moses how the Children of Israel were to prepare for, and escape, the tenth and final plague.

"Speak ye unto all the congregation of Israel, saying, In the tenth day of this month they shall take to them every man a lamb, according to the house of their fathers, a lamb for an house: Your lamb shall be without blemish, a male of the first year: ye shall take it out from the sheep, or from the goats: And ye shall keep it up until the fourteenth day of the same month: and the whole assembly of the congregation of Israel shall kill it in the evening. And they shall take of the blood, and strike it on the two side posts and on the upper doorpost of the houses, wherein they shall eat it. And they shall eat the flesh in that night, roast with fire, and unleavened bread; and with bitter herbs they shall eat it. And thus shall ye eat it; with your loins girded, your shoes on your feet, and your staff in your hand; and ye shall eat it in haste: it is the LORD'S Passover. For I will pass through the land of Egypt this night, and will smite all the firstborn in the land of Egypt, both man and beast; and against all the gods of Egypt I will execute judgment: I am the LORD. And the blood shall be to you for a token upon the houses where ye are: and when I see the blood, I will pass over you and the plague shall not be upon you to destroy you, when I smite the land of Egypt." Exo 12:3-13)

In order to be saved from the death angel a perfect animal without blemish was to be slain by and for every family unit of the children of Israel. The blood of this innocent victim was to be brushed onto the two doorposts and the lintel above the door. All the Children of Israel who—by faith—followed God's instructions were "passed-over" by the death angel, and were subsequently set free from Egyptian bondage, which is a "figure" of man's enslavement to sin. Any family—Hebrew or Egyptian—whose doorposts and lintels were not marked with the blood of an innocent animal victim received a visit from the death angel that awful night. It is a shameful thing in retrospect to admit that in my years as a

Catholic I believed the Jewish Passover was a memorial of their "passing over" a dried-up Red Sea.

For a third example of sin atoned for by the shedding of innocent blood, fast-forward to the children of Israel freed from Egyptian captivity and established in the Promised Land. While in the wilderness they had been instructed as follows: *"Also on the tenth day of this seventh month there shall be a day of atonement it shall be an holy convocation unto you; and ye shall afflict your souls, and offer an offering made by fire unto the LORD."* (Lev 23:27) On that day—the only day in an entire year—the high priest entered the Temple's Holy of Holies in which were the Ark of the Testimony and upon it the Mercy Seat. The high priest would take a bullock and two goats, each without spot or blemish: *"And he shall take of the blood of the bullock, and sprinkle it with his finger upon the mercy seat eastward; and before the mercy seat shall he sprinkle of the blood with his finger seven times. Then shall he kill the goat of the sin offering, that is for the people, and bring his blood within the veil, and do with that blood as he did with the blood of the bullock, and sprinkle it upon the mercy seat, and before the mercy seat."* (Lev 16:14,15)

Then, after cleansing the Holy of Holies the high priest: *"…shall go out unto the altar that is before the LORD, and make an atonement for it; and shall take of the blood of the bullock, and of the blood of the goat, and put it upon the horns of the altar round about. And he shall sprinkle of the blood upon it with his finger seven times, and cleanse it, and hallow it from the uncleanness of the children of Israel. And when he hath made an end of reconciling the holy place, and the tabernacle of the congregation, and the altar, he shall bring the live goat:"* (Lev 16:18-20) The high priest was then instructed to *"…confess over him all the iniquities of the children of Israel, and all their transgressions in all their sins, putting them upon the head of the goat, and shall send him away by the hand of a fit man into the wilderness: And the goat shall bear upon him all their iniquities unto a land not inhabited: and he shall let go the goat in the wilderness."* (Lev 16:21, 22)

God shed the blood of innocent victims in the Garden of Eden to obtain coverings for Adam and Eve's sinfulness. It took the blood of innocent victims in Egypt to cause the death angel to "pass over" the children of Israel. It took the blood of two innocent victims and a "scapegoat" on the tenth day of the seventh month every year to atone for the nation of Israel's sins. It took the precious blood of our innocent, sinless Lord Jesus Christ, shed **once** on Calvary, to pay in full the debt for sins—past, present, and future—of each and every sinner who believes Him to be both the Lamb of God and the "scapegoat" that takes away the sins of the world in every generation.

In each of the Old Testament examples cited, God's sin solution was accepted by faith. Adam and Eve could have rejected God's animal skin coats, preferring to hang onto their fig leaves. Had this been their choice, their sins would not have been covered, and *"the wages of sin is death."* (Rom 6:23) By faith they accepted God's solution and were forgiven. The children of Israel could have rejected the smearing of blood on their doorposts and lintels, choosing rather to hide all firstborn in a closet or cellar. Death and continued captivity would have been the result. By faith they did as instructed, thereby escaping the death angel and were freed from Egyptian captivity. By faith the high priest did as he was told on the Day of Atonement each year, thus obtaining God's forgiveness of his and the nation's sins for another year.

It was and is God's prerogative to choose the method of sin atonement. And from the very beginning, He chose the shedding of innocent blood. In my years as a Catholic I was not aware of these important facts from the Old Testament, which, we are told, was written for our learning. So, in my mind, the only association of blood with Christ's death was the fact that a body deprived of its blood ceases to live. I knew Jesus was referred to as the *"Lamb of God that taketh away the sin of the world,"* (John 1:29) but I never associated that appellation with the necessity that innocent blood be shed to atone for sin.

Catholics who would be freed from the bondage of "fig-leaf" works, must—from the foregoing—be made to understand that by faith in Christ's shed blood, He becomes their offering for sin, their propitiation (full payment) for sin, and their advocate (attorney) with the Father. This—not Holy Communion—is the God-directed, biblical way to receive the Lord Jesus. This is the act of faith that brings the new birth, the forgiveness of sins, adoption as children of God, and the indwelling of Christ's Holy Spirit unto everlasting life. **"He came unto his own, and his own received him not. But as many as received him to them gave he power to become the sons of God, even to them that believe on his name: Which were born not of blood, nor of the will of the flesh, nor of the will of man, but of God** (John 1:11-13) Faith in anything or anyone else is NOT FROM GOD!

Here, then, is the crucial question for Catholics—for all religionists—who truly are concerned with where they will be spending eternity: IN WHAT OR IN WHOM ARE YOU PLACING YOUR FAITH? *"I* (Jesus) **am the way, the truth, and the life: no man cometh unto the Father, but by me."** (John 14:6) Faith placed in the Roman Catholic church, or any other denomination, is NOT

FROM GOD. Religious organizations are not the "way;" Jesus is. *"Sirs, what must I do to be saved? And they said, believe on the Lord Jesus Christ and thou shalt be saved, and thy house."* (Acts 16:31, 32) Faith placed in water baptism is NOT FROM GOD. It is simply the visible expression of the faith that has been placed in the Lord Jesus Christ.

"For there is one God, and one mediator between God and men, the man Christ Jesus;" (1 Tim 2:5) Faith placed in Mary the mother of Jesus or deceased persons designated "saints" by Rome is NOT FROM GOD. No matter how high Mary is exalted by Rome, she cannot intercede for, nor can she save, a single sinner. *"Neither is there salvation in any other* (name but Jesus)*...for there is none other name under heaven given among men, whereby we must be saved."* (Acts 4:12) Faith placed in Mary is NOT FROM GOD *"I, even I,* (Jesus) *am the LORD; and beside me there is no saviour."* (Isa 43:11)

Faith placed in sacraments or other works to obtain or influence salvation is NOT FROM GOD. *"Not by works of righteousness which we have done but according to his mercy he saved us, by the washing of regeneration, and renewing of the Holy Ghost;"* (Tit 3:5) Faith placed in Mass attendance, recitation of rosaries, wearing scapular medals, doing nine first Fridays and/or five first Saturdays, going to Confession and Communion, these are works and are NOT FROM GOD *"For by grace are ye saved through faith and that not of yourselves: it is the gift of God: lest any man should boast."* (Eph 2:8, 9)

Faith placed in temporal punishment suffered in Rome's "Purgatory" to cleanse, purify, and make fit for heaven is NOT FROM GOD *"But if we walk in the light, as he is in the light, we have fellowship one with another, and the blood of Jesus Christ his Son cleanseth us from all sin."* (1 John 1:7) Only the precious blood of Jesus cleanses from sin. Confessing Him as Savior and Lord places one "under the blood" that cleanses, the blood that causes eternity's death angels to "pass over" believers when the religious but unregenerated are cast into the lake of fire. *"But the fearful and unbelieving and the abominable, and murderers, and whoremongers, and sorcerers, and idolaters, and all liars shall have their part in the lake which burneth with fire and brimstone: which is the second death."* (Rev 21:8) Who are the fearful? They are those deceived Catholics who—no matter how exemplary their lives—live always in the fear that they may fail to make heaven. Yet they fear even more to seek peace in the divine Word of God. They choose the "fig leaves" of Catholicism and reject the shed blood of Christ. Who are the unbelieving? They are all those—Catholics included—who have rejected the Word of God, accepting instead the words of men.

"Verily, verily, I say unto you, He that entereth not by the door into the sheepfold, but climbeth up some other way, the same is a thief and a robber." (John 10:1.) *"Then said Jesus unto them again, Verily, verily, I say unto you, I am the door of the sheep"* (John 10:7) *"I am the door: by me if any man enter in, he shall be saved, and shall go in and out, and find pasture.* (John 10:9) Catholic Church teachings are filled with many different paths to salvation; many different doors to the "sheepfold." But there is only one path and one door—Christ Jesus our Lord is both. He is the "Way" and He is the "Door." Faith placed anywhere else but 100% in His atoning sacrifice is faith misplaced, and is NOT FROM GOD.

Good works, good deeds, holy living are not to be trusted to obtain or assist in attaining salvation. *"…the wages of sin is death; but the GIFT of God is eternal life through Jesus Christ our Lord."* (Rom 6:23) Only through our Lord can everlasting life be experienced. Only through His work, and not through any work of ours, is forgiveness of sins and reconciliation with a holy God. As the precious blood of a dying Christ ran down into the soil of Golgotha's hill, much more was about to happen than the swinging open of heaven's gates. A miraculous exchange, an incredible trade, was about to take place, one that astounded even the angels in heaven. God the Father, in His infinite mercy and love, gathered together all our sins and all the rest of the world's sins and laid them on His beloved, only begotten Son, until His Son literally became sin in all its filth and ugliness. He then lifted from Jesus His sweet, sinless, compassionate righteousness and wrapped it in the pure white garment that now clothes each repentant sinner the instant he or she comes to Christ for justification. What an unfair exchange—our putrid sins for His divine righteousness! Jesus collecting "the wages of sin—death"—in our place, that we might have everlasting life clothed in His sinless righteousness.

Catholics are very close to being born again when they come to understand this miraculous exchange. Scripture describes it as follows: *"**He** (the Father) **hath made him** (Jesus) **to be sin for us, who knew no sin; that we might be made the righteousness of God in him.**"* (2 Cor 5:21) God's solution to man's sin problem was the precious blood of His only begotten Son, not sacraments, Masses, or other religious piety. God's solution was to give born again believers His own spotless righteousness, without which no one can come into His holy presence. God's solution was to junk men's old natures and supply them with brand new ones. *"**Therefore if any man be in Christ, he is a new creature; old things are passed away; behold, all things are become new.**"* (2 Cor 5:17) God's solution had nothing to do with religion.

"For God so loved the world, that he gave his only begotten Son, that whosoever believeth in him should not perish but have everlasting life." (John 3:16) God's Word makes no mention of religion, no mention of sacraments, no mention of popes empowered to add qualifying conditions to His rules. God's Word says **WHOSOEVER**. It says **whosoever believes**. It says all those **"whosoevers" will not perish**. It says their reward—fully guaranteed, not by mere men, but by God Himself—will be **forgiveness of sins** and **everlasting life**. *"I am the resurrection, and the life: he that believeth in me, though he were dead, yet shall he live: And he that liveth and believeth in me shall never die."* (John 11:25, 26)

A loving, merciful God saw the helpless, sinful condition of His creatures and sent His only begotten Son to die and—through death—become *"the propitiation for our sins: and not for ours only, but also for the sins of the whole world."* (1 John 2:2.) Three days later, an angel announced: *"Ye seek Jesus of Nazareth, which was crucified: He is risen; He is not here:"* (Mark 16:6)

The suffering Jesus depicted on Catholic crucifixes is not the Jesus of Christianity. Nor is He the Jesus Rome says is being sacrificed anew in every Catholic Mass. The Jesus of Christianity is RISEN! The old rugged cross is empty! The sepulcher has been vacated! **The work of redemption is finished**. Penances given to the Catholic faithful after they've gone to Confession are absolutely worthless. Sin—all sin—already has been paid for. And because all sin is black in the eyes of a holy God, there are no "mortal/venial" sin distinctions. Hell welcomes for all eternity both the unregenerate "little white liar" and the mass murderer. But neither need go there. Each has the opportunity to experience the "new birth" our Lord spoke about to Nicodemus.

This new birth does not happen as a result of being part of a religion—Catholic or otherwise. It is not brought about by immersion in water. It comes about by faith in the fact that Jesus, the Son of God, is the promised Messiah, the Savior of the world. And that kind of faith comes not from the declarations of popes, bishops, etc., but from the precious, priceless Word of God. The Sword of the Lord.

He, we are told, was the spotless "Lamb," the "Lamb" without blemish, the only acceptable sacrifice for man's justification. Born in a lowly stable or cave on the outskirts of Bethlehem, Judah… *"He came unto his own, and his own received him not."* (John 1:11) They were looking for a King. He came as a carpenter. They wanted freedom from Rome. He said He would free them from their sins. They said He was a blasphemer. He fulfilled over 300 Old Testament prophecies. *"But as many as received him, to them gave he power to become the sons of God, even to them that believe on his name:* (John 1:12) **Which were born not of blood, nor of the will of the flesh, nor of the will of man, but of God."** (John 1:13)

It is Jesus, not Catholicism, who gives believers the adoption as sons of God and joint heirs with Him of heaven and eternal life. The infamous Council of Trent, (AD 1545-1563) condemned and condemned and condemned. An incredible 125 condemnations (that never have been abrogated) were decreed against any and all who opposed Rome's man-made dogmas and insisted on a return to Biblical principles. But… **"God sent not his Son into the world to condemn the world; but that the world through him might be saved. He that believeth on him is not condemned: but he that believeth not is condemned already, because he hath not believed in the name of the only begotten Son of God."** (John 3:17, 18) Believing "on" Him means accepting as truth and doctrine HIS WORD—the BIBLE—not the words and doctrines of mere men.

Believing "on" Him means placing total trust on HIM alone for justification, sanctification, salvation, and advocacy with our heavenly Father. **"Cursed be the man that trusteth in man.** (Jer 17:5) In the final chapter 24 of the book that bears his name, Joshua challenged the children of Israel to decide whom they would serve, the gods of the heathen nations or the God of Abraham, Isaac and Jacob. He said: *"…as for me and my house, we will serve the LORD."* (Josh 24:15) He informed them that a wrong choice would bring God's judgment. *"If ye forsake the LORD, and serve strange gods, then he will turn and do you hurt, and consume you, after that he hath done you good."* (Josh 24:20) Then the children of Israel replied: *"…Nay; but we will serve the LORD."* (Josh 24:21) The road to destruction is paved with good intentions, a fact well known to Joshua. He replied to them as follows: *"…Ye are witnesses against yourselves that ye have chosen you the LORD, to serve him. And they said, We are witnesses.* (Josh 24:22) *"Now therefore put away, said he, the strange gods which are among you, and incline your heart unto the LORD God of Israel."* (Josh 24:23)

The Catholic faithful, for the most part, have a zeal to serve the Lord. But there is a false goddess among them that must be put away. There are false prophets and false doctrines among them that must be abandoned; false hopes that must be replaced by **"CHRIST in you, the hope of glory:"** (1 Col 1:27) Their one true ally is not the parish priest, the local bishop or the pope in Rome. Their one true ally is the infallible, inerrant Word of God—the holy Bible—the Sword of the Lord. Until they are willing to discard the paper-thin trappings of religion and put on the whole armor of God, they have little chance of reaching the Promised Land of heaven.

"Wherefore take unto you the whole armour of God, that ye may be able to withstand in the evil day, and having done all, to stand. Stand therefore, having your loins girt about with truth and having on the breastplate of righteousness: And your feet shod with the preparation of the gospel of peace; Above all, taking the shield of faith wherewith ye shall be able to quench all the fiery darts of the wicked. And take the helmet of salvation and the sword of the Spirit (Lord) *which is the word of God."* (Eph 6:13-17)

The Sword of the Lord is the Word of God. It is the eternal weapon upon which are impaled the myriad heresies of Catholicism. *"For the Word of God is quick, and powerful, and sharper than any two edged sword, piercing even to the dividing asunder of soul and spirit, and of the joints and marrow, and is a discerner of the thoughts and intents of the heart."* (Heb 4:12) One by one, the Sword of God's Word dispatches all of the following man-made doctrines decreed by Rome as extra-biblical revelations from God:

1] The priesthood including the papacy; 2] papal infallibility; 3] transubstantiation of the bread and wine; 4] the sacrifice of the Mass; 5] baptismal regeneration; 6] aural Confession; 7] Purgatory; 8] indulgences; 9] mortal/venial sin; 10] temporal punishment; 11] the Immaculate Conception; 12] the Assumption of Mary; 13] Mary, mother of God; 14] Mary, queen of heaven; 15] Mary co-mediatrix, co-advocate, co-redeemer; 16] canonized "saints;" 17] the sacraments.

Catholics who are putting their trust in their Catechism's teachings, need to be reminded of Christ's promise repeated in each of the synoptic Gospels: *"Heaven and earth shall pass away: but my words shall not pass away."* (Mat 24:35; Mark 13:31; Luke 21:33) Catechisms, Books of Mormon, Korans, all will pass away. The Bible—God's Word—is eternal; it will never pass away. It is not "just a bunch of words." It is the only inerrant revelation of God and His truth to sinful mankind. Catholics who say "I don't care what the Bible says, it's not what the Catholic Church teaches," are expressing their utter disdain for the very Son of God they claim to worship, for He is the eternal Logos, (John 1:1) the Word, the incarnate Christ, in writing that can never be altered or erased.

As noted earlier, most Catholics express a certain zeal for God. But rather than accept the free gift of HIS righteousness through faith in Christ's FINISHED Calvary work, they are going about trying *"to establish their own righteousness,"* (Rom 10:1-3) atone for their own sins, and climb up another "way" into the heavenly sheepfold. In His great commission to His disciples, our Lord said: *"…TEACHING them to observe all things whatsoever I have commanded."*

(Mat 28:20) What Christ Jesus commanded is clearly stated in the Word of God. Any doctrine not clearly stated therein was not commanded by our Lord. Catholics who read, study, and believe God's Word as revealed in the holy Bible, not only can be saved, they almost certainly WILL be saved. *"So shall my word be that goeth forth out of my mouth: it shall not return unto me void, but it shall accomplish that which I please, and it shall prosper in the thing whereto I sent it."* (Isa 55:11) God's will and God's pleasure is in delivering sinful mankind from the grasp of Satan. *"The Lord is not slack concerning his promise, as some men count slackness; but is long suffering to us-ward, not willing that any should perish but that all should come to repentance."* (2 Pet 3:9) *"Who will have all men to be saved and to come unto the knowledge of the truth."* (1 Tim 2:4) God wants salvation for all, and it is in His divine Word—not men's teachings—that salvation will be found.

Many years ago I was educated in a Jesuit university. One of the required courses for my discipline was "Logic," and, though much of what was covered now escapes me, one thing I learned never has. That which has stuck with me all these years is the logical law of contradictory statements: "When two statements contradict each other, only one of those statements can be true; both may be false, but only one of them can be true." It works like this. Two people are looking at a vehicle. One says, "That vehicle is red." The other says, "No, the vehicle is green." Here, both contradictory statements are false because the vehicle is **black**. But, if one says "That vehicle is black," and the other says, "No, the vehicle is green," only the first statements is, or can be, true because the vehicle is, in fact, black. The other is false and can never be anything but false.

My decision to leave the Catholic religion some twenty years ago was largely based on that logical law of contradictory statements. As I delved ever more deeply into the Word of God, I came to realize that Roman Catholic doctrines and Scriptural Christianity are not "on the same page," as it were. Rome's teachings **contradict Scripture** from Genesis (creation) to Revelation—the millennial rule of Christ. Since the Word of God is truth and will never pass away, any doctrines or teachings that contradict it HAVE TO BE FALSE.

Example. Catholic doctrine teaches participation in three works called sacraments—Baptism, Penance and Eucharist—is mandatory for salvation. God's Word says *" For by GRACE are you saved through faith; and that not of yourselves: it is the gift of God: not of works, lest any man should boast."* (Eph 2:8, 9) God's Word says: *"For God so loved the world, that he gave his only begotten Son, that whosoever believeth in him should not perish, but have everlasting life."* (Joh 3:16) God's Word says: *"Not by works of righteousness which we have done, but according to his mercy he saved us, by the washing of regeneration, and renewing of the Holy Ghost."* (Tit 3:5) God's Word says: *"That if thou shalt confess with thy mouth the Lord Jesus, and shalt believe in thine heart that God hath raised him from the dead, thou shalt be saved."* (Rom 10:9) God's Word says: *"For whosoever shall call upon the name of the Lord shall be saved."* (Rom 10:13) God's Word is contradicted by this Catholic teaching. God's Word is true. This Catholic teaching **must be false**.

Example. Catholic doctrine teaches that the Mass is "**is the unbloody sacrifice of the body and blood of Christ,**" and "**is the same sacrifice as that of the Cross.**" It teaches that each time the Mass is performed "**the work of our redemption is carried out.**" God's Word says: *" But this man, after he had offered one sacrifice for sins for ever, sat down on the right hand of God;"* (Heb 10:12) God's Word says: *"For by one offering he hath perfected for ever them that are sanctified."* (Heb 10:14) God's Word says: *"By the which will we are sanctified through the offering of the body of Jesus Christ once for all."* (Heb 10:10) God's Word says: *"Who needeth not daily, as those high priests, to offer up sacrifice, first for his own sins, and then for the people's: for this he did once, when he offered up himself."* (Heb 7:27) God's Word says: *"I have glorified thee on the earth: I have finished the work which thou gavest me to do."* (John 17:4) God's Word is contradicted by this Catholic teaching. God's Word is true. This Catholic teaching **must be false**.

Example. Catholic doctrine teaches that "**the Blessed Virgin is invoked in the Church under the titles of Advocate, Helper, Benefactress, and Mediatrix.**" God's Word says: *"For there is one God, and one mediator between God and men, the man Christ Jesus* (1 Tim 2:5) God's Word says: *"But now hath he obtained a more excellent ministry, by how much also he is the mediator of a better covenant, which was established upon better promises."* (Heb 8:6) God's Word says: *"And for this cause he is the mediator of the new testament...."* (Heb 9:15) God's Word says: *"And to Jesus the mediator of the new covenant."* (Heb 12:24) God's Word says: *"And if any man sin, we have an advocate with the Father, Jesus Christ the righteous."* (1 John 2:1) God's Word is contradicted by this Catholic teaching. God's Word is true. This Catholic teaching **must be false**.

One after the other, Catholic doctrines consistently contradict what is taught in the Word of God. And it is the Word of God—the Sword of the Lord—that contains our blueprint for eternal life with God. *"...the holy Scriptures are able to make thee wise unto salvation through faith which is in Christ Jesus."* (2 Tim 3:15) *"So then faith cometh by hearing, and hearing by the Word of*

God." (Rom 10:17) Over the past twenty years, I have come to believe that devout Catholics are very much like the five unwise virgins described by our Lord in the following parable:

"Then shall the kingdom of heaven be likened unto ten virgins, which took their lamps, and went forth to meet the bridegroom. And five of them were wise, and five were foolish. They that were foolish took their lamps, and took no oil with them: But the wise took oil in their vessels with their lamps. While the bridegroom tarried, they all slumbered and slept. And at midnight there was a cry made, Behold, the bridegroom cometh; go ye out to meet him. Then all those virgins arose, and trimmed their lamps. And the foolish said unto the wise, Give us of your oil; for our lamps are gone out. But the wise answered, saying, Not so; lest there be not enough for us and you: but go ye rather to them that sell, and buy for yourselves. And while they went to buy, the bridegroom came; and they that were ready went in with him to the marriage: and the door was shut. Afterward came also the other virgins, saying, Lord, Lord, open to us. But he answered and said, Verily I say unto you, I know you not." (Mat 25:1-12)

The **lamp** Catholics are equipped with is **religion.** It looks good; appears able to get the job done because God is part of it. *"Thou believest that there is one God; thou doest well: the devils also believe, and tremble."* (Jas 2:19) But the lamp of religion is worthless. It's a product of ambitious men who've provided an inferior **lamp fuel** for it called "**works.**" And there simply is not—in the entire world—enough fuel of "works" to get a bearer of the lamp of religion into the "Marriage Supper of the Lamb." (Rev 19:9)

The wise Catholic will trade his or her lamp of religion for the **Lamp of God's Word**. This lamp is fueled by the "oil of gladness" with which Jesus—the Logos, the Word—was anointed by our heavenly Father: *"Thou hast loved righteousness, and hated iniquity; therefore God,* (Jesus) *even thy God* (the Father) *hath anointed thee with the oil of gladness....*" (Heb 1:9) The Word of God is fueled by the oil of gladness—the Lord Jesus Christ. That oil is a divine compound of love, faith, trust, comfort, guidance, correction and joy. It's the only oil that can light a born again Christian's lamp all the way to the "Marriage Supper of the Lamb."

"Thy word is a lamp unto my feet, and a light unto my path." (Psa 119:105) To the Catholic who is trusting in religion for eventual (after Purgatory) salvation, the greatest blessing he or she can receive is a hunger for the Word of God. In the final analysis, God's Word is the one and only way a Catholic will ever be able to: *"come out from among them, and be ye separate, saith*

the Lord, and touch not the unclean thing; and I will receive you. (2Cor 6:17) ***"Thanks be unto God for his unspeakable gift."*** (2 Cor 9:15) The Amazing gift of GRACE!

> Amazing **Grace**, how sweet the sound,
> That saved a wretch like me;
> I once was lost but now am found.
> Was blind but now I see.
> Twas **Grace** that taught my heart to fear,
> And **Grace** my fears relieved;
> How precious did that **Grace** appear,
> The hour I first believed.
> Through many dangers, toils, and snares
> I have already come;
> Tis **Grace** has brought me safe thus far,
> And **Grace** will lead me Home.
> When we've been there ten-thousand years,
> Bright shining as the sun,
> We've no less days to sing His praise,
> Than when we've first begun.

May God's Amazing Grace be shed upon you and yours…and upon all with whom you share "The Sword of the Lord," and "the Lamp of God's Holy Word."

0-595-65682-X